T0338812

ROYCE'S MATURE ETHICS

Royce's Mature Ethics

Frank M. Oppenheim

UNIVERSITY OF NOTRE DAME PRESS
Notre Dame, Indiana

Library of Congress Cataloging-in-Publication Data

Oppenheim, Frank M., 1925–
  Royce's mature ethics / Frank M. Oppenheim.
    p. cm.
  Includes bibliographical references and indexes.
  ISBN 0-268-01642-9
  1. Royce, Josiah, 1855-1916—Ethics.   I. Title.
B945.R640656   1993
171—dc20   92-53531
                                                CIP

Dedicated
to the
Logos - Spirit
and the
Members of Its Body

Contents

Preface

Since Josiah Royce's death in 1916, Americans have entered two world wars and the age of nuclear energy, space exploration, and computerization as well as the post-cold war era. The question easily comes to mind, then: "Why examine Royce's final contribution to ethics in that so far away 'classical age' of American moral philosophy?" Were Royce alive today, he would, I believe, enjoy this question. He might counter, "The rich concrete whole of human life embraces our unique selves as bonded to nature, other human selves, and something superhuman. This whole sets the unavoidable context for the new possibilities opening up on our pilgrimage of bodily birth, growth, decline, and death. When starting ethics, then, how can we find a set of questions that keeps us open to this rich whole of life?"

Royce's thoughts and questions are especially relevant if, in eagerness for a so-called clarity, one begins ethics with specific questions. By contrast, the mature Royce taps into humankind's basic motives and all-embracing interests to locate a fitting set of initial ethical questions. Yet ethicists can trap themselves into studying a part of ethical life, or even an abstraction of a part. Thus they miss that concretely lived "whole mix" of ethical life that includes its passivity of being called and changed by others as well as its activity of self determination.

By contrast, when the popular mind uses such words as "life" and "death," "good" and "evil," "love" and "ought," it possesses a richness of concrete experience and a subtle association of meanings that call the philosopher to recognize them. Royce had learned to respect this sense of the ethical life in ordinary folk. Writing to Professor Arthur O. Lovejoy in 1912, he recorded his esteem of their ethical common sense:

> The popular mind is deep, and means a thousand times more than it explicitly knows. The philosopher's endless task is to find out what this deep mind means, and to tell what it means.[1]

In his final course in ethics, Royce emphasized the need to respect this rich variety of ethical experiences and judgments. He also highlighted the need to approach ethics in a corresponding variety of ways. He told his students, "Nowhere is pedantry or a love of mere uniformity more out of place than in ethics."[2] This mature openness to both the simple depth and rich variety of ordinary ethical life marked Royce's experiential way, especially in his later years.

From the start one needs to demarcate the range included by the term Royce's "mature ethics." On the basis of the dawning of his "religious insight" in early 1883, I divide his intellectual development into his "pre-formed" (1855–1882) and "formed" (1883–1916) periods. This insight into an All-Knower provided Royce's thought with a central orientation which he thereafter never changed fundamentally. Later his mental striving seems gradually to have achieved two other maximal insights: into the individual (1896) and into the community and its Spirit (1912). Relying on these three maximal insights, I formed the hypothesis that the Harvard years of Royce's "formed" thought-growth are fittingly subdivided into three sub-periods: the early Royce of 1883–1895; the middle Royce of 1896–1911; and the *mature* Royce of 1912–1916.[3]

I focus on the intellectual and moral maturity that Royce manifested from 1912 to his death. Physically, he underwent an apoplexy attack in early 1912 from which he recovered mentally with amazing resilience even if it left him physically enfeebled. For instance, he produced his most insightful masterpiece, *The Problem of Christianity*, within a few months in late 1912. The maelstrom of World War I surprised and confused both Royce and many other thinking Americans. But the colleague who knew him best, William Ernest Hocking, along with Royce's students and family members, recognized that from 1912 to 1916 Royce had reached the zenith of his intellectual and moral growth.

During this mature period, Royce employed an epistemology of inter-pretation for his ethical reflections. It presupposed a community of embodied "minded beings"—to use Charles Peirce's term. Its temporal process, while freezing past deeds into irrevocability, opened up new possibilities for present choice, and confronted human selves with bodily death at some future date. This ethical life was to be energized (and in part guided) by the community-members' moral will to interpret and be interpreted. It was to be guided still more by the interpreter-spirit of each community, and indeed by as many of such spirits as there were greater, hierarchically arranged communities receiving their direction from the overall Universal Community and its Spirit. In this context, then, Royce's mature ethics called each human self to discern the "eternal" present in its practical here-and-now choice, in its current "mode of moral action." This means 'seeing' the Chinese Tao and 'touching' it.

Unfortunately, the mature ethics of Royce has remained twice hidden. A pair of obstacles has impeded a fair grasp of his late ethics. For one thing, the decades of post-1916 ethical investigation have successively deposited new strata of questions upon Royce's ethics. In this way instrumentalism, linguistic analysis, ethical non-cognitivism, and deconstructionism have been flood currents which buried Royce's ethics beneath their later deposits. Then, too, if any fossils of Royce's ethics were excavated, anthologists usually drew them from the familiar but nearly exhausted veins of either Royce's first major work, *The Religious Aspect of Philosophy* (1855), or from his most popular work, *The Philosophy of Loyalty* (1908). These, however, formed the "Pre-Cambrian" or "Miocene" deposits of his early or middle thought. He himself later criticized these deposits as, respectively, too crude in method and too popular for a discerningly refined ethic.[4] The typical "samples of Royce's ethics" found in anthologies are not extracted from those final five years when Royce's Peircean insight was producing a new "mother lode" of transformed value.

Besides these historical overlays and less than optimal selections in anthologies, an amazing variety of people's attitudes and mental styles have hidden Royce's mature ethics. Some misperceive it as a largely voluntaristic striving for loyalty that lacks any inquiring and practical Deweyan-like intelligence. Some brand it Schopenhauerian or Hegelian, and thus "not genuinely American." (The latter do not take time to discover that Royce's mature ethics is distinctively American since it draws mainly from Peirce and James and from the Californian uniqueness of "that man from Grass Valley," Royce himself.) Others brush aside his mature ethics in their belief that any ethics that goes beyond description of feelings into the normative realm of stating what people should do has to be pretentious. Still others recall the middle Royce's slogan, "Be loyal to loyalty!" Mistaking this as an abstraction, they regard his ethics as based on either a meaningless cliché or at least a needless mystification.

Finally, for their part, deconstructionists tend to blast into "airy abstractions" Royce's late concrete endeavors both to identify an essential ethical ideal and to highlight that central ethical life which integrates freedom, goodness, and duty. Their attack against such "futile foundation hunting" results in a notable emptiness, even if it reasserts, contrary to their intent, the reality of that historically processing community which the mature Royce made central to his ethics. Let us, then, leave these many weak misinterpretations and glance quickly at the major themes of Royce's mature ethics in order to see their strength and balance.

In late August 1915, Royce wrote to his wife Katharine (then visiting their son and daughter-in-law in Hurley, Wisconsin), "I have now written out the two opening lectures in full—the hardest for me—of my University Extension Course [in Ethics]."[5] Royce's admission of great mental effort drew me to reread the second of those lectures—the only one of the original pair that is still extant.[6] Fortunately, its introduction summarizes the first lecture which treated two ideas in his newly discovered triad of "leading and most fundamental ethical ideas": *Freedom* (or autonomous self-determination), *the*

Good (or union with what would make one's life eminently and genuinely happy), and *Duty* (or "this idea of obligation to follow some will not my own, to obey, to be bound by laws which are not of my own making").[7] He told his audience at Boston University:

> We cannot live our moral life without them [these three leading ethical ideas]. But with them we can live only at the expense of inner and outer warfare, *until we learn how to harmonize them.*[8]

Back in 1912 Royce strove to integrate the three most essential "Christian ideas" (of community, lost individual, and atonement) by means of the idea of Grace. Similarly now in 1915, he recurred to his fundamental ethical theme of "harmony" to synthesize within a transformed loyalty his newly appearing triad of basic ethical ideas.

In his first lecture Royce had clarified for his audience the meaning and role of the ideas of Freedom and the Good. The first led to self-determination (or, as the poet Henley put it, of "being captain of one's soul"), insofar as external fortune, destiny, and God allowed this. The idea of the Good revealed the need for embracing an overall goal in life (which, as one's chosen goal, establishes one's life-plan, gives meaning to one's life, and makes one a Self). Royce had started with the motives and interests that give rise to these basic ideas. Then he identified how Freedom led to "Henley's problem" and Goodness to "Everyman's problem" (of finding wherein lies genuine happiness).

Having finished his summary, Royce turned to "Emerson's problem" of the origin of Duty, that third basic ethical idea.[9] Here Royce sketched a *most mature synthesis of the ethical life* as integrated by these three ideas. Royce quoted the lines in Emerson's poem "Voluntaries" where in response to Duty's low whisper, "Thou must," the dutiful soul of the patriotic youth responds, "I can." Then in a page that despite its length deserves full quotation because of its centrality to his mature ethics, Royce synthesized the three ideas:

> When he [the patriotic youth] says, "I can," he says what includes indeed a great defiance of mere destiny [in response to Henley's problem of self-determination]; but his attitude is obviously humble as well as defiant, submissive as well as proud, conscious how ignorant he is about what, after all, is really good for us mortals in the way of mere luck and of chance happening as well as of natural attainment. The dutiful spirit leaves to what it calls God the art of making the great triumph, of solving Everyman's problem [of the Good that creates genuine happiness], and of reconciling the poor individual man whose head fortune so often leaves bleeding, to the blows of chance which he is sometimes too weak merely to defy.
>
> Now just *this strange union* of patient acquiescence with resolute self-expression, this harmonizing of a certain piety towards what the dutiful soul

regards as divine, with a kind of sharing of Henley's vigorous self-will,—this unearthly confidence that, beyond all sorrow, all shall be, for the dutiful, somehow good, despite the fact that the dutiful soul does not always feel sure about what the true solution of Everyman's problem is, all this, which the dutiful answer "I can," as uttered by Emerson's Youth, puts into words, constitutes one very serious ground why our time has so often lost its power to understand what duty, apart from the actual winning of good fortune, really means, and how one can be high-spirited, although dutiful.[10]

Echoing through this lengthy passage are *new* themes in Royce's ethics —themes not clearly announced even in his ethics of *The Problem of Christianity* (1913). Expositors of Royce's ethics have not attended enough to these themes that we here simply indicate. First, Royce's use of "duty" in this text can tempt a reader to think misleadingly that Royce is here simply borrowing Kant's central ethical idea. Instead, in this second lecture, one of Royce's main tasks is to show how the idea of duty arises, not primarily from pure practical reason, but from concretely lived experiences of the past, once they are recognized as irrevocable.

Then, too, the term "mortals," hints that Royce's "philosophy of life" had become enriched by growing into a "philosophy of life and death." In 1915 Royce thought that a balanced ethic required the moral philosopher to consider all the goods and evils of human life, especially the basic ones of life and death, as these affect both body and moral self.

Thirdly, the quotation rings out the individual self's bondedness to nature, fortune, societies, and God. This is the concrete, particular, and real network of its ethical life. If moral philosophy divorces itself from this network, it becomes a mere abstraction.

Fourthly, the emphasis of the paradoxical ingredient in "this strange union" highlights the personal, interpersonal, and communal dimensions of Royce's maturest ethics. Furthermore, his terms "divine" and "unearthly confidence" suggest the religious aspect permeating his ethics. And lastly, the text offers a self-portrait of the much battered, Job-like Royce in his final year. Because of these and other new themes in Royce's 1915–1916 ethics, and because until now these themes have not been brought to a public forum for careful study, the present work seems needed.

The reader deserves a caveat on the tentativeness of the present work. It is conditioned on the extant Royce writings available to me in 1992. For years I have searched diligently for some lectures that are missing from Royce's 1914 Berkeley Series and especially from his 1915–1916 Extension Course in Ethics. If in the future any of these missing manuscripts are discovered, their light will qualify the findings here expressed.[11]

In this preface, we surveyed some obstacles preventing many from focusing on Royce's mature ethics (from 1912 to 1916). We found those who merely label Royce and end up libelling him. Later we glimpsed a "synoptic view" of Royce's enriched maturest ethics. Since most of this richness lies unpublished, our procedure calls us to map out the intricate context from which this mature ethics grew. Then we must uncover, step by step, the contextual ingredients entering into the final form of his ethics, including its nexus with his mature theory of knowledge and metaphysics. This calls us to be more empathetic with Royce's intents and more critical in handling his texts. Beyond his published texts, we need to examine his many unpublished manuscripts on ethics, especially those of his final years, and also the Royce Family Papers recovered in 1988 from an attic in Crystal Falls, Michigan.

Before doing all of this, however, we need to taste enough of Royce's life to see how his family, his surroundings, and chiefly his own choices nurtured ethical life in him before 1912. I believe with Royce, Fichte, and William James that a person's philosophy arises from one's unique personality. Hence, while appreciating the difference between theory and lived life, I find experience constrains me to believe that a philosopher's personal life affects both the basic attitude he or she takes toward life and one's self-positioning toward the world. From this basis one looks upon and tests the various ethical theories and upon it one ultimately rests one's case.

Genuine empathy with Royce and his texts requires both appreciative insight and critical distance. If with such critical appreciative empathy we can watch how Josiah grew in genuine ethical life—that is, in the commitment to, and in the art of discerning interpretation required by such a life—ours will be, in my opinion, a breathtaking experience.

Herewith I gratefully acknowledge permissions granted for the first publication of some privately owned Roycean materials and for the republication of other materials by Harvard University Archives, Houghton Library of Harvard University, the University of Chicago Press, the University of Wisconsin Press, and to Peter J. Hare, editor of *Transactions of the Charles S. Peirce Society*, to Nancy Hacker, Richard Hocking, Alexander R. James, James Royce and Josiah Royce, III.

This book is the fruit of so many Royce researchers, fellow Jesuits, and reference librarians that any attempt to credit them all will surely omit many who deserve recognition. For all that, however, I must express my indebtedness to professors Gladys Bournique, John Clendenning, Bruce Kuklick, John J. McDermott, Ignas Skrupskelis, and John E. Smith; to Xavier University and the Chicago Province of the Society of Jesus for their trust and support; and to the Jesuits of Xavier, of the John Courtney Murray Writers Group, and of the Jesuit Renewal Center at Milford, Ohio, for their manifold helps; to the late David J. Hassel, S.J., and Sr. Helen C. Swift, S.N.D. de N., for their critical observations on earlier drafts; and to the faithful helpfulness of the archivists and librarians at Harvard University, Xavier University, and many other Roycean deposits. Despite such help and faithful supports, the inaccuracies that remain are mine alone.

Frank M. Oppenheim
Xavier University

New Year's Day, 1993

1. Eighty Years of Responses to Royce (1910–1990)

American philosopher Josiah Royce embodied and advocated the individual spirit of genuine loyalty in a beloved community. Born in 1855 of English immigrants who had joined the gold rush of 1849, Josiah grew up in California and drew from it and his mother a spirit of being independent, earnest, and reverent—a spirit he acknowledged in himself.[1] When he graduated from the University of California at Berkeley in 1875, he had spent his first twenty and most impressionable years in California—the first decade in and around Grass Valley, his mining town birthplace, and the second decade in and around bustling San Francisco and Oakland.

After a year of graduate studies in philosophy at German universities and two more at the Johns Hopkins University, Royce returned for four more years, 1878–1882, to his *alma mater* in Berkeley as an instructor in English composition. In late 1880 he married the younger daughter of socially prominent Judge Head, Katharine, who soon presented Josiah with a son Christopher. During these Berkeley years Royce personally engaged in deep and intense philosophical work, despite the philosophical barrenness he felt stifling him there.

Invited by William James to Harvard's philosophy department in 1882, the young adventurous Josiah relied on his felt talent and strength to risk a step that would otherwise have been foolhardy.[2] Assured of only a one-year appointment, Royce brought his wife and child across the continent to Harvard and her relatives in the East. After one year as lecturer, he secured another, soon became an instructor, and eventually attained professorial rank. As for his relationship with William James, the two of them influenced each other's thinking for decades and grew in a friendship deep enough to withstand the radical philosophical differences that eventually emerged.

During his thirty-four years at Harvard (1882–1916), Royce fostered the growth of philosophical thinking in students, colleagues, and the educated class generally. He became America's foremost example of philosophical idealism. Thanks to his own originality and the insights he borrowed from Charles Sanders Peirce, Royce created in his final years a unique version of idealism. Its distinctiveness lay in its interpretive way of knowing, its

1

engagement with the mystery of life and death, its intouchness with the realism of concrete process, and its anti-nominalistic pragmatism.

With his central argument to an All-Knower in his first major work, *The Religious Aspect of Philosophy*, Royce's career at Harvard began to rise. It peaked, as far as popularity went, with his 1899–1900 Gifford Lectures, *The World and the Individual*. From 1900 until Royce's death, the contrary and increasingly popular philosophical movements of the realists and neo-realists so sidelined Royce's mature work that his masterpiece of 1913, *The Problem of Christianity*, drew little attention at the time.

After this background, we begin our survey of the main interpretations of Royce from 1910 to 1990.[3] With the exception of some essays in *Festschrifts* honoring Royce,[4] the various philosophical styles dominant in America since 1910 have created differing interpretations of Royce, most of them negative.

At the start a bird's-eye view may help. Very little research focused upon Royce's philosophy from 1910 to 1950. The few exceptions usually stereotyped it as foreign and outdated. From 1950 onwards, a gradual dawning of interest began. Presentations of Royce's thought after 1950 freed it of some stereotypes and revealed an empathetic approach more faithful to his concerns and insights. Only since 1960 have some of the tools needed for accurately interpreting Royce's thought become available—a critical annotated bibliography, the publication of his letters, and a balanced biography. Only since 1960, therefore, has the study of Royce's thought been carried out with increasing discipline and care.

THE PERIOD OF NEGLECT

From 1910 to 1950, interest in Royce sank to near oblivion for three major reasons: Royce himself, contrary trends in philosophy and culture, and obstacles to Roycean research. A brief initial development of these reasons may prove helpful.

Royce's quaint appearance, often prolix style, and challenging message did not attract academic Americans as much as did Emerson or William James. Then, too, in his maturity Royce concurred with C. S. Peirce that at its start philosophical reflection requires a certain pregnant vagueness to forestall premature foreclosures. He also agreed with Peirce that deep philosophizing will create boredom in most minds. Neither of these tenets pleased thinkers wanting to make philosophy scientific through an initial clarity and distinctness on precise but interesting new questions.

Secondly, by 1910 the pragmatists and realists smeared Royce systematically.[5] From 1920 onwards professional philosophy became increasingly technical and infighting between neo-realists, philosophical naturalists, and logical positivists left little room for Royce's thought in leading universities. Members of these schools usually judged Royce's problems and method no longer specific and precise enough to merit attention. Moreover, historians of American philosophy sheared Royce of his unique and distinctive traits in order to propose him as a typical sample of American absolute idealism.[6]

As for American culture in the first half of this century, secularism grew and its naturalists wanted a pragmatism without traditional religion. Yet a religious tone was prevalent in Royce's writings.

Finally, the few professors then interested in examining Royce's thought encountered many obstacles. After Royce's death fourteen years passed before Harvard Archives received his unpublished papers. There they were guarded with strict permission requirements and remained unarranged chronologically.

Our initial survey, then, of the factors leading to the general neglect of Royce until about 1950 notes his partly deserved unpopularity, some contrary trends in American philosophy and culture, and obstacles to careful research in Royce. A more thorough examination of these factors seems called for.

Royce's Partly Deserved Unpopularity

Unavoidably or unwittingly Royce himself occasioned some opposition and later neglect. Royce's Harvard colleague and friend of thirty-four years, George Herbert Palmer, knew Royce as a Socrates-like figure:

> His appearance was strange. His short stocky figure was surmounted by a gigantic round head well sunk in his shoulders. The top of it was sprinkled with red hair, while the strongly freckled face seemed to himself and to every stranger unparalleled in homeliness. . . . His clothes, of no particular fashion, seemed to have as little to do with him as matter with mind. His slowly sauntering gait was characteristic.[7]

However superficial a criterion, attractive looks counted even then.

Again, Royce's prolix style of lecturing often bored his audience. He confessed this when penning a line of the epitaph he humorously proposed for himself: "He [Royce] died from an excess of loud garrulity."[8] Because he needed to supplement his yearly professor's salary of $3,500, he offered hundreds of outside public lectures at a fervid pace.[9] This demand often kept Royce from achieving concise, well-polished utterances. When perhaps too many of these lectures or articles appeared in print, some readers failed to distinguish between the Royce who thus "kept the pot boiling" to feed his family and the Royce who in other publications revealed how rigorously he thought and wrote at times.

In these more disciplined writings, however, the middle and mature Royce sometimes incommoded readers by adopting that initial vagueness needed to prevent a premature closing of questions. Moreover, in these same essays, Royce sometimes used technical language and frequent qualifiers and distinctions. These features did not make him easier to read.

More seriously, the depth and scope of Royce's thought provided a stronger reason for neglecting him. One may recall that after yet another of the Cambridge Conferences by Charles Peirce, he and Royce were wont to converse on abstruse logical and metaphysical questions into the wee hours of the night like two Olympians.[10] The scene may remind one how few thoughtful Americans—both in and beyond academe—could keep pace mentally with these two godlike thinkers. Difficult as it is to grasp faithfully a truly gifted mind, it is far more difficult to achieve a "fair understanding" of a genius and to feel genuinely at home in his mind.

Then, too, some felt Royce's reputation tainted. From 1885 to 1892 an unfortunate argument had grown between Royce and Francis Ellingwood Abbott about the latter's philosophical competency.[11] Charles Peirce publicly backed his classmate Abbott while William James publicly supported his friend Royce. Lawyers, local gossip, and the media stirred the pot still more. Royce had by then become a well-ensconced professor at Harvard. Abbott, scion of a well-regarded Cambridge family, had been ordained though he no longer exercised the ministry. Thus many cultured Bostonians regarded the Californian outsider as ruthlessly keeping Abbott from achieving a berth in Harvard's philosophy department. Echoes of the fracas lingered long.

In his final years Royce acknowledged that he had lived in more self-conceit during his middle years than during his final decade when he advertised his fallibility more often.[12] Nor in his middle period did he reveal that gentle humor and playfulness which so frequently marked his mature period.

Moreover, unlike James and Dewey, Royce related to his students in such a way that he formed no school of disciples. Instead, he evoked in them a creative independence of thought and rewarded their reasoned disagreement from his own positions. This method of teaching forestalled the rise of any Roycean movement that might have propagated his ideas through the first half of the twentieth century. Of course, some of his students—independent thinkers like Hocking, C. I. Lewis, Marcel, and others—acknowledged their indebtedness to Royce but certainly trod their own unique paths.

Finally, Royce styled himself a rebellious non-conformist and came across as an outsider.[13] As a deeply dyed Californian, he never quite fit in with cultured Boston. As a thinker, he spoke of the religious aspect of philosophy when the trend was turning increasingly to materialism. As a nondenominational Christian coming from a biblical thought-world, he contrasted with many professors for whom the Bible was no longer a most familiar source.

His nonconformism also showed itself in his choice of starting points. He began the history of modern philosophy with Spinoza rather than Descartes. He began formal logic, not as Russell and Whitehead had done, but by insisting on including modes of action among its starting elements. In psychology he divided psychic activities, not chiefly according to James's triad of feelings, knowings, and conations, but according to an increasing intimacy shown in sensitivity, docility, and initiative.

In all these ways, then, Royce did not fit in easily and somewhat put off his audience.

Contrary Trends in American Philosophy

Labels need context and distinctions to be used fittingly. Nevertheless, a comparison and contrast of bare labels about Royce may orient the reader to the present survey of views. What labels, then, did Royce apply to himself?

In his early years he styled himself a Californian, a truth-seeker, a doer of deeds, one called to be independent, earnest, and reverent. In his middle span he saw himself as more Kantian and Fichtean than Hegelian, as an absolute voluntarist and pragmatist, as a psychologist, a mathematician, and especially as a formal logician. In his final period he called himself far more of a Peircean than a Hegelian, a Christian metaphysician and a metaphysical idealist of the life of the "spirit,"[14] an idealist called "to be as realistic as possible,"[15] one who pointed to the Logos-Spirit of the beloved community like John the Baptist, one who was not merely romantic and mystical but especially a teleologist striving for a more exact definition, and finally a nonconformist disposed to a certain rebellion despite being wholeheartedly devoted to the beloved community.

The labels imposed on Royce by others offer an interesting contrast. William James had called Royce various things. He was "the Rubens of philosophy"—that is, a sketcher in broad strokes who needs a wide canvas but avoids the depth and detail that careful analysis requires. Royce was the defender of the imperial Absolute with its block universe and "belongs essentially among the lighter skirmishers of philosophy." Before his death in 1910, James had charged Royce with monistic absolutism, Hegelianism, rationalism, and vicious intellectualism.[16]

After Royce's death in 1916 and America's entry into the war against Germany, others multiplied their labels against Royce. He was branded Hegelian, German, foreign, non-American, romantic, transcendentalist, and a sterile intellectualist.

A sketch of the history of American philosophy from Royce's coming to Harvard until 1950 may prove more helpful than these conflicting labels. As mentioned, American idealism reached a kind of zenith from about 1880 to 1905. Shortly thereafter, the popularization of William James's *Pragmatism* produced a new trend.[17] It was bolstered by realists like Bertrand Russell and Santayana both of whom held ultimate physical reals independent of knowing minds. It was also bolstered after 1910 by the new realists (R. B. Perry and others), and after 1920 by the critical realists (Drake Durant and others).[18] Both these groups held that at least some objects exist independently of a knowing consciousness and are not altered by being known. They differed because the critical realists denied that the mind perceives or knows external objects immediately or directly.

As American philosophy moved into the late 1920s and 1930s, Deweyan naturalism became the dominant trend. It sealed nature off from any divine impingements or other "pre-existent reals." If guided by the felt quality of ongoing communal experience, its logic of inquiry into nature of this sort proved fruitful indeed in scientific, technological, educational, and political contexts. To Deweyan naturalists and humanists, Royce seemed to show a broken-backed dualism and spiritualism.

Chiefly after World War II, the influence of the Vienna circle gradually spread into many American universities. These positivists stressed scientific rigor in philosophy with empirical verifiability as a norm. To them Royce's thought seemed nonempirical and therefore flaccid.

Moreover, during the first half of the twentieth century, a strong animus operated in secular universities against thinkers who used the core of the traditional religions as their matrix for reflection. This animus against traditional religion so dominated academic hiring then that only those young philosophers with secularistic (later positivistic) outlooks could teach in the leading departments. Young philosophers interested in philosophizing from the perspective of Royce, Hocking, Emerson, or Whitehead could not as a rule find any positions open to them.

Given the trends indicated in the foregoing brief sketch, one rightly expects that from 1910 to 1950 most of the interpreters of Royce would present marred versions of his thought. Often a preoccupation within the rising tides of Jamesian pragmatism or Deweyan naturalism or a later positivism accounted for these warps. Nevertheless, rather than one-sidedly faulting the pragmatists and naturalists, one needs to sense their feeling of having for decades been despised by certain idealists who assumed the posture of "protectors of the faith."[19] A closer look at this main stream of anti-idealism seems needed.

Around 1910, R. B. Perry, Royce's junior colleague at Harvard, continued James's attack by initiating the New Realist movement. He pictured idealist Royce as imprisoned in an egocentric predicament—a predicament in which, as Royce soon pointed out, both realist and idealist alike were inescapably imprisoned.[20] In this way, Perry and his group of new realists launched their attack against the Absolute of Royce's middle period. This occurred shortly before Royce transformed his Absolute into the processing Universal Community and its Spirit of interpretation. Moreover, when these logically honed new realists charged Royce's work with imprecision, they did not distinguish between his popular and academic works.

Then in 1912 Arthur Lovejoy launched his own attack with innuendos that Royce's philosophy was an "imposture" and that Royce himself was one of those so "religiously-minded or irenically disposed philosophers" that he could not do "philosophy as a science."[21] Thus, when Royce published his *Problem of Christianity* in 1913, his greatest work fell largely on inattentive ears. Clendenning informs us:

Although Royce must have received other letters of congratulation and approval, *The Problem of Christianity* did not make a considerable impact upon intellectual circles. *The World and the Individual* had prompted a chorus of opposition, but *The Problem of Christianity* was politely reviewed, warmly praised, mildly criticized, and otherwise ignored.[22]

Soon the concerns of World War I drew attention away from Royce, especially from the philosophical work of his Peircean period (1912–1916). Because American "patriotism" then surged to a high that continued into the 1930s, the "realist smear" of Royce took stronger hold on the American intellectual circles.[23] As a Hegelian absolutist, was not Royce foreign in his thought, and so perhaps an enemy in disguise, or at least a non-American? Ironically, this "Germanizing" of Royce associated him more with his colleague, Hugo Münsterberg, the promoter of Prussia, and less with the pluralistic and democratic William James, his deepest (though sometimes acerbic) friend in philosophy. In this way Royce became branded as the un-American purveyor of a dangerous imperialistic absolutism.

After 1918, professors who had struggled through the trauma of World War I looked forward to their own peacetime pursuits. Most of them had little interest in what happened to Royce's thought just before America entered the war. This became increasingly the case once they and their students became involved in the more immediately pressing matters of the "roaring twenties" and the following years. Three of Royce's students, George Santayana, Ralph Barton Perry, and George Herbert Mead can serve as instances.

Santayana had gradually become disaffected towards Royce. He gloried in William James's romantically induced revolt against the basis, pedantry, and cant of what he called "the genteel tradition." Its ethos had, in his eyes, dominated America too long. He classified Royce within this tradition and during his middle and mature periods continued to level imprecise charges against Royce.

Before leaving Harvard's philosophy department permanently in 1912, Santayana had delivered his influential address, "The Genteel Tradition in American Philosophy." He softened this address only slightly when he revised it for an East Coast circulation which appeared in his *Winds of Doctrine: Studies in Contemporary Opinion*. He continued his attack in various essays, especially in his well-known *The Genteel Tradition at Bay*.

Santayana traced the roots of the genteel tradition to Calvinism and transcendentalism. He found that

> persons with no very distinctive Christian belief, like Carlyle or like Professor Royce, may be nevertheless, philosophically, perfect Calvinists. . . . Calvinism, essentially asserts three things: that sin exists, that sin is punished, and that it is beautiful that sin should exist to be punished. . . . He [the Calvinist whose conscience is "agonized"] oscillates between a profound abasement and a paradoxical elation of the spirit.[24]

Whatever similarities link Royce and Calvinist Jonathan Edwards, the dissimilarities ought to have kept Santayana from suggesting the philosophical identity of Royce as a perfect Calvinist. The identification presupposes that each of Royce's finite human selves, by living in some supposed "block universe," is wholly predestined from the start. Yet in Royce the human self possesses genuine initiative and a "common reasonable human nature." The latter is neither fatally flawed by sin nor predestined beforehand either to heaven or to hell. Moreover, the pioneer openness and unpredictable modes of action in Royce's logical system certainly create no block universe and his doctrines of grace and atonement contradict the concept of a vindictive divine being.

After an eight-year interval, Santayana in his *Character and Opinion in the United States* intensified his attack on the genteel tradition.[25] As a target he chose the Absolute of Royce's middle period, rather than the Spirit of the Universal Community of Royce's later thought. If Santayana had carefully examined *The Problem of Christianity*, he would have detected the change in Royce's method and message after 1912.

For his part in the opposition, Perry charged that Royce's idealism imprisoned the knowing subject in an inescapable solipsism.[26] In his *The Thought and Character of William James* (1935), Perry made Royce depend on James for his ideas and career. In this work Perry transfigured Royce into a foil for James, intensifying the differences between them. This led him to differ from James's appraisal of those differences. To create this opposition, Perry omitted many key qualifiers and essential nuances in Royce's correspondence with James, even as he fixed upon Royce such labels as "block universe" and "absolutist."[27]

As a third instance, Royce's pupil, George Herbert Mead, paralleled Perry's path of gradually distancing himself from Royce. Abandoning the tone of his earlier more appreciative essay, "Josiah Royce: A Personal Impression," Mead in 1930 portrayed his former teacher as un-American, as one whose "philosophy belonged . . . to a culture which did not spring from the controlling habits and attitudes of American society.[28] Negative moves such as these definitively set the mold for later interpretations of Royce.

In 1933, an influential rejection of supernaturalism appeared in "A Humanist Manifesto," signed by thirty-four leading American thinkers, including John Dewey, John H. Randall, Jr., and Roy Wood Sellars.[29] These religious humanists regarded a theistic creator, worship, and prayer, along with body-soul dualism as outdated. Without naming Royce, many of their strictures struck at his doctrines of grace, atonement, and of love coming "as from above." Moreover, by constructing a naturalized language and making it dominant, they backstaged users of biblical language, like Royce.

A year later, John Dewey recommended hastening the natural withering of "religions" by emphasizing the experiential quality of "the religious." He concluded that faith in the latter "has always been implicitly the common faith of mankind. It remains to make it explicit and *militant.*"[30] Concerning the religious aspect of philosophy, therefore, Dewey wanted philosophy not to arise from "a religion" but to possess the "religious quality" experienced in feeling the great community. Royce had also agreed that philosophy should not arise from "*a* religion" yet required more of "religion" than a felt religious quality. For he held that the religious action of praying to interpret "in germ . . . contains the whole meaning of the office, both of philosophy and of religion."[31]

Obstacles to Roycean Scholarship

Besides Royce's own partly deserved unpopularity and the contrary currents in American philosophy, a third factor hindered a fair appraisal of Royce. To better understand the near oblivion of Royce from the 1920s through the 1940s, one needs to tally up the then-current obstacles to sound Roycean research.

With the exception of *The Spirit of Modern Philosophy* and his *Philosophy of Loyalty*, Royce's works had gone out of print by 1930. How different it was with William James and even Charles Peirce!

In 1915–16, Royce himself and his assistant, Fergus Kernan, sorted the unpublished papers of the recently deceased Peirce. Within two decades Paul Weiss and Charles Hartshorne were assiduously editing these papers into six volumes.[32] Except for two posthumous volumes edited by Loewenberg, Royce's papers lay uninvestigated during the dozen years following his death.

Mrs. Royce guarded some in her Cambridge house; Loewenberg held some in California under her tutelage. When Mrs. Royce finally gifted most of Royce's papers to Harvard Library in 1930, they remained in its Treasure Room practically unexamined until the mid-1950s.[33] Then, J. Harry Cotton's researches finally called public attention to the treasure in these largely unpublished papers.

Although the first collection of William James's letters appeared within ten years of his death, it took more than fifty years after Royce's death before Americans gained access to Royce's letters through John Clendenning's landmark edition. A similar phenomenon occurred regarding the definitive biographies of these two philosophers. Perry's monumental *Thought and Character of William James* was published within twenty-five years of James's death. Seventy years would pass after Royce's death before Clendenning's *Life and Thought of Josiah Royce* appeared in 1985.

The other research tools were marked by a similarly lengthy time-lag. Editions of Williams James's major works have almost always been readily available. By contrast, just as in the 1930s, so in the early 1980s publishers were letting most of Royce's works go out of print. Even a modest collection of Royce's basic writings did not appear until 1969. Perry's *Annotated Bibliography of the Writings of William James* appeared in 1920, whereas Ignas Skrupskelis's definitive annotated bibliography of Royce's published writings did not appear until 1969. Besides this lapse of time in the publication of needed Roycean tools, other obstacles prevented research into his thought.

What little attention Royce's philosophy did receive from 1916 to 1950 focused almost exclusively on his early and especially his middle-period works. The late works fell under an almost total eclipse. Moreover, according to Bournique's study, those who evaluated Royce's philosophy before 1950 were not familiar enough with Royce's thought or were insufficiently disciplined in their method of treating it.[34] She found that most of the secondary literature on Royce fails to measure up to A. O. Lovejoy's requirements for sound methodology when tracing out a history of ideas. That is, the procedure and expression of these studies are marred because their authors want to tell it their way rather than enter faithfully into Royce's mind.

In several ways these studies about Royce revealed a lack of scholarly formation in their authors. They failed to contextualize Royce's thought within the problems through which he and his fellow Americans were then living. They lacked the techniques needed to analyze his thought rigorously. Moreover, they often failed either to define their purpose accurately or to set Roycean texts in their proper chronological setting. For example, quotations from 1885 appeared with those from 1913 without cautionary flags to the reader. Studies of particular aspects of Royce's thought are often marred by inattention to the whole synthesis of a certain period—one that then affected every part of his philosophy.

In addition, Bournique found that most appraisers of Royce have been preoccupied with a certain mode of philosophizing or with a certain subjective interest. This has led them to overemphasize one point and blinded them to other equally important aspects of Royce's complexly woven thought. She also found that too many of these secondary studies were marked by an "unintended naivete." They expected him to meet contemporary standards of style or interest. Or they supposed that his thought could only be true or interesting if it could be shown relevant to present problems.

EARLY POSITIVE ASSESSMENT

Some early appraisals were positive. William Ernest Hocking, Gabriel Marcel, Mary Whiton Calkins, Jacob Loewenberg, Morris Cohen, and Clarence Irving Lewis published some of the more influential positive evaluations of Royce.[35] Following Royce's preference for no disciples, however, each of these thinkers neither simply built on Royce's basic positions nor developed his thought further. Instead, all of them created their own independent philosophies.

Arguably, Royce's student, colleague, and friend, William Ernest Hocking, became the most effective early promoter of Roycean research. Born in Cleveland in 1873 and reared in the Midwest, Hocking pursued his education by alternating between work-place jobs and schooling in academe. Equipped with a doctorate in philosophy from Harvard (1904), he first taught at Berkeley for two years (1906–1908) and then at Yale for six more. In 1914, he was called to Harvard where he taught philosophy until 1943. Hocking's interests in international law, Christian missions, and governmental policies, as well as in Royce, generated many books and scores of articles until his death in 1964.[36]

As a graduate student in 1903–04, Hocking held, contrary to Royce, that we immediately grasp the reality of the other person in dialogue. When Hocking ventured to present this thesis to Royce, he feared the worst. To his surprise and delight, Hocking found Royce insisting that he be true to his own insight rather than following Royce.[37]

Before 1916, Hocking knew it unfair to label the mature Royce with catch-phrases like "monist" or advocate of a "block universe." For Hocking held in his hands a late—and still unpublished—letter from Royce that countered such stereotyping.[38] It described how, despite all the necessary determinations imposed on the world from environment, education, and historical trends, freedom and chance kept emerging in many areas from Royce's unique individuals.

In 1916 Hocking countered the trend to brand Royce's philosophy as that of an aprioristic "block universe." He pointed out that the mature Royce attenuated his Absolute by having it operate within the motives of history and experience even while it exercised an ultimate moral intent and exigence.[39]

In a memorial after Royce's death, Hocking highlighted Royce's "large humanity and kindness" and the "decided trend to ethical and social applications" in his thought after 1908. He witnessed in Royce "an added vigor of production" after 1912—despite Royce's slight stroke and the spiritually oppressive nightfall of World War I.[40]

In 1929–31 Hocking conducted two Harvard seminars on Royce's philosophy. In 1932 he published a penetrating study of Royce's ripest epistemology and metaphysics.[41] At the same time he prepared Royce's Last Lectures on Metaphysics (1915–1916) for publication. When the Depression and anti-idealistic currents in philosophy forestalled this aim, he entrusted its eventual publication to his son, Richard.[42]

Through the years Hocking's own perception of Royce developed. Even in 1939 he still regarded *The World and the Individual* as Royce's chief work. Yet by the 1950s he pointed with Gabriel Marcel to the *Problem* as Royce's more significant contribution.[43] Hocking was also sensitive to the stages of Roycean scholarship. In the 1950s he indicated the importance of using all of Royce's unpublished writings—even the "scraps"—so an authentic retrieval of this American thinker could be achieved. In his final decade, he saw the need to emphasize the hitherto neglected logical aspect.

Hocking provided many services that have helped researchers come to a more empathetic and objective grasp of Royce. He emphasized the need of first coming to know the person, Royce, rather than just the philosopher. He also underscored the growing empiricism in the thought of the mature Royce. This empiricism carried its own kind of realism, particularly in ethics—a type of realism that had also revealed itself in Royce's earlier writings. Besides this intensified empiricism, Hocking also recognized in Royce a foreshadowing of the twentieth-century philosophical movements of existentialism and phenomenology.[44]

He also served Roycean scholarship by insisting on the need to recognize that Royce's thought moved through alternation—what Hocking called the "ballistic swing of his [Royce's] ideas." This alternation grew out of, and paralleled, Royce's two early and perduring interests: "science and mathematics on one side, literature, especially poetry, on the other."[45]

Accordingly, Hocking pointed out that the middle Royce's refutation of mysticism as a metaphysical conception of being in no way meant that Royce rejected mysticism as a style of life. Instead, both Hocking and Royce wanted everyone to respect that "one necessary postulate" in every lived form of mysticism; namely, that "reality may be, and ought to be, approached in worship."[46]

Concerning Royce's ethics, which saw external meaning inescapably embodied in a community's cause, Hocking remarked:

> And if, as Royce maintains, that external meaning is from the first the divine being, whether or not we consciously so define it, our rule of life becomes also, to this extent, an "ethics from above."[47]

Hocking saw that Royce's ethics arose from human nature and "as from above." Textual evidence for this interpretation lay in the Problem's use of experiential data and Royce's declaration that genuine loyalty comes, if at all, "as from above," in a way beyond explanation.

While serving in the French Red Cross during World War I, Gabriel Marcel (1889–1973) was led to study Royce through his interest in idealism. Invited by the editors of La Revue de Metaphysique et de Morale to bring Royce's thought to their French audience, Marcel examined all of Royce's works available in France in 1918–1919 and published his analysis in a series of four articles.[48]

Marcel quickly detected the significance of the mature Royce. So, omitting the young Royce, he chose to start his appraisal from The World and the Individual and to extend it fully into The Problem of Christianity. Working simply from the internal evidence of the Problem, Marcel detected that:

> Royce's most profound and original thought found only in his latest writings the means of expression which it not only needed to be communicated, but even to be essentially understood.[49]

This recognition that Royce's mind had undergone some radical transformation before writing the Problem constitutes, in my opinion, Marcel's greatest service to Roycean research.

In the quotation cited, Marcel referred to something more than the mature Royce's far simpler and deeper style of writing in the Problem. Rather, Marcel referred mainly to Royce's late mental metamorphosis whereby he developed a triadic espitemology and metaphysics. These brought Royce's complex mind to a new method, medium, and message. Through these Marcel (and others) could finally understand the harmony of the many deep and original tendencies in Royce's mind.

In other words, Marcel meant that prior to 1912 not only had Royce inadequately formulated his philosophy, but also that until then he had inadequately thought through his philosophy. For Royce needed the new medium of interpretive knowing to discover the method of interpretive musement as the most fundamental process of knowing. Then he could offer to others his transformed message which Marcel detected.[50]

Mary Whiton Calkins, professor of philosophy at Wellesley College after 1903, largely concurred with Hocking's appraisal of Royce. Even while acknowledging parallel themes in Hegel and Royce, she claimed Royce's complete independence from Hegel.[51] In this way she countered the popularized stereotype of Royce as a "Hegelian." She emphasized four "peculiarly Christian features" in Royce's teaching and witnessed to the transcendence *and* immanence of Royce's God.

Nevertheless, Calkins also erected some obstacles to interpreting the mature Royce. By focusing on his statement that *The Problem of Christianity* was in essential harmony with his earlier writings, she disregarded Royce's adjoined witness that it also contained "unexpected results," "a distinctly new interpretation," and "novel views." This led her to select the works of Royce's early and middle periods as her main focus of study.

Jacob Loewenberg, who served as Royce's assistant in the early 1910s, promoted a wider acquaintance with Royce. He published Royce's early essays and his 1906 lectures on modern idealism. He created several studies of Royce's later thought and recorded personal memoirs of being Royce's student and assistant.[52] By carefully studying the early Royce's manuscripts and published essays, Loewenberg documented how many of the themes and procedures of the middle and later Royce were seminally present in the youthful Royce.

This significant service, however, also contributed to the trend of focusing on the early or middle Royce, thus distracting later scholars from the mature Royce. Moreover, since Loewenberg was convinced that Royce had written far too much, he wanted researchers to restrict themselves solely to the writings Royce himself had judged worthy of publication. On this he disagreed with Hocking.

Morris R. Cohen, Royce's assistant in 1905–06, published a largely positive, even if frequently overlooked, appraisal of Royce's thought. These essays were re-edited and published posthumously in his *American Thought: A Critical Sketch*.[53]

Cohen judged, "It is Josiah Royce's great insight to have recognized the community as the central fact of most religious worship."[54] Cohen grasped the importance of Royce's later works. He ranked Royce's "Principles of Logic" as the logical work most important for philosophy. He detected both "that the unity of the absolute becomes in Royce's later writings the unity of a community, indeed, the unity of a federal republic" and that in the *Problem* "the Spirit of Community replaces the Absolute." He found "an analysis of the inadequacy of individualism and the recognition of human solidarity . . . even more significant in Royce's later writings."[55]

Failing to weigh the discipline that a Roycean community exerts upon detached individuals, Cohen situated Royce in the more liberal movement, without adding the qualifications needed. Then, too, he reported inaccurately that because of Royce's emphasis on the social element in religion, Royce showed "a disregard of the question of individual freedom and responsibility."[56]

Clarence Irving Lewis, Royce's pupil and an outstanding American logician, zeroed in on Royce's late logical writings and called attention to the importance of System Sigma for grasping Royce's distinctive system of order. He highlighted Royce's critical choice to start logic differently than Russell and Whitehead had done and, also unlike them, to include "modes of action" among the basic elements of logic. Lewis recognized the distinctive "pathfinder" character of Royce's logic and suggested that System Sigma probably "contains new continents of order whose existence we do not even suspect."[57] The constancy and flexibility of Lewis's late social ethics, with its pragmatic apriori and its four imperatives, reflects much of Royce's mature ethics.[58]

In 1932 Clifford Barrett edited *Contemporary Idealism in America* and dedicated it to Royce. In it G. H. Palmer sketched a personal reminiscence of Royce and C. M. Bakewell and W. E. Hocking contributed essays of particular significance for Royce scholars[59]

In sum, from 1910 to 1950, the thinkers just reviewed pointed to Royce's insights and sometimes to the importance of his mature period. They did this while trodding their own ways of thought against the prevailing currents of philosophy.

INTERPRETATIONS OF ROYCE SINCE 1950

We can view the return to Royce movement of 1950 to 1990 in three phases, each with its leading scholars. First came those who turned the tide, especially John E. Smith. Next came scholars such as Bruce Kuklick who used formal logic or linguistic analysis to achieve yet more precision in Roycean studies. Finally, John Clendenning, John J. McDermott, and the editors of the University of Chicago Press created the initial tools needed for these studies.

Turning the Tide

According to Bournique, interest in Royce revived after 1950 for three reasons: American thinkers grew discouraged with logical positivism and linguistic analysis and concerned about the arational ethic often connected with these modes of thought. Then among historians of American thought after 1950, there gradually grew a history of ideas methodology which promoted definitive editions of classical thinkers and careful attention to their own quotations seen in context. Finally, a small circle of Roycean scholars emerged.[60]

In 1950 John E. Smith, professor of philosophy at Yale, published *Royce's Social Infinite*, which evoked the dawn of a new period of Roycean interpretation.[61] Smith highlighted the dynamic structure as well as the purposeful wills at work within the mature Royce's community of interpretation. In numerous books and articles since 1950, Smith has brought Royce's thought into focus and underscored its significance.

For example, his chapter on Royce in *The Spirit of American Philosophy* provided a much needed and reliable presentation.[62] So, too, did his study of Royce's Self.[63] In his Introduction to the University of Chicago edition of *The Problem of Christianity*, Smith showed that in the *Problem* the Spirit of Christ pervades the universe far more actually and intimately than Hocking and Calkins had given Royce credit for. Scarcely anyone, then, has labored more to win a fair hearing for Royce and to make his thought, especially his mature thought, intelligible.

Also in 1950 occurred the publication of *The Social Philosophy of Josiah Royce*, edited with an introduction by Stuart Gerry Brown.[64] Brown soon edited and introduced another Roycean anthology, *The Religious Philosophy of Josiah Royce*, published by the same press in 1952.

Max H. Fisch, in his influential *Classic American Philosophers*, included Royce in his six American sages of perduring value.[65] This proved a significant countercultural move and provided Royce with some acceptance in academic circles. Ranking Royce this way, however, carried its price. He later became accepted, often enough, as simply a sample of the idealist tradition in American thought. The unintended result was that in introductory undergraduate courses, Royce often came across as a lesson rather than as the unique individual he was.

In 1951, too, Daniel S. Robinson published *Royce's Logical Essays*.[66] It gathered under one cover Royce's hitherto dispersed studies in logic. This collection emphasized Royce's stature as one of America's top ten logicians.

Soon J. Harry Cotton published his dissertational study of *Royce on the Human Self*.[67] This called attention to one of Royce's most central ideas. It also showed the scholarly importance of employing unpublished manuscripts.

In 1956 Regnery produced the English version of Gabriel Marcel's *La Metaphysique de Royce*. This American translation did more than extol Royce's philosophical achievement since it became pivotal in calling attention to Royce's thought.[68] After writing this work on Royce in the late 1910s, Marcel had grown disenchanted with both idealism and empiricism and created his uniquely individual, anti-systematic "approaches" to metaphysics. These flowered, for instance, in his *Metaphysical Journal, Being and Having*, and in *The Mystery of Being*, his Gifford Lectures of 1949–1950.

In 1956 Marcel looked back almost forty years to his early work on Royce's metaphysics in order to prepare a foreword to its English edition. In it Marcel selected several Roycean treasures that he had mentioned in the original edition but which he now saw as needing fresh highlighting.

First, he identified the heart of the mature Royce's transformation— parallel to, yet diverse from Marcel's own dialectic of love:

> It was through an epistemological theory of the interpretation of signs that Royce was led, in *The Problem of Christianity*, to his triadism and to his conception of a process of interpretation encompassing an infinite series of interpretive acts.[69]

Here Marcel spied how fruitful was the triadism in Royce's "I-thou-it" dialogue.

He also drew attention to Royce's "Doctrine of Signs."[70] This Doctrine, which pervades the universe of processing selves, offered Marcel a basic clue for discerning in general which message the Spirit of the Universal Community is continuously communicating to finite minded members.

Finally, recalling his original study of *Loyalty, Sources*, and the *Problem*, Marcel had this to say about the ethics of the mature Royce:

> I should like to stress the particular and lasting value of Royce's philosophy of loyalty. Here, I am sure, Royce effectively contributed to the advancement of ethics in a concrete direction which is in profound accord with the demands of contemporary thought.[71]

Marcel saw that a mid-twentieth-century person needed a sound and effective remedy against the cancer-like spread of "detached individualism" which Royce saw infecting Western civilization. Long before the current decades of "selfism," then, Marcel pointed out that Royce's doctrine and art of loyalty offered his contemporaries an antidote and, even more importantly, a practical healthy way to simplify and fulfill the call to integrate their ethical lives.

Marcel's review of Royce's metaphysics, however, had its limitations.[72] He chose to analyze Royce's thought without careful portrayal of Royce's intellectual development. Opting to publish his own youthful reflections on the philosophy of this Harvard philosopher, Marcel did not, for the most part, put Royce in center stage by quoting him directly and at length.

Although Royce himself had in the end focused on interpretations, Marcel preferred to expose what he called Royce's "metaphysical conceptions." He also chose to present Royce's thought in the abstract form of metaphysical theses. In this way Marcel failed to convey the fire that energized Royce's continuing empirical researches and his passionate pursuit of life in its concrete uniqueness. Ironically, the anti-systematic Marcel tried to portray the thought of Royce as a finished system. The mature Royce, however, had claimed that every philosophical system, his own included, had to be inadequate and capable of being further interpreted.[73]

Despite his praise of Royce's thought in 1919, Marcel eventually adopted a detached posture towards it. By 1956, he clearly pursued his independent path and soon regarded Royce's philosophy as "outdated" (*depasseé*) and "hardly useful."[74] Nonetheless, the limitations of Marcel's youthful interpretation and his subsequent self-distancing from Royce remain relatively insignificant. They pale when compared to the widespread attention which the English version of Marcel's work received and the impulse it gave to many Roycean researchers in the United States. These included such Roycean scholars as David Casey, Peter Fuss, Charles Hartshorne, Edward Jarvis, Jacquelyn Kegley, Mary Mahowald, Frank Oppenheim, Daniel Robinson, Ignas Skrupskelis, and John E. Smith. The work of at least two of these scholars deserves notice here.

In his *The Moral Philosophy of Josiah Royce*, Peter Fuss endeavored to explore Royce's significant contributions to ethics, rather than to examine further the logical, religious, or social thought of Royce the polymath.[75]

A few years later, in his, "Royce and the Collapse of Idealism," Charles Hartshorne focused on the middle Royce and drew a significant distinction.[76] He differentiated between Royce's sound idealistic starting position and the subsequent additions he made to it. Hartshorne claimed that, in their criticisms of Royce, William James, R. B. Perry, and G. E. Moore had missed Royce's sound idealistic starting position, even while they accurately attacked the additions he built upon that position.

The studies of Royce by Smith and Marcel, and shortly thereafter by J. Harry Cotton and Daniel S. Robinson, called on later scholars to do a higher level of research in investigations of Royce's work. Their studies set in motion the demand for competent tools so that a more precise kind of research could be done. They also invited and supported studies of particular aspects of Royce's thought.

Modeling a More Precise Study of Royce

When one turns to Bruce Kuklick's works on Royce, one enters a new and better world of Roycean scholarship. Kuklick's studies achieve a far greater extent and depth of treatment. He enjoys an empathy for and understanding of Royce that enables him to expose selected aspects of Royce's thought faithfully and to create illuminating commentary. He leads a reader to appreciate how Royce's *Sources of Religious Insight* (1912) have a deep import for philosophy of religion.[77] He points out that for the mature Royce interpretation defines the individual member's relation to the community. As such, it differs from, and makes a significant advance over,

Royce's earlier epistemological doctrines of self-representation and of the discrimination that reveals a "between" element. Kuklick also clarifies how Royce's idea of loyalty developed between his publication of *The Philosophy of Loyalty* and that of his *Problem of Christianity*. In this period Royce moved from loyalty as a simple devotion to a cause into his later view that loyalty is a two-way reality operating between a community and its members.

Nevertheless, in my estimate, Kuklick's perspective has three shortcomings. First, Kuklick does not seem to appreciate the transformative effects of Royce's Peircean insight upon his subsequent intellectual development. Second, Kuklick asserts that Royce "developed no new ideas, . . . [suffered] a decline in intellectual achievement. . . [and by 1916] verged on senility."[78] Third, Kuklick so emphasizes the logical aspect of Royce's philosophy that he decentralizes its ethico-religious interest into simply another area of applied logic.

Kuklick's view of the senescent Royce rests heavily on Horace M. Kallen's record of Royce's physical aspect during a brief meeting with him in May 1916.[79] Kuklick's view, however, omits the appraisals of Royce's intellectual vigor during his final years made by persons nearest him day-to-day, such as Palmer and Hocking, Kernan and Loewenberg. They witnessed that, despite aging and physical enfeeblement as well as some psychic depression, Royce's intellectual prowess grew during the final years. This is evidenced by his pioneer studies of Peirce and Nietzsche, his masterful articles in Hastings's *Encyclopaedia*, his 1913–14 Seminar in Comparative Methodology, and, perhaps most tellingly, his three published efforts in logic and theory of knowledge from this period.[80]

A third shortcoming arises from an unbalanced emphasis on logic in Royce after 1898. Kuklick's firsthand experience with Royce's logical manuscripts correctly convinced him that after 1898 logic influenced Royce's thought ever more profoundly. Kuklick's concentration on logic, however, seems also to have dominated his perception of Royce's mind. For Kuklick gives slight credit to Royce's early witness that religious problems, which first drove him to philosophy, "of *all* human interests, deserve our best efforts and our utmost loyalty."[81] Kuklick also gives slight credit to Royce's non-logical works written after the *Problem*.

In sum, a sympathetic reader of Kuklick and of his stress on logic might fail to recognize that Royce's *Problem of Christianity* is intended essentially as a work in the philosophy of the Christian religion. Thus, although Royce employed his logic throughout the *Problem*—even if he kept it from the view of his ordinary audience—the *Problem* stands primarily as a work in ethics and philosophy of religion rather than as a work in logic.

Such shortcomings as these, however, dim considerably when set within the overall contributions of Kuklick and other historians of American philosophy, like Andrew Reck and Murray G. Murphey.[82]

In the "Josiah Royce" chapter of *A History of Philosophy in America*, Murphey, a colleague of Kuklick at the University of Pennsylvania, has raised Roycean investigation to a new level. Here he corrects some earlier Roycean interpreters by rightly recognizing *The Problem of Christianity* and *The Sources of Religious Insight* as among Royce's most remarkable works. Moreover, Murphey highlights realistic elements in Royce's thought. He accurately points up the need to examine Royce's *Outlines of Psychology* if one wants to grasp Royce's nexus between attention and will. This nexus leads to Royce's view of an idea as a plan of action and hence to Royce's plan of a loving action as his principle of individuation. Murphey well describes Royce's absolute pragmatism and Royce's constituents of the moral will, rather than of a merely natural one. Best of all, perhaps, Murphey carefully exposes the content and significance of Royce's 1905 and 1910 works in logic.

I was struck, however, when Murphey dedicated only ten of his sixty-five pages in this chapter to the *mature* Royce. Although he documents Royce's acknowledgment of dependence on Peirce's early articles for the second part of *Problem*, Murphey, like Kuklick, offers no hint of familiarity with Royce's public acknowledgement in 1914 of the fact and import of his "Peircean insight" two years earlier. Yet Royce saw this insight as supplying a new light and real force to his mature ethics and philosophy of science. Furthermore, Murphey does not mention that Royce estimated his Peircean insight to be *as* earthshaking *as* was his religious insight of 1883.

As a result, even in his section entitled "Christ and Community," Murphey becomes preoccupied with that logic and epistemology of a community of interpretation found in chapters 11–13 of the *Problem*. Royce developed those chapters, however, simply as a tool to face directly and persistently the pressing problem of Christianity. Thus preoccupied with logic, Murphey largely fails to grapple with Royce's central intent in the *Problem*—namely, to be *principally* a philosopher of the Christian religion rather than a logician.

Murphey shows a final variance from Royce when describing the latter's idea of community as "most difficult and most fundamental."[83] For Royce ranked the idea of atonement as the "most hopelessly problematic, of the three [Christian ideas]" and as "especially foreign for the modern mind."[84] Moreover, although the idea of community is fundamental in the sense of embodying itself into the reality of community by the process of interpretation, nevertheless, when disloyalties tragically tear a community apart, only atonement can and does restore it. So Royce described atonement as "the function in which the life of the community culminates" because in it alone does community find its authentic, most life-giving center.[85] Royce's idea of atonement, then, has a solid claim for being viewed as "most fundamental," as well as "most difficult."

Creating the Tools Needed for Roycean Research

The third phase of the Royce revival began in 1968 when the University of Chicago Press launched its Royce series with the republication of *The Problem of Christianity* in a one-volume edition, introduced by John E. Smith. Next, the University of Chicago Press published the much needed two-volume gathering of *The Basic Writings of Josiah Royce*, thanks to the insight and energy of editor John J. McDermott. Both in this work, as well as in his other studies, McDermott has shown himself an outstanding Royce scholar.[86] He locates the center of Royce's life and thought in the moral dilemma of how to reconcile a good God with the world's flagrant evils. He emphasizes the Puritanism in Royce whom he sees in close intellectual relationship with Jonathan Edwards. Sensitive to Royce's own appraisal, McDermott finds that in the *Problem* Royce finally brought to the center of his philosophy his long-standing insight that community is achieved *only* by "reverence for the relations of life."[87] In addition, McDermott points out that struggling for one's loyal cause against evil is also central to Royce's ethics.

McDermott's edition was enriched by the careful bibliography of Royce's published works crafted by researcher, Ignas K. Skrupskelis. Skrupskelis also contributed to Roycean scholarship by documenting Royce's highly nuanced position on obedience and authority.[88]

The very next year the University of Chicago Press published John Clendenning's edition of *The Letters of Josiah Royce*.[89] This allowed readers to discover Royce the person with his basic interests and without the stereotypes and gifted researchers with an indispensable tool for seeing the development of Royce's thought. Using this basis, Roycean scholars, like Mahowald, Jarvis, and myself soon produced studies of specific aspects of Royce's thought.[90] Clendenning next contributed the long awaited full-length biography of Royce. This and the preceding research tools allowed me to publish *Royce's Mature Philosophy of Religion*, which evidenced the import of the religious, ethical, and logical dimensions of Royce's late thought.

Unexpectedly, in 1988, a rich collection of Royce family documents was discovered in Crystal Falls, Michigan, and acquired in 1989 by Harvard University Archives. Containing correspondence coming to Royce from contemporary philosophers and his own letters to his family, as well as a few other Royce manuscripts, photographs, and much family correspondence, this Crystal Falls collection provides a significantly richer context for Royce research.[91]

Admittedly, this rapid survey has omitted many contributors to the evaluation of Royce's thought—for instance, contemporary scholars like Robert Burch, David Casey, Robert Corrington, and Jacquelyn Kegley. Yet the survey may show how the dialectic of contrasting views of Royce from 1910 to 1990 has made the "essential temperament" of that man from California gradually become appreciated more accurately.

2. Royce's Personal Moral Development

To map out and measure the moral growth of a person calls for care and empathetic understanding. Our attempt to do this with Royce gets the help he supplied in 1915 when he identified free self-direction, goodness, and duty as the three leading ideas in ethical life.[1] In his last ethics course, he applied these ideas to individuals and communities as moral agents. The three ideas guided both his mature philosophy of loyalty and his art of loyalty. The latter required "constancy, tolerance, and resolving conflicts of loyalties" for the practical embodiments of these ideas.[2] In brief, then, by observing how Royce grew in his sense of free self-direction, goodness, and duty throughout his life but especially in his final decade, we may discover how his personal life signaled what "being loyal to loyalty" meant.

As mentioned, Royce's childhood was spent in the mining town of Grass Valley, California. He lived there in an orderly and affectionate home that contrasted with the harsh and blustery atmosphere of a recent gold-rush town. His home had its share of tensions due to the frequent absence of his father, its condition of poverty, and the labors shouldered by his mother, Sarah Eleanor. She influenced him predominantly along strong moral, intellectual, and religious lines. She taught children both in her own home and at the town school. She supplied young Josiah with as many books as her means allowed, nurturing a reading habit that became voracious. She practiced religion earnestly, communally (at home and church), and a bit fanatically at times.[3] Although Sarah Eleanor had quasi-mystical experiences, her daughter Ruth described her as "intensely spiritual" to avoid the common misinterpretations of the term "mystical."[4]

His father, Josiah Senior, was an amiable eccentric, deeply religious but inept as a provider. He often sold produce in far-off mining areas. By his absences he evoked in Royce a permanent longing for a father figure.[5] Even during the rare presences of his father, Josiah found him more of a negative model. True, he had shown the courage and adventurous spirit of a '49er and reinforced Sarah's example of religious dedication. He failed, however, to

23

show his son how to be a man, how to conduct a career, how to treat one's health, and how to avoid becoming a biblical fundamentalist.

Royce was "not a very active boy. . . [having] no physical skill or agility" due to a congenital asthmatic condition which made his health frail.[6] Moreover, he was socially restricted to the company of his mother and three sisters during his childhood. His mother did not allow him to associate with either the rough and ready miners of Grass Valley or its handful of boys his age (for as yet the town had few families).

About 1860 the Royces relocated at Avon Farm, more than a mile from town. This increased Josiah's isolation from male companions and called him to think and behave more on his own. Often his only escape from his female home-environment was walking alone in the woods. During these hikes, when he found "the vestiges left by the former diggings of miners, saw that many pine logs were rotten, and that a miner's grave was to be found in a lonely place not far from my own house," his profound musing about decay and death made him wonder how people could call his community *new*.

Religiously, young Josiah was frequently immersed in home Bible-reading and psalm-singing, both of which he enjoyed. The family Bible, displayed on the living room table, so fascinated him that at an early age he made its Apocalypse his first independent reading. However, he did not often enjoy his attendance at church and Bible-school on Sundays—things that stimulated his spirit of independence and nonconformism. He later recalled how heresy-refuting preachers "more than once . . . used to quicken my wits by the hostility which they awakened in my mind and to arouse my boyish fury by their dogmatism."[7] Many social irritants seem to have fueled this long-remembered rebellion: the required regular attendance, the dogmatism of the fundamentalist preachers, the cover-up primness of Sunday dress, and the "scent" of the church-goers' presumed self-righteousness.

The Civil War influenced Royce's sense of country. Accounts of war inspired imaginary battles for his solitary games.[8] Sharply increased war-prices confronted the family and his mother eked out contributions to aid the wounded.[9] Later he recalled:

> My earliest great patriotic experience came at the end of the civil war, when the news of the assassination of Lincoln reached us. Thenceforth, as I believe, I had a country as well as a religious interest. Both of these were ineffective interests, except in so far as they were attached to the already mentioned enthusiasms, and were clarified and directed by the influence of my mother and sisters.[10]

In 1866, the Royce family moved to San Francisco. They were poor and young Josiah frail. Once typhoid fever quarantined him inside a woodshed where he lay shivering "in a straw bed on the dirt floor covered only by an old quilt."[11]

He was enrolled in Lincoln Grammar School which emphasized physical fitness, military drill, and group supremacy over individuality. Royce, "redheaded, freckled, countrified, quaint, and unable to play boys' games,"[12] was teased and disciplined by the other boys to recognize their group rules. With these he had to comply, even in a withdrawn sort of way, if he were to survive socially. This seared his consciousness with male demands not of his own choosing.

Moreover, his quick mind and particularly his self-righteous "preaching down" to them only irritated them the more. This further promoted both their reactions against him and his own inner rebellion against them, despite his outer compliance. As yet he was not fully sensitive to this dynamic.[13] However crude the values governing their practices and customs, the group held the overwhelming majority and thus reflected "the majesty of the community." If Josiah had previously been treated as "special" and reared to be an independent Californian, he learned at Lincoln Grammar School that he too was obliged to meet at least the minimal demands of a tolerably good group. In this way, the idea of duty, as one's response to the authority of a community, was inculcated more memorably into young Josiah.

In his thirteenth year, Josiah encountered a challenge to his attitude toward the sacred book of the Christian People. On New Year's Day, 1869, Sarah Eleanor presented her son with the gift of a new Bible. Along with it, this evangelical Christian, who was Josiah's first and most influential "teacher of philosophy," offered to this impressionable lad the witness of her "tough love."[14] For on the book's inside cover she had inscribed her poem that started, "Remember, love, who gave thee this," and ended:

> A Mother's blessing on her son,
>   Goes with this holy thing;
> The love that would retain the one,
>   Must to the other cling.
> Remember! 'tis no idle toy,
>   A *Mother's* gift! Remember boy!"[15]

No soft sentiment here. The alert adolescent grasped clearly both the message of the poem, "If you love me, love the Bible," and its inherent warning: "If you cease clinging to the Bible, you lose my blessing."

Part of Josiah's lifelong loyalty to his mother involved a clinging to the living core of the Christian Scriptures, even amid an increasingly rationalistic environment. However much he might later use higher criticism to refine biblical legends, myths, and reported histories, he would remain loyal to what he later called its "sword of the spirit."[16]

In high school and college, Royce experienced his free self-direction more and more. The way he chose to write or declaim gradually won him recognition. Quite independently he kept revising his program of studies at the University of California. During this period truth-seeking became a dominant trait in Royce. For instance, he broke with the traditions of his family by preferring the experiential evidence of evolutionary science because it seemed more true. As indicated in many of his essays of the early 1870s, he strove passionately toward understanding each topic more fully and fairly. Truth-seeking became explicitly a dominant theme in his writings in the late 1870s when he returned to Berkeley as an instructor. He then published articles that showed how actively this motive operated in his intellectual development.

Royce's year of study in Germany reveals an almost incredible, self-imposed commitment to work, to mastering German, to taking twice as many graduate courses as is ordinarily done today. Later at the Johns Hopkins, he became readily familiar with Schopenhauer, Spinoza, Kant, and contemporary philosophical literature, exulting in the work. Having finished a doctorate in philosophy but lacking a position, Royce settled for a place in Berkeley's English department, where he continued with patience and "stick-to-it-iveness" for four years.

Here he met Boston-born Katharine Head, whose father, Edward F. Head, had graduated from Harvard and later brought his wife and two daughters to California, where he currently served as superior court judge of San Mateo County. The marriage of Katharine and Josiah followed in late 1880. After the birth of their first son and the good news of Harvard's offer to Josiah of a one-year appointment as lecturer, Katharine too was eager to return to her relatives in the Boston area. On this slim offer from Harvard, Royce ventured to pack up his wife and infant son Christopher and traveled by rail across the country to Harvard where he began teaching three courses in September 1882.[17]

1883-1905

At Harvard Royce committed himself unceasingly to work. In mid-January 1883, his intellectual experience attained a climactic insight that lay—not like Buddha's in some mystical illumination—but rather in a rational realization that the whole system of finite judgments requires an All-Knowing Constitutor of all judgments (both true and false). When publishing his argument, Royce wrote that every possible finite error

> implies a judgment whose intended object is beyond itself, and is also the object of the corresponding true judgment. But two judgments cannot have the same object save as they are both present to one thought. . . . Only as present to an including thought are they either true or false.[18]

This "including thought" is or points to an actual infinite All-Knowing Judge who actually constitutes the infinity of all finite truths and all possible errors. Otherwise, the ultimate condition for the possibility of our experienced actual error would be lacking and thus our actual finite error would become impossible, which is contrary to fact.

Looking back at his breakthrough to this religious insight, Royce later acknowledge that by it "I had definitely passed over from my earlier sceptical position to the constructive Idealism that I have ever since endeavored to work out."[19] Scarcely anything else in Royce's first twenty-five years at Harvard affected his moral character so deeply as did this religious insight, his awareness of the reality of a superhuman type of consciousness. It became a religious duty for Royce to seek truth with all his energies, in every way possible. The resultant productivity was astounding. Within five years, it included, besides a full-time teaching load, three major books, many articles and reviews, frequent public lectures, and a breakdown.

Due to the unexpected death of historian W. W. Crane, Jr., Royce was asked in 1883 to write a history of California in addition to his work as a lecturer in philosophy and his own writing. First, Royce sought advice from Bernard Moses, Berkeley's history professor, whether to undertake this work in history. Although "affection for the task" and need for money moved Royce to say yes, he said he was far more moved "by the good that would be done me if I undertook to examine the moral and general significance of just that set of concrete facts."[20] His subtitle to the work, "A Study of American Character," revealed his basic intent: to grow as a moral philosopher by doing an ethical case study. As for method, he would approach ethics experientially rather than follow the *a priori* deductive method of many ethicists.

In *California*, his main focus would be "just that set of concrete facts" which created the state between 1846 and 1856. His chief interest would be neither the ethics of individuals nor the ethical demands exerted by the common good of California, the United States, or the international community—indispensable as these dimensions were for his task. Rather he wanted to focus on the factual network of developmental processes, attitudes, customs, laws, cultural backgrounds, biases, and other societal institutions which interlinked the Spanish, Anglo-American, Indian, and Chinese peoples as they interacted in California during this period. This work reveals Royce's growing sensitivity to the way a complex social infrastructure affects the ethical life of different groups and their members. This interest in the ethics of cultural and political economy led him to draft lectures on the topic in the mid-1880s. Later, after his visit to Australia in 1888, he initiated comparison-contrasts of our cultural and political economy with that of Australia.

Contrary to his anticipated "amusement for leisure hours," Royce found how exacting and tedious it was to gather enough clues to create an evenly balanced historical picture. He admitted it was "fearfully hard to seek truth in these [historical] matters."[21] He found that writing history, unlike philosophy, required many hours in various archives, tiresome hunts for documents, irksome interviews with some of the personnel involved, cross-checking with historians of different perspectives, and sustaining their criticisms. Certainly his self-confessed "respect for thoroughness" only increased all his labors.[22] Yet usually he could laugh with a correspondent about his own gaffs and the attacks of nettled readers.

Professor George Herbert Palmer's choice of a leave of absence during 1883–1884 made a second year at Harvard possible for Royce. He took over Palmer's advanced course in ethics. For this, he engaged in a historical study of Ancient, Hebrew, and early Christian ethical thought. As a historian of philosophy, Royce knew the importance of seeing ethical questions in their cultural setting. As a philosopher examining Christian ethics, he suspended his judgment about anything "supernatural" in Jesus, yet remained "without any hope of ever satisfying himself with any one of the many particular natural explanations [about Jesus]."[23] By making these comparative historical studies of ethical systems and cultures, Royce undoubtedly sharpened his own insight into the key turning points of ethical life and theory.

For the academic year 1884–1885, no position opened for Royce. During this third year he managed to stay on at Harvard only by accepting some piecemeal work in forensics and English composition. Meanwhile he waited for the overseers of Harvard to recognize the merits of his just published *Religious Aspect of Philosophy*. To his relief, Harvard did recognize him with an assistant professorship in philosophy in April 1885.

Royce's cross-country research on *California*, his ongoing controversies about interpreting early California history, and his seeing the final draft of this manuscript through publication left him exhausted. He chose to rest by writing a novel. In February 1888, he collapsed, feeling the whir of a "devil in the brain." He confessed to having "joined the too great army of scholarly blunderers who break down when they ought to be at their best."[24] To restore his health, he took a health-cruise to Australia.[25]

Returning by way of California, Royce found that his father had meanwhile died. Back in Cambridge, Royce found his own family soon expanded from two to three boys. (Christopher was born in 1882, Ned in 1887, and Stephen in 1889.) His letters reveal how he grew more attached to these boys, increasingly interested in observing their psychological growth, and, as professional duties allowed, readier to invest time with them on hiking or boating vacations. However, as early as 1890, Royce's doctor indicated that Christopher's psychic health might deteriorate. Thus a concern began for Josiah and Katharine—a worry that would mount in the next two decades until Christopher had to be confined three years before his death in 1910.

After Katharine's pregnancies—all of which involved complications that alarmed Josiah—she took primary charge of rearing the three boys. In financial matters Josiah was hardly shrewd and later when Katharine broke her leg, Josiah meant well but was inept in running the house in her stead. Both highly valued their professional lives—he in his career as a philosopher coming to international eminence, she in hers as a gifted pianist in her home with her beloved boys, as a social hostess in Cambridge, and particularly as a linguist and translator who supplemented the needed family income.

Katharine's was a "vivid personality...gifted with a picturesque speech which she did not hesitate to employ."[26] She once described her husband to a student as a "funny-looking man" and poked fun at his metaphysical profession. Their married life had its deep tensions, quarrels, and disappointments. At times she scolded not only the boys of the neighborhood but Josiah as well. Escaping from the often volatile atmosphere of his home, Josiah took almost all his trips alone—often becoming an absentee father in his turn. Eventually his mature sketch of the "tragedy of love" surfaced such experiences of isolation and misunderstanding:

> What constitutes, in this present world, the pathos, the tragedy of love, is that, because our neighbor is so mysterious a being to our imperfect vision, we do not now know how to make him happy, to relieve his deepest distresses, to do him the highest good.[27]

During their final decade together, Josiah's idealism was increasingly attacked, Christopher was confined and died, Josiah's health declined, especially after his stroke, and the war crushed his dream of a Great Community of nations. Yet through and perhaps because of all these sufferings, Josiah and Katharine evinced a tender and deepening compassionate love for each other, their two surviving sons, and a retarded grandson.[28]

Royce's salary at Harvard was meager indeed, especially before his Gifford Lectures. He wrote to a friend that his college salary barely kept him out of the poorhouse.[29] With the expanse of his family, Royce gave more public lectures to supplement his income. For example in the spring of 1898, Royce offered six Cambridge Conferences on "Aspects of Social Psychology" and ten lectures to the Twentieth Century Club of Boston on the "Social Factors in the Development of the Individual Mind."[30] This repeated public lecturing undoubtedly led to that already mentioned "excess of loud garrulity" about which Royce quipped—half in jest, half in earnest—in the mock obituary of himself offered as a get-well gift to William James during the latter's illness at Rye in England.

At the end of the century, in the midst of his preparation of the Gifford Lectures, he received an invitation to a vacation from Mrs. Mary Dorr, a long-standing friend. His reply reveals how dutifully he regarded himself bound:

> The Gifford Lectures . . . are, or ought to be, . . . the effort of my life. If I cannot do them rightly, I shall do much more than fail; I shall be a false servant of Harvard. If I do not do them rightly, I shall be false, also, to the friends who have obtained for me this high trust, and to the cause of serious thinking on Religion and to the public concerned. To say this is . . . only to say that this trust concerning a very sacred task has been put upon me; and now I must live up to it.[31]

Few passages express so clearly Royce's sense of the urgency of duty. This wholehearted practical dedication to creating his Gifford Lectures exacted many hours of labor. In particular, he toiled to bring his lengthy, undelivered Supplementary Essay to completion. Again, dissatisfied with his already delivered Second Series, he strove for a radical restructuring of those lectures for publication. In all of this, however, the central factor was Royce's total commitment to do the best he possibly could in his profession.

As he reached middle-age, the words of his youth, "It is good to strive," expressed an increasingly treasured value in his life. It took a striving still more exacting to bring three inner factors into a life-giving balance: his drive for more knowledge, his intouchness with affectivity as central to human living, and his wholehearted decisiveness of service. Only in 1912, when he broke through to the fecund interpretive musement inspired by Peirce, did he finally attain the integrated and balanced pursuit of the goal he desired.

Royce's striving also involved the struggle to maintain relationships—with personalities like Katharine and Christopher within his own home; with colleagues like Palmer, Peirce, and Münsterberg; with currently dissenting, former students like George Santayana, G. H. Mead, and R. B. Perry; and, perhaps most trying of all, with some not so friendly opponents like F. E. Abbott and G. H. Howison, and his most challenging critic and closest philosophical friend, William James. All this striving kept testing the mettle of his spirit—sometimes unfortunately in his stinging reviews of Abbott or in his overburdening of editor Howison with an appendix longer than the contributions of the four initial panelists.[32] But usually his spirit became further disciplined and eventually mellowed.

After his Australian journey, Royce intensified his study of ethics. Having completed his *Spirit of Modern Philosophy*, he planned to produce a book on ethics.[33] As an editor for the *International Journal of Ethics*, he reviewed dozens of books on ethics and surveyed ethical thought annually.[34] He applied his philosophy to the practical problems of life in public lectures and in essays. Some of these were eventually collected in *Studies of Good and Evil* and *Race Questions, Provincialism, and Other American Problems*. Many of these unveiled his strong aversion to racism, to America's penchant for war, and to the intellectual superficiality and fadism of many so-called educated Americans. This further grasp of ethical life had to affect, at least indirectly, his own ethical attitude, commitment, and life.

From 1887 to 1906, death touched Royce more closely than in his childhood encounter with a miner's grave. Now close acquaintances died— often in pairs or clusters. In 1887, his two close friends in Berkeley and Baltimore, Edward R. Sill and George B. Coale, died. In 1889–1990, he lost Mary, his oldest sister, and Judge Head, his father-in-law. Then in April 1891 brute chance struck his mother, when a stranger in the postoffice at San Jose ran into her so hard that her head knocked against the wall. She never fully recovered but died in November 1891. This happened just after the climax of the controversy with Abbott, when articles abusive of Royce were circulated abroad and the Harvard Corporation was asked to remove him from the faculty.[35] In 1901 Royce knew a triple loss—in May his mother-in-law died in his own home and in July Joseph LeConte and John Fiske, two close associates of his earlier work, passed on. In 1906, when Royce served as honorary pall-bearer for two Harvard colleagues, their "passings," like those just mentioned, intensified his characteristic "cult of the dead."[36] This series of deaths summoned his ethical reflection to keep confronting the deepest challenge in ethical life: the problem of evil, particularly as encountered in death, and the enigma of an afterlife. In response, he created and revised his address, "The Problem of Job," and his Ingersoll Lecture of 1900, *The Conception of Immortality*.

One of the most attractive features of Royce's developing moral character was his mental and spiritual openness. By moving amid a changing nature—hiking on mountain trails, sailing in changing seas—he fostered a watchful readiness for surprises, especially as he grew older.[37] He also read broadly—history, mathematics, psychology, languages, medicine, geography, anthropology, and most of all, philosophy. He subscribed to German papers and to the *Leader* from Australia. He read Kant and Hegel in the original. He handled Greek and Sanskrit easily. He quoted the Latin of Vergil's *Aeneid* from memory. As one of only a handful, he both understood the abstruse lectures that C. S. Peirce delivered at Harvard and conversed with him on logical topics as an equal.

His ambition sometimes outran his awareness of his own limits. For instance, he had plans for many books which were never brought to publication. In 1888 it was a critical construction of philosophy in three volumes; then, individual books on Theodore Parker, Goethe, and Hegel, and a full-length study of Hegel's *Phenomenologie*. In 1892, it was to be a work on ethics; and later still, a masterwork on logic, which he had to abandon for health reasons after 1912.[38]

His openness also disposed him to feel his need for correction. In 1902 he accepted Peirce's recommendation that he should study logic and invested fourteen years in logical research. He circulated preliminary drafts of his *Spirit of Modern Philosophy* and *Sources of Religious Insight*. Before going to Scotland for the Gifford Lectures, he used his well-known metaphysics course (Philosophy 9) to test out his theory about conceptions of reality. Generally he was open to suggestions from his editors and publishers about titles and contractual arrangements. Though he did not often use Peirce's term "fallibility," the maturing Royce increasingly showed his awareness of the inescapable human tendency to err. As Royce grew older, he also further "discerned things of the spirit."

After his Gifford Lectures, Royce's truth-seeking drive led him into almost countless hours of study and research in logic and its relations with mathematics. He identified certain "absolute truths" within the consequences that follow from various initial axioms. Working off of the Erlanger Programme, Royce detected, apparently upon a cue from Peirce, how significant was the work of the English logician, Alfred Bray Kempe. This led Royce to the creation of his System Sigma and his masterful article, "The Relation of the Principles of Logic to the Foundations of Geometry" (1905). His dedication to logic led on to his outstanding work, *The Principles of Logic* (1910), and his "An Extension of the Algebra of Logic" (1913).[39]

1906–1916

Royce saw that all genuinely loyal persons (or, in his sense of the term, all "Christians") are called to meet the problem of evil in a distinctive way. Going beyond a merely stoical acceptance of their sufferings, they are to use these to enter into atoning activity, the hallmark of authentic loyalty.

> The value of suffering, the good that is at the heart of evil, lies in the spiritual triumphs that the endurance and the overcoming of evil can bring to those who learn the hard, the deep but glorious, lesson of life. And of all the spiritual triumphs of life that the presence of evil makes possible, the noblest is that which is won when . . . [going beyond Stoic endurance], one is willing to suffer vicariously, freely, devotedly, ills that he might have avoided, but that the cause to which he is loyal, and the errors and sins that he himself did not commit, call upon him to suffer in order that the world may be brought nearer to its destined union with the divine. In brief, as the mystics themselves often have said, sorrow—wisely encountered and freely borne—is one of the most precious privileges of the spiritual life.[40]

This solution to the problem of evil has "expressed itself in the lives of the wisest and best of the moral heroes of all races and nations of men." Royce thus manifested his gradually dawning conviction that sufferings, if idealized into sorrows, have a religious mission in everyone's life: that is, they then become "a source of religious insight," as Royce would interpret them in a chapter unique in philosophical literature in his *Sources of Religious Insight*.[41] Here Royce entered profoundly into human suffering and showed how, by idealizing one's sufferings into sorrows, a hope arises that brings energies to atone. Soon he spoke of atonement as "the function in which the life of the community culminates."[42]

Royce's later years were marked by tragedies and suffering. In 1906, he wrote his editor at Macmillan that illness in his family had kept him from examining a manuscript for them—a likely reference to the growing problem of his first son Christopher.[43] In the autumn of that year, William James mentioned to Royce the neighborhood rumor that Christopher had suffered a nervous breakdown and been sent to a sanitorium. Royce branded the rumor false, even while guardedly admitting that Christopher's problem had "caused us some care."[44]

In May 1907, Christopher first needed restraints. Seeking counsel from a number of medical experts, Royce obtained treatment for his son both at home and elsewhere. By August, Royce admitted to James the high cost of medical care for Christopher—a sum he might as well have poured into the sea "for all the good it did to the poor boy."

Striving to pay for Christopher's treatments, Royce undertook many extra lectures, in addition to his regular load at Harvard and Radcliffe. From November to April in both 1906–07 and 1907–08 he provided teachers with an introductory course in ethics that met twice weekly.[45] Undertaking to teach two courses in philosophy at Yale in 1907–08, Royce had to take the train down to New Haven and back each Saturday. Royce drained himself this way to keep out of "pauperism, which I of course regard with peculiar horror." He clearly remembered how he had broken down from excessive toil in 1888 and faced the worrisome prospect of the dire consequences he might visit upon Katharine and his sons if he again broke under his extra burdens or died and left them completely bereft.[46]

In January 1908, Christopher had to be committed to the Danvers sanitorium. Royce wrote James:

> But there are some things that are beyond speech,—at least for me. . . . Please do not talk to me more than is necessary about the matter, when we meet. . . . [I find Christopher] pathetically amiable and intellectually intact (as to mathematics, chemistry, etc.) as he is, [yet burdened by] . . . one or two nests of confused ideas, and of helpless misjudgments, [along with] . . . a general failure of will,— a large aboulia, as to all the critical enterprises of life,—viz. undertaking a

calling,—striking out for himself, etc. . . . The prognosis is of course bad. . . . The whole affair has been of course far worse than the death of our first-born could have been. We have long had to envy those who have thought their own afflictions very hard. . . . We have fought our fight, and lost. We shall keep on fighting, and try not to make any outcry. . . . I try to . . . hold onto my two other boys . . . I don't ask comfort. The only comfort to look for is not of this visible world. But at least I am not a "shallow optimist" . . . nor do I change my mind as to our problem of evil because I am hard hit.

But the poor boy will probably never see any of the light that I had been longing and fighting to have him see. And the way is a long and dark one for us all.[47]

Christopher remained in the sanitorium for several years, dying there in 1910.

There were other difficulties in Royce's family life during his last years. He himself suffered a stroke February 1, 1912. Six weeks later Royce described the episode:

For a day or two after the attack there was some somnolence and confusion. Then there followed, of course, a good deal of depression and moodiness, with a general emotional flabbiness. And there were naturally plenty of headaches. But there was never any motor paralysis, or serious interference with mental processes of any level. I soon took to my usual interests and plans.[48]

Although he would speak of the matter with cheerfulness and humor, referring to his "dilapidated head piece," he recognized that the attack was serious. However he had other problems which occupied his thoughts. His son Ned and new daughter-in-law Elizabeth Randolph had been causing him mounting concern. Royce cherished Elizabeth, an artistic, physically weak, and "ineffective" young woman and had been recently concerned for her health during her first pregnancy.[49]

In the late spring of 1912, this young couple gave their infant son Randolph, who proved to be mentally handicapped, into the keeping of Josiah and Katharine. There were signs that their marriage was beginning to unravel. Royce wrote to a friend:

Both of them are . . . in may ways, babes. —As I feel myself also a babe. . . . Nor can I do anything myself but sit by while these conditions aim to wreck both of these young lives.[50]

Royce also suffered the foreboding that Ned, under the doubled pressure of both making his career in music and enduring these marital difficulties, might crack and go the way of Christopher. After moving from several instructorships, Ned finally found a position at Middlebury College, Vermont, initiating a music department there. Randolph, however, stayed with his grandparents.

Royce's third son, Stephen, was a geologist in the mining region of Upper Michigan. In January 1915, Stephen and his wife Marion lost their first child "Petsy," after only a few months of life. They were further burdened by Marion's ill health, large medical bills, and financial straits caused by wildly fluctuating prices of iron ore. Besides companioning this young couple in their loss, Josiah and Katharine supported them financially as far as they could. Josiah penned many letters of introduction or recommendation to secure positions for his sons.

With losses, memories, concerns, and parental pains, Royce and his wife savored the bitter tragedy of life.[51] Through it all, however, both of them loved their children tenderly, cared for them persistently, and encouraged them steadfastly. As Royce had earlier written:

> The family ties, so far as they are natural, are opportunities for loyalty; so far as they are deliberately chosen or recognized, [they] are instances of the choice of a loyalty.[52]

His griefs, disappointments, and worries led him to refine his practical loyalty to family and pressed him to muse more closely upon family. To belong to a family constituted the human self's first and most basic relationship in time and function. This natural relationship embodied the logical relation *epsilon* (ϵ), the most fundamental of Royce's logical relations. The relation of belonging to a family diversified itself according to three different "modes of (ethical) action" proper to the communications occurring between husband-and-wife, parent-and-child, and siblings. Embodied in these three modes of natural belonging Royce found that three distinct logical pair-relationships arise in series from the fundamental ϵ relation.

Royce also found that the logical pairs underlying husband and wife, parent and child, and sibling relationships corresponded, respectively, to his three "leading ethical ideas": goodness, duty, and autonomy. He further examined how these three familial relations can become "dangerous dyads" infected with estrangement and how only a servant-like atoning mediation can promote their reconciliation. When upon this basis he later described the three kinds of loyalty needed in family life, he showed how much further he had developed his loyalty doctrine, even since its development in the *Problem*, three years earlier.

In addition to the pain and disappointment Royce suffered in his family circle, he faced estrangement from friends and colleagues during the final years of his life. As pragmatism mounted in popularity, Royce felt his success and acclaim slipping through his fingers. He saw poignantly that this loss was caused most of all by William James, his close friend and colleague for a quarter century. When James resigned from Harvard in 1907, Royce sensed the growing decline of what had been Harvard's great department of philosophy.

Despite his desire to improve his friendship with James, Royce decided to criticize James publicly for lacking an adequate philosophical perspective on truth. The criticism was leveled, with James in the audience, during Royce's seventh lecture on "The Philosophy of Loyalty," December 8, 1907.[53] James replied with a brief statement, "The Meaning of the Word Truth," at the annual meeting of the American Philosophical Association that same month. Not waiting for the published *Proceedings*, James had this four-page statement printed and circulated, sending a copy to Royce. Although he could not take exception to James's positive statements, Royce was appalled at the inadequacy of James's position:

> My general objection to your view is that it is not the *whole* truth about truth.
> It leaves out essential aspects. This objection [of mine] has never been met or
> even touched in any of your statements.[54]

A few months later, Royce strove to maintain and increase his philosophically strained friendship. To James, "one of the dearest of my friends, and . . . one of the most loyal of men," Royce drafted his famous tribute while looking even more faithfully toward genuine loyalty:

> What I personally owe him [James], then I most heartily and affectionately
> acknowledge. But if he and I do not see truth in the same light at present, we
> still do well, I think, as friends, each to speak his mind as we walk by the way,
> and then to wait until some other light shines for our eyes. I suppose that so
> to do is loyalty.[55]

James thanked Royce for paying him such a high tribute but then added:

> I am sorry you say we don't see truth in the same light, for the only thing we
> see differently is the Absolute, and surely such a trifle as that is not a thing for
> two gentlemen to be parted by. I believe that at the bottom of *your* heart *we*
> see things more alike than any pair of philosophers extant! I thank you anyhow
> from the bottom of mine. Affectionately yours, Wm. James[56]

James's jest about the Absolute as a trifle showed a brief loss of touch with Royce's most vital religious insight. Despite the affectionate gratitude conveyed, James's note bore some sting.

How deeply this note affected Royce may not be ascertainable, but he was certainly pained profoundly by James's final neglect of his Heidelberg address.[57] Royce had drafted this essay most carefully as a coherent theory of truth, integrating the instrumental, pragmatic, and objective motives operating in individuals and communities that search for more truth. James's neglect might be partially understood by his preoccupation with his own Hibbert Lectures, "A Pluralistic Universe" in 1908 and early 1909. Yet a year later when he recorded in his diary "Royce gives me his Heidelberg address," James evidently noticed Royce's invitation to examine this essay. Perhaps because James was by then trying to accomplish as much creative work as his condition allowed during his final months, he seems to have given it no more than a cursory reading.[58] This unusual disregard remained a thorn in Royce's heart for his final eight years.

In late December 1909, Ralph Barton Perry attacked Royce's idealism in a paper called "The Ego-centric Predicament." In this way the New Realists, borrowing the mantle of James's *Pragmatism*, began their anti-Roycean campaign.

In 1910, after the death of both his son and his friend James, Royce threw himself into his work—a busy academic year, commitments to writing, and a schedule of external lectures heavier than usual. This last included a 1910–1911 course in the philosophy of religion at Yale, where he received an honorary degree. Soon at Sanders Theatre he delivered a perceptive and widely acclaimed Phi Beta Kappa address on "James the Philosopher." Royce also made various preliminary presentations of his general philosophy of religion, which soon led to his *Sources of Religious Insight*.[59]

Sometime around 1911 Royce drafted an article for Hastings's *Encyclopaedia*, entitled "Error and Truth." During its preparation Royce seems to have experienced the fatal flaw in idealism at that precise foundational point upon which he had built his philosophy. He confessed:

> Precisely with regard to the problem of the possibility of error, . . . the idealistic theory of truth and error has proved to be, thus far, most incomplete.[60]

Trying to resolve this problem, Royce specified seven "Conditions of a solution of the problem of error"—a list that climaxed in his final condition:

> (7) A revision of Hegel's dialectical method, a synthesis of this method with the empirical tendencies of recent Pragmatism, a combination of both with the methods of modern Logic *seem*, in their combination, to be required for a complete treatment of the problem of error.[61]

Here Royce's "seem" expresses more than a tentative recipe for a new solution. It also reveals Royce's discovery that he had lost his way intellectually in thinking through the radical starting point of his philosophy: the problem of the possibility of error. He felt himself groping about but as yet could not find his way, for he was still caught in a theory of knowledge that remained basically dyadic. This radical difficulty would frustrate him until his "Peircean insight" in mid-1912.

Meanwhile, contemporary events concerned him. In the American Philosophical Association's planned discussion on "The Relation of Consciousness and Object in Sense Perception," the committee had selected the questions and slanted the definitions of terms to favor the realist view. Royce saw the result as "a riot of philosophic anarchy."[62] In November 1912, another professional vexation arose. Arthur Lovejoy, Royce's former student, charged neo-Fichteans with "imposture"—a charge most of his readers took as targeted at Royce. Royce asked Lovejoy for a clarification. In his response, buried in the final pages of a later issue of the *Journal of Philosophy*, Lovejoy withdrew the abusive term, yet inserted the innuendo that as a philosopher Royce was insincere and philosophized mainly to comfort hearts.[63]

However, neither this concern nor his own physical breakdown in early 1912 kept Royce long from his work. He had previously promised to apply his general philosophy of religion to the special case of Christianity.[64] Before his breakdown he had contracted to deliver the Lowell Lectures in the fall and he looked forward to giving the Hibbert Lectures at Oxford.[65] Once he had sufficiently recovered from his attack, he became increasingly absorbed in the problem of Christianity for these two lecture series.

Four years earlier, however, he had already returned to Christianity's religious problems—those that had first driven him to philosophy and also promoted his moral development. For already in 1908 he had discovered that Christianity's vital and vitalizing energies lay in Christ's living attitudes both towards the Father's love for each individual human person and towards the consequent "infinite worth" of every person. He also found this vitality in the reasonably interpreted doctrines of the Church's main symbols: the Incarnation and the Atonement.

For Royce, incarnation occurs in the present moment insofar as finite human selves freely allow God to be born within themselves by consenting to "transmute transient and temporal values into eternal meanings"—that is, "in so far as humanity looks godwards" in its choices. This free turning to God and acceptance of his will is the enfleshment of "our unity with the universal purpose" of God, a moral incarnation of the Logos.

Confronting the problem of evil, Royce had found that atonement has its bases in the divine Spirit's plan and in the finite selves' transmutation of their sufferings. In its plan for a reasonable world, the Spirit intends "that you should not remain what you now are." Finite selves are to go beyond a mere endurance of their sufferings by turning them into blessings for others—that is, by their "willingness to suffer vicariously."[66]

As Clendenning pointed out, Royce's deeper and more purified grasp of these two Christian doctrines both enabled him to experience God's companionship within his own perennial sense of loneliness and prepared him to meet the deeper tragedies soon to come in upon him.[67]

In his recuperation of 1912 when Royce began preparing for his Hibbert Lectures, he delved especially into theologians. He also systematically reviewed the earlier and later published writings of Peirce, searching for the pattern that governed the latter's intellectual development. Inspired by Peirce's way of weaving his simplest ideas (of firstness, secondness, and thirdness) into a theory of interpretation, Royce gradually caught sight of a new triadic epistemology. Our best insight into just what Royce then underwent derives from his own public account of it given two years later at Berkeley.[68]

Royce acknowledged that only with his "new review" of Peirce's theory of knowledge in 1912 had he observed how closely it was connected with the things "I had been trying to formulate in my philosophy of loyalty." Royce also acknowledged that when he brought this Peircean theory of knowledge to bear upon the ethical aspect of philosophical idealism, he found that his [Royce's] mature ethics "got a new concreteness, a new significance, and a new relation to the methods and to the presuppositions of inductive science."[69] Royce discovered that Peirce's method of interpretation and his "three simple ideas" gave his own late ethics a new life and depth. Accordingly, the "mature period" of Royce's thought (1912–1916) begins with this "Peircean insight."

So, in the summer of 1912 when Royce took four two-week cruises on fruit steamers to and from Port Limon, Costa Rica, he found that while he sat quietly in the stern, he enjoyed the most suitable conditions for musing creatively on Christianity and for drafting his lectures. By September he had written seven of these and with a leave of absence for the academic year 1912–13 was able to finish all sixteen before leaving for Oxford at the end of December.

Meanwhile Santayana had resigned from Harvard's philosophy department, further weakening it. As a senior faculty member, Royce inherited Santayana's unfulfilled task of recruiting new faculty. During his 1913 stay in England, Royce scouted among Britain's many talented thinkers. In these delicate exchanges, however, he admitted feeling like a disappointed bachelor who proposes often and is rejected just as often.[70]

Back in Boston, Royce discovered that Santayana had seen to the wider publication of his "Genteel Tradition in American Philosophy," as mentioned. The republished version was softened only slightly. It treated the middle Royce with satire and failed to engage with the mature Royce of the *Problem*.

Royce's own work, *The Problem of Christianity*, received reserved reviews, although generally favorable.[71] Most of his reviewers disappointed Royce by missing his main point: how should Christianity come to grips with the accelerating rate of change in the modern world? Instead they charged him with downplaying the historical Christ, with failure to identify a visible embodiment of the Beloved Community, and with not being specifically Christian enough. These and other rejections added to Royce's strong sense of failure.

Ironically, the labor of thinking through the lectures of the *Problem* had made him even more aware of his own deepest ethico-religious needs, as well as those of humankind. He saw more clearly than ever that he personally, like every human self, needed union with a higher communal life. He, too, felt deeply divided and separated from this higher life. Like so many people, his failures in external success, his frustrations in relating to family, friends, and associates, and his awareness of his own limits and shortcomings made him feel his moral burden and his failure in attaining the full moral integrity he longed for. He experienced that these deep needs were not yet fully satisfied. He, too, had still to search for deliverance from this moral burden.[72]

Because his son Ned had accepted a position at Vermont's Middlebury College, Royce's interest in this small liberal arts college intensified from mid-1913 on.[73] When the Carnegie Foundation tried to classify this college as "either entirely funded and controlled by the State or in no way funded by the State," Royce sensed that this excessively tight dichotomy would work injustice. He rose to the defense, envisioning the college as a "province" that was being threatened with identity-loss by larger institutions. He gathered data, read reports and correspondence, and then drafted "Provincial Independence of Middlebury College," a letter later utilized by the American Association of University Professors as a model for defending the academic freedom of small colleges.[74] Discerning the different roles of variously sized institutions, Royce defended the smaller ones' right to a fitting independence and the larger ones' duty to provide effective subsidiarity to the smaller ones.

Royce's desire to promote logic and scientific methodology occasioned a double frustration. Despite his lengthy preparations, he now recognized that his frail health and other commitments prevented him from creating the major work in logic he had committed himself to. In 1908 he had agreed to bring Federigo Enriques's *Problema della Scienza*, a leading study of scientific methodology, to an English-speaking audience. His wife Katharine had translated the less technical parts. In June 1912, Royce finally completed translation of the technical parts and drafted an introduction.[75] However, the work was not published until 1914.

Royce had become thoroughly familiar with Bertrand Russell's *Principles of Mathematics* and *Principia Mathematica* (co-authored with Whitehead). He admired the power, depth, and stoical calm of Russell's mind, especially as revealed in his articles "The Essence of Religion" and "A Free Man's Worship."[76] These qualities led Royce to recommend Russell to the Lowell Institute as a lecturer. Although the two men differed radically on the starting elements of logic, on Germany, and on ethics, Russell thought Royce's logical work sufficiently important to invite him to take part in a Mathematical Congress in August 1912.[77] When Russell was a week late in arriving at Harvard for the spring semester, 1914, Royce filled in. To orient

Russell's students, Royce contrasted objectively two theories of knowledge—Russell's dyadic type over against Peirce's triadic theory.[78] Royce's mental breakthrough of 1912 into Peirce's theory had just freed Royce from his earlier tight dyadism and transformed his subsequent philosophizing into the flexible pluralism of a pathfinder. While Royce considered Russell "too nominalistic," Russell was said to have remarked of Royce, "The label is still there but the bottle is empty."[79] However, according to Clendenning, "Russell liked Royce ('tho . . . a garrulous old bore') because he listened to 'whispers from another world'."[80]

In their final years of life, Royce could not well convey to Peirce the deep affection and indebtedness he felt for him and Peirce could not fully recognize his bond to Royce. In May 1913, when Peirce was dying of an incurable illness, Royce sent him the two volumes of his *Problem of Christianity*. He later reported that the enfeebled Peirce had responded by giving the work "a reasonable and an unexpectedly careful, although necessarily a very summary attention, and my interpretation of him gained on the whole, his approval."[81] But sickness and distance hindered that high-level of thought exchange which both wanted and which Peirce had requested more than a decade earlier when the preoccupied Royce had had to decline.[82] In the spring, 1914, when news of Peirce's death reached him, he took prompt steps to obtain and retrieve Peirce's papers. With his assistant, W. F. Kernan, Royce did a first survey of Peirce's unpublished papers and drafted an article on Peirce for the *Journal of Philosophy*.[83]

World War I broke out while Royce was at Berkeley, lecturing in its summer school. He felt it part of his moral commitment to shelve his prepared material and give his audience genuinely relevant materials. His planning and redraftings of his hew lecture, "War and Insurance," revealed a full dedication both to his present particular community—his audience at Berkeley's Philosophical Union—and to the Great Community of humankind endangered by war. By creating this lecture, he embodied loyalty, "*the willing and practical and thoroughgoing devotion of a person to a cause.*"[84]

The war also challenged Royce's relations with his two German colleagues at Harvard—Kuno Francke and Hugo Münsterberg. Francke, curator of the Germanic Museum, was torn by a conflict between loyalty to his homeland and to the whole of humankind. Even though his sympathies naturally inclined to Germany, Francke clearly set higher priority on the Great Community, which he wanted effectively promoted, no matter which side won the war. Admiring such genuine loyalty, Royce supported and strengthened Francke.[85]

Münsterberg, on the other hand, became a loud proclaimer of Prussia's cause and a well-known apologist of Germany's intimidating terror (*Schrecklichkeit*). In this case, Royce terminated a long-standing friendship, even taking an occasion in winter to run Münsterberg off a narrow footpath in the Harvard Yard into the snow. To this proven pro-Prussian propagandist and foe of humanity, Royce showed a face fierce with moral indignation. This was *not* the mature Royce's usually gentle, even kindly and playful behavior towards the friends of humanity, but his moral response to one who preferred the interests of a bully nation to those of the whole human family of nations.[86]

The war years (1914–1916) evinced special efforts from Royce. Besides his regular class lectures, plus his extension course in ethics, and his drafting of philosophical articles—including four significant ones for Hastings's *Encyclopaedia*—Royce wrote several occasional pieces on the war and was twice invited to address the public on this topic. In his famous addresses at Tremont Temple in Boston, he rose up with a prophetic fire, like Amos of old, and thundered against "the spirit of international immorality," against a Germany whose face was that of brother-killing Cain; against a "Germany [which] as at present disposed, is the wilful and deliberate enemy of the human race."[87]

He had arranged to teach the academic year of 1916–1917 and even sketched ideas for a second extension course in ethics at Boston University.[88] However, in late August Royce became seriously ill and was confined to bed for three weeks where, among other things, he mused on "the cult of the dead."[89] He died on September 14, 1916, in the presence of Katharine his wife and Kernan his assistant. The cause of death was set down as arteriosclerosis.[90]

During his last decade Royce applied Peirce's theories of interpretation, signs, and mediation to contemporary problems such as family relations, insurance, and war—trying to balance individual and communal freedoms, duties, and goods; trying to adjust fittingly to the different kinds of loyalty required by different situations; and trying to discern a reconciling path in conflicts of loyalty. Royce's sadness over the difficulties and tragedies within his own family circle, within his profession, and within the world community are aptly reflected in his own words:

> The greatest evil of human social life lies not in the elemental greed, the selfishness of men, but in their failure to understand one another.[91]

3. Royce's Early Ethics to 1895

Contrasted with Royce's many courses in logic, metaphysics, and theory of knowledge during his thirty-four years at Harvard, his formal courses in ethics at Harvard and Radcliffe were relatively few. They occurred chiefly from 1883–1888, in 1913, and then in his 1915–16 Extension Course in Ethics at Boston University. However he continuously whetted his interest and competence in ethics by a variety of activities. As book-review editor for the *International Journal of Ethics* from 1891 until his death, he read ethical works omnivorously. He served in symposia on ethical issues and lectured publicly on ethical topics. Many of these lectures he gathered into his "applied ethical works" as guides for practical living, all of which can be viewed as applications of the overall ethical doctrine which he published for a popular audience in *The Philosophy of Loyalty* (1908).[1]

Royce's ethical thought divides into the reflections of his pre-formed years (1863–1882) and those of his formed years (1883–1916). These latter or Harvard years subdivide into an early period defined as following his religious insight of the reality of an All-Knower in 1883, his middle period following his insight into individuality in 1896, and a mature period following his 1912 Peircean insight of signs and interpretation, of community and its Spirit.

ROYCE'S PRE-FORMED PERIOD (1863–1882)

At age eight Royce wrote a remarkable composition, "Pussey Blackie's Travels." In it young Josie narrated the adventurous journey of his cat and its eventual return home. Into this story he blended the journeying, decision-making, and quest for self-identification characteristic of ethical life. After Lincoln's assassination, thirteen-year-old Josiah examined the ethical question of tyrannicide. He based his almost universal prohibition upon a religious and communitarian context. As an undergraduate at Berkeley, his articles, "The 'Holy Grail' of Tennyson" and "The Life-Harmony," presaged both his quest for an ethico-religious ideal and his discovery of the moral insight.[2]

As an instructor at Berkeley, Royce had developed several influential ethical themes prior to his insight of 1883. In particular he drew from Goethe's *Faust* a basic principle:

43

Im Anfang war die Tat, i.e., the essence of life and being is activity. This activity is not on the one hand simple blind force (*Kraft*), nor on the other hand pure subjective thought (*Sinn*) but the living union of both as seen in the work of the individual moment. . . . The individual moment is the Real; but it is so only in so far forth as it denies itself, strives to pass out over itself, to plunge on into a future. . . . Such continual striving from one moment to another is the Universe itself.[3]

"In the beginning was the Deed" became practically the motto for Royce's emphasis on choice, on striving, on not clinging to the present, on heading into the future. All these marked his activist and voluntaristic ethics.

However, he counterposed his stress on the active with an even more important "*submission* to a conceived other consciousness."[4] He integrated these active and passive responses by emphasizing that in ethical life resigning oneself to one's small share in the Ideal life (necessarily completed by others and dependent on them) is preeminent over "courageous striving to that ideal." Only by such resignation could one avoid the selfish pursuit of character. One needed to let go and allow Nature to employ one as a tool for creating "her vast moral structures."[5]

Other ethical themes mark Royce's earliest writings. He was convinced that earnest human endeavors are required for social change. He was committed to liberty and natural rights. And he kept wrestling with the problem of pessimism.

From 1882 to 1895, Royce developed from a young Harvard lecturer into a professor of the history of philosophy. This period stretches from a maximal insight in January 1883 through his struggle to produce his first major book, *The Religious Aspect of Philosophy* (1885), through his more popular *The Spirit of Modern Philosophy* (1892), until just beyond his "Conception of God" address (1895). Overall during these thirteen years, his ethical depth and precision grew and became more nuanced. Yet during this period his dyadic method, his dialectical rhetoric, and his insufficient experience as a professional ethicist still constricted him.

To confine one's study of Royce's early ethics to published works almost forces one to concentrate on *The Religious Aspect of Philosophy*. Thus both Royce's early efforts to fashion a socio-economic ethics and his development of an integral ethics during the decade after *Religious Aspect* are overlooked. We will start by counteracting this, at least in brief.

LECTURES IN SOCIO-ECONOMIC ETHICS

His 1884 lectures reveal that Royce viewed ethics as far more than a program for simple self-development or the better building of interpersonal relationships.[6] Ethics also had to bear upon social structures and the political economy. Royce found inadequate both the plans for "new socialisms" proposed by people like Henry George and the uncurbed competition of American capitalism which was corrupting both government and business in that era. He saw that widespread urban poverty and ecological devastation required sacrifices of personal freedom if America were to create a better life for all. Every utilitarian search for the greater material and cultural welfare of the greatest number had to fail if it did not emphasize the even more urgent need that every citizen undergo an ethico-religious transformation.

He also saw that the collectivist schemes of the reformers must fail because they adopted as their basis, not a community, but a mere collectivity whose parts simply behaved as functions within a mechanical whole. These socialists forgot about the need to foster the deepening free individualization of every member within the nation's community life. Royce proposed a restructuring of society's institutions upon the basis of a central doctrine: America is an organism, a community with a mind, values, and demands of its own. The great task, then, was both to educate people to the insight that this community needs and deserves each one's unique service and to evoke from all citizens a wholehearted commitment to this community.[7]

Nine years later Royce worked out another lecture series, entitled "Some Recent Tendencies in Ethical Doctrine." Expecting to fashion a book from them, he presented some of them at Thomas Davidson's Summer School in Glenmore, New York. At least two of these lectures concerned a right restructuring of the social order.[8] However, Royce chose *not* to publish most of these ethical lectures, perhaps because he increasingly appreciated the difficulty of fitting the principles of ethics into societal applications.

THE RELIGIOUS ASPECT OF PHILOSOPHY

As published, Royce's *Religious Aspect of Philosophy* revealed his desire to climb into a Harvard berth—one he already had taken considerable risks to obtain. More significantly, however, it signaled his desire to offer Harvard undergraduates some intellectually warranted guidance for their lives. He, William James, and George Herbert Palmer had been struggling against an atmosphere of materialism, popular agnosticism, and moral skepticism, intensified by recent guises of evolutionary theory. These trends and his students' needs, as set within the traditional, almost entirely Christian perspective and culture of Royce and his audience, formed the matrix for the *Religious Aspect*. This matrix also included his previous prodigious reading of most English philosophers, German thinkers, and some French authors. For this work, the young Royce had woven the context of his ethical reflections out of contributions drawn from the British empiricists, but more from Schopenhauer, and most from Kant. He also credited many neo-Kantians (especially Lotze, his teacher), English idealists like Caird and Green, and not least of all, his American colleagues, Palmer and James.

Royce recognized that the outer form of the *Religious Aspect* might be considered "a sort of roughly sketched and very incomplete Phenomenology of the religious consciousness."[9] Accordingly, he acknowledged his decided debt to Hegel but judged he could not "call himself an Hegelian" (x). Royce later felt that even in 1892—the date he designated as the high-water mark of Hegel's influence upon his thought—Kant and Schopenhauer were influencing his thought more than Hegel.[10]

Religious Aspect was assembled from some fresh material, large excerpts from previously published articles, some previously drafted but unpublished manuscripts, and many of his lecture notes from 1883–84, touched up for inclusion. Since Royce had neither written it continuously nor had time to revise it well, ambiguities and misleading statements arose to cloud his expression and to promote misunderstandings. Nonetheless, a unity of design operated through its art, method, and doctrine.

The Art of 'Doing Ethics'

The commitment he stated in this work—to philosophize "reverently, fearlessly, and honestly" (5)—simply echoes the pledge he had made in his 1879 "Meditation before the [Golden] Gate" to do his reflections earnestly, independently, and reverently.[11]

Among these attitudes, the independence of the young Royce involved an extreme self-reliance—perhaps designated more accurately as "Pelagian." He felt few of the limitations which the elder Plato discovered about human reasoning and about the human need for a divine word as a second boat to cross life's stormy seas.[12] Instead, at this stage in his life, Royce insisted, "We want to work out our own salvation by our own efforts" (6).

His early style also included an almost mechanistic alternation that viewed a doctrine first objectively and then subjectively in its author's mind-set. Royce later acknowledged, "With this alternation of repulsion and attraction, my studies in philosophy have always proceeded."[13] Here he used the term "alternation" to describe his way of criticizing a theory. That is, Royce first adopted a scientific point of view to examine a thinker's position objectively, but later sought psychologically to grasp what led this thinker to adopt such a position.

Method in the *Religious Aspect*

To appreciate Royce's perspective, one needs to enter his neo-Kantianism and that phenomenism to which it committed him. Royce chose to center on the meaning discoverable in our distinguishing between right and wrong (20, 172). Thus, like Kant, he emphasized duty. Kant had used the God of his third postulate to maintain a balanced moral order. Somewhat similarly, Royce anchored his "Ideal of all ideals"—the will to harmonize all harmonizable finite wills—in his Righteous Ruler. This use of religion to promote dutiful living reveals one way in which the young Royce was a pragmatist.

Royce presupposed so great a difference between the "judgements: *This is,* and *This is good"* that "they have to be reached by widely different methods of investigation" (23).[14] Hence, one could not move from natural grounds to the realm of ideals. He began therefore from *moral* experience, the realm of ideals as found within experienced meanings (466) rather than from sensibly experienced natural facts or "bare externalities."

Because in Book One Royce looked to the future and stressed practical living, he found himself on the level of ideals and oughts. Accordingly he held, "Our interest is, first of all, with the ideal in its relation to human life" (18). As befitted the method of an idealist, Royce gave priority to the ideal over the real (22). He found this realm of ideals lying within the conditions required for moral skepticism itself. The very hesitation one experiences when confronted by two conflicting ideals is an expression of the more deeply governing Ideal of all ideals: to somehow harmonize all conflicting wills that can be harmonized, to somehow have all of them live by "one soul of many a soul" (168). When by deeper reflection one grasped the underlying intent that necessitated the emergence of this Ideal amid conflicting lower ideals, one won the moral insight.

Guided by this Ideal of all ideals, Royce moved in Chapter VII to find the fitting moral principles and attitudes needed for the organization of human life. For this he relied in part upon the inescapable natural tendencies within human selves towards the ideals of highest love, art, science, and political life (212). These more determinate ideals were to serve as touchstones for testing whether the requisite universality of intent perdured within particular chosen aims. To guide the application of the principles thus derived to human life's practical issues, Royce wanted to rely on the soundest available scientific findings (172–177).

Generally, then, Royce's method lay in searching for a moral ideal (Book One) before searching for a religious truth [about reality] (Book Two). In the first or ethical part of his search, Royce chose to use a dialectic of opposites to find a middle course. He first faulted two moods:

an over-skepticism and an excessive reverence, since each impeded a critical religious philosophy (9–13). Next, he identified and dialectically criticized the opposed beliefs of ethical dogmatists and ethical skeptics. After this "clearing away of the brush," Royce had to overcome the illusion of a self-centered perspective if the moral insight were to be won, even briefly.[15] When finally won, "The moral insight discovers harmony as an ideal to be attained by hard work" (162).

Viewed in more detail, the ethical dogmatists claimed to know that the ultimate goal of human life lay specifically in X or Y or Z. The ethical skeptics claimed all ethical knowledge impossible and thus sowed pessimism. Against the dogmatists Royce showed that people choose diverse ultimate goods. Against the skeptics he discovered a knowable and constant meaning within the distinction people make between right and wrong—a distinction in which he found the heart of the ethical problem (20).

As we saw, the early Royce began his philosophical ethics from the hesitation one feels on encountering conflicting wills. Inside this hesitation he found the unavoidable intent to somehow harmonize these wills if possible. But this intent could be unavoidable only if within it one were also intending, still more intimately and necessarily, a community of universally harmonized wills. Royce's analysis of the intentionality of finite will, then, grasped reflectively a necessary intent within the hesitation of a moral skeptic.

Royce chose *ideal-analysis* as his way of approaching this moral insight, rather than psychology or traditional ontology. If the psychological evidences of Professor Bain and Mr. Galton provided him with coherent confirmation (135–136), these lay on the perimeter of Royce's approach.

In this connection, Royce's usage of the term *"realize"* (and its derivatives) in Chapter VI calls for clarification. Earlier in Chapter II, "realize" had meant to embody an ideal, to render it actual in concrete life (22). But in his summary of Chapter VI, for instance, Royce says, "Moral insight . . . consists in the realization of the true inner nature of certain conflicting wills that are actual in the world" (168; with 138, 166, and *passim* in this chapter). So, in Chapter VI "realize" and "realization" seem Royce's groping words of 1883 for grasping intellectually, not some ontological nature or some merely psychological behavior, but the *logical* relations of many finite wills to their conflicting ends and their teleological meanings ("vectors") which necessitate the rise of that Ideal of all ideals, the universal harmony of wills.

Royce here presupposed a second, connected, interpersonal sense of "realize" when he chose Shelley's line to thematize this chapter: "Love is like understanding, that grows bright, Gazing on many truths" (131). For Royce also here described what it means to "realize the other" in interpersonal relationships:

When thou hast loved, hast pitied, or hast reverenced thy neighbor, then thy feeling has possibly raised for a moment the veil of illusion. Then thou hast known what he truly is, a Self like thy present Self. (159)

As early as 1883, then, Royce sensed that for the "realization of the other's internal life" and for the loving loyalty dependent on it, one needed at least implicitly to grasp intellectually the unavoidable teleology in minded beings to want a harmonious Universal Community.[16]

Nor was the ideal of harmony "already implied in the nature of these blind, conflicting wills" (162). That had been the ontologically based "hackneyed error" of many earlier traditional moralists from Socrates to Bentham, Mill, and Spencer (163–168). Royce did not look for a common ontological structure ("nature") in human appetency. Rather, knowing that without conflicting ideals, ethics would have no work to do (165–166), Royce set his fully idealistic route through the analysis of ideals that conflict—both within oneself and between oneself and others. His analysis of these ideals would uncover the highest of all ideals: the harmony both of all ideals sought and of all wills seeking ideals.

Royce found flimsy those efforts of naturalist ethicists who try to build ethics upon a "science of human nature." They are like boat-builders who set the steam engine in place before having laid the keel (167). Instead, a science of human nature should enter, not at the very start of ethics, but later on to guide the application of its already won central insight into the various areas of human life. Thereupon, one would move on to organize that life harmoniously.

The methodic circle of Royce's foundational ethics, then, traced the following path: to find the meaning within ethical skepticism and thus to recognize that "the true inner nature of certain conflicting wills that are actual in the world" lies in a "will to harmonize" them so far as possible. This means "to act, so far as may be, as if one included in one's own being the life of all those whose conflicting aims one realizes" (168–169). Having reached this ideal of a living community of wills that are somehow to be brought into harmony, Royce moved in the second half of his methodic circle to search for the real knower of our moral insight, "the Judge of our ideals, and the Judge of our conduct, . . . not only an infinite Seer of physical facts, but an infinite Seer of the Good as well as of the Evil" (433–434). Thus, the second half influences the first half reciprocally.

Another perspective may cast light upon the method of moral analysis Royce employed in Book One. Try to analyze your conceptual meaning of circle. You will find you cannot grasp it *simply*—that is, just by itself. Instead, you must also grasp a whole network of necessarily implied concepts—such as those of point, curve, radius, and plane.[17] Similarly, in his epilogue to the *Religious Aspect*, Royce described his overall movement in its Book Two: "Our special proof for the existence of an Universal Thought has been based, in the foregoing, upon an analysis of the nature of truth and error *as necessary conceptions*" (476, emphasis added). With equal accuracy he might have described his method in Book One as basing the special proof for the existence of the Moral Insight upon an analysis of the nature of many interacting ideals, and of hope, doubt, and despair—all viewed as *necessary conceptions*. In their network of logically implied concepts, they necessarily include that of the highest ideal—the harmony of all wills—and that of the most central means—the requirement (duty) to promote the further realization of that ideal.

In sum, then, having completed his search for the moral ideal (Book One), Royce then drove down to its religious ground in an actual All-Knower (Book Two). Just as his method in Book One searched out the conditions necessary for the possibility of ethical skepticism, so too his method in Book Two searched out the conditions necessary for the possibility of error.

Ethical content

For Royce the central problem of ethics lay in the way we read the significance of our experienced distinguishing between right and wrong (20). His claim to know the truth intrinsic to this distinction had its root in Royce's religious insight—a nexus deserving notice. Perhaps Royce's explicit movement from Book One to Two obscures the implicit movement whereby his religious insight influences his search for a moral ideal.

The All-Knower's appreciative knowledge of *Itself* as highest and wisest Reality gives finite selves their highest ideal and grounds their distinction between right and wrong (434). In Its moral life the All-knowing Judge primarily appreciates Itself as most real, wisest, and best. But It cannot do this unless It also simultaneously sees as erroneous or immoral every finite judgment and decision not consistent with Its primary vision. These latter the All-Knower cannot but see and detest, even if It tolerates and overcomes them in Its larger process. The All-Knower's Self-valuation as one who is of supreme worth and as one who cannot but know and hate moral evil (untruth, unlove, and injustice) is *worthy* of being seconded by all finite minds and of being imitated appreciatively through their distinguishing similarly between right and wrong (8, 466–467). Here lies the basis of the early Royce's ethical cognitivism.[18]

Thus, in the order of worth, the inmost center of Royce's All-Knower lies not in the Absolute's speculative knowing (as in Aristotle's Thought-thinking-Thought) but in Its valuational knowing (as in the prophet Amos's Righteous Judge). The origin of the human Ought, then, lies in the *worthiness* of this wisest All-Knower to be imitated freely by finite appreciators. In so doing, the latter constitute their moral selves by distinguishing similarly between right and wrong (8).

When sketching the "general ethical problem," Royce noticed the struggle involved in opting to make one's basic good either *survival* or something *better than survival* (24–25). One might interpret survival physically or culturally, on either personal, racial, or national levels. But adopting survival as one's basic good carried with it the demand to become ever more skillful and clever in order to survive. Skill and cleverness, however, are not morality. Instead, adopting something better than survival as one's basic good opens one up to living in union with something greater than oneself. It also makes reasonable the sacrifice of one's lesser goods, even of bodily life, for this something greater. Thus one not merely survives but also flourishes, according to the intent of the Righteous Judge who so guides universal process that the "divine spark" of each human self may grow without end.[19]

As Kant had done before him, Royce also pointed out the *relativism* that results whenever one tries to base the moral ideal on any heteronomous norm—whether this be the will of God, universal Reason, or Conscience in general (32–60). Besides the capriciousness of settling upon one of these heteronomous norms, there is the illusion of our seemingly permanent grasp of them. This reminded Royce of his boyhood valuation of Grass Valley as "my home always there," which had proven illusory (55). Older and wiser, he now commented, "There is no known limit to the caprice and to the instability of the human will" (168). To ground ethics on such norms, then, is to relativize it.

The absolute moral ideal must instead be found by reflecting upon that intentionality of willing the End which necessarily underlies a human self's three, serially experienced, psychic states: (1) the willing of two or more conflicting ends, (2) the hesitancy experienced in not wishing to extinguish any of them, and (3) the resultant skeptical pessimism that arises from despairing of one's own realizing these conflicting ends (138–145). Thereupon Royce pointed out how to penetrate to the meaning underlying this triad of psychic states:

> . . . if you reflect [more deeply] on all this, you see that in truth you . . . really have still a highest aim. You seek unity. You desire the warfare to cease. You have an ideal. All this is, to be sure, a physical fact, dependent on your nature as a voluntary being; but it is not valuable just for that reason alone, but for the reason that, in discovering this fact, you have discovered . . . that you are in possession of an ideal [that you] cannot get away from. (143–144)

This deeper reflection reveals the unavoidable teleological thrust to harmonize all ends and all willings of ends. From this alone emerges one's inalienable

"Ideal of ideals." One discovers at bottom that this intentionality directs one to the "highest good" (144–145).

Absolutely, then, for each one of us, "my Ideal very simply means the Will to direct my acts *towards* the attainment of universal Harmony. It requires me to act with this my [moral] insight always before me" (141). In brief, then, this intentionality within one's *hope-despair of good* is as central for Royce's moral insight as is the intentionality within one's *search-doubt of truth* for his religious insight.

A decade later, when looking back on the *Religious Aspect* as his "poor first effort at construction," Royce appraised its strengths and weaknesses in a letter to G. H. Howison.[20] He treasured the positive insight "indicated" in the work. He regretted the misleading methods used in both its ethical and religious parts, because they occasioned "many unnecessary misunderstandings." He wrote:

> It has more crudities of method than I for my part any longer care to count up. . . . On the whole [however,] I care more for the line of thought there indicated (i.e., in my Chap. XI [The Possibility of Error]) than for anything else that I have ever done, although I admit that unless very much developed, supplemented, and supported by the treatment of allied problems, this line of argument will never mean to others what it does to me. . . . The ethical doctrine I now hold in [a] decidedly modified and supplemented form.[21]

THE SPIRIT OF MODERN PHILOSOPHY

In his *Spirit of Modern Philosophy* (1892), Royce claimed no "technical exactness," since he simply intended to persuade by a popular "sketch" (341, 471).[22] Yet he showed that he had decidedly modified his epistemology. His was a new distinction—not a dichotomy—between the world of description (objective and abstract, for the sciences) and the world of appreciation (concretely personal and valuational, for ethics and aesthetics) (388–389, 411, 418, 426). Through this distinction he kept the determinism that science needs from denying the freedom that ethics needs (433).

In contrast to *Religious Aspect*, Royce had supplemented his current philosophy by cultivating the history of philosophy. Thus he had won that "decided advantage which the historical fashion of philosophizing always possesses as against the dialectical fashion" (xi). His studies as professor of the history of philosophy had led him to his kind of "radical empiricism" long before William James broached the term. Royce called for an intensified noticing of the present moment, "The individual moment is the Real." It is charged with energies from the past and future and enriched with its own rich potentials and actualities. These he later sketched as the sensitivity, docility, and initiative of the present moment.[23] Secondly, Royce's hope of winning "creative wisdom" through these studies (xii) oriented him to a future that extended far beyond the short-range expectations of popular pragmatism. Moreover, his experience was deeply dyed by his commitment to serve wholeheartedly humankind's prolonged forward thrust of gathering future generations to such communication and cooperation as will strengthen their moral bonds and shared life into one Great Community. Thirdly, Royce's empiricism explored backwards much farther than any just "received" Humean impressions or any historically acquired associative habits. Recognizing the influence of these currents, Royce's empiricism also sought saving contact with two more purified streams. It required the input of the millenia-long wisdom traditions of the evolving human race. In particular, it also required the entire reflective experience of the philosophical community in dialogue down through the ages.

Almost ten years after *Religious Aspect*, Royce saw more clearly that finite consciousness must face towards the future if it is to have ideals, values, and thus any ethics (431). The idea of community was becoming more pronounced and even his new idea of individuality was beginning to surface (433-436). Along with these developments, however, the problem of the relation of the finite self to the Absolute All-Knower was becoming more acute (373-374). Royce found great help towards solving this problem during his study of the first volume of Ernest Schroeder's *Algebra der Logik*. Around 1891 he recognized with Schroeder that the consistency of any universe of disclosure required a Self-reflecting series of viewpoints.[24] Hints of this insight already appeared in *Spirit of Modern Philosophy* (375). Royce's idea of an infinite self-representative series, coupled with his budding notion of individuality, cast further light on the problem of human immortality that he was already examining more closely.[25]

This work also showed Royce's sharper and deeper philosophical encounter with the problem of evil. For him evil included both moral sin and the irrational caprice of fortune (440-471). His own experiences of personal and familial tragedies in recent years occasioned this more acute and profound grasp. Now he saw evil as offering an opportunity to reach genuine spirituality if one courageously endures it, wills to resist it, and wrestles with it, by seizing it at the throat through "a binding of the strong man by being stronger than he" (263).

Royce's psychological studies had meanwhile alerted him to another aspect of the problem of evil. Human consciousness is so limited in its time-span and perspicacity that the universe must ultimately appear morally meaningless to finite human selves (469). Brute chance, blind chaos, and a seemingly ultimate farce lead the true pessimist to deny any underlying moral order (447). Hence, of all adults, and especially of ethicists, Royce required that *seriousness* of will which becomes good by recognizing and detesting moral evil (440–441).[26] He also faulted religious optimists and mystic escapists for lacking this seriousness (441–454).

No moral order can exist without such seriousness. This Royce unveiled in four steps (455–461). At the lowest, moral life has about it the seriousness and risk of a game because we can lose the moral game. Secondly, since "moral evil isn't a mere dissonance in the world-symphony... [but] is through and through regrettable, diabolical" (458), the only fitting attitude towards it is our stern hatred of moral evil. Thirdly, our ongoing experience of temptation, or latent sin, makes moral life still more serious. Finally in his holiness God seriously hates and detests sin. He thus supplies the ultimate ground for the seriousness of the moral order (460).

By 1892 Royce had also come to see how the attacks that the ignorant or wicked make upon the good serve an epistemological function. Earlier, when Royce had urged his friend, Edward Roland Sill, to desist "casting pearls before swine, [since] they only turn and rend you," Sill had replied, "Ah, Royce, but one doesn't *quite surely know* that they were pearls that he cast *until he feels the tusks*" (467 emphasis added). By their attacks upon genuinely good persons the ignorant or wicked unintentionally provide an authenticating sign of how highly valuable a service the good are indeed making. In *The Spirit of Modern Philosophy*, Royce had discerned this portion of his later "doctrine of signs."

Starting this work, Royce sketched the heart of his idealistic philosophy:

> This theory is that the whole universe, including the physical world also, is essentially one live thing, a mind, one great Spirit, infinitely wealthier in his experience than we are, but for that very reason to be comprehended by us only in terms of our own wealthiest experience. (17)

Concluding this work, Royce summarized:

> We have found in a world of doubt but one assurance—but one, and yet how rich! All else is hypothesis. The Logos alone is sure. (471)

By so doing Royce suggested a "forced option" at the start of philosophy (xviii). Being human requires one to have some faith—naturalistic, agnostic, religious. Hence, one cannot avoid working from some faith when starting philosophy—a faith that necessarily carries with it some metaphysical position. Even the cautious religious agnostic cannot avoid exercising some belief that lacks a belief in God. Thus, holding that one must begin metaphysics as either a realist or an idealist, Royce clarified:

> ... a doctrine remains, in the metaphysical sense, idealistic, if it maintains that the world is, in its wholeness, and in all of its real constituent parts, a world of mind or of spirit. The *opposite* of an idealist, in this sense, is one who

maintains the ultimate existence of wholly unspiritual realities at the basis of experience and as the genuine truth of the world—such unspiritual realities for instance as an absolute "Unknowable," or, again, as what Hobbes meant by "Body." (xvii)

At the start of philosophy, then, one's methodological practice is either idealistic (= theistic) or realistic (= atheistic and materialistic). For Royce this fundamental option would perdure through the decades. In 1913 he would assert that when, from many possibilities, we definitively choose our bearing towards the universe, there can be only one right attitude towards reality. It is the generally theistic attitude of a loyal creative response to the Spirit of the Universal Community.[27]

In the final chapter of *The Spirit of Modern Philosophy*, entitled "Optimism, Pessimism, and the Moral Order," he presented his 1892 view of ethics (435–471). In it he revealed a bi-polar emphasis. Subjectively, a sound ethics depended on one's adopting a reasonably criticized attitude towards the world and its problem of evil. A person had to choose a course lying between two extremes. On the one hand, one had to avoid an enthusiastic or merely pious optimism. On the other, one had to avoid that lethal pessimism which persuades to a complete relativism and skepticism in ethics and impedes any ethical cognitivism.[28] Objectively, a sound ethics depended, despite the presence of evil, on an extant moral order that is ultimately rational because rooted in the Logos (439, 454). This order actually bound human selves in real relations of rights and duties.

REPRESENTATIVE ARTICLES (1893–1895)

From 1891 through 1895 Royce created seven articles of his own on ethics and revealed some of his ethical views in his 1893 "Lectures to Teachers." Besides these activities, Royce drafted thirty-six reviews of ethical works while serving as book-review editor. The varying approaches, questions, and paradoxes of these authors familiarized Royce with the complexities of philosophizing about ethical life. Having to read them carefully and to criticize them reflectively made him grasp more clearly and firmly the central simplicity and distinctiveness of ethical life.

Turning to three of Royce's ethical articles that culminated his early period, we find in "Tolstoi and the Unseen Moral Order" a rarely noticed yet revealing piece of Roycean discrimination. In his latter period Count Tolstoy revolted against the existing social order which prized above all its technologically focused scientific progress. Eccentric as Tolstoy's ethical opinions were, Royce judged it instructive to contrast Tolstoy's Christian ethics with the realistic ethics of such thinkers as Spencer, Wundt, and

Paulsen. These latter lacked the universality needed for an ethics for *all* people. Royce found:

> The creed of the ethical realist is, after all, when too one-sidedly insisted upon, a creed for just the times and the nations that enjoy general prosperity and progress, and for them only in so far as nearly all things go well with them. Hence ethical realism has never been the creed of the world's prophets and martyrs.[29]

Ethical realists do not "keep us alive to the absolute ideals" as do such loyal "servants of the Invisible Moral Order" as Antigone and Socrates.

After passing through a period of despair, Tolstoy turned for guidance to the common folk, the peasants. They "live confident of an abiding good because they are sure that God, of whom indeed they know very little, has sent them here for his own eternal ends." Tolstoy recognized:

> ...that in the idea of a benevolent Infinite, whose order is perfection, but whose plan is too high for us mortals to know, lies the true solution of the problem of the worth of life. All is indeed vanity, except the service of this plan.

Reading the Gospels, the elderly Tolstoy found in the Sermon on the Mount both this plan and the guidance he longed for. As a thoroughgoing doubter, Tolstoy also recognized that "no natural order as such—be it a selfish or a social order—can answer the demands" for such a plan and order. For ultimately "either [human] life has no sense, or its sense is given to it by its place in some infinite and all-embracing plan." Thus recognizing that "our natural human life is full of illusion and mischief," Tolstoy accepted both Gospel requirements: negatively, to renounce the merely natural aims, and positively to love all beings so sincerely that non-resistance to violence followed.

Tolstoy was significant for Royce's ethics at this time because he focused on the unseen moral order, required attention to the Eternal, and emphasized the need to manifest the benevolence of the Eternal Absolute in one's life and deeds. However, Royce, reluctant "to lose sight of the significance of ethical realism," sought a more balanced position. He preferred to value the guidance science gave in applying ethical principles to current problems.

In a second study, "The Knowledge of Good and Evil," Royce examined the "delicate ethical question as to how far 'the knowledge of evil' contributes to moral perfection."[30] His answer arose from his interpretation of life as "a balance of opposing tendencies." Physical life exhibits this balance. It should be expected, then, "in all forms of the higher life, and, in particular, of the moral life."[31] Unlike innocence, attained moral goodness "is only won through a conflict with the forces of evil." This conflict requires a rather deep knowledge of evil—a knowledge that unfortunately often leads to sin. But whether it involves only that knowledge of evil experienced in rejecting a temptation, or also that further knowledge of sin felt through sinning and its consequences, "the knowledge and presence of evil form, in very manifold and complex ways, a moment in the consciousness and in the life of goodness."[32]

The significance of Royce's insight here needs emphasis. Contrary to later views that regard the good as a "simple" and therefore undefinable, Royce saw goodness as a "triad"—both in our true awareness of it, and in our ethical creation of it in practice. That is, he recognized that to regard the idea of the good as a "simple" was the mistake of the romantic poets—one into which the early Tennyson fell.[33] For the idea of the good is inseparable from the ideas of evil and of a consciousness that appreciates good *and* detests evil. Similarly at the practical level, the good ethical intent must avoid the lure of the pure good—that is, of the distant ideal (the "Holy Grail"). It must focus rather on finding God in the present—that is, within that *mix* of good and evil which requires brave struggling to create the better in the now. The good here present lies in actual talents and potentials, while the evil lies in human limits, nature's resistance and caprice, and sinful intents and structures. Royce's view of this triad of good-evil-and-conscious-response led him to define his "best man. . . by virtue of his readiness to take his part in the struggle against evil."[34] In this way the Royce of 1893 grappled with the problem of evil from its epistemological side.

Third, in summer 1894, Royce delivered a highly significant address "Meister Eckhart" to the Plymouth School of Ethics.[35] Royce's earlier studies of Spinoza and of the "Moral Insight" in the *Religious Aspect* had hinted at some kind of metaphysical mysticism intrinsic to his way of philosophizing. The influence of this study of Eckhart perdured with Royce until his death, yet Royce remained opposed to Eckhart's withdrawal from present experience of human social interactions. This study revealed Royce's interest in the mystic's viewpoint and several themes in particular echo through Royce's later works.

With his doctrine of the Godhead's ineffable Mystery (or "silent wilderness") Eckhart opened another door for Royce, beyond Lanman and Schopenhauer, onto the apophatic view of traditional monotheism—that is, its recognition that the Godhead cannot be named or uttered. For Eckhart the Absolute is Mystery (the "wilderness of Godhead") that is *"no-thing"* and *does nothing*, so that "It" can be neither comprehended rationally nor expressed articulately. Its determinate "manifestations"—whether infinite Trinity and the three Persons or finite spark-like images of God—all pulsate with a life of empathetic sensitivity, of synoptic insight, and of committed benevolence. In his "Eckhart" article, Royce portrayed the Absolute both as super-rational Mystery, as most fully alive, and as capable of being experienced concretely, at least by the mystics. Thus, because of his recent recognition of how descriptive knowing depends upon its appreciative base, Royce no longer conceived the Absolute simply in the logical way he had done in *Religious Aspect*; namely, as the All-seeing Rational Thought who first judges propositions and thereupon is led to know the minded proponents of them.[36]

The notion of the finite self as a "spark or glimmer of the Godhead" (*Fünkelin*) became a governing idea with Royce. It would soon become a central factor in his new American idea of individuality and perdure with him into his final lectures on metaphysics.[37] As "sparks of the Godhead," they image God in finite ways, yet because each finite self is also a "little point" (or *Pünctelin*), it differs uniquely from both God and every other self.[38]

Of the many ethical insights Royce saw as flowing from Eckhart's Absolute, three seemed especially noteworthy: grace, salvation and virtue.[39] In Eckhart Royce encountered the Christian theme that a human self's actual union with God comes only if "God acts on us" (296). Human discipline and dispositions are needed, but union with the divine comes as a miracle of God's gracious Self-gift to us.

Again, Eckhart held that to be saved the soul must in some sense rise above knowledge. In their mystical experience, when souls "in some measure attain God" (287), they reach beyond knowledge of the determinate and are opened to an encounter with the awesomely Holy Mystery. For Royce this view "supplemented" his *Aufklarung* rationalism. The soul was saved from an ultimately vain and meaningless life *only* through this totally personal and deeply transrational union with the Godhead.

Once this union was gained, it required an ordering of the *Fünklelin's* concentric "lower powers"—first of its intellect and will, then of its more embodied powers of the senses and desires. Only as so ordered would the self expand in spiritual freedom (292). And only with self-control and discipline could this expansion occur.

Moreover, according to Eckhart, virtues empowered the self on two levels to achieve and maintain this ordering of the good person. In general, the unseverable pair of virtues are "departedness of soul" (*Abgescheidenheit*) and the actively practical virtues (that the *wayfarer* needs).

Rest-filled *Abgescheidenheit* consists in that God-centered inner solitude which makes one indifferent to earthly fortune. For it looks "heavenward only, to the absolute home of mystery" (293). In contrast, the actively practical virtue looks earthward to strive and endure amid temporal process and bodily encounters. *Abgescheidenheit* animates practical virtue as the soul vitalizes the body's parts. Or, as Royce further illustrated their connection:

> For the inner man, in his *Abgescheidenheit*, stands as a sort of Aristotelian unmoved mover, beyond this tempestuous sublunary world of finite passion, never, during our earthly life, destroying but vitalizing the lower nature. (294)

Focusing upon each of the two virtues, Royce first described the foremost and innermost.

> *Abgescheidenheit* is the special virtue related to the centre or Spark of the soul. As so related it is a virtue higher even than charity. The man who has it . . . sees all as God's will. The Godhead is all in all to him, and the peace that passeth understanding. . . . *Abgescheidenheit* does not strive or cry, but it calmly and with absolute assurance, prays, or, what is the same thing, irreversibly determines and declares in its peace, that God's will shall be done on earth as it is in heaven. (293)

This indispensable reference to "on earth" is precisely what keeps the soul's "absolute freedom from the bondage of the creature" from degenerating into quietism. For in the mystic's language, "on earth" means the world of the soul's "lower powers" where it must meet challenges to its growth and encounter pain and passion, temptation and sorrow. At this less central level, the good person:

> . . . appears to be not at all an ecstatic quiestist, but a strenuous, busy, virile, essentially practical being—a man of hard sense, fearless of speech, vigorous in maintaining his cause, indifferent to the mere form of good works, little disposed to fasting, to going barefoot, or to other non-essentials of the religious life, [but] much disposed to helping the brethren. (295)

This portrait startlingly anticipates Royce's initial (and admittedly inadequate) definition of loyalty in his *Philosophy of Loyalty* (1908).[40] Yet, after discerningly hunting for worthy causes, Royce ended *Loyalty* by showing the ethical centrality of a kind of "departedness of soul" (*Abgescheidenheit*). For only by maintaining union with the Eternal could one fulfill Royce's finally integrated definition of loyalty by manifesting the Eternal in all one's deeds.[41]

In sum, then, the ethical ideas of the early Royce came to still fuller flower after he had completed *Religious Aspect* and *Spirit of Modern Philosophy*. His recently devised distinction between knowledges by description and by appreciation, along with the distinction between their corresponding worlds, permeated his thought. For Royce, one could not know a natural fact descriptively unless one appreciatively knew its social verifiability. Inferring correctly that the communal knowing which appreciates ethical values and bonds must underlie and sustain one's descriptive knowing of physical facts, Royce concluded, "social consciousness is ethical before it is physical."[42]

All these striking developments in Royce's ethical thought as he approached the end of his early period have deserved careful study. They deepened and enriched the ethical ideas of *Religious Aspect* and *Spirit of Modern Philosophy*. They startle an attentive reader because they are pregnant with insights that will emerge in the middle and mature periods of Royce's ethics.

4. Royce's Middle Ethics (1896–1911)

Royce's middle ethics (1896–1911) arose from his second maximal insight—his "startlingly 'original' (let us say 'American') theory of individuality."[1] Taking Ernst Schroeder's previously mentioned cue (that a consistent universe required a Self-reflecting series of viewpoints), Royce reached this insight into the free Self-individualization of the Absolute in 1896 and published it in the 1897 edition of *The Conception of God*.[2] He applied this insight into individuality to the finite self mainly in *The World and the Individual* and *The Conception of Immortality*.

FACTORS AFFECTING THE ETHICAL LIFE

The Full Individual

Royce knew that individuality requires *uniqueness*—a reality that is complex, subtle, and even supra-rational. Instances of mistaken identity prove this. His survey of the history of philosophy taught him the inadequacy of the previously proposed principles of individuality: location in space and time, sense presentation, or concepts arranged ever more specifically. To reach the true ultimate meaning of "the individual" he had to push beyond its commonsense, conventional, and logical meanings which never got beyond general ideas and thus missed uniqueness.

If a First Individual were found, it could individualize finite selves and they could individualize themselves through relation to this First Individual. Royce's problem then was "how to get the first individual" (257). He wrote:

> The concept of an individual *in the full sense* is a limiting concept [*Grenz Begriff*], not corresponding to any fact of our conscious experience. . . . Our goal [the ever sought but never attained limit] is the envisagement of the one real individual, viz., the whole universe.[3]

By rooting his concrete concept of the "individual in the full sense" in Will or Love, it became teleological, ethical, and unique. He stated:

> I propose to show that the Principle of Individuation, in us as in reality, is identical with the principle that has sometimes been called Will, and sometimes

61

> Love. . . . Divine Love. . . individuates the real world wherein the Divine
> Omniscience is fulfilled. (259)

Royce's theory of individualization presupposes the Absolute as the unique First Individual, which in its Self-constitution intends the universal process of all finite individual selves. Among these, minded selves intend, at least inarticulately, this Absolute Object as their ever-present living context. Thus they are started on their ethical task of consciously individualizing themselves within the one concrete process of forming the Universal Community.

Many kinds of love, of course, are *not* individualizing—e.g., love of pleasure, of profit, of power over other persons. Yet truly loyal kinds of love—a mother's love for her child, the love of one's vocation, and one's wholehearted love for God—are among the ethical organizing interests of life and involve an exclusive element (264). Hence the category of individuality is ethically significant. As Royce summed up:

> In brief, it is such affections [of love] that, as they give us the consciousness
> of the One, henceforth tend to make our world one, and hence, by infection,
> to individuate for us every object in the world. (265)

Royce rendered the *community* aspect of his individualization theory clearer in his Cambridge Conferences of 1898. Here, when pointing out why atomistic accounts of the ethical individual are fatuous if they claim for him a "sacred dignity," Royce told his audience:

> Individuality is indeed sacred; but if you need at least two individuals, real
> or ideal, in order to get a consciousness of individuality, then the sacredness
> belongs to the situation in question, and consequently to both the individuals in
> common, and not to either of them alone. Here lies the fundamental basis, not
> only for a general objection to every form of anarchism, but also for a specific
> criticism of countless modern ethical attempts which depend upon taking an
> individual alone by himself and then considering him as an isolated but still
> sacred ethical being.[4]

Royce soon clarified the positive side of this communal relation. The reality of the "cause" to which a finite self dedicates itself must somehow be a unique individual. Even though human selves conceive their causes in a general way, the reality of their cause cannot be a mere type. Otherwise, their cause could neither serve as an object of "true loyalty" nor individualize the dedicating self. For Royce a cause is a community and a community is as much an "individual in the full sense" as is any ethically committed human person. Since one's cause, taken concretely, is really a "unique individual," it individualizes the finite self dedicated to it. The finite self may view its cause in different ways. One's cause may be a beloved person viewed as member of one's communal life (e.g., one's wife *qua* co-constituting one's conjugal community). Or one's cause may be one's concretely experienced community life in which many selves participate.

The requisite triadic structure can be discerned in this ethical doctrine of individuality. Neither the individualization process nor genuine ethical individuals arise without three realities bound in ethical relations: a finite self (an *I*), an other finite self (a *thou* that, as "cause-and-member," both calls and extends to a concretely individual community), and a First Individual (the Absolute that constitutes Itself through its passionately loving choice of this universe and no other). In this presupposed triadic ethical community, *A-B-C*, lies the importance of Royce's "individual in the full sense." For a human self (*A*) is ethically individuated as unique by its preferential and exclusive choice of another human self (*B*) as co-related with *A* to a community, *in accord with* the ultimately individualizing intent of the Absolute Self (*C*) for Its co-constituted and thus individualized finite selves.

Hence, the ethical encounter within an I-Thou interpersonal relation is central of Royce's meaning of an "individual in the full sense." For only by relating to a pair of existent others does a Roycean self freely constitute itself into such an individual. The one other is a particular finite self, consciously experienced and lovingly chosen. The ultimate Other is the Absolute Self, intended simultaneously yet usually unconsciously in each choice and thought of a finite self. If the latter intends the one real universe (intended in an individualizing way by the Absolute Self) and at the same time intends and chooses some other finite self, it promotes its own proper individualization.

This choice involves a preferential love whereby the finite self is definitively oriented toward that beloved and no other. Preferential affirmation of the paired others as the object of one's wholehearted devotion and love implies an exclusion of any other finite object from *such* free love by the self. Its distinctively loving will and feeling of devotion transform the self thus communally related into a unique individual even as the finite beloved is transformed into a uniquely appreciated individual.

Since reason deals with concepts, it cannot successfully analyze this individuality which lies beyond concepts. On what basis, then, does the self exclude all other finite others except its chosen beloved? To constitute "this one" as an "object of an exclusive interest" the finite self must will "this and no other."[5] Such an act contains a central core of positive love of its object but also includes a negation of all finite others so that its love can be preferential. To explain the psychological basis for this exclusion, Royce pointed to unconscious instincts of feelings:

> The "no other" of the individual's nature comes to mind by virtue of exclusive but unconscious instinctive bases of feeling whereby any other case, viewed as

a rival, gets rejected as impossible. These bases later get [= become] in science more explicit. They never become absolutely clear to us mortals.[6]

The roots, then, of Royce's middle period ethics can be found in this second maximal insight and in other lesser insights found in his pertinent writings of 1896 to 1903.[7] In response to the chief work of this period, *The World and the Individual*, Peirce judged it "a prominent milestone upon the highway of philosophy" and particularly treasured its notion of the self as a "dynamo of ideas."[8] But criticizing Royce's dialectal use of a deductive mathematical method in metaphysics, Peirce urged Royce to study logic, especially the kind that arises from experienced facts.[9] Heeding Peirce's advice, Royce studied logic during his remaining fifteen years and thus strengthened his new insight into individuality. In this individualizing intent, however, a psychological infrastructure and an enlightened reason had their roles to play.

Three Psychological Functions

Sensitiveness, docility, and originality, the basic triad of the middle Royce's *Outlines of Psychology*, necessarily support each moral choice.[10] Pre-ethical consciousness arises for Royce, as for James and Dewey, from habits, instincts, and insightful intelligence. Ethical consciousness presupposes a human self's present susceptivity towards the current situation. It also requires a high degree of docility in fidelity both to current guides and to generally productive habits acquired in the past. Except for Ignas Skrupskelis,[11] expositors of Roycean ethics seem to have omitted the docility dimension in Royce's ethics—namely, a highly sophisticated kind of obedience. Opposed to any merely blind obedience, or to an obedience in which one prostitutes oneself into an object wholly controlled by an external other, Royce sought the ground for the right to accept and follow another's directive. He found it in the coincidence of the aim of the external authority with one's own life-plan. As Royce told his University of Illinois audience:

> The power to which I am to yield must commend itself to me as in conformity with my own voluntarily accepted purpose, or else my submission to that power will be merely a surrender to a major force, and not an ethically valuable act.[12]

To exercise authority ethically, then, the person in authority may not be wholly external to the obedient selves cooperating in community, but has to identify with the members' personal growth as expressed in their basic life-plans and desires.

Besides sensitivity and docility, however, originality also calls for attention if psychological balance is to be achieved. In Roycean moral decision making, originality plays a distinctive role—both by way of instinctive feelings and impulses as well as through the free creation of values. The human self lives by emergent emphases and selections. Its instances of originality, then, arise pre-ethically in impulses and feelings, and ethically in the free initiation of values. Impulse, instinct, and a certain restlessness spark the self's quest for novelty. When a "groping" procedure is needed to create a uniquely new entry into the future, originality initiates it.[13] By preferring to focus more upon originality than upon sensitivity or docility, Royce maintained the primacy of subjectivity. For each human self expresses and further realizes his or her unique individuality by the responsible initiative which it exercises in its ethical decisions.[14]

Royce knew that we remain "frail and ignorant human beings, who see through a glass darkly." Hence, the only successful way to decide complex practical issues lay, not in mainly trusting abstract reasons and ethical formulas, but in relying ultimately on "a happy instinctive choice and wholesome sentiment."[15] In Royce's eyes, if the self is genuinely loyal, then its instinctive choice will be "happy" and its sentiment will be "wholesome." Clearly, what Royce here taught about complex ethical decision making parallels the doctrine of Fichte and William James that one's own personality ultimately controls each philosopher's "fundamental option" and Aristotle's rooting of sound moral choice in "right desire." Like philosophy itself, the ethical act reveals its author's unique personality even more than do his objective reasons. For a self's individuality lies in the unique "tilt of the triad" of its sensitiveness, docility, and originality.

Needed Qualities of Intelligence and Reasoning

Contrary to most voluntaristic presentations of Royce, he himself placed increasing emphasis upon inquiry and enlightened reason as indispensable for the individual's ethical act. In fact, the desires to further clarify meanings and to seek more truth are so characteristically Roycean that it boggles the mind to encounter presentations of his loyalty that make it a blind sort of ethics. As a human truth-seeker and competent logician, Royce appreciated reason's power and worth along with its limits and weakness. If for him the ultimate determinant of ethical choice lay in the unique free individuality of the human self, he always wanted that choice to be as intelligent and reasonable as possible. For him sound ethical choice must artfully synthesize the directive, "Be simple as a dove and crafty as a serpent."[16] Any so-called loyalty unwilling to search for more truth shows itself spurious. Ordinarily Royce wanted reason to work to the full to reach as intelligent an insight and as comprehensive a wisdom as humanly attainable. In his 1898 Cambridge Conferences, he said the goal of our Western moral endeavor lay:

simply in finding any tie, any relationship, any office, however humble, such as brings light, makes definite, the life of your fellows, [such as] gives harmony and organization, increases (instead of decreasing) the tie that binds men together. The cunning contrivance, the careful thought, the scientific discovery, the well-ordered household, the faithfully fulfilled office, these constitute the regions where your goal is to be fulfilled.[17]

In order to fulfill "your goal," inquiry and enlightened reason are indispensable.

Yet Royce simultaneously felt the limits of reason. One can so cherish its clear articulation that one forgets that abstract concepts necessitate a loss of union with the concretely real. Reason can confuse its fallacious shadows with its real light, its formulas with its preformulated insights, its continued (but no longer needed) deliberations with needed decision making. In 1899 he told a Vassar audience:

> I constantly see the mischief done by an unwise exaggeration of the tendency to reason, to argue, to trust to mere formulas to seek for the all serving word; in brief, to bring to consciousness what for a given individual ought to remain unconscious.[18]

Such Roycean phrases as "enlightened loyalty" or "rational loyalty" occur frequently.[19] Even the receptive side of reason found a place as shown in his attitude during the closing days of his argument with William James about an adequate theory of truth. Each maintained respect for the other and for the other's differences from himself but chose "to wait until some other light shines for our eyes."[20] In general, then, Royce emphasized the need for docility and discernment, for criticality and discrimination within the moral act.[21]

Hindrances to Ethical Life

Among various hindrances to ethical perspective and life, Royce became, at the turn of the century, notably sensitive to selfishness. He began hinting that at its center ethical life needed a radical transformation consisting in the way one turns or does not turn one's attention.[22] In childhood and adolescence, one necessarily looks on oneself as the center of one's world, thus falling into an "inevitable illusion of perspective."[23] While saving the personalistic grain of truth in this illusion, one must be freed from the illusion and the "natural selfishness" it causes. One must undergo a kind of Copernican revolution, or transformation, in one's ethical viewpoint. For one needs to recognize and live by the truth that every other human person is as valuable as oneself and that the Universal Community of minded beings is even more valuable than oneself.[24] Royce also identified, in 1898, two other major obstacles to the kind of thinking his ethics required:

From our modern point of view, the ethical interpretation of the universe is hindered by two especially serious difficulties . . . : the general presuppositions of modern naturalism . . . [and] our incomplete appreciation of the meaning and the essential limitations of the human type of consciousness.[25]

Modern naturalism presupposes that organic matter causally determines any "minded spirit." Lacking an awareness of authentically free self-determination, naturalism reduces ethics to a sociological study of rationally approved behavior. Secondly, we block our entry into genuine ethical life by not taking adequate account of how consciousness *as human* is marked by goal seeking and a quite limited time-span.

So far we have explored how Royce's insight into individuality, his three psychological functions (of sensitivity, docility, and originality), and reasoning (both appreciative and descriptive) affect the roots of ethical life. We also noticed the three hindrances to that life. With this background, we begin to investigate some dimensions in those roots themselves: (a) the environment and growing self-consciousness, (b) the moral self, (c) the development of moral consciousness, (d) the indispensable struggle with evil, and (e) the human self's union with the Eternal in the practical.

THE ROOTS OF ROYCE'S
MIDDLE PERIOD ETHICS (1896–1903)

The Environment and Growing Self-consciousness

In his search to uncover the growth of moral consciousness, Royce countered the tendency to focus only inwardly. He emphasized that this growth also depends on each self's interaction with its environment which is to be taken broadly to include nature, other selves, communities, and one's particular situation in life.

In two of his earliest works—in *California* and in *The Feud of Oakfield Creek*, Royce had situated his concrete examination of moral characters within specifically Californian environments. In these works he showed how ecology shapes moral consciousness.[26] Shortly after his health cruise to Australia, he published his explicit awareness of this, "The mountains of a country often predetermine its poetry, and even its thinking. A land where nature is original has more chance of developing original men."[27]

One's psychosomatic skills and habits provide an environment closer to moral life than nature itself. Royce pointed out how athletics develop skills and habits of fair play, team spirit, and cooperation that help evoke moral consciousness. If well directed, athletics provide training and challenges that call strongly for growth in self-control and moral awareness.[28]

He also highlighted those skills of intelligence which careful chess playing and alert classroom exercises develop. These, too, can strongly support moral growth. As examples of acquired skills and habits of deportment and will, Royce turned to British administrators in racially tense Jamaica. These men habitually maintained great reserve in speech even as they strongly stressed communal actions—for example, building new roads and houses. In this way they improved the situation, won the respect of the Blacks, and reduced hostilities.[29]

One's community and system of communities influence one's moral growth even more than environing nature, psychosomatic skills and habits. These variously hierarchized communities call, test, and hone the moral self. Amid these communal impacts, one can endeavor to become *more* loyal, especially more loyal to the growth of moral life among all people. If one does so, then the preferences one insists on in conflicts of loyalty increase one's moral self-consciousness. The experience of these conflicts calls a person to harmonize the rights and duties of individuals and societies, to maintain an appreciative awareness of other persons, and to embody within one's present decision the wisdom of past traditions and the creative possibilities of feasible expectations for the future.

The Individual Moral Self

In such ways, then, nature, skills, and habits, along with one's relation to a system of communities, constituted the environment for one's moral growth. In this context, Royce started building his ethics from his 'American' definition of the individual. He also had to purify his meaning of Being beyond its first three inadequate conceptions. In his Gifford Lectures of 1900, Royce fashioned his interpretation of the human moral self in accord with his fourth and final conception of Being. His series of conceptions of Being had run from the realistic, through the mystic and the critical rationalist, to his own ethical individualist interpretation of Being. Realists claim that the self is a unit essentially independent of all other selves (or things) and consequently an unrelated "separated being" whose interests are essentially only its own. But according to this realist view of an individual, the self cannot rationally come to recognize, beyond its own caprice, any responsibility to other selves or to God or to any absolute Ought.[30] This "realist" view, then, makes ethics unintelligible and impossible.

According to the mystics, the individual human self should eventually dissolve into God. By such a view no finite individuality will in the end withstand the all-absorbing Absolute. Then, according to the critical rationalists' interpretation of Being, the individual is supposed to be a finite rational agent equipped with rights and duties and operating in an objective moral order. But the rationalists' abstract universalized concept of an individual lacks uniqueness and thus cannot contain that unique purpose which makes a person an individual. On Royce's final view, the individual is essentially a concrete life-plan set in a community context. One gains one's individuality by relating to God for individuality is a unique expression of personal response to the divine purpose.

Royce's critique of the three previous views together with his own final position became clear in his summary in *World and the Individual*:

> It is precisely the restoration of individuality to the Self which constitutes the essential deed of our Idealism. For us the Self has indeed no Independent Being: it is a life, and not a mere valid law. It gains its very individuality through its relation to God; but in God it still dwells as an individual; for it is an unique expression of the divine purpose.[31]

Although one knows by experience that one exists, one never knows directly just what one is, except insofar as one glimpses one's present Self *being sent* to some Other (287). Since a human self's life-plan cannot be fulfilled in the present life, one's true self cannot be a datum, but is for us an ideal to be approached in the future. Moreover, the human self depends most intimately "upon both natural and social conditions" (290). Only as aware of the reality of other selves and as interested in their distinct and mutually contrasting life-plans, can it hope to fulfill its own unique life-plan. It does so only by recognizing how its life-plan differs from those of other selves (289).

Many implications follow from the communally based unique life-plans of finite individual selves: respect for others' different individualities and freedom, recognition of reciprocal rights and potentials, and recognition of individual demands. That is, if others, too, are unique communally based individuals, ultimately one may not demand this or that unique act of them, even if one may have to demand it of oneself. For although the individual self depends for all its general characteristics on its relations to societies and to nature, nevertheless, its own individuality lies in its unique way of blending these general characteristics into its own self-chosen uniqueness (293). In brief, the individual of Royce's middle period is an ethical self, knowable only in terms of meaning, of task, and of intent to become a unique self.

In 1900, then, Royce's "fourth and final," love-based, ethical definition of an individual self arose within the context of the self's dynamic relations to many others. These others included the self's chosen ideal, which energizes its life-plan and calls the self to realize ever further the uniqueness of its individuality. These others also included God, and (as expressions of His Self-diversifying will) all other minded beings, the whole of nature, and the objective Ought which regulates finite selves in the moral universe. Because of his restlessly penetrating mind, however, Royce would not long remain satisfied with his notion of individuality.[32]

By interpreting the human self this way, Royce transcended the popular view that ultimately an individual has only its own interests. His American theory of individuality (based on the creative love that organizes the interests of a life in an individuating way) reveals the ethical significance of Royce's kind of individuality.[33] Because this ethical love selects one and only one "other" as the beloved object of its devotion, it creates a conscious life-world which co-individualizes all other realities according to one's own individual self-constitution. Royce thus built "interests beyond the self's own interests" into his definition of the individual. Because of such extended interests, once the human self selects perhaps its family, or art, or God as its own beloved object (or "cause"), this now individualized self has interests in whatever its world embraces. If its "cause" is open, its interests reach out to everything in the whole universe—all its minded members, non-minded natural selves, the Universal Community, and the Interpreter-Spirit of this Community. This is its shared moral life to which we now turn.

Evolution of Communal Moral Consciousness

In 1901, Royce lectured on the work of John Fiske, who had popularized evolutionary theory.[34] Using this base, Royce saw that moral consciousness, nurtured in a series of widening communities, evolves in four stages. With each of these stages Royce linked in this lecture "the four ethical lessons that Fiske most frequently draws from his study and interpretation of the evolutionary process" (35). The first centers on the shared consciousness between mother and child. The long period needed for an infant's brain to evolve successfully to support moral consciousness requires a mother's care and love. But since the mother meeds protection, ties between father, mother, and child arise to preserve the family and thus the race. To support and protect the family, subsidiary communities arise in series with their own kinds of shared consciousness: clan, tribe, nation, humanity. In a striking cameo Royce portrayed this first stage:

> . . . thus all civilization develops, in a sense, about the bed of the helpless infant. And the sense of duty grows from this same root. In consequence, our idea of duty is primarily an idea of helpfulness to those whom we love. And this accounts for the evolutionary origin of the sympathetic aspect of morality. All ideals of kindliness thus have their source in an unselfish fondness for fellow beings that need help. (38)

Each subsidiary community, however, makes reciprocal claims on the family members and requires services—perhaps even one's life, should it come to war. Royce continued:

In second place, if the clan is needed to protect the mothers and the babes, natural selection, in favoring the best knit clans, favors not only the sympathetic, but the sterner virtues—the virtues of loyalty to the clan...in the form of courage, and of obedience to the voice of the clan or the tribe. (42)

At this second stage, duty directs human selves not only to help the family members they love but also to so adhere to a larger community that it is able to withstand the eliminating selection of evolutionary nature.

Such development, however, requires members to create and share a meaningful worldview. As the third stage of shared moral consciousness, this shared view enables members to develop priorities for various private and common goods in order to meet the sacrifices needed. Seeking to understand the things and events it encounters, each member forms a shared conception of the whole world in terms of its group traditions and its interests in the ideal. It takes part in its group's skills, sciences, philosophy, and religion as instruments towards a meaningful worldview. These instruments lead the member irresistibly to conceive the universe—at first crudely, but then more rationally—as the expression of that same power which appears in its own consciousness as the struggle for the better. Thus one conceives one's duty to God and becomes willing to sacrifice some private ends for the goods of an unseen world. In one's highest aspiration one views God as a source of superhuman good (43–47).

Fourthly and finally, history and evolution show that any good attained here on earth comes only step-by-step, slowly, "through the infinite patience of God's manner of work." At the most practical level, then, one needs to be not only cooperative, but also patient. In terms more realistic than pleasing, Royce recalled the millions of millenia it took evolution to produce humankind and noted:

> You must not expect the ideal ends to be attained by sudden revolutions, by vast reforms, by swift processes. You must learn to labor and to wait. . . . Let the rebellious reformer remember, then, the Age of Reptiles, and learn to trust in God and be patient. (48, 50)

Involved in the evolution of the whole world community, we mortal selves must adjust our shared consciousness practically to fit the pace and long-range hope of this Universal Community.

If we summarize these four levels of shared moral consciousness by translating them into imperatives, we can grasp them in more familiar Roycean formulae. First, like a mother with her infant, simply "be loyal" to shared life as your cause. Second, "be loyal to loyalty"—to a maturer level of life in the supporting communities. Third, "be loyal to the superhuman divine life"—in your and Its atoning struggle to realize the better.[35] Lastly, "be loyal in your practical cooperation"—by being patiently faithful and decisive.

Facing the Problem of Evil With Steady Ethical Intent

As Royce saw it, ethics had to be a "study of good and evil" because moral good arises only through one's encounter with evil and victory over it. In 1896, in presenting his revised version of "The Problem of Job," Royce asked his colleagues, in the light of "the hypothetical perfection of God," to look at the dark side of things, both steadily and without the usual defensive self-deceptions. No more gulling themselves, for example, into believing "that sin, disease, death, degradation, oppression, weariness, despair, madness, wounded affection, and the other tortures of our finitude are comparatively exceptional phenomena."[36] In his paper Royce clarified the psychological bases needed to study the problem of evil. He focused on the unavoidable blendings of attraction and aversion in human psychic life. These phenomena of blendings lead a person to "love his own hates and to hate his own loves in an endlessly complex hierarchy of superposed interests in his own interests" (21). After listing many instances, Royce maintained that:

> this organization of life by virtue of the tension of manifold impulses and interests is not a mere accident of our imperfect human nature, but must be a type of the organization of every rational life. . . . But I insist that, in general, the only harmony that can exist in the realm of the spirit is the harmony that we possess when we thwart the present but more elemental impulse for the sake of the higher unity of experience; as when we rejoice in the endurance of the tragedies of life, because they show us the depth of life, or when we know that it is better to have loved and lost than never to have loved at all, or when we possess a virtue in the moment of victory over the tempter. (23)

Royce held that as long as one views God as an external power, as Job did, the problem of evil cannot be solved. Instead, Royce offered an insightful answer to this problem: recognize God as internally present to us and as suffering with us to produce the higher good.

The Human Self's Union with the Eternal in the Practical

Freed from misleading theories of atonement, in "Job" Royce recommended focusing on "the immortal soul of the doctrine of the divine atonement" (14). This implied, however, that "God's life could not be perfected [in this life] . . . without suffering, without ill, without woe, evil, and tragedy" (24–26). Such an immanent God is marked by the practical eternity of the Hebrews, not the detached and deedless eternity of the Greeks. Royce put it this way:

> He [God] is not remote from you even in his eternity. He is here. His eternity means merely the completeness of his experience. But that completeness is inclusive. Your sorrow is one of the included facts. (26)

Seven years later, in "The Eternal and the Practical," his presidential address to the American Philosophical Association, he further clarified this idea. For his human ethics-building, then, Royce clung tenaciously to our human experience of evils, both moral and amoral (e.g., fortuitous evils). Unless one started from them and from the selves who grapple with them—the one Eternal and many temporal selves—an ethicist could not be faithful to human experience.

In retrospect, them, our exploration has unearthed the roots of Royce's middle-period ethics: (a) an intouchness with one's environment taken broadly; (b) an individual moral selfhood teleologically "sent to others" (to one's ideal, nature, other persons, the future, and to God as the source of the human self's individuality); (c) a communal moral consciousness that develops through relations of extension and subsidiarity; (d) a steady victorious encounter with evil; and (e) a union with the Eternal in each deed of the human self. In these ways the middle Royce counterbalanced the dynamisms of nature and society, of individuality and loyalty to community, of freedom and responsibility, of good and evil, and of the finite and infinite.

THE STEM OF THE
MIDDLE ROYCE'S ETHICS (1904–1908)

From 1904 to 1908, Royce again began attending more directly to ethics. In 1906 and 1907, he lectured on ethics at Harvard's Summer Schools, at the Universities of Illinois and Yale, and at the Lowell Institute. By doing so, Royce's grasp of ethics became "somewhat deep-going and transforming."[37] Understandably, then, in the preface to his most popular work, *The Philosophy of Loyalty* (1908), he acknowledged, "One learns a good deal about ethics as one matures" (ix). The simple style of *Loyalty* hides how skillfully Royce balanced the complex dynamisms of ethical life just mentioned. Accordingly, we first examine the balance achieved there, then point out several noteworthy features in *Loyalty*, and conclude by observing four themes that Royce began sounding in these years.[38]

First, in *The Philosophy of Loyalty* Royce aimed to purify the meaning of loyalty gradually until he reached its full and final intent. Too frequently, commentators either simply convey Royce's preliminary definition of loyalty (16–17)—although he cautioned it was only "partial and provisional"— or merely offer his first and final definitions (357) without indicating that his intervening series of mutually enriching definitions develops as an expanding helix. Unfortunately such approaches keep the reader from entering into Royce's method of a step-by-step series of ever more integrated interpretations of loyalty and from noticing Royce's progressively enriching series of more than a dozen definitions.[39]

Secondly, in *Loyalty* Royce identified certain requirements for ethical life (201). One must dedicate oneself to a cause and serve it. One must be purified from misleading individualisms and from specious loyalties in order to reach that life-giving balance of the mature moral self which Royce called "real individuality" and "true loyalty." One must also make "promoting loyalty in *all* persons" the objective criterion of one's moral life. This norm reveals as immoral any preying upon others or any lack either of respect or of universality of intent. And one must develop one's universal rational consciousness into a conscience both decisive and faithful.[40] Among necessarily fallible human beings,[41] Royce found an example of such true loyalty in General Robert E. Lee (193–196).

Thirdly, Royce had to apply his theory of loyalty to solve certain American problems and to suggest ways of encouraging Americans to grow in the art of loyalty.[42] Otherwise, his doctrine of loyalty, however well designed, would remain inadequate.

Finally, Royce felt he could offer a complete exposition of his philosophy of loyalty only if he traced its relations with truth, reality, and religion.[43] This explains why he could not settle for William James's pragmatism of the passing moment and why he held that sincere loyalty necessarily involved some religious belief—"at least a latent belief in the superhuman reality of the cause" (386, 391).

The following points also deserve notice about Royce's *Loyalty*. He found the wellspring of ethical life, as well as the fountain of all the traditional and contemporary virtues, in the spirit of loyalty—that spirit of being loyal to universal loyalty. Moreover, by 1908, Royce was becoming increasingly concerned about the art of loyalty as a complement to his philosophy of loyalty. This art would empower one to reconcile the conflicts of loyalty encountered both within oneself and between oneself and others. It also would guide the pedagogy of training others in loyalty.[44]

Then, too, in Chapter VII, "Loyalty, Truth, and Reality," Royce exposed the inadequacies of James's theory of truth. He did so by using implicitly the "three motives of truth." He would soon render this theory explicit in his famous address to the Third International Congress of Philosophy at Heidelberg in 1908. According to this theory, for a genuinely loyal choice to be truthful, it had to "fit" three norms:—the individual subject (as the individualist norm), the changing outer world (as the pragmatist norm), and the objective truth of the real universe (as the classical idealist norm).[45] Moreover, in Royce's critique of James something else occurred. Here Royce argued about the more fitting interpretation of Peirce's pragmatic maxim. For here, in effect, Royce was asking James, "In clarifying our conceptions of truth, which of us two is more faithful to Peirce by considering all the practical consequences that conceivably might result necessarily from the truth of our conceptions of truth?"[46]

In these years Royce displayed his four new themes. First, he attached great importance to his "synthesis of individualism and loyalty which constitutes our whole ethical doctrine" (200, 79–80, 95–96). To effect this synthesis he had to purify both individualism and loyalty from their "chance and misleading associations" (viii, 15, 77). Then he had to test their balance by discerning whether a particular present stress on both did or did not promote genuine "unity in the spirit." Thus he already foreshadowed his mature triad of individual, community, and loyalty, all governed by the unique spirit of genuine loyalty.

Secondly, in his Urbana Lectures of 1907, Royce examined personality-ideals. Which ideal does a human self select? How does life's series of trials gradually reveal the shortcomings of various ideals? Consequently, what series of moral ideals can be expected?[47] Life, society, and fortune bite into one's personality so deeply that any truth-seeking self gradually detects the limits of the moral ideal that he or she has currently accepted. Hence, at Urbana Royce sketched how these pressures propel civilized selves through a phenomenology of moral ideals—from hero, through ascetic saint and rebellious titan, to loyal suffering servant. Although human selves differ in codes, customs, and religions, their pathway to moral growth involves a common pursuit of an ever more purified loyalty. One discovers early that only a few can realize one's youthful ideal of becoming a hero who serves a group. So the human self resolves to achieve something possible for all— that inner greatness of close union with God. That is, he resolves to become what Royce called a "stately self." But this ideal of becoming a holy one lacks a needed orientation to the human community. Moreover, if carried out completely, it would lead the self to becoming completely absorbed in God and thus to deny the value of its own unique personality.

Thus purified into at least some sense of the dignity of the "unconquerable soul," one grows by emphasizing one's own individuality and independent will. One seeks to become a titan. One wants most of all to be captain of one's own soul and, despite all adversities, to hold one's head "bloody but unbowed." Continuing experiences, however, soon school the self to the shortcomings of the titan ideal. Its sense of a superiority over others and of its own self-righteousness feels false. So this stage, too, must be transcended by adopting an ideal of equality to, solidarity with, and service of all fallible human beings.

Gradually, then, one who develops morally draws the best from his three former ideals. From the hero, he draws service to the community. From the saint, relation to the Holy and Eternal. From the titan, appraisal of one's unique worth. Then one concretizes these into a fourth and final moral ideal. He chooses to become the genuinely loyal self who as suffering servant builds up communities. Like Royce's earlier fourth conception of being, this fourth personality-ideal reinstates itself if one tries to deny its relevance for moral growth within the human situation. In such a loyal servant of community, then, Royce found the one ideal that can continuously attract a human personality to ever fuller development of the self even while calling it on to that continued dedicated service of others which is needed for raising the level of community life.

Thirdly, in *The Philosophy of Loyalty*, by "conceiving duty in terms of the conception of loyalty" (viii), Royce revealed how his ethical thought was moving beyond both deontology and teleology into a more comprehensive ethics of responsibility. In *Loyalty* he drew increasingly upon Aristotle's notion of the *fitting*.[48] This resulted in Royce's heightening focus upon both a fitting synopsis of percepts, concepts, and individualized knowings and an apt synthesis of feeling, intelligence, and will as indispensable ingredients of ethical choice.

Lastly, Royce's setting forth of what he then called "loyalty to loyalty" became "the most significant part" of his philosophy of loyalty (viii).[49] He preferred the term "loyalty" to "love" for several reasons. "Love" was even more ambiguous, insufficiently inclusive because caught in the context of the Christian "twofold commandment of love," and often equated with either mere benevolence or sterile sentiment of a religious not-of-this-world attitude. Instead, Royce chose "loyalty" to connote that human and worldwide decisiveness and that thoroughgoing service which genuine moral life requires.[50]

He had already shown that the moral life requires every person to dedicate oneself wholeheartedly to a cause. Only thus could a person give meaning to one's life and gain guidance for it. In his next move he revealed the radical demand central to his ethics—a demand he expressed in the often misunderstood directive, "Be loyal to loyalty" (118). Royce began by countering the traditional conception of loyalty that pits it against individual liberty. For people usually associate loyalty "with moral situations in which some external social power predetermines for the individual, without his consent, all the causes to which he ought to be loyal" (200). By contrast, Royce distinguished between only one absolute requirement and many modal freedoms:

> But in our philosophy of loyalty there is only one cause which is rationally and absolutely determined for the individual as the right cause for him as for everybody,—this is the general cause defined by the phrase "*loyalty to loyalty*." The way in which any one man is to show his loyalty to loyalty is, however, in our philosophy of loyalty, something which varies endlessly with the individual, and which can never be precisely defined except by and through his personal

consent. I can be loyal to loyalty only in my own fashion, and by serving my own special personal system of causes. (200–201)

This gave conscience a wide range of freedom to fulfill the only cause that each individual is morally obliged by rational will to embrace; namely, to evoke, respect, and promote loyalty in all minded beings. Royce explained it as follows:

> . . . the general principle of loyalty to which all special choices of one's cause are subject, is the principle: Be loyal to loyalty, that is, do what you can to produce a maximum of the devoted service of causes, a maximum of fidelity, and of selves that choose and serve fitting objects of loyalty. (201)[51]

A more succinct and significant ethical statement by the middle Royce can hardly be found. He packed into this sentence so may of the central dynamics of ethics: an emphasis on morally productive action, a universal intent and concern for the moral life and growth of all selves, one common rational obligation with room for individual freedom in the manner of fulfilling it, an aspiration for the better, and a discernment of the fitting.

One might object, however, either that the slogan "Be loyal to loyalty!" catches attention but needlessly mystifies, or that "Be just to justice!" or "Be caring about caring!" summarize ethical life just as effectively (144–145). Royce responded to objections like these in a letter to Professor Frank Thilly, after thanking him for his careful review of *The Philosophy of Loyalty*.[52] In it Royce stated more clearly than before that "Be loyal to loyalty!" indicated as no other motto could what genuine ethical life required of a human self. To be genuinely ethical, a self had to be fully self-conscious, communally related, and truly individual. In the following excerpt from his explanation to Thilly, the most operative phrases are "on a logical level" and "an essentially self-sustaining process" of rationally reflective self-consciousness:

> I don't agree with you that "justice to justice" or any analogous generalization, could stand anywhere nearly on a logical level with my own "loyalty to loyalty." The ground of that generalization of loyalty which I undertake lies in the intimate relation of loyalty to the very essence of self-consciousness, so that it is only when loyalty takes on the "reflective" form, as an essentially self-sustaining process, that it becomes at once truly universal, and truly individual. Justice and other fragments of loyalty cannot receive any such reflective form in any adequate way.[53]

In its logical structure, self-consciousness is a self-representative series. The ethical transformation of this structure is found in loyalty to loyalty. One can only want genuinely to be loyal if one is dedicated to developing serially the life of loyalty in oneself and in all other community members. Thus the intimate logical relation of *ego, alter,* and community at the heart of self-consciousness requires the triad of loyalty to loyalty as its ethical transcription.

Royce told Thilly that for self-consciousness to become "at once truly universal, and truly individual," it must reach the "reflective" form of the loyal life by being loyal to itself wherever found. For only in its reflective form can it become "an essentially self-sustaining process," which maintains, corrects, and develops itself. Characteristic of such practical rational self-consciousness is the process of committed decisiveness. Logically, then, Roycean ethics centers on a triad: two poles (individual and member) integrated by an interpreting spirit. For each human self's membership relation to the Universal Community contrasts with its need to be faithful to its own unique and true individuality. Unless these two poles are not only felt and understood, but also synthesized by the "spirit of loyalty," there will be no morality (viii).

Negatively, this process keeps rational self-consciousness from being drawn down by the various inclinations it experiences. The human self is unfortunately able to act primarily from feelings or from mere intelligence, or to concentrate on its individualistic self, or to lose true self-identity by settling merely into conventionality or organizations or mystic wholes. Positively, if paradoxically, this process of serial moral development keeps the individual human self directed in fidelity to the hierarchy of communities which it serves. It does so by promoting a still further fidelity both towards the true uniqueness of this individual self and towards the nature it has in common with other human selves.

In his own moral life as a philosopher, Royce found that "doing ethics" involved a striving to harmonize this paradoxical variety of opposites. Moral philosophy had its own specific encounter with the problem of evil. Thus three years after writing *Loyalty*, Royce summarized its moral philosophy from the perspective of this striving towards harmony:

> My philosophy of loyalty . . . is an endeavor to harmonize individual right with social duty, private judgment with a willingness to accept a certain sort of external authority, the personal consciousness with the voice of our wiser moral traditions.[54]

Royce suggested that each loyal self experiences this same call to strive to harmonize and to integrate the many polar oppositions in his or her moral life. For one has to find a way to be both unique and social, autonomous yet open to some external guide, open to moral traditions yet sensitive enough to one's long-range future to be critical of them and thus enabled to be true to oneself in the present situation. As Royce moved into his final years, this sense of struggle amid conflicts and dissatisfactions, along with his striving to overcome them in peace and hopefulness, increasingly marked his life and moral philosophy.

THE BLOSSOMING OF ROYCE'S
MIDDLE PERIOD ETHICS (1909–1911)

Royce's lectures at Pittsburgh and at Smith College in 1910, his letter to a future daughter-in-law, and his Bross Lectures of 1911 on "The Sources of Religious Insight" portray the full flower of Royce's middle-period ethics. From these we assemble a series of perspectives that displays how brightly his ethics had bloomed before his apoplexy attack of early 1912.

The Essence of Loyalty

Tirelessly Royce kept trying to disabuse his audiences of inadequate ideas of "loyalty." The term sounded so familiar to them that few suspected the richness and novelty he meant to insert into it. To his Pittsburgh audience, for instance, he displayed various inadequate understandings of loyalty. Some thought Roycean loyalty meant mere unselfishness, or pure benevolence, or subservience, or blind obedience to authority. Others identified it with a conservatism that resisted reforms and progress, or with an absorption in mere tasks without adoration or inner personal cultivation of the spirit.[55]

They missed the essence of loyalty because its accidental robes distracted them. The essence of loyalty lay in a spiritual attitude which fittingly embodied the spirit of loyalty. Echoing the evangelical distinction between life and letter, between spirit and law, Royce told his Pittsburgh audience, "The dutiful spirit is indeed precisely a spirit. No letter is able exhaustively to characterize it."[56]

To better identify this spirit Royce grew increasingly interested in the art, as well as in the philosophy, of loyalty. He sometimes described this art with the recurring theme of the truth-seeker:

> . . . the art of loyalty is the art of discovering what your own rational will is, and of then discovering how to be true to that will, whatever [be] your tumult, your moods, or your life.[57]

Here Royce focused on that rational self-knowledge, gained by inquiry, which is an indispensable, yet often underestimated, aspect of his loyalty. For his loyal person has a clear eye, an intelligence that is rationally discerning. This person strives to maintain and increase rational self-consciousness. Throughout a series of ethical choices, his or her truth-seeking moral will works at its interpretive task and keeps inquiring what promotes greater loyalty among more people. If the person tries to deny this unique "principle of increasing harmony," he or she will experience a performatory contradiction whereby the unavoidable moral light of this principle will reassert itself within him or her. For the person undeniably appreciates the goodness of promoting the genuine life and its growth in all people. By committing the self to this purpose as to its own general cause, the person gains light and guidance for his or her particular choices.

On the other hand, if the loyal person somehow becomes estranged from oneself, this rational commitment to promote loyalty universally drops from his or her consciousness. A certain blindness then arises and keeps the person at the level of being simply loyal. For the while the person is unable to taste the goodness of the former rationally self-conscious dedication to making others and its own self more loyal. In brief, to be true, one's loyalty must be enlightened, discriminating, and discerning.

Where Thomas Aquinas described the vital center of ethical life in terms of practical wisdom (or *prudentia*),[58] Royce sketched such rational inquiry in terms of "being considerate."

> Of course you are considerate. You try to think over the doubtful matter carefully, to weight consequences, to dwell upon the principles of your art, to avoid caprice, to surrender mere self-will, to look to your highest cause, to remember how all the loyal need your good example and your help in the spirit of faithfulness. You try, in short, to bethink you, in Wordsworth's metaphor, of that spirit which preserves the stars from wrong. But if, when all the most universal and lofty considerations have been thought over, if when all insight has been fairly tried, the matter still remains doubtful,—then one duty remains, and that duty is indeed certain. You must decide for yourself, and fear not, and act out your decision. This is loyalty. And without such personal and practical decisiveness, loyalty is but a dream.[59]

For all Royce's stress on searching for more light, intelligence is not enough. Faithful decisiveness is also required. For this, however, the loyal person's love of his cause must be of a certain kind.

> The loyal person wants to judge only as the cause needs to have him judge. Of course he uses, therefore, his own judgment; but he uses it with a perfectly objective principle [his cause] to guide him.[60]

Through the love of one's cause (and thus of the community whose cause it is), the loyal person is given a "perfectly objective principle to guide him" and thus is raised above any mere affection for another individual as such. In this way Royce emphasized how loyalty is greater than love of an individual:

> . . . love for any one human being is never the whole of loyalty. True love is simply the warm light which loyalty throws over your relations to your fellow servants in a common cause. Thus mother love, when it is a true and loyal love, is simply the will that the child should in time become, through the services that mother love offers, a faithful fellow servant of the common cause,—of the home, of the family, of the social order, of humanity. No love that is not inspired by a loyalty that is larger than any merely individual affection, is an offering worthy of the person to whom it devotes itself. In turn you yourself

want nobody's love who does not view you as such a fellow servant of a common loyalty.[61]

This subsidiarity of various "common causes"—from the home of the mother down to humanity itself—manifests both a "true spirit of loyalty" within her loyal love and a direction to a community beyond humanity.

Since some people are only aware of human causes, whereas others also recognize in their system of causes a direction to the divine, Royce taught the women of Smith College to distinguish between two forms of loyalty:

> ...the highest values in the life of the past have depended upon two forms of loyalty; namely, religious loyalty to the unseen superhuman world, and humane loyalty to the ties that the visible world suggests.[62]

Sometimes he referred to religious loyalty as superhuman, and to humane loyalty as natural. Sensitive to the ways in which superstition has mingled with "faith in the unseen" and how conventions, now antiquated (like waging war), have nourished natural humane loyalty, Royce pointed to the discernment between the true spirit of these two loyalties and their false accretions as "the question of questions for a modern philosophy of life."

In late 1910, Elizabeth Randolph, Royce's future daughter-in-law, asked for his help with some vexing questions. Royce sent her a copy of *Loyalty* and promptly responded to this talented and sensitive artist. Wishing he "could effectively condense it [his book] all into a word," he succeeded in carving a classic cameo of his 1910 philosophy of loyalty. In Appendix A we present it within a few pages.

In it we also find a vignette of Royce dealing interpersonally with Elizabeth in a way that makes palpable his art of loyalty. He preferred the resonance of her heart to any thoughts of his own. He pointed out to her the radical choice she and all have when interpreting life. He emphasized the opportunity which life offers to be of help to others. For, according to Royce, one's life has meaning simply because one's help is needed.

The Sources of Religious Insight

The fullest flowering, however, of Royce's late middle-period philosophy of loyalty occurred in the concluding chapters of his *Sources of Religious Insight*. In these Royce identified three dependable authenticating sources of religious insight: the spirit of genuine loyalty, the religious mission of sorrow, and community life in the unity of the Spirit. Royce focused on the bond between ethical and religious life, on the "fitting" as an ethical norm, and on the way this entailed a practical mysticism. Quite familiar with the ongoing strife between ethicists and religionists, Royce thought it wiser to stress the bond between the life of ethics and religion. He searched for a "way of reconciling our need of a grace that shall save with the call of the moral life."[63] He found it in a "certain type of morality that, in and for itself, is already essentially religious so that it knows nothing of this conflict between duty and religion" (181). He thus showed that "[w]hat a narrower way of living can divide, a deeper and truer mode of living can unite." Such a religious ethic

> is a sort of consciousness which equally demands of those whom it inspires, spiritual attainment and strenuousness, serenity and activity, resignation and vigor, life in the spirit and ceaseless enterprise in service. (181)

This type of morality searches to fit one's finite will into the intent of the infinite will. As Royce put it, "Your search for salvation is a seeking to adjust yourself to this supreme will" (159). Finding the "light that leads kindly" and fitting in, one step at a time, with its lead, constituted the late Royce's kind of practical mysticism. He described it this way:

> However ignorant you are, you are, then, in constant touch with the master of life; for you are constantly doing irrevocable deeds whose final value, whose actual and total success or failure, can only be real, or be known, from the point of view of the insight that faces the whole of real life, and with reference to the purposes of the will whose expression is the entire universe. (159)

The heart of this religious ethic, therefore, is more than genuine loyalty since it lies in its *spirit*. As Royce put it:

> The spirit of true loyalty is of its very essence a complete synthesis of the moral and of the religious interests. The cause is a religious object. It finds you in your need. It points out to you the way of salvation. Its presence in your world is to you a free gift from the realm of the spirit—a gift that you have not of yourself, but through the willingness of the world to manifest to you the way of salvation. This free gift first compels your love. Then you freely give yourself in return. (206)[64]

Moreover, in the *Sources*, Royce's reexamination of the problem of evil plumbed new depths. In its chapters V and VI he treated more clearly and thoroughly than previously how oppressive physical powers confront, persecute, and hurt loyal persons and how these latter respond creatively under such oppression (209–210). Underneath such dire oppression, these loyal sufferers manifest a breathtakingly courageous endurance. Here Royce sounded a major thesis: "Adversity and loyalty are inseparable companions" (252–253).[65] The loyal sufferer not only has compassion and comforts those who are oppressed but actually enters into their dying so that through death a new and higher life will arise. Given the linguistic limits imposed in the *Sources* by its "philosophy of religion in general," this is as close as Royce could come to what explicit Christian language calls the "Pascal Mystery."[66]

The *Sources* centers around "the Religious Paradox," that problem of how a fallible human self validly discerns a genuine divine communication (20–25). The paradox focuses upon the "assurance that the believer already knows the essential marks by which a divine revelation is to be distinguished from any other sort of report" (23). In the concluding chapters of *Sources*, after identifying "the Spirit of loyalty" as the heart of ethical life, Royce revealed an inner dialogue between that Spirit and the spirit of a finite self, its own "divine spark." In this context he developed further criteria for discerning true and false loyalties, some negative, some positive (192–197, 205). To be genuine, loyalty cannot: (a) contemn the loyalties of other people; or (b) prey upon their loyalty by deprivation or manipulation; or (c) restrict their freedom from choosing any cause to which they can be loyal (204). Positively, he added the criteria of what could be called "spiritual freedom," "resonance to the loyal spirit wherever it blows," and "non-regretableness." Royce described the active detachment of spiritual freedom this way:

> . . . the warrior, if rightly inspired, is as ready for life as for death, is as ready for peace as for war; and despises defeat as much as danger—fearing only sloth and dishonour and abandonment of the service. (194)

Concerning one's resonance to the song of the loyal heart wherever it sounds, Royce held:

> The other test is whether the warrior is ready to recognize and to honour, with clear cordiality, this same spirit when it is manifested in another calling, or in another service, and, in particular, [when it] is manifested by his enemy. (194)

A prerequisite for the third positive criterion is a calm reflective review of one's whole life. In this context one finds that one cannot regret wanting to promote loyalty in all selves:

> . . . the principle of loyalty, if rightly defined and served by you—served with the whole energy and power of your personal self—is a principle that upon any enlightened survey of your life you can never regret having served. This, then, is what we were seeking—an absolute moral principle, a guide for all action. (205)

With its presupposed enlightened survey, this *non-regretableness* constitutes both an illuminating signal of the Absolute that one experiences at the core of his moral life and a distinctive benchmark of Royce's ethics in 1911.

To summarize, then, in the *Sources* Royce had developed his ethics far beyond his 1896 insight into individuality and beyond *The Philosophy of Loyalty* (1908). His mind had kept seeking for an ever fuller, still fairer understanding of ethical life.

Such intense searching, however, exacted a price from his mind and body. Around late 1911, Royce's mind felt uneasy about one basic point in idealism—neither about its "statement of the ideal of truth," nor about its "conception of truth as the teleological harmony or adjustment of a partial to a total view of experience and its meaning."[67] Rather, the now-felt inadequacy of the very basis from which he had started his idealism began turning into a neuralgic point. In his article, "Error and Truth," he was driven to confess:

> Precisely with regard to the problem of the possibility of error, that is, of disharmony between the demands of any partial interpretation of experience and that which is revealed and fulfilled by the whole of experience, the idealistic theory of truth and of error has proved to be, thus far [1911] most incomplete.[68]

Despite this acknowledged mental nadir, Royce still hoped to find a fuller, more satisfactory answer to explain the possibility of error. He concluded the article by setting down seven conditions for such an answer—the seventh pointing to the breakthrough which was soon to dawn. Meanwhile, amid such intense searching, frustrations, and external tensions, his body gave way. With his apoplexy attack of February 1, 1912, Royce's middle period ended.

In his convalescence of early 1912, Royce reached out to review the writings of his friend, C. S. Peirce. Little did he dream that the intellectual insight being thus occasioned would equal the transformative power of his first maximal insight of 1883.[69] For the "Peircean insight" initiated his mature period and provided him with a new medium of thought, a new philosophical message, and a new manner of expressing it. Because this insight transformed Royce's theory of knowledge and metaphysics as well as his ethics, we need first to examine the relations of his mature ethics with his transformed epistemology and metaphysics of 1912–1916.

5. Nexus with His Late Epistemology and Metaphysics (Part One)

Occasionally Royce spoke of his ethics as the foundation of his epistemology (or theory of knowledge) and of his metaphysics.[1] In other contexts he described his epistemology and metaphysics as founding his ethics.[2] We need to contextualize both manners of speech into Royce's way of philosophizing after 1912. A comparison may clarify. In the human organism, breathing, brain activity, and heartbeat depend on each other for the life and health of the organism. Similarly, at least in Royce's post-1912 philosophy of life, his ethics, epistemology, and metaphysics interconnected vitally.[3] Hence, we need some account of how the mature Royce integrated these three disciplines.

If for a clearer presentation we treat Royce's epistemology and metaphysics in two separate chapters, the reader deserves a caveat. Royce constantly linked his metaphysics and theory of knowing during his last course in metaphysics. Accordingly, the reader is invited to go beyond our separate treatment and create a synthesis of Royce's mature epistemology, metaphysics, and ethics.

For Royce all three of these disciplines developed out of his religious insight of 1883, which he called "a necessary and absolute principle of philosophy."[4] We need, then, first to follow him to this insight, especially as he reinterpreted it in 1916 after its many periodic transformations. So, in the present chapter we will first revisit Royce's argument to the religious insight, then examine his final theory of knowledge—particularly, interpretation as a fundamental kind of knowledge and the problem of truth—and show how this theory connected with his mature ethics. In the next chapter, dealing with his final metaphysics, we will summarize his Last Lectures on Metaphysics, highlight the gist of his 1916 article "Mind," survey the resultant themes of his metaphysics, and then see how Royce's metaphysics of 1916 interacted with his final ethics. We assume that Royce's logic and interpretive musement supported all three disciplines.

ROYCE'S 1916 ARGUMENT TO THE ALL-KNOWING
SPIRIT OF THE UNIVERSAL COMMUNITY

Royce's argument of 1883 to an All-Knower and its religious insight continued to undergird his metaphysics. Yet, while maintaining its central life, this insight developed through stages that paralleled the growth of a butterfly. In particular, Royce's Peircean insight of 1912 transformed the argument of 1883 but did not change its essential life. To appreciate it, then, in its 1916 garb, we need to notice, first, some prolegomena, then Royce's efforts to rephrase the argument after 1883, and finally, his last enunciation of the argument in 1916.

PROLEGOMENA TO ROYCE'S ARGUMENT

To build a context that enables a person to understand Royce's argument honestly one needs to adjust to it by giving fair consideration to more than a dozen contextual antecedents.

1. Since philosophies arise from people's different temperaments, as Fichte, James, and Royce taught, certain people will easily grasp whatever cogency Royce's essential argument to an All-Knower may have. Other temperaments , however, will either see no cogency in it or see it only dimly.

2. The *whole* Royce created his fundamental argument from the possibility of error. Royce as a logical, ethical, practical, mystical, and Christian epistemological metaphysician entered into this argument and left the marks of these dimensions upon it. Consequently, attempts to express his argument in phrases of purely formal logic, or of mystical sensibility, or of an anti-materialistic polemic necessarily fail because they reduce Royce to one dimension. Rather, since all the dimensions of his personality created the argument, they all need to be taken into account.

3. For each person, the problem of God's reality is a "live, forced, and momentous option," to borrow William James's terms.[5] Hence, to reason objectively on this problem, the honest searcher must become intellectually free enough to be ready for either a "yes" or a "no" solution to it. But a person naturally resists calling into question the whole of his or her past and future life—whether as a believer, an unbeliever, an agnostic, or a puzzling fluxing mix of all three positions. So, the searcher into Royce's argument needs to attain enough intellectual freedom to treat honestly and fairly the evidence offered.

4. Even if Royce himself in 1883 had not yet shifted his mode of thinking explicitly to an *interpretive* epistemology, he had surely done so by 1915. At this later date, he stressed the need "to revise our metaphysical

ideas" (12/2).[6] This occurred if one shifted one's habits of thinking from a primarily conceptual or perceptual mode of thought into a primarily interpretational mode. For instance, the mature Royce cautioned his audience that they must counter their habit of defining truth and reality in merely conceptual terms (1/4). If his argument were to function for them, they would have to shift to a concrete interpretive context and consider truth and reality in their essentially social setting. He required this profound revision in one's way of philosophizing if anyone wished to understand him fairly.

5. Because Royce's argument calls for a series of judgments, it cannot function in the atemporal atmosphere of mere percepts or concepts. When a person shifts from an erroneous to a true judgment, he or she has to grasp the temporal process involved in this interpreted shift. It reveals through its temporal process the interpreter's evaluative preference for truth over error, and thus the functioning of the ideals of "beauty, duty, and truth"[7] in this process of completing a comparison.

For example, first, a factual judgment: "Today the president works in his Oval Office." Secondly, "But he's actually spending today out at Camp David, as I discover from television and newspapers." Thirdly, by comparing the second judgment with the first I judge, "I erred in my first judgment, since I have more evidence for the second. From this experienced recognition of actual error, and the teleological shift to a true*r* view, one can begin to search for the conditions that make actual error possible.

6. In Royce's philosophy, reality is essentially social. This thesis contradicts the nominalism of most people who ignore the basic reality of some communities and what Peirce called "real generals" such as objective tendencies, types, and habits.[8] For most people the only real beings are individuals. Robert Bellah has described a "detached individualism" that dominates Americans' attitudes and thoughts and rises out of an "ontological individualism" that claims the world is composed ultimately of individuals only.[9] The mature Royce called this latter uncriticized belief "nominalism" (3/9, 10/14) and recognized it as blocking his argument to an All-Knower.

By contrast, in the *Problem* Royce had asserted explicitly the dual ultimacy of the ideas of the individual and the community.[10] Finding that his fundamental "doctrine of the two levels" governed reality and consciousness, he pointed out:

> two profoundly different grades, or levels, of mental beings,—namely, the beings that we usually call human individuals, and the beings that we call communities.[11]

Hence, only to those acknowledging the communal nature of truth and reality could Royce's argument to an All-Knower make sense.

7. If "mental beings" include individuals *and* communities, then truth, too, has to be essentially social. Since truth lives only in an appeal from one judging mind to another within a community of mental beings, it can never exist in an individual mind as such. It can live only in a triad of minded beings; that is, in the shared life of the appealer, appealee, and the communal "mental being" or community that embraces them both.

8. The person who tests Royce's argument with traditional logic may fault it for not being classifiable as primarily a deductive or inductive argument. But this critique, although on target *qua* classification, fails to notice that Royce here argues in a Kant-like "transcendental" way, as John Smith has pointed out.[12] That is, Royce searches in it for the indispensable conditions which make actual error possible.

9. In addition to Royce's tracking of prerequisite conditions for error, he also interweaves two other noteworthy logical strands into his argument: the "necessary connections" of concepts and an argument from performative contradiction.

A person cannot think of the meaning of circle unless he or she also knows what is meant by point, curved line, plane, radius, and equality, since these concepts are "necessarily connected" with the concept of circle. Similarly, one cannot think clearly of the meaning of *doubt* unless one also knows what one means by error (possible and actual), truth, and judgment, along with hope and despair and their underlying affects: love and fear. So, logically speaking, Royce's argument also relies upon the necessary connections of these concepts correlative to those of doubt and discovered error.

Moreover, even in 1883, Royce's argument employed seminally what in 1916 he called his "reflective method" with its implicit "reduction to absurdity." By this method he showed that any attempted denial of his argument involved an affirmation of it because the denial constituted a performative contradiction. If I deny that my actual error implies the reality of an All-Knower, I either address my denial to some other mind, or my denial is void of meaning. But if this other mind is fallible, our fallible community of addresser and addressee requires an All-knowing Mind to embrace and constitutively judge all possible errors as truly errors. Hence, my original denial of an All-Knower simply reinstates the truth of the All-Knower's reality.

10. Some thinkers are surprised that several moral dimensions also permeate Royce's argument. First, suppose a person interprets that his or her judgment, "*X* is *Y*," is indeed true. Then that person is morally responsible for affirming this judgment as true.[13]

Again, anyone making a judgment of the form "*X* is *Y* " appeals intrinsically to some other mind. The validity of this appeal, however, requires honesty between appealer and appealee—that is, a morally sound interpersonal relatedness. Royce clarified by expanding the realities underlying this judgment (4/25).[14] First, "[I say] (it is true that) X is Y." And by a second expansion: "[I say honestly to some other mental being, and ultimately to a final Court of Appeal] (that it *is* true—insofar as a finite human self can interpret truth, even if always tentatively and serially—) that X is Y." For a sound, essentially social judgment, honest communication (or veracity) is a moral must; otherwise, the community involved tends into a "people of the lie."

Still another moral aspect appears in Royce's argument. For he affirms there is "one and only one right attitude" for making any judgment; namely, his "third attitude of will."[15] The genuine loyalist has the morally fitting attitude of lovingly embracing the universe—warts and all—and through his or her judgments of working constructively with its processes.[16] Only out of such a loving loyalty for the whole universe do sound judgments arise. They cannot arise if one's attitude of will is excessively individualistic—like the self-affirmer devoid of respect for all other persons and communities or the escapist who withdraws from community involvement.

11. Again, when a sick, enfeebled Peirce wrote in his final year to Royce about "reasoning," he witnessed that his own pragmatism:

chiefly goes to improve the *security* of inference without touching what is far more important, its *Uberty* its full-breasted richness or fecundity]. It doesn't for instance seem to have any thing to say as to our exaltation of *beauty*, *duty*, or *truth*. . . . I am going to insist upon the superiority of Uberty over Security.[17]

Through a distinctive evaluation, reasoning *exalts* (or values highly) these three ideals and strongly disvalues ugliness, irresponsibility, and falsehood. When Royce pointed to the "ideal that guides the truth-loving interpreter" as indispensable for reasoning,[18] he concurred with the dying Peirce's desire to "insist upon the superiority of Uberty over Security" in reasoning. So, if Royce chose to reason to a supposed most-exalted Reality, some Uberty-producing evaluative response is needed to animate his argument about Being and truth.[19]

12. The logical core of this response had to include the "numerous not-relations" marking that negative theology which, according to Royce:

very volubly characterizes a set of unsymmetrical distinctions of value, of preciousness, of grades of being, and of processes of emanation, which . . . depend for all their interest upon the fact that the mystic presents to us something of which he can say that it is best known 'when most I feel there is a lower and an higher.' [20]

13. Royce's argument starts from a true judgment about one's actually erroneous judgment. Hence, anyone who *confuses* truth with probability or certitude or verification will both confuse Royce's argument and find it confusing. Royce found many of his readers and audiences confused in this

way—including William James, whom Royce saw as confusing truth with verification and probability (5/13). The absolute character of a judgment, as either true *or* false, may not be watered down. Thus judgments about past but distant persons or events are either true or false—howsoever probable, or "historically verified," or subjectively certain they may be under different definable aspects. The same holds true of judgments about present occurrences and experiences. Concerning judgments about future choices, we cannot as yet know them as either true or false, since the truth about future free choices has yet to come to our judgments.

14. Prolegomenon 13 suggests the need to notice the difference between the mature Royce's view of God and Aquinas's *totum simul* view of God. Drawing upon the Greek notion of the incorruptible (*aphtharton*), Aquinas employed a classical understanding of Being as fundamentally unchangeable. In the First Part of his *Summa Theologiae*, the God of Aquinas partly echoes the neo-Platonic view of the *Nous* (Mind).[21] The latter contains not only Plato's universal Forms, but also all ideas of *individual* persons, things, and events. Accordingly, such a neo-Platonic God has to see simultaneously the whole of reality in its every individual detail (= *totum simul*). To do so, however, and yet also be immanently provident, such a God's insight has to view the world from the end of history, too, and behold it in its uniquely individual entirety to which it has developed. Such a requirement, of course, tends to put sequence and stages in the knowing of such a God whose provident care would have to know the choices of finite individuals both before and after they occur. Thus the God of Aquinas's *First Part* knows quite differently from the interpretive way whereby Royce's Spirit of the Universal Community knows Being in a teleological process. So, the mature Royce avoided this dilemma of a *totum simul* God.

Various Expressions of Royce's Argument

If a person responds empathetically and critically to the foregoing *prolegomena*, he or she can readily grasp Royce's argument to an All-Knower from the possibility of error. Royce found his argument close to Augustine's: "since a truth exists, therefore, the Infinite Truth exists."[22] Even in his *Religious Aspect of Philosophy*, Royce expressed this argument in many ways.[23] He revised and reaffirmed it in many of the writings of his remaining thirty-three years.[24]

In summer 1914, Royce described how genuine loyalty creates a distinctive kind of interpretive knowing which holds its own religious insight. He told his Berkeley audience:

> . . . in and through and above all these special forms which the loyal spirit takes, we all, precisely in so far as we are loyal, *come into some genuine touch*

with one and the same reality, with one and the same cause, with one and the same live spiritual reality. To this one cause all the loyal are, according to their lights, faithful.[25]

The Universal Community of Interpretation is the ultimate reality contacted by all genuinely loyal agents. In this form of the argument, what I call Royce's mediated metaphysical mysticism stands out more clearly.

A Final Expression of the Argument in 1916

When Royce revisited this argument in 1916, he may by his brevity have effectively alerted his audience to its gist as he then viewed it. For in his 1915–16 metaphysics class he had chosen to do something quite atypical for Royce—offer them a sketch of his own intellectual autobiography. Having reached in his story the first year of his teaching at Harvard, Royce recounted what had—exactly thirty-three years earlier—moved him on January 11–12, 1883, out of his earlier skeptical view of only a postulated world to the reality of an All-Knower. He had found himself with present experience and a "world of the postulates"—that is, a world that seemed necessarily to have extension and a past and future. But *why* must consciousness build itself up this way? Through what Royce described as "a somewhat insistent self-criticism," he came to the following considerations. Acknowledging his ignorance about why he must think his "world of the postulates," Royce told how this

> led me to the decided reversal of point of view which followed. My postulates may be mere attitudes toward the real. If that is the case, then error is at least possible. but what would be an error? . . . This led me to the doctrine of the nature of error as involving *interpretation*. I said to myself, this view which I set forth about the nature and conditions of error is true or false. Whether it is true or false, we have here a teleological situation which brings the thought of the moment into contact with a type of consciousness which is not the merely human type. (1/11)

Royce then read from his own notes written on January 11–12, 1883, recording his discovery. In the 1916 version of it just given, we find his mediated metaphysical mysticism based on the world of true and false judgments and the inescapable sociality of minded beings. Central to it, too, is the Mind that in determinatively constituting the systemic order of all true judgments has likewise to grasp the infinite universe of all possible errors—that is, a reflective All-Interpreter. In this way, then, Royce found it to be true that this Mind serves as an indispensable condition for the possibility of any actual error that human beings experience. He also expected his students to "summarize the argument (set forth at length in the lectures) . . . regarding 'the Possibility of Error'."[26]

ROYCE'S FINAL THEORY OF KNOWLEDGE

Around fall 1915, Royce created his article "Mind" for Hasting's *Encyclopaedia*.[27] In it he offered what is arguably the clearest and deepest revelation of his most mature theory of knowledge and metaphysics.[28] In "Mind" he dedicated four sections to epistemology before feeling prepared to communicate his "metaphysics of mind" in a final section.[29] Here, then, in our précis of "Mind," we will follow Royce's order by first describing the epistemology of his final year. In this epistemology the problems of the basic kinds of knowledge and of truth deserve special attention.

Is Interpretation a *Basic* Kind of Knowledge?

In "Mind" Royce began by noticing how many complications have beset epistemology and hence impeded ethical theory. Among these, the traditional twofold division of knowledge into perception and conception—while of great importance for science and metaphysics—has put philosophy and ethics into a dyadic straightjacket ever since Plato. These two basic kinds of knowledge cannot grasp life, temporal process, signs as signs, and especially, uniquely individual minds in community.

For example, the acute William James constricted himself within this traditional straightjacket with his division into "knowledge by acquaintance" and "knowledge about." Perception generates the former knowledge which is sometimes called "immediate knowledge." Conception generates the latter knowledge by using "abstract ideas" (which include many judgments and inferences). Philosophers have known that usually we experience a mingling of these two modes of knowing, even though some, like Bergson and James, have proposed the ideal of "pure (or radical) experience," while others, following Plato, have proposed "pure reason" (without input from sense experience).

By 1913 Royce saw that only Peirce's establishment of *interpretation* as a third fundamental kind of knowing had finally released philosophy from the dyadic straightjacket just described. While using percepts and concepts as its needed elements, interpretation moves concretely beyond these (through a reading of signs) to life, especially to mental life, to the concrete meaning of life, and thus to the individual decisions of moral life.

What then is interpretation? As a mental process, it *completes a comparison of ideas*—for instance, a comparison of one's present self with that of some *Alter* (other self or mind). To illustrate, when a person understands a spoken or written language, "what he perceives is some signs or expressions of an idea or meaning, which in general belongs to the mind of some fellow-man" (152).[30] Royce asserted that if I hear someone cry "Fire!" I get my percepts and concepts, but I also interpret the cry "Fire!" as a sign indicating an idea not my own which refers to a mind distinct from my own. I can misread the sign—prankster? manipulator?—or I can complete the comparison of possible interpretations of his cry "Fire!" by consulting a wiser community than my present self—the crier directly, or others nearby, or perhaps the community of my memories of this other's consistent way of behaving.

The psychic states I can perceive are only my own—not those of the crier—since only he can perceive his psychic states. And surely my concepts of him and of fire are too abstract to supply adequate contact with the unique concreteness of this individual cry. Nor can a union of percept and concept suffice because these static elements cannot know the mental motion needed to complete this comparison of signs—a temporal process. Likewise, within Peirce's three basic kinds of commonsense and scientific reasoning—abduction, deduction, and induction—an interpretive process operates.[31] Whether viewed in their minute uniqueness or in their integration within the overall process of scientific inquiry, these three kinds of reasoning exhibit interpretation within the temporally staged comparison and contrast they presuppose.[32] Therefore, a different, fundamental, and irreducible third kind of knowledge refers a person through a temporal process of reading signs to the psychic intent, meaning, feeling, or interest of his or her neighbor. Royce continued:

> In fact, we come to know that there are in the world minds not our own by interpreting the signs that these minds give us of their presence. This interpretation is a third type of knowledge which is closely interwoven with perceptual and conceptual knowledge, very much as they in turn are bound up with it, but which is not reducible to any complex or combination consisting of elements which are merely perceptual or merely conceptual. (153)

All social and interior conversations require this interpretive process of knowing.

The typical *objects* of interpretation "are signs which express the meaning of some mind" (154). These are quite different from the objects of perception (sense data and subjective feelings) and from the objects of conception (kinds of things and their relations, such as likeness or equality).

When the incoming sign is first encountered, the receiver knows with certainty that the idea it carries is not then his own. Despite this certainty, however, is not interpretive knowing as fallible as are perception and the process of conception? Royce's affirmative response led him to point out the community-building inescapably present in interpretation:

> . . . whenever one is led to attempt, propose, or believe an interpretation of a sign, he has actually become aware, at the moment of his interpretation, that there is present in his world some meaning, some significant idea, plan,

purpose, undertaking, or intent, which at the moment he discovers its presence, is from his point of view not identical with whatever idea or meaning is then his own. (155)

Accordingly, he described interpretation as:

> ...the essentially social process whereby the knower at once distinguishes himself, with his own meanings, ideas, and expressions, from some other self, and at the same time knows that these selves have their contrasted meanings, while one of them at the moment is expressing its meaning to the other. (156)

Interpretation, then, is essentially social but also teleological—that is, it possesses "a directed 'sense'," the bearing of one minded being *toward* another intended mind.

To sum up, then, interpretive knowledge is: (1) an interpreter's expression, of (2) the meaning or idea carried by a sign from another mind, and (3) addressed or directed to a third mind to which the interpreter construes or reads the sign.

What happens, however, when interpretation is directed to oneself? Like all other interpretations, self-interpretation encapsulates a knowledge of temporal process (or of lived time, felt concretely). Royce taught that if interpretation occurs within an individual persons's mind, one "finds oneself" or "gets one's bearings." For example, when one reads the meaning of a past jotting in one's memorandum book for the current day, one grasps the relation of one's past to one's future through one's present knowing. For then the signs from one's 'past self' and one's 'future self' are compared by one's 'present self'. To become an interpretation, however, this comparison must go beyond a mere finding of likeness or unlikeness in these 'selves', since it must break through to recognize some identity; that is, it must also make a judgment of identification.

At this point in his article "Mind," Royce took up James's example of a person lost in the woods whose idea of home supplies the "leading" whereby the person eventually finds his way out of the woods and discovers his own home. Royce pointed out that in this instance James omitted that "aspect of cognition which is [as] equally pervasive and significant" as are its percepts and concepts:

> For by what process does the wanderer, when he reaches home, *recognize* that this home which he finds is the very home that he had sought? Not by a mere presence of a 'home-feeling,' not by a perception which, merely at the moment of home-coming, pays the 'cash' then required by some then present conception of home, but by a process involving a comparison of his ideas about his home, at the moment when he reaches home, with his memories of what his ideas *were* while he was lost in the woods and while he still inquired or sought the way home. (159, emphasis added)

In the contrasting case, where the wanderer finds a house *not* his own, he also interprets that he has to search yet further. That is, he makes a negative judgment of identification about this house through a process that must also embrace a grasp of temporal process.

Recognizing with Peirce this third fundamental kind of knowledge, Royce indicated its fruits, since he grasped its "consequences...at once familiar and momentous for the theory of knowledge" (155). Without such cognitive processes of comparing ideas of one's past and present and future, one *could never even begin to form a coherent view either of oneself or of other selves.* As Royce put it, "Our ideas both of the Ego and of the Alter depend upon an explicit process of comparing ideas" (160–161). In this process one recognizes something the *same* as what one sought in some past moment and hoped to find in one's future self. This identifying comparison and recognition founds one's knowledge of "I." The same process is used similarly in coming to a judgment of identification whereby one recognizes another person. In that case one says eventually, "He (or she) is indeed the *self-same* sign-sender."

This process of interpretation, then, integrates several functions: a comparison of signs from distinct selves (from the same individual or from distinct persons), an awareness of temporal process, a recognition of coherence (sameness or constancy), and a judgment of identification. Only through this distinctive and irreducible interpretive process can we know "the self, the neighbor, the past, the future, and the temporal order in general" (161).

Approaching his bonding of epistemology with metaphysics, Royce taught that we know two facts: that various minds exist and which kind of beings minds are. How, then, are preception, conception, and interpretation related to our knowledge of these two basic facts?

Royce began his response by pointing out that the purchase which theory of knowledge has for helping people understand metaphysical problems is felt most of all in "the metaphysics of mind." Here much confusion has reigned historically because thinkers have created various hypotheses without first determining whether mind can be known adequately by perception or conception or their combination.

For example, someone might propose *soul* as an object adequately conceived—e.g., as in Aristotle's conceptual definition of soul in his *De Anima.* Or, someone might describe soul through perception, as something immediately perceived in the activities of a living organism. Or again, one might describe soul as an object of a certain kind of interpretation yet fail to keep his or her language in parallel with this third kind of knowing. In all three cases confusion would arise. For instance, continued Royce, when William James tried to define the truth of his pragmatic hypotheses about mind, his pragmatism showed its greatest inadequacy. For the direct verifiability he expected and required could not be had in the case of mind.

Instead, one can only hope to interpret (through more or less probable judgments) what the mind of one's neighbor means or intends. Hence, any 'working hypothesis' about my neighbor's mind can never be "converted into the cash of experience." For neither immediate acquaintance nor any abstract universal idea can verify the uniquely individual mind of one's neighbor.

According to Royce, when William James claimed that one knows that another mind exists *by analogy* with one's own mind, he followed a well-known but misleading philosophical tradition. For here James's position was not verifiable. It both overlooked the brute experience of being confronted with ideas not one's own and rejected the realistic correspondence of the neighbor's existent mind as related to one's own.

Likewise, Bergson's metaphor of converting bank notes into cash proved itself most inadequate when it came to knowing mind. Instead, *conversation* is the far apter metaphor, since in it the truth of an interpretation gains "relative, but never immediate, verifiability" (165). During the felt temporal process of a social conversation, I become aware of encountering ideas not my own but only partially expressed in signs. "I offer a further expression of what to me they seem to mean," and I suppose my expression has better clarified to myself both the meaning of the sign and the idea of the mind which gave expression to the sign.

Furthermore, since the sign I have already received carries a meaning not yet my own but expressed only partially so far, my interpretive effort essentially tries to read this sign further. What I offer at the moment, however, has to be an incomplete interpretation which requires still further interpretations. Thus, in conversation I am led to give my interpretation back to the neighbor who has sent the sign in the hope of seeing whether it elicits a new expression from me that is basically in line with the expression he directed to me.

Without gaining any immediate verification of having rightly grasped his mind, my demand that my interpretation be correct is satisfied precisely insofar as my ever-incomplete interpretation "leads to a conversation which remains, as a whole, essentially 'coherent' despite its endless novelties and unexpected incidents" (166).

As his conclusion to the epistemological section of "Mind," Royce made a statement which is understandable in the light of the foregoing, even if it amounts to a Copernican revolution in theory of knowledge, "*The essence of. . .intelligent mental life and of all spiritual relations not only depends upon, but consists in, this coherent process of interpretation*" (167, emphasis added). Even if James's pragmatism were to 'work' sometimes in physical nature, it does not 'work' in one's dealings with another mind. In the latter case, the telltale criterion remains whether a social intercourse between minds 'retains genuine coherence'.

When synthesizing the interpretive process at work at the heart of a conversation, Royce required his audience to notice:

> ...that this Alter, with which I have to deal, both in reflecting on my own mind and in seeking for new light from my neighbor, is never a merely single or separable or merely detached or isolated individual, but *is always a being which is of the nature of a community*, a 'many in one' and a 'one in many.' A mind knowable through interpretation, . . . in so far as it possesses genuine and coherent unity, tends. . . to become essentially. . . many members, one body; many gifts, but one spirit [Romans 12:4ff]. (167–168, emphasis added)

Royce interprets mind—whether in a single individual or in a pair of dialoguing individuals—as constituting by itself a community of sign-sending and sign-receiving selves. The unity and life of such a community lies in the communal process of interpretation—that third basic kind of knowledge.

How Do We Know Truth as True?

Turning to Royce's Last Lectures on Metaphysics, we find him stating emphatically, *"The question of metaphysics is the question of the sense in which statements are true"* (5/23). Eight years earlier Royce had carefully crafted his address, "The Problem of Truth in the Light of Recent Discussion." If William James paid scarce attention to this key article—though invited more than once by Royce to do so—John Dewey detected its importance.[33]

Royce came to focus on truth because, as he told his students, "Our conception of what it is to be *real* is inclusive of what it is to be *true*" (5/23). Here Royce's "conception" means "interpretation" since for him the ideas of truth and reality are essentially interpretive (12/4). As he told his students:

> For a rational being *unaware* of his past and future and of his fellow beings— no matter how intelligent he was and how clearly he could conceive his propositions—*there would be no idea of truth.* (12/4)

Unfortunately, however, besides failing to view truth and reality interpretively, many people confuse what it is to be true with what it is to be verifiable, or probable, or even with being certain. Royce insisted on keeping these four dimensions of cognition clearly distinguished.

To distinguish truth from verifiability, Royce used the example of a creditor who, worried about the solvency of his bank, went to it and asked to withdraw his deposit. When the bank clerk brought him the cash desired, the worried man said, "If you have it, I don't want it; but if you don't have it, I want it very badly." The clerk offered him a momentary verification which did not satisfy the trouble depositor. The truth the depositor needed to know was whether his bank *continued* to be solvent when he was not asking for his money. He wanted the perduring and security-producing truth, "My bank has been and will continue to be solvent." However much the mere offer of cash verified the bank's present solvency, verifiability ought not to be confused with the truth the depositor sought (5/20). Royce asked:

> What is the truth of your ideas at the moment when you *don't* test them?" Unless they have a truth which is *beyond* what you test, they aren't what you want them to be. (5/20)

To distinguish truth from probability, Royce stressed the absolute character of objective truth and the variable flow of probability (11/18). Using a personal illustration, he said:

> It is an absolute truth now that I shall, or shall not be alive the first of January next [1916]. . . . I was alive January last [1915]; statements about the past are either true or false. That truth will forever remain; nothing will ever alter it; it is irrevocable. But the *probability* that I *was* alive on the first of January 1915 may become in various degrees less and less if somebody has reason to make the historical statement. (11/18)

To distinguish truth from certitude, Royce showed that, *pace* Schiller, one could believe in absolute truth without believing in absolute certainty. "[W]hile the uncertainty of human propositions is a good reason why we shouldn't burn men at the stake, the truth or falsity of the statements is not a mutable matter" (11/18). Royce regarded the truth of a judgment as something which is distinct from whether it feels sure to oneself. A political candidate may say he "knows" he will be elected but later turn out to be defeated. Without knowing the truth, he had subjective certainty concerning an erroneous opinion about a future fact.

Royce regarded William James as driving together all the difficulties about truth and certainty by letting present experience take care of certainty and putting all the difficulties on the shoulder of truth. Present experience may put you in possession of the living truth, but, countered Royce, "such truth shifts and is mutable." He then asked:

> Does the effort to put all the difficulties on the shoulder of truth really aid us in our theory of knowledge? You "know" so many things that aren't so, and subjective certainty often runs counter to the truth. Must we not expect to recognize that distinction? . . . When we seek the truth we do not mainly seek confidence. (12/8)

By insisting, then, on the difference of truth from certainty and probability and verifiability, Royce kept truth anchored in a grasp of the real through an objective and eternally true judgment.

He found thinkers like Joachim, James, and Russell omitting from their theories of truth "the social aspect of the consciousness of truth." Royce, however, regarded the "essentially social relations" found in any purported knowing of truth to be "the most critical matter of all" in any theory of truth (12/11). He soon clarified what he meant by the "essentially social relations" in every true judgment:

> Beliefs are true or false only from the point of view that recognizes an *interpreter*. The mind of the interpreter is needed as well as the mind of the believer; and the mind of the interpreter must be so related to the object as to be able to define the correspondence of the believer and the object; otherwise there is *no truth or error*. (12/11)

The basic triad indispensable for truth, therefore, consists in: (1) an object specifically intended by a believer, (2) the believer who asserts something about that object, and (3) the interpreter who confirms the union of the believer's assertion with the object intended. As Royce put it:

> Thus every belief is not only a belief about its object, but also a belief about its interpretation, about what it really means. It is an appeal for confirmation to someone who knows what it is aimed at. (12/11)

The asserter's two beliefs and the interpreter's insightful knowing constitute the triad indispensable for truth. This is what the mature Royce called "the most critical matter of all" in any theory of truth.

NEXUS OF THIS EPISTEMOLOGY
WITH ROYCE'S MATURE ETHICS

How, then, does Royce's late epistemology connect with his mature ethics? A response can be cast in a thesis and commentary format.

1. The mature Royce's method of interpretive musement and his version of Peirce's doctrine of Signs transformed his philosophy of loyalty. As Royce acknowledged in his Berkeley Lectures of 1914, that after finally grasping Peirce's theory of knowledge, "I observed its close connection with what I had been seeking to formulate in my philosophy of loyalty."[34]

2. Royce's late theory of truth required, among other things, that if a proposition were to be true, it had to *cohere* with the universal context of true propositions. In ethics, an interpretive judgment of identification is needed to guide each sound moral choice. That is, when one judges interpretively, "This act (X) better fits my genuinely loyal self," one both identifies "this act X rather than Y or Z" and identifies the genuineness of his loyal self to lie, in part, in relationships to many communities. Because of these judged propositions of identity, then, Royce's mature ethics had to involve an interpretation of how the proposed action related fittingly with one's "divine spark" of selfhood, with others, nature, and the Spirit of the Universal Community.

3. Hence, Royce's theories of interpretation and truth called him to an *ethics of responsibility*. One knows one's own life-plan by interpretively grasping one's "triplicity of present, past, and future selves," each responsive to the other two. Moreover, one lives socially as "a being who responds to communication with companions" (11/27). So, unless one both interpretively knows one's life-plan and interpretively responds to others in society, one cannot generate an intelligent accounting to oneself of one's choices—i.e., be responsible.

Then, too, all of the triads needed for ethical life require truth-seeking interpretations. Royce's most basic triad of sign-sender, sign-receiver, and sign-interpreter realizes itself in the subordinate Roycean triads: (a) of object, believer, and interpreter; (b) of dialogue-partner, self, and interpreter; (c) of past, present, and future selves; and (d) of many other communities of interpretation (10/9, 10/26). But all these triads demand truth-seeking in their interpreters under pain of being irresponsible.

4. Royce's "will to interpret" *intends to unify these communities* of interpretation by promoting truth in them. Only through such a truth-seeking, unity-promoting will can these communities become and remain ethical. Thus arises the need for finding or creating *fitting* responses to the minded beings and signs involved in these processing communities. Accordingly, Royce's "will to interpret," the heart of his communities of interpretation, supports his late ethics of responsibility, his "ethics of the fitting."

5. Royce nevertheless presupposed a *special kind of interpretation*, when speaking of the knowing which rises from the genuinely loyal love of a community. For genuine loyalty creates a distinctive kind of interpretive knowing. The reader may recall how genuine loyalty contains a religious insight. "[P]recisely in so far as we are loyal, . . . we all . . . come into some genuine touch with one and the same live spiritual reality," the Universal Community.[35] The concretely real cause of the Universal Community lies present within all the genuine special causes to which the loyal dedicate their lives. Thus genuinely loving loyalty puts one in metaphysically mystical touch with this "same live spiritual reality."

So Royce retained his kind of mediated metaphysical mysticism to the end, even as he swept aside the many deviant or adolescent forms of parapsychological and religious mysticisms. In brief, because the truly loyal self lives bonded intrinsically to the Universal Community and its Spirit, it has an "eye" not found in a "morally detached individual," however shrewd or skillful the latter prove in ordinary interpretation. This special kind of interpretation makes the genuine loyalist adept at discerning signs, at appreciating values and disvalues, and at mediating between alienated selves, because the genuine loyalist operates *in the unity* of the Logos-Spirit of the Universal Community.

6. Of necessity this special kind of interpretation *works concretely*. For instance, when remembering one's past deed, the genuine loyalist detects whether it has or has not fitted into one's overall plan of life. Looking to the future, such a self detects whether one's intended deed will cohere with one's plan of life and produce more good than ill. In both instances, quiet discerning of the fitting reveals some "coming in touch with" the mystery of one's Self and its embraced cause, and thus with the underlying cause of the Universal Community. If the reader recognizes how passionately the "in-touchness" of such interpretation works, he or she will discern how wide of the mark those come who charge the mature Royce with "barren intellectualism."[36]

7. If concrete experience, loyal love, and mediation play their roles in any of Royce's ethical communities of interpretation, so, too, does *language*. He saw language as distinctively affecting the way members interpret communication in their community. In his final year, Royce told his students, "A language which always passes through groups with a tendency for the *interpretation* to become predominant, tends to become wiser than any of the people who speak it" (10/23). A group's language tends to transmit to an individual member the consciousness of what is the best in the tradition of its wider linguistic communities, *if* the individual listens deeply and seeks for the wisest in that tradition.

For instance, when a small community, like a family in San Francisco, uses language in its dialogic interaction, it responds to a series of languages that undergird larger communities—the language of its "province" (e.g., California), of its overall politico-economic community (e.g., the United States of America), of the still larger community of English-speaking peoples, and of that more extensive linguistic community whose roots carry messages from its Anglo-Saxon and its Hebraio-Graeco-Roman traditions.

In another instance, Royce pointed to persons called "founders" of the world religions. Before they appeared on the scene, previous "ages of development of the collective consciousness" of humankind had built up in languages a treasure house for use by these founders of religion. Thus when they used a particular language to dialogue with their disciples, they relied upon their community's language freighted with its traditional religious wisdom. Hence, the world's great religions were generated as much by this language-based communal religious consciousness as by the individual founders (10/26).

In review, then, this chapter has focused on Royce's argument to the All-Knower—some needed preconsiderations and its various forms until 1916—then sketched his theory of interpretive knowing and truth, in order to see how his late epistemology interacted with his mature ethics. Now we need to turn to the vital bond between his late metaphysics and ethics.

6. Nexus with His Late Epistemology and Metaphysics (Part Two)

ROYCE'S FINAL METAPHYSICS

The mature Royce had called his audience beyond an ontological metaphysics and even beyond a subject-centered metaphysics.[1] While recognizing some values in these earlier stages, he invited his readers to a third and radically different kind of metaphysics that started from a community of interpreting selves. If one tries to understand Royce according to either of the two previous, but now transcended stages for doing metaphysical thinking, the chance of success is minimal.

Royce's 1915–16 course in metaphysics and his 1916 article "Mind" offer perhaps the most promising entries into the final form of his metaphysics. The foregoing chapter showed Royce's reasons for making interpretation become the general method governing his metaphysics. The historical and dialectical logic of this interpretive method was itself governed by Royce's System Sigma, outlined in his *Principles of Logic*.

In this chapter, then, we will first carefully survey his Last Lectures on Metaphysics and the metaphysical section of his article "Mind." Then, after drawing from these their main theses, we can show how Royce's final metaphysics connected with his mature ethics.

Survey of the Progressive Argument

During the first semester of his Last Lecture on Metaphysics (1915–1916), Royce employed his recently developed "social approach" to metaphysics and used *The Problem of Christianity* as a text. Because of the essential sociality of both reality and truth, Royce judged that this "social approach" *founded* the "logical approach" of his second semester's work (4/25). He held that the "essentially social relations" in any purported knowing of truth are "the most critical matter of all" (12/11).

In the first semester Royce strove to lead his students' minds out of their dyadic ways of thinking—out of their preference for percepts and their tendency to conceive truth and reality abstractly. His aim was to lead them into the thick world of interpretive knowing. This world always involved a community of minded beings engaged in an interpretive process. It implied the working presence of the Logos-Spirit of the Universal Community.

Beginning experientially, Royce invited his students to encounter four problems: (1) Ego and Alter (or the self and the *socius*); (2) the Individual and the Group; (3) the Existence of Other Minds; and (4) the Nature of the Community (10/7–10/19). Within these experienced problems he showed them several significant dimensions of social reality.

At work within the Ego-Alter relationship and within one's present, past, and future selves is the dynamic dialogue of a community of interpretation. Then, too, truth and reality are essentially social because they can exist only in a community of minded beings. (This was a thesis Royce confessed he could not get his opponents to accept.) Thirdly, since the judgments of human interpreters can only be made in time, human judgments have to involve some felt sense of temporal coherence (or constancy). Since neither present perception nor abstract conception can convey such knowledge, only a communal and concretely operating interpretive process could supply this grasp of real coherence. Finally, as Peirce had shown in his essays of 1868–69 and Royce had come to see, reasoning grounds even the simplest judgments.[2] An interpretive reasoning lies at the heart of the abductive, deductive, or inductive processes that secure even our simplest judgments. Moreover, they are integrated within an overall process of communal interpretation.

In the second semester, Royce employed his "logical approach," using *The World and the Individual* as his text.[3] A most general survey of this semester reveals that Royce led his students through a dialectical (and painfully precise) process of interpretation.

While indicating some shortcomings of the first three "historical conceptions" of Being—now better styled "interpretations" or "Ideas" (3/23)—Royce garnered something precious from each of them. He found that these three "Ideas" of Being do not attend enough to the concrete purpose (teleology) at work within each judgment. So, he used his idea of a finite individual interpretation to read its ultimate purpose in the unique Individual Reality, which is the processing universe.[4] Finite interpretations of Being need to become more conformed to this overall truth-constituting interpretation of the Spirit-Interpreter of the Universe who sees the whole process in its monism of purpose and its pluralism of realizations (5/25). Hence, Royce claimed that his method was not primarily eliminative—finding fault with the first three interpretations of Being and so settling on his fourth and final interpretation (5/23).

We move now to flesh in this scanty outline. Royce employed contemporary thinkers to model the first three interpretations of Being: Santayana,

Bergson, and Russell, respectively. He then showed that their views were inadequate for the world's unique factual process.

Royce was fully aware that many regarded his portrayal of the First Conception of Being as a straw man—the "realism" which held that beings existed wholly independently of mind (4/29). Yet surprisingly, Royce judged this position so fundamental that he examined it with exceptional care and then returned to it later in the semester to reinvestigate it with his students.[5]

Royce saw the First (or "realist") Conception of Being buttressed by two distinct yet related positions: metaphysical realism and classical nominalism. Metaphysical realists hold that beings are wholly or almost wholly independent of mind. Put otherwise, beings have no internal, but only external relations with truth and minds. The key difference between realists and idealists lies in the fact that realists view external relations as more important while idealists view internal relations as more important (5/4).

Shifting from the question of independence between things and minds to the perspective of individual and community, the classical nominalists hold that there are only two realities: individual things and words; and since words derive from individuals, ultimately only individuals are real. Hence, classical nominalists hold that all communities are merely derivative collections of individuals and that habits, types, and tendencies (what Peirce called "real generals") are merely products of the mind.[6]

Through a careful linguistic analysis of Santayana's essay, "Some Meanings of the Word 'Is'," Royce highlighted Santayana's sharp distinction between essences and existents and the independence of both from minds that know them.

Santayana declared that the great metaphysical distinction is that between the essences and the existents, a distinction which can be defined in terms of perception and conception (3/23). In his view the existence of things and their essences are mutually independent. Hence, because of this independence no kind of ontological proof can be used to show from an essence whether a thing exists or not. Royce added:

> *This kind of independence seems to be the very essential feature of the realism that Santayana exemplifies.* The consequence of viewing the thing in that way is to insist upon a certain independence of the existence from the question of whether they are known or not. (3/23)

The consequence of holding, with Santayana, a complete dichotomy between essence and existence is the "realist" position of the total independence of beings from mind. Santayana's dyadic theory of knowing led him to this, since he claimed to grasp essences by conception and existents by perception. Thus his epistemology kept him from entering into signs and process, and particularly into that dialectic of interpretation whereby reason proceeds from essence to existence in all judgments of identity. Royce soon showed that this unavoidable form of the ontological argument could not be based on present experience only (3/2).

He began by showing that every *what* has its *that* and every *that* has its *what*; or, more explicitly, that no essence can be essence without its kind of existence and no existence can be existence without its kind of essence. Royce taught, "There is no more important issue between realism and idealism than . . . [the adequacy of Santayana's position that] existence adds no new character to the essence it hypostatizes" (2/29). Royce judged that Santayana distinguished too sharply between essence and existence because one cannot understand that essence is not existence without knowing what we *mean* by existence—i.e., grasping the essence of existence within a perceptual judgment—and thus Santayana overlooked the reciprocal relation binding the two. This implicit nexus between essence and existence supplied an essential feature of Royce's idealism in which any pair of opposites is necessarily related to a broader context that holds them, e.g., essence and existence to mind that knows them, ego and alter to community that enlivens them, possible and actual to a necessary being that undergirds them.

Royce taught that one's choice of metaphysical method depended on whether one sees that judgments of identification inevitably move from essence to existence since they involve principles (3/2). In these frequent judgments a kind of "ontological argument" operates necessarily. It is so named because of Anselm's example but, unlike Anselm's, is not used as an argument to God's existence (3/4). Royce went on:

> Applied to mere conceptual objects [like divine being or counterfeit gold] the ontological proof is indeed vulnerable. Applied to your experience you use it all the time. (3/4)

You use it whenever you judge that something not now experienced is real— your deep self, the world, the historical past, the expected future, or your neighbor's mind (3/2).

Royce took up the case where one says of an approaching person, "That's my brother!" (3/4) This judger has the perceptual experience, "I see a man who looks very much like my brother." But he could not have evidence for reaching his identifying judgment unless he *also* implicitly employed the negative existential universal judgment, "No other individual in the whole world could look so much like my brother without actually being my brother." Such reasoning, however, moves from the essence of such a world (as excluding all other exactly similar persons) to the existence of one's brother (as alone coherent with such a world). This is a kind of ontological argument.

Reversing his tactic, Royce asked, "Why do you rule out the hypothesis: 'there was no past and all memory is false'?" He replied that your sense of the *very nature* (or essence) of the past requires that it be real, and then continued:

> The *very nature of the past forces on you that there was some past. Whatever happened happened.* . . . The very essence of induction depends on presupposing that the essentials of your account of time, the past with its irrevocable character, the future with its yet expected character, these represent existence. *Your evidence about nature and man and whatever else you are dealing with involves the ontological proof.* (3/4)

In this way Royce came to what he called his non-Anselmian "relational form of the ontological argument."[7] In every judgment the Predicate possesses a relational essence binding it to the Subject through the judger's purposeful process of judging.

For example, if one enters the denoument of Homer's story and says with the suitors, "That is Odysseus!" he reaches the truth of this judgment by using both present experience and also *evidence* which involves more than present data. For beyond one's perception of present data, his or her evidence for this judgment requires a grasp of an unchangeable past fact and a reliable memory (e.g., "This is the man who just shot that bow with stunning accuracy") *and* also relies on a negative universal existential principle (e.g., "This world has such a nature that no one could shoot this particular bow with such stunning accuracy as this man just did and yet be someone other than Odysseus").

Focusing with Santayana on ordinary existents, Royce asserted, "Whoever takes his existents as space-time individuals has on his hands the problem of the identification of individuals" (3/9). He spoke "not merely of a conceptual identification, but of an identification *of the sense of a process*—as identifying, for example, the Odysseus whose story had brought him through a long process (Troy, wanderings, and now a someone standing in beggar's garb and drawing the bow before the suitors of his wife).[8] Likewise, identifications of oneself, a natural object, an essence, and a neighbor's mind require a similar grasp of the felt coherence of a process (3/14–3/18).

At this point, conceptualistic readers may feel irritated by Royce's evident if implicit call for a revision of the principle of non-contradiction. Interpreting as "most significant," the thesis from Hegel's *Logik* that "identity *is* difference," Royce replied in advance:

> [Y]ou can hardly tolerate [this thesis] if you regard knowledge wholly from the conceptual side, but . . . if you are thinking of a knowledge of interpretation—not only knowledge of, but through and by means of processes in time—[then Reason] . . . regards the *variation* of essence as of its very nature. It is

never engaged with a mere distinction and identification of essences. Identity is difference if it is recognizable identity. (3/14)

In sum, when one judges, his intended purpose of asserting an identity must first recognize the differences of S and P and then transcend these before coming to the identifying union of S and P which fits the judger's purpose; (e.g., 6 + 7 = 13). Since every judgment requires the identification of S and P, it rests upon a "relational essence," which grounds people's unavoidable use of the "relational form of the ontological proof" in all their judgments.

More particularly, each causal judgment (wherein, for example, one infers from an existent animal track in the snow to the existence of an animal that made it) relies on what G. H. Howison fittingly called the "illative relation." This works within the universal negative existential judgment that this world's nature is so unique that it does not tolerate a genuine animal track being made in the snow without the existence then of some animal that produced it. As Royce put it:

> My whole point is this: Whenever one existence is supposed to give you ground for inferring another existent, then the ontological proof is used, insofar as this relational system (of which the evidence and that of which it is the evidence form parts) is a system such that the world cannot but contain it. (3/16)

Thus through the indispensable presence of the "relational form of the ontological proof" in existential and causal judgments, Royce showed that beings cannot be independent of knowing minds, that the world of the reals is a world of spirit. In this way Royce found inadequate the First (or "realist") Conception of Being, the position that beings are wholly independent of mind or at least not dependent on it through internal relations to minds and truth.

Turning next to the Second Conception of Being, advocated by Bergson, James, and Eckhart, Royce endeavored to empathize with the anti-conceptualist approach of these pure perceptionists. While admiring those who claim to have had mystical experiences, Royce said that such non-mediated knowing does not ordinarily characterize human selves during their pilgrim search in this life—whatever might be its relevance for experience in some transcendent life.[9] During his ten lectures on mysticism Royce found Eckhart's position most intelligent. Although mysticism usually ends in the absorption of finite individuals within the Godhead, Eckhart had avoided the metaphor of a droplet losing its identity when flowing into the divine ocean, but favored what Royce translated into the metaphor of ships that come to reach their haven in the Godhead, without losing their finite individual uniqueness.

Royce next moved to the Third (or Critical Rationalist) Conception of Being, using Bertrand Russell as its model. According to Royce, this Conception "says the reality of things not merely is *consistent with* but *consists in* the truth of certain propositions about them" (5/9). The reality of being consists in the truth of propositions about it, not in the object of those truths.

Royce pointed out how this Conception wisely renders the *reflexive* nature of judgment explicit. That is, it focuses on the crucial roles played by the unexpressed factors in every judgment; namely: "[*I say* (to some Alter) *that it is true that*] X is Y." Yet Royce saw that this attempt to make a judgment fit in consistently with a whole system of propositions that *would be* true of some world might attain valid truth but not necessarily factual Being. For this Conception put one in contact with worlds of *possible experience.* Royce knew that, however helpful this Conception has been for science, this third path, based on concepts and their unions in true propositions, was *not enough* to put one in living contact with the individuality of the Real.

The human knower, however, wants to get beyond "as if's" and postulates about the Real and have his judgments correctly hit, not just possibilities, but factual Reality in all its individuality. As Royce in the end confessed to his students:

> I have never found Being at any moment. It is the essence of Being that it is always the object of a quest. I never find it; I am always in the position that I am profoundly dissatisfied with the experiments that I make upon what it is *to Be.* They are all particular and special. What I want is Life, the whole of Life, not defined in terms of virtual entities, not defined in terms of sense-presence in experience, but Wholeness in some other sense.
>
> To put the matter in that way is to give you the very essence of the spirit of idealism. (5/18)

Hence, only a finite will that wants to be conformed to, and corrected by the Unique Individual Whole can supply this needed fitting metaphysical attitude towards Reality as a factual whole. But this attitude and the purpose it embodies can only live in a concrete process of communal interpretive knowing. Hence, one's Fourth Conception of Being must unceasingly embody this quest for the Wholeness of Being in an unending interpretive process, that exists as an appeal to the Whole of Reality and an openness to be corrected by It.

Having intensely studied Peirce's scholastic realism during the past four years, idealist Royce now concluded his last metaphysics course on a surprisingly realistic tone:

> The whole discussion [of our course] depends on the effort to find out the sense in which I am the acknowledger of a world, not only in some wise external to myself, but of a world whose nature is such that the whole purpose of my undertaking is that I should conform to its ways. . . .The whole intention with which we can approach idealism is the intention *to be as realistic as we can.* (5/20, original emphasis)[10]

In sum, then, what resulted from Royce's two-semester course in metaphysics in 1915–16, in which he employed his "social" and "logical" approaches to metaphysics? From the "social approach" (first semester) his students learned that they always live in communities of interpretation. Besides percepts and concepts, interpretations are indispensable for philosophy—viewed both as a method and as a life. Using this essential sociality of reality and truth as a foundation, Royce then led his students into the "logical approach" (of his second semester). Here his students learned that since they sought to know Being's unique factual Whole, they needed to adopt a loyalty-based interpretive attitude towards Reality that was grounded logically in the relational form of the ontological argument. This metaphysical attitude expresses itself in a fallible, corrigible, cognitive process (interpretation) that seeks to become more conformed to Reality as the individual factual Whole of Being in process.

Survey of Royce's 1916 "Metaphysics of Mind"

Within this overall metaphysics, we can now concentrate on what Royce in 1916 called his "metaphysics of mind."[11] (One can approach his mature "metaphysics of physical nature" through his philosophy of natural science.[12] One needs to remember that for Royce any physical object is essentially social—verifiable by a community of minded beings—and that all human knowing of nature is limited by the time-spans of its human investigators.)

After 1912, Royce had at long last discerned a theory of knowledge that fitted "minded beings." So by 1916 Royce felt equipped to examine metaphysical theories of mind. First, he exposed the "predominantly perceptual theories"—animism, hylozoism, Hindu experiences of Atman, Bergsonian *elan vital*, and Schopenhauerean will to life. He faulted them all because they supposed that mind can be perceived immediately. But "Peirce so well insisted that no one of us has any purely perceptual knowledge of his own mind" (172).

Next, Royce examined the "predominantly conceptual theories," to which philosophers who seek systematic completeness tend. They can arrive at their conceptual theory of mind either by abstractly rational or by more inductive paths. Within this kind of theory, Royce located Aristotelian vitalism, mind-matter monisms, and various monadologies. All of these are "characterized by the assertion of the existence of many real and more or less completely independent minds or selves" (173).

With a certain pragmatic humor, Royce added that no one has observed what difference it would make if one's mind were an Aristotelian 'entelechy' or a Leibnizian monad or a monistic reality composed of mind-matter.[13] Moreover, none of these theories offer much promise of becoming more verifiable than they have been in the past. Since "a mind is essentially a being that manifests itself through Signs," these conceptual theories cannot be verified inductively by immediate perceptions (174).

Instead, as *signs*, minds demand interpretations which necessarily relate a mind to other minds, thus forming a community (174). Accordingly, Royce inferred:

> A world without at least three minds in it—one to be interpreted, one the interpreter, and the third the one for whom or to whom the first is interpreted—would be a world without any real mind in it at all. (174)

In this way Royce finally reached a metaphysical theory of mind based on interpretation—even though he found this theory still inadequately developed in 1916. He identified a pre-Peircean trace of this kind of theory in some former religious consultations of oracles. Then, alternating the lenses of his interpretive musing between 'self' and 'community,' Royce confined his interpretation of mind to its phenomena as he, perhaps more clearly than ever before, compressed his own "metaphysics of mind" into the following noteworthy statement:

> . . . mind is an object to be known through interpretation, while its manifestations lie not merely in the fact that it possesses or controls an organism, but in the fact that, whether through or apart from an organism, it expresses its purposes to other minds, so that it not merely has or is a will, but manifests or makes comprehensible its will, and not merely lives in and through itself, as a monad or a substance, but is in essence a mode of self-expression which progressively makes itself known either to its fellows or to minds above or below its own grade. (175)

In this passage Royce mused on minds communicating in community in a way that revealed many of his most central themes: life, purpose, will, signs, series, temporal process, embodiment, levels, modes of action, community of communication, and that unique individuality which even internal relations cannot exhaust, since a minded being "lives in and through itself, *as* a monad or a substance," even though its life lies essentially in self-expression.[14]

Further, by indicating that mind can be defined by freely using two approaches, Royce also suggested the "fecundity of aggregation" that might result if one alternated one's lenses of 'self' and 'community' when defining mind:

> . . . mind is, in all cases where it reaches a relatively full and explicit expression, equally definable in terms of two ideas—the idea of the self, and the idea of the community of selves. (176)

Unfortunately, in the history of philosophy, both 'self' and 'community' have been "too often viewed as reducible either to purely perceptual or to purely conceptual terms." This reduction, of course, shortcircuits a metaphysics of mind. Yet experience shows that the two ideas of the individual self and community are "peculiarly adapted to interpret each other, both to itself and to the other" provided such interpretation is carried out in the spirit of a beloved community (177–78).

Thematic Approach to Royce's Final Metaphysics

After surveying Royce's Last Lectures on Metaphysics and "Mind," we can examine the content of Royce's 1915–1916 metaphysics by way of theses and some accompanying comment.

1. Truth and reality are essentially social, lying in a series of communities of individual, processing and communicating minded beings. Hence, two opposed metaphysical starting points are inadequate: (a) the claim that ultimately reality consists of individuals only (metaphysical nominalism), and (b) the claim that beings exist wholly independent of mind (extreme realism).

2. Within this uniquely individualized factual universe of ours, individual members of individual communities engage in communicating their individually intended meanings. If these meanings converge on common idealized past or future events and deeds, the members enjoy the communal mental life of a "community of memory" or "community of hope," respectively.[15]

3. Royce held, "The universe consists of real Signs and of their interpretations," and again, "On the whole, to be is to signify, to express a meaning" (5/25).[16] Being is the actuality of sign-sending and sign-receiving. Being is not ontological substance. To be is to engage in communication of various sorts, to exercise the power of initiating, interpreting, or receiving meaning between minds. All this semiotic world forms a temporal flow of some constancies and many chancy events.

4. The All-knowing Logos-Spirit is the central Interpreter of its Universal Community of interpretation (2/17). The centrality of the Logos renders Royce's universe, for all its errors and evils, ultimately intelligible and meaningful (12/2).

Subordinate to this processing Universal Community and to its mediating Spirit, a series of less comprehensive communities of interpretation operate. Within these lesser communities, "minded beings" engage in interpretations and direct or misdirect their processes of communication and cooperation. At the human level, each of these individual minded selves possesses a "common reasonable human nature" guided by common instincts and needs.[17] Among these, the moral instincts of truth-seeking, patient courage in the face of evil, and the furthering of harmony and unity among selves holds pride of place.

To continue downward in Royce's "metaphysical geography," below human minded selves come merely conscious selves (non-human animals and plants), then so-called inanimate selves (inorganic compounds and elements), down to the least sub-atomic particles. Each of these selves pulses with something resembling consciousness and has its own limited perceptual time-span.

5. As this Logos-Spirit is Sign of its source, so too are all finite selves Signs of their source, the Logos-Spirit. For each finite self is both a divine spark (*Fünkelin*) and a unique individual (*Pünctelin*) (5/11). As Signs, finite minded selves both send and receive signs to and from each other (10/9).

According to the mature Royce's "doctrine of Signs," the Spirit uses the leading ideas of Time, Interpretation, Community, and the World as Community to guide all the selves (minded and non-minded) in this processing universe.[18] Primarily it uses these basic ideas to heal dissonances and instill unity into the world process. The Spirit also employs Royce's so-called "Christian" ideas—the Signs of genuine community, humankind's fallen condition, atonement, and grace—to guide minded selves more accurately, as well as to reconcile and transform them into a Beloved Community within the Universal Community.

One can hear the ethical and religious demands that emerge from this metaphysical matrix when Royce mused as follows:

> This essentially social universe, this community which we have now declared to be real, and to be, in fact, the sole and supreme reality,—the Absolute,—what does it call upon a reasonable being to do? What kind of salvation does it offer to him? What interest does it possess for his will? If he accepts such a view of things, how should he bear himself towards the problem of life? To what ideas of his own does such a view offer success? How can he bring such a view into closer relations with ordinary human experience?[19]

Such a whole process rightfully calls finite minds to cooperate and coordinate their choices to promote the overall intent of the Spirit of the universe. Only in this way can they fulfill their own inmost interests and individuality.

6. Anything real must be internally related to mind (or to Logos), even if our limited minds fail to grasp its intelligible relation to mind. The fitting relation to mind makes true knowledge the heart of the Roycean universe, especially the truth of the Logos who constitutes itself and its processing world of interpreting selves.

7. Hence, the *logo*-centric predicament of reality—that whatever is real is tied to mind—has central importance in Royce's late metaphysics.[20] Royce's insight that any reality has to relate vitally to mind constituted his basis for so persistently criticizing the extreme realism of the First Conception of Being. The latter supposes selves wholly independent of mind, like atoms

that, while hermetically sealed-off and lacking any internal relations, possess only external spatio-temporal relations.

8. Implicit in every idea is the *"relational form of the ontological argument."* For each idea selects its object and thus reveals itself as a teleological essence seeking existential embodiment. As its purpose, it "chooses" its object as the specific target it means. Hence, every act of mind (or idea) has in it an unavoidable teleology. For every idea is a state of consciousness "which, when present, is then and there viewed as at least the partial expression or embodiment of a single conscious purpose."[21] Each idea, then, has its unique aim or internal meaning, as well as its embodiment or external meaning. Since an idea is an internal meaning seeking its ultimate fulfillment, by inversion, "The world is the expression of the idea" (5/27).

9. From this teleological view of an idea, metaphysics must ask *"in what sense* are statements true?"[22] For the interpretation of reality includes an interpretation of the meaning of truth (5/23).

10. Royce's fourth and final interpretation of Being suits a pilgrimaging, never-satisfied, seeker of that truth which comprehends the uniquely individualized universe.

11. Hence, to the question, "What then is the nature of metaphysics?" Royce replied in his lecture of May 18, 1916:

> Metaphysics turns not on a perception of the real [as Bergson and James say], nor on a conception of the real [as Russell and Santayana say], but on an interpretation of the real, which is ruled by the general thesis that the world contains its own interpreter; that while no moment of experience, no deed, is satisfactory, and the final is nowhere faced, and while there never is the final advice to be given, we still can declare that the nature of the complete interpretation is definable in terms which the reflective method can frame.

For the mature Royce, then, metaphysics is the reflectively defined interpretation of what the complete interpretation of the real world is.[23] This interpretation of an interpretation is ruled by the general thesis that the world contains its own interpreter.

12. It follows, then, that Royce's universe is, as he described it in 1916, "both monistic and pluralistic" (5/25). The Logos-Spirit's intent and chronosynoptic vision make it monistic. The infinitely diverse modes of action by all selves, individual and communal, make it pluralistic—especially through their diverse modes of interpretation and misinterpretation.

NEXUS OF THIS METAPHYSICS WITH HIS ETHICS

How, then, does Royce's metaphysics of 1916 relate to his mature ethics? Again we cast our response in a thesis and commentary format, while continuing the numeration of theses to emphasize their dependence on his metaphysical positions.

13. At the close of his 1916 metaphysics course, Royce stated, "*The very recognition of Being is itself an estimate. The categories of metaphysics are from the first teleological*" (5/27).[24] He soon clarified how an estimate of Being lies in its very recognition. Unlike the extreme realist who views the world as a detached spectator, supposedly unaffected by it, Royce, the "realistic idealist," exists by interpreting the world and by being interpreted by it. He concluded this course by summing up:

> So our answer to the various positions which I have indicated is that the whole problem of Being is essentially a teleological problem, and that to have a world is *to estimate it either spasmodically or systematically.* (5/27, emphasis added)

The emphasized phrase can be interpreted subjectively and objectively. Both interpretations reinforce each other as regards the presence or absence of teleology in the world.

Subjectively, one can know the world by means of disorganized haphazard insights ("spasmodically") or by means of a tentative yet synoptic interpretation of a set of ideas ("systematically"). In the latter, teleology operates by moving a genuine truth-seeker to a tentative philosophical vision of the whole.[25]

Objectively, to know Being is to interpret it as either chaotic and absurd ("spasmodically") or as ordered and intelligible ("systematically"). In the latter, teleology is manifestly at work. In all these human interpretations, then, one makes an estimate. But only the Logos-Spirit fully knows the true interpretation of the universe. Hence, what we mean by the "real world" is that Spirit's "true interpretation" of this our problematic situation wherein we have unavoidably to estimate the "real world."[26] In this way, then, Royce's mature ethics arises from an interpretive, value-appreciative kind of knowing.

14. The teleology of minded selves' quest of Being translates itself ethically into Royce's *emphasis on moral striving* and his call for unending moral growth.

15. The basic attitude one adopts towards life and the world as well as one's consequent assertions and deeds operate as world-altering Signs inserted into the universe. Hence, one's *choice of a basic ethical "attitude of will"* and one's injection of it into the universe through one's assertions and deeds becomes radically significant in moral life.[27]

16. *The norm of ethical life* within a community of mental beings is genuine loyalty whereby a member so dedicates oneself to one's particular and universal communities that he or she is open to contribute to and be enriched by at least this pair of communities.

17. The encounter of human selves with the problem of evil is "the most important moral aspect of the world" (5/27). The philosophical task is to *interpret the problem of evil* more and more into the main lines of the universe of the Logos-Spirit. In this way one employs the problematic situation into which human selves are immersed as part of that atoning process which tends toward an ultimate reconciliation of finite conflicts. To dodge the problem of evil by supposedly transforming it into the merely practical problem of "how to get rid of particular evils" is to fail in one's vocation as a seeker of wisdom, a philosopher.

18. Confronted with evils, with those seemingly absurd elements in the universe,[28] *one needs to trust* that despite human selves' limited views, the Spirit of the Universal Community embraces, reconciles, and governs finite selves through these evils because of its chronosynoptic interpretation of the universe. Hence, Royce's late ethics issues the radical call to human selves that they acknowledge the Logos-Spirit practically by their exercise of trust and hope.[29]

19. Royce's late ethics echoed the *alternation* of his "social and logical" approaches in metaphysics.[30] An exclusive reliance on the idea of community or on the idea of individual self will lead to ethical imbalance. If one overworks the idea of community, the uniqueness of individuality goes underdeveloped. If one stresses the uniqueness of individuality too much, Roycean ethics loses its leading category, the idea of community. Discerning the lead of the Logos-Spirit became the pathway to balance in the whole of his most mature ethics.

In a brief closing summary, then, the reader may discern, through the Signs offered in this and the previous chapter what a rich and complex epistemology and metaphysics of 1916 interacted with Royce's mature ethics. In epistemology his development of Peirce's theories of interpretation and of Signs permeated Royce's final ethics. In metaphysics he fruitfully married his social and logical approaches and by his reflective method let them influence his ethics. The novelty generated both by his advances in logic after 1902, by his series of major insights into various fields of philosophy, and especially by his maximal insights into the reality of the All-Knower, into individuality, and into Peirce's doctrines of interpretation and of signs, witness to that unique creativity distinctive of a "classical American philosopher."[31]

7. Royce's Methods in His 1915–1916 Ethics

Few things so confirm William Ernest Hocking's thesis that the mature Royce became increasingly experiential and concrete in his philosophizing than a reading of Royce's extant lectures from his 1915–16 Extension Course in Ethics.[1] Through these lectures we can examine how Royce directed his ethical reflection in his final year. Our sketch starts with Royce's empirico-historical method, then enters into his properly ethical method, and finally turns to his overall method of interpretive musement.

ROYCE'S EMPIRICO-HISTORICAL METHOD

In the *Problem* Royce had fine-tuned his empirico-historical method. It moved firmly and powerfully from its initial in-touchness with experienced instincts, interests, and motives toward identifying serially the needs expressed by these experienced facts—first, psychological needs, then the ethical ones, and finally the religious needs. In his final course in ethics, Royce did not overlook the psychological or religious dimensions present there. Yet he focused principally on the ethical needs and ideas expressed by the human instincts, interests, and motives that give rise to human ethical life. Some evidence may document such a broad claim.

Surrounded by reports of World War I, Royce drafted the Programme for his "Introduction to Ethics" course to be offered at Boston University during 1915–16. In it he set down that the course would especially emphasize how the problems treated in his *Philosophy of Loyalty* were related both to the social problems of his day and to the question of "how far morality relates to the conduct of nations as well as to the conduct of individuals."[2]

A first browsing through Royce's lectures from this course conveys a sense of rich empirical detail. He did more than drop hints of his familiarity with, and anxiety about, the events of World War I. In order to correct that symbol of duty emphasized by Kant—the apparently steadfast order of the "starry heavens above"—Royce employed the recently observed catastrophic explosion of a star in the constellation Perseus. He set this unpredictable

117

space event within the span of the many light-years needed to carry it to our notice. For Royce the explosion symbolized the totally novel or brutally casual events in human ethical life.

Then, too, he revealed his clear grasp of Titchener's recent research on complex pleasure/pain experiences with their accompanying intricate "feeling tones." Yet he subjected Titchener's generalizations to penetrating criticism. For this, Royce employed his own series of experiences with one ardent and vivacious young lady. Although she had been the shining, very attractive center of an assembly for the display of art, she had honestly experienced it all as boring. So she felt an intricate mixture of inner ennui and the pleasure of success. Royce completed the account by showing how she had matured into a still more creative woman by her gradual increase in self-discipline.[3]

Royce packaged his three leading ethical ideas—autonomy, goodness, and duty—within the then-familiar figures of the Captain (with "head blood-ied but unbowed") from Henley's poem "Invictus," of Everyman (from the medieval morality play), and of the responsible Youth who responded to the whispering voice of patriotic duty (in Emerson's poem "Volun-taries"). Royce's references to numerous figures from Greek antiquity—Antigone, Solon, Sophocles—touched off chords familiar to minds schooled in the classics. His use of references to Shakespearean characters—Portia, Juliet, Ophelia, Desdemona, Rosalind—bonded him with his largely feminine student-body.

His rich experiential data, however, was not merely casual and illus-trative. Without an investigative interpretation of cases, the mature Royce did not study ethics. Thus, he examined the history of the case and the facts in it relevant to ethics. By such an empirico-historical procedure, Royce aimed to find concrete signs of his three leading ethical ideas. He wanted concrete cases both to instantiate these ideas and to confirm his overall hypothesis that these principal ideas arise from each self's inquiry into its own mystery as it interacts with the mysterious communal selves of some communities. Thus, generally, in Antigone he found an instance of autonomy. In his boyhood from his Berkeley neighborhood, he traced the birth of the idea of duty. In the case of a mother-and-daughter's quarrel and subsequent reconciliation, he identified goodness lost and later restored through loyalty to companionship.[4]

A closer look at Royce's handling of these three cases supports these claims. As regards the story of Antigone, he first recounted its series of events. Her brother had been slain in battle fighting against her uncle Creon who became king and forbade that this "enemy" be buried. Antigone felt it a sacred duty to bury her brother. In this way she and the king became estranged. Obeying an eternal law higher than the king's, Antigone defied him and secretly buried her brother. Arrested, she was threatened by King

Creon with death. Then she asserted herself with a "loyal independence" based on the freedom which her religion gave her. Thus, in her free loyalty to what she perceived as a divine command, she underwent death. Royce's way of focusing upon this classic story emphasized how in that loyalty distinctive of siblings special emphasis must be given to their equal freedom of self-direction.

From his Berkeley days of the early 1880s, Royce recalled a friendly five-year-old neighbor boy, a relative of the Head family, who frequently visited Royce.[5] Although sometimes obstinate and aggressive, the lad was usually thoughtful and docile. Walking into the barn, the boy unexpectedly found in the hay a queer mess—a litter of new-born kittens. In a sudden outburst, he picked up a club and wiped them out completely. Soon, upon encountering strong social disapproval, the little fellow began to learn his lesson. Later, when needlessly reminded of his misdeed by some elder, he asserted defensively, "But I'm not killing kittens *now!*" He thus stated the problem of evil in the way of a child but not yet as a moral being. Aware that his past deed could not be undone, he gradually came to see that it did not fit into the kind of person he wanted to become. Later still, when as a youth he resolved to make himself the kind of person that henceforth would never kill kittens again, he started to constitute himself a moral self.

Royce observed that if the lad nurtured this seed of moral self-constitution, he would germinate the idea of duty. Of course, such moral development would take time. The five-year-old would have to grow into Emerson's kind of youth—one who, despite other voices inviting him to pleasures and ease, would hear and obey the clear voice of duty, however "still and small."

In his analysis of the case Royce sketched how family and tradition influenced the child socially. He pointed out how the lad's individual consciousness passed through stages and what role his temperament and character played in this growth. Rarely has the time-filled process of the interpretation intrinsic to moral development been so carefully and clearly etched. In this way the mature Royce instanced concretely how he used his empirico-historical method.

Again, in his mid-year examination Royce asked his students to solve the case of a desperately estranged relation between an apparently fraudulent mother and a suspicious daughter.[6] He involved himself in a most detailed study and reinterpretation of this problem. Twenty years earlier Royce himself had encountered this revealing case and now confessed how badly he then had bungled it. Preoccupied at the time with an ethics of virtue, he had regarded the case as primarily one of dishonesty. In 1916, however, with his Peircean insight into the all-pervasiveness of interpretation, he saw it as a case of restoring and increasing the good of comradeship (community) between mother and daughter—that is, of promoting an instance of life's full-breasted richness, which Peirce called *uberty*.

In his 1916 rerun of the case, Royce carefully sketched the facts and ignorance of facts involved. The daughter gradually grew suspicious that her mother was embezzling funds from the bank. She feared that her mother was a criminal and that she herself might lose her moral integrity by complicity. In this situation she felt anguished and ashamed. This led the daughter to cease communications with her mother. At this point Royce asked his students to identify which problems of loyalty were here involved. He concluded, "Show how: (1) The idea of Independence; (2) the idea of the Good; and (3) The idea of Duty stand related to the ethical needs of these two women."[7]

In his written "Comments" on this case and on the ways his students handled it, Royce atoned for having misinterpreted the case in the 1890s. By 1916 he had grown more reverent toward the two persons involved and thus could mediate atonement more skillfully. Instead of letting aretaic thinking focus his analysis too sharply upon honesty and dishonesty, as he had done earlier, Royce sagely considered the good of increasing a loving loyalty between the two women.

His suggested solution may have surprised many of his proper Bostonian lady students. For he called the daughter to that kind of whole-hearted devotion to her mother that would impel the daughter to first pluck out the plank from her own eye before daring to help remove any possible mote from her mother's. Royce recommended that the daughter actually confess to her mother her fear that she had tempted her mother to embezzle funds out of love for her daughter whose career she desired to promote. Only by leaping psychologically into her mother's life and interpreting it positively could the daughter escape from the imprisoning fears and shame that had paralyzed her morally. Certainly, to trust her mother this way presupposed a loyalty to the mother-daughter relationship and an empathetic love for her mother that was strong enough to make this leap. Royce's "Comments" on this case, then, demonstrated quite clearly his empirico-historical method of interpretation.[8]

ROYCE'S DISTINCTIVE ETHICAL METHOD

Convictions Basic to this Method

The distinctive ethical method that Royce used in his final year arose from some of his abiding convictions. Briefly, these included: to recognize Being is to value it; to be a human self is to have "a common reasonable human nature";[9] to become conscious of Being is to interpret two, mutually ultimate "levels" of reality—that of the unique individual self and of the community. The latter lay in a series of communities leading into the Universal Community.

A closer look at these convictions provides an entry into Royce's most mature and distinctive ethical method. In his final metaphysical lecture in 1916, Royce made a bold proclamation about the union of fact and value:

> The world isn't first given to you as a datum and afterwards estimated in virtue of the fact that you as a being with certain interests, and standing outside of that whole realm of existence, find some things in it good and some things evil. *The very recognition of Being is itself an estimate. The categories of metaphysics are from the first teleological.*[10]

In experience as lived, fact and value are integrated, since a person recognizes Being as better than non-Being. Here Royce saw that when Hume dichotomized "is" and "ought," he left the realm of lived experience. By conceiving Being and duty abstractly, he constructed a chasm that conceptualistic thinking could not bridge. Hume's fact-value dichotomy arose, then, because he failed to employ interpretive knowing which, according to the mature Royce, can alone reach Being. Contrariwise, if one recognizes Being through interpretation, one simultaneously estimates the value of Being. It radically satisfies one's drive for truth and goodness. This estimate requires one to further fulfill this drive. In other words, one's prizing of Being reveals one's duty toward Being—that is, to respect the worth of Being.

Not every kind of interpretive knowing, however, can reach Being. The human self must pass through and beyond the earlier psychic dispositions characteristic of the "first and second attitudes of will" and adopt the morally requisite "third attitude of will."[11] The first two attitudes are the self's affirmation of the will to live and win its aims, and secondly, the will's resignation whereby it denies its will to live and refuses to get involved in worldly projects that have come to seem ultimately futile. Only if one transcends these two attitudes by dedicating oneself to a particular genuine community and "falling in love with the whole universe," can genuine interpretation arise. Hence, if and only if Royce's interpretive labors were animated by this third attitude of will, could he fittingly engage in his maturest method of ethical consideration and judgment.

When specifying the third principle of his philosophy of loyalty in 1914, Royce had already described this distinctive kind of interpretation, the "soul" of genuine loyalty:

> . . . in and through and above all the countless social forms in which we are accustomed to interpret to ourselves our relation to the community which we learn to love . . . we all, precisely in so far as we are loyal, *come into some genuine touch with one and the same reality*, with one and the same cause,

with one and the same live spiritual reality [of a communal solidarity which is our life-source or mother].[12]

The loyalist's contact with a "live spiritual reality" recalls that kind of mystical touch through loyal interpretation which Royce in his middle period had retained from his dialectical purification of "the four conceptions of Being." This mystical touch gave no immediate union with the Absolute, no individualistic shortcut to it, and no adolescent escapism from the labors of successive interpretations. Yet Royce's living and genuine in-touchness with a genuine community which other loyalists were also contacting constituted a live mystical union.

Besides this basic conviction about an interpretation of Being that simultaneously knows and appraises it, Royce was also convinced that his notion of the human self had to include "a common reasonable human nature."[13] If he did not construe the human self in this way, the idea of duty could not appeal to it.[14] Since Royce's interpretation of the human self was that of an ethical reality based on one's choice of a plan of life, "nature" in the phrase above could not point to something ontological or to an unknown Lockean substrate. Rather, it meant that temporally flowing, psycho-social, living center which interprets ethically the mysteries of self and community.

These mysteries became the focus of the third and final conviction basic to his ethical method.[15] By interpretively investigating his "two levels" (of individual self and community)—which in their bi-polarities of Being and consciousness are ultimately unfathomable—Royce came to identify his three leading ideas in ethics. These ideas must operate in any self-consciousness that is rational and genuinely moral—whether at the level of self or of community. The self's willingness or unwillingness to serve the community determines the health or sickness—the genuine loyalty or estrangement—of self towards community.[16] To interpret the self's or community's swing from health to sickness and back again to health, Royce mused alternately upon the two mysteries of self and community. As bonded to or estranged from the Universal Community and its Spirit, this pair of cooperative "levels" set the parameters of Royce's final ethical method. He also applied his strategy of alternation to the on-going cyclic consideration of how his three leading ethical ideas bore upon the health or sickness of the basic relationship of self-and-community.[17]

Royce's Implicit Description of His Ethical Method

In the Programme published for his 1915–1916 Extension Course, Royce included sections on ethical ideals and problems. From these sections and his three outlines for the course we can glean a fair estimate of how he intended to carry out his final investigation in ethics. In the Programme he wrote:

> In Ethics we have to deal with the rational definition of our *ideals themselves*, with estimating their relative worth, and with the endeavoring to discover what is the highest ideal.
>
>   The problems of Ethics which are to be especially emphasized in this course will be:—
>
>   1. The problems discussed in Royce's "The Philosophy of Loyalty."
>
>   2. The general question of the relation between these problems and what are usually called the Social Problems of our day.
>
>   3. The question especially suggested by the situation of the human world at the present moment, namely, the question as to how far morality relates to the conduct of nations as well as to the conduct of individuals.[18]

The remainder of the Programme identified "Other questions" that pertained to the "Ethics of Individualism" and to "Conscience"—most of them being questions of "How far . . . ?" These questions sought to discover the vitally tense balance which needs to be identified and maintained between communities and between their members.

As the Programme showed, then, Royce's final ethical endeavor aimed to define rationally the moral ideals (of self-direction, duty, and the good); to grade their relative worth; and to try to identify the highest moral ideal, which he had earlier called "being loyal to loyalty."[19] His endeavor to define moral ideals rationally implied his logical approach and a normative aim for his ethical method.

In his 1915–16 course in metaphysics Royce's "logical approach" employed what he called the "reflective method." It used a *reductio ad absurdum* to establish the truth of a proposition.[20] In his concurrent Extension Course in Ethics, I find a similar reflective support operating in Royce's logical approach to his ethical method. At his sixtieth birthday celebration, he described his logical approach in general as his

> fondness for defining, for articulating, and for expounding the perfectly real, concrete, and literal life of what we idealists call the "spirit," in a sense which is . . . perfectly capable of exact and logical statement.[21]

In his course in metaphysics, he was showing how the reflective method within his logical approach gradually reduced to absurdity anyone asserting that "there is a last prime number" or that "the side and diagonal of a triangle are commensurable."[22] Similarly, in his ethical method the same kind of reflection within his logical approach reduced to absurdity anyone asserting that "I should *not* seek truth, good, and beauty" or that "I should *not* be dutiful." Reflection on such assertions made undeniably clear their unavoidable preambles which are usually left unexpressed. If these preambles were highlighted, the full assertion would read, "*I say it is true that* I should not seek truth, good, and beauty, or be dutiful."

At this point, however, Royce did not search into the unavoidable motives in our "common rational human nature," as a naturalistic ethicist might. Rather, he adhered to the unavoidable logical relations within the preambles: "I say" and "it is true that." For the "I say" can be meaningful only if it is addressed to other selves, to some community of co-minded beings, in an appeal for confirmation or disconfirmation of what I utter. But the lived logic within this appeal says it is truer, better, and more beautiful to seek unity with a community that saves my assertions; otherwise the unavoidable appeal is meaningless. So, too, the lived logic within this appeal says that the community of other minded beings are worthy of my appeal and I in responsiveness am duty-bound to them to make this appeal. Hence, my assertion "I should *not* be dutiful" implicitly asserts "I should be dutiful"—a logical contradiction made explicit through a *reductio ad absurdum*.

Similarly, the preamble "it is true that" exposes not only the experienced difference between truth, error, and indifference to both, but also a "mode of logical action" which embodies a preferential option for truth. As Royce had said in his final metaphysical lecture, "The very recognition of Being is itself an estimate. The categories of metaphysics are from the first teleological."[23]

We see, then, that Royce's ethical method was marked distinctively by its cognitive endeavor. He intended, not simply to map various emotive meanings unavoidably involved in ethical statements, but also to win knowledge of moral ideals, to define them rationally, and to understand their relation to ethical problems. We see, too, that the mature Royce insisted that ethics not settle for any merely descriptive task. As an ethicist, Royce had ethical norms to identify and to define by clarifying interpretations guided by the logic of his System Sigma.

Turning from ideals to problems, we notice that Royce's announced method of handling ethical problems was to relate the problems of his 1907 *Loyalty* with the social problems of his day. He required that the latest contemporary insights from the social sciences enter into his ethical consideration. For instance, because of the interests common to ethics and political science, psychology, and sociology, he required the students in his extension course to read and report on *The Great Society*, by Graham Wallas, a contemporary sociologist and political scientist. Royce urged his students to compare and contrast the data from the social sciences with that of ethics.[24] In his recent seminars on scientific methodology, in which professors and graduate students from a wide range of disciplines participated, he had experienced what Peirce called "the fecundity of aggregation" of minds. This led Royce to recommend that his students in this extension course enrich their study of ethics by some critical interdisciplinary dialogue.

Royce's still extant outlines, programme, and five lectures from this course reflect his sense that he could not expect the same kind of exact logical rigor and analysis from these extension course students as he did from his Harvard students of metaphysics. Yet through the simple analysis and synthesis of his opening lectures he carried out his own logical approach to ethics. For there he reflectively interpreted the meanings of his principal ethical ideas: self-direction, the good, and duty. Then, when he proceeded to interpret these ideas in the context of his students' familial, national, and international communities, he revealed his "social approach" to ethics.

Furthermore, he wanted to let the present situation of World War I supply input for his ethical investigation. This wartime situation might either further deform or possibly correct the many deviant types of individualism rampant at the time.[25] This situational input seemed particularly pertinent to his "social approach" to ethical investigation. Because Royce held, unlike the majority of ethicists around him, that communities existed hyper-personally as realities just as ultimate as real individual persons, he concluded that communities were also morally responsible for their choices. For example, if such a community elected the institutions and officers of its national government, it became morally responsible for the wartime choices which its people made through its government. As Royce put it, "Society in its united capacity has its own ethical problems and ideas, its task to control itself, to seek the true good, and to do its duty."[26]

Royce's outlines for the course also revealed his strategy of alternation. He wrote "that all ethical ideas should be both socially and individually applied."[27] Accordingly, he planned to give three lectures to the individual, then three to communities; then he would apply another ethical idea to individuals in three lectures, and later four to the community. His strategy of alternation was alive and well.

Another distinctive feature of the mature Royce's ethical method was the "leading" role played in it by his three principal ideas. That is, Royce's three ethical ideas are leading, not only in the sense of being fundamental and directive, but also in the methodologically significant sense that they lead into three different kinds of ethical interpretation.

Specifically, if one allows the first ethical idea of autonomy to enspirit one's interpretation, it becomes marked by the interactions of selves freely directing themselves within communities. Hence, the tone of such interpretation becomes that of free sign-senders, calling to each other, requiring mutual respect, and trusting selves co-responsibly to search for and find the fitting ways in and for community.

Secondly, if one employs the leading idea of goodness as one's main key when interpreting an ethical life-question, the themes of goal and pilgrim home-seeker come to the fore. Then considerations of means and ends, of cause and plan of life, of good and evil come to center stage.

Lastly, if one allows the ethical idea of duty to lead one's interpretation, the themes of universal law, of rights and wrongs, and of codes and rules tend to occupy the interpreter's attention.

In my estimate, much of the significance of the mature Royce's ethical method lies in his synthesis of these three styles of ethical interpretation and in his alternation of their usage. From each of his three leading ideas arose a distinct "spirit of interpretation," each integrated within the Logos-Spirit of life. Overall, then, his general inquiries were: What is more vital and life-giving? What tends to estrange the life of genuine loyalty or even to corrupt it? Thus he subordinated all three styles within his overall interpretive search for the more vital, for what more wisely fits that union of those two mysteries of the individual self and of the Universal Community. He viewed this union as mediated by a series of many intervening communities and their apposite "spirits of interpretation."

Moreover, because Royce "deeply prized" his final letter from Peirce, it must have significantly affected his late ethical method.[28] In that letter Peirce witnessed that the security of inference (which pragmatism ensured) was far less important than the *Uberty* of inference—its full-breasted richness. Peirce linked the Uberty of inference to "our exaltation of *beauty, duty,* or *truth.*" This series of norms closely paralleled Peirce's previously hierarchized norms of logic, ethics, and aesthetics.

I suspect, then, that Peirce's calling Royce's attention to "our exaltation" of these ideas and ideals alerted Royce in 1915 to examine more carefully both those ordinary people whom he found "fail to admire and extol the idea of duty" as well as those "moralists . . . [who] glorify the majesty of duty" but confuse it with the majesty of a seemingly well-ordered, law-abiding nature. Surely Royce sensed that the motives behind "our exaltation of beauty, duty or truth" deserved the closest ethical scrutiny.

I further suspect that Peirce's letter stimulated Royce to find and identify his three principal ethical ideas. That is, at the level of logic, a required ethical norm lay in the idea of rational autonomy—that is, of directing oneself coherently. For by adopting a cause (with the plan of life it generates) and by being faithful to it through actual choices, one gives a basic consistency to one's life. At the level of ethics, the idea of duty supplies another required moral norm. Lacking this responsibility to self and community, a person slips into the status of a "detached individual." Finally, at the level of aesthetics, the idea of goodness, taken in its widest sense, constitutes a third indispensable moral norm. For if the idea of goodness does not direct one's ethical life, one lacks a commitment to the better. One would thus experience no demand to expand one's ethical outreach to embrace all true communities, including even the Universal Community. Aesthetically, then, as well as logically and ethically, Royce's mature method in moral philosophy recoiled from the ugliness of any self-enclosed life. For, deviant individualisms of any form walled oneself off from the Universal Community and its saving influence.[29] The self's pilgrimage homeward was genuinely autonomous, dutiful, and beautiful only if the home it intended embraced all minded beings in community.

ROYCE'S OVERALL METHOD OF
INTERPRETIVE MUSEMENT

The mature Royce employed his general philosophical method of interpretive musement in his seminar on comparative scientific methodologies, in his philosophy of religion, in metaphysics, and in ethics. Since a detailed study of this method has been published elsewhere,[30] here we will simply: (1) examine an instance of Royce's usage of interpretive musement; (2) trace Peirce's intellectual presence in it; (3) form an abstract summary of this method; and (4) conclude with Royce's own late cameo of his maturest, experientially interactive method of interpretive musement.

An Instance of Interpretive Musement

Royce's overall method of interpretive musement can be grasped concretely if we follow him in his lecture, "The Idea of Duty," the first of his surviving extension course lectures.[31]

Throughout the lecture, his aim is clear: "to help us to a better understanding of how and why the idea of duty differs from the other great ethical ideas" and to "point the way upwards and inwards" (9). Here Royce's overall intent to use interpretation serially to further clarify our meanings of basic ideas echoes his philosophical aim perduring since the *Religious Aspect* and *The World and the Individual*. Royce started from Emerson's description of duty's low whisper of "Thou must" to the patriotic youth who replies "I can" (1–2). Royce then begins his dialectical process, "The idea of duty widens and deepens its scope for your vision the more you view it in the light of objections" (2). So directed, he moves from thesis to antithesis, according to his strategy of alternation, in search of a more purified notion of duty. Thereupon, he expands his purview by taking in a Sign of true witness from the poet Sill that some ethical expression of the idea of duty belongs to everyone's interest in life, as do their drives for freedom and the good

(7–8). He then contrasts the motives behind our drives for freedom and the good over against the less attractive idea of duty, that obligation to obey, to follow some will not my own. Royce's drive to unify then leads him to try to harmonize these conflicting motives (8).

The objection that duty is difficult is strengthened by the objection that it is an increasingly unpopular idea. Responding with his interpretive comparison and contrast, Royce examines the short-range view of the fate of the idea of duty during the last fifty years (4–6), and then contrasts it with its role in the civilizations of ancient Greece and Israel (7–8). Upon this wider basis for interpretation, Royce moves to discern why so many at present cannot understand what duty really means (10). He sees that people have been blinded by falsely identifying the external success they desire (good fortune) with the genuine meaning of duty.

Then, on a second endeavor, Royce finds that Wordsworth and Kant used images of the steady stars above as symbols of our constant duty (11–15). Through a contrast with the explosive in Perseus, Royce interprets that this association of image and duty tends dangerously to lead people into making too close a parallel between natural laws and the moral law. Royce discovered a "glaring contrast between what the idea of duty demands in the moral realm and what the explosive collisions and wrecks of the physical world appear to show to our senses" (15).

When Royce next turned to examine how the idea of duty slowly develops in an ordinary child and youth, he revealed his preferential option for the ordinary rather than for the sublime and stately (16). Here he again employed his empirico-historical method, as we saw, upon a neighbor boy whom he remembered from his years in Berkeley (17–18). Most significant in this examination of the "boy who killed the kittens" was Royce's use of a series of Signs coming from one's own past deeds and from the dead, from experienced memories and the discovery of the irrevocability of the past, as well as from a serial reflection upon these Signs (21–22). This led forward to the youth's recognition that his future would be regrettable if he again so acted (23). Thus arose in the youth the idea of duty, founded on the most fundamental law of the universe:

> the law that the past is irrevocable,—a law without which neither my own will nor my independence, neither my fortune nor my defiance of fortune, neither nature nor mind—and neither gods nor men, have any being or sense or meaning whatever. (25)

In this case of ethical reflection, then, the richness and thoroughness of Royce's interpretive musement is striking. It is indeed a penetrating musement marked by an insistence on clarification, on playful freedom, on alternation, and on not resting upon previous answers but pushing on to still better ones.

Peirce's Intellectual Presence in Interpretive Musement

Earlier we sketched how Royce's "deep prizing" of Peirce's letter intensified the mature Royce's commitment to triadism and to the pursuit of inferential *liberty*. Peirce's profound influence also appeared in two other ways that affected Royce's interpretive musement. Communion with Peirce's mind guided Royce as he generated his three outlines for his extension course. And in the basic interpretation creating these outlines, Royce used Peirce's pattern of inquiry that passed from doubt to belief.

In September 1915, after writing out his first three lectures in full, Royce judged by interpretation that if he let himself be guided by their basic lines of thought, he could handle most of the remaining lectures orally. Then pausing to reflect upon the entire extent of those lectures and to trace out their course, he created from his successive musements three "Outlines for the University Extension Course."[32] He likely intended to muse upon their respective merits and shortcomings in order to reach a still better guide for the course.

These outlines show that he intended to center upon genuine loyalty in the life of an individual self and in that of a true community. To this end he would first ponder with his students how the three leading ideas of ethics constitute aspects of the loyal life. Then applying them alternately to individual and community life, he would examine the different roles that these ideas played in the ethical life of individuals and communities. Series of planned reconsiderations characterized his expected musement and in them he aimed gradually to grapple with current social problems and the international conflict then raging. The outlines bespeak a passional logic to win a still fuller and fairer grasp of genuine loyalty—a passional logic redolent of Peircean interpretation.

In sum, then, these outlines could not have arisen by approaching the course mainly from percepts or concepts. Only an interpretive musement that generated Royce's series of three outlines could effectively lead his students step-by-step to appreciate more fully the rich life of genuine loyalty.

Royce's Programme witnesses that Peirce won still more intimate entry into this course. Royce had found intrinsic to interpretation a scheme of moving from doubt to settled belief—like Peirce's pattern of problem-solving inquiry. Royce had been led to view the mysteries of self and community as the most basic matrices of ethical life and reflection. In this he partly followed Schopenhauer musing over his own self-identity in the Dresden gardens. As Royce told the story:

> The question: "Who am I?" is inevitably and closely related to each of the ethical questions that we have so far faced in these lectures. . . . Therefore we, in these lectures, as surely as Schopenhauer in the Dresden flower-gardens, are

trying to find out who and what we are. . . . [T]his question . . . interests us all because all ethical questions are bound up with it. . . . At the moment when the officer said: "Sir, who are you?" Schopenhauer observed that, to him, the Self was just then a mystery. He therefore said: "I wish that you would tell me who I am." Well, that was, as far as it went, a good answer to the question of the officer. So I hold; and thereon I shall found a large part of our later ethical thesis.[33]

Royce also found as great a mystery in the community. Like the self, it too had to serially identify itself. Each human self and community, in its encounter with its own psychic, social, and physical environments, finds direction arising from its instincts and needs. As a human self or community experiences life, however, it finds that part of its mysterious existence consists in encounters with conflicts, pains, tragic surprises, failures to integrate, felt estrangement from others and from oneself, and even death. These "bumps and bruises" generate puzzlement, heighten a sense of mystery in both self and community, and unleash deep questions. Such encounters awaken a sense of obstacles and of limits, even amid the self's or community's partly autonomous direction of its choices of response.

From the mysterious depths of self and community, then, how do Royce's three leading ethical ideas arise to give guidance? How do they make some sense out of these jarring encounters with the problem of evil? How do they cast some light upon the radical ethical question: "Who and what am I?"

From these experiences of resistance, the self and community experience a puzzlement that might be formulated as, "Even within these felt limits, am I free to form my own life-plan and course?" In this way the idea of autonomy dawns into explicit consciousness.

Secondly, the encounters with adversities highlight how chance and fortune can help or harm one's existence outside one's control. The wonderment arises, then, whether somehow beyond the ravages of fortune some kind of lasting happiness or goodness can be achieved. In this way, the largely illusory idea of happiness (as one of good fortune, passing pleasures, and avoidance of present pains) is transmuted into an initially enriched idea of human happiness that is profound enough to include pain and sorrow. The latter idea can function as a guide to one's supreme good.

Lastly, the experience of being involved in an environing process far larger than oneself leads one to ask, "Is something greater than myself directing me, worthy of my response, and requiring my cooperation?" And so the idea of duty dawns in consciousness.

Within such interpretive musements, then, we see the pattern of Peirce's inquiry process clearly at work. The musement begins from puzzling encounters and moves through various interpretations to settled belief. Without losing his originality, then, Royce showed himself profoundly influenced in 1915–16 by Peirce whose unpublished papers he was then examining in Emerson Hall.

An Abstract Summary of the Method of Interpretive Musement

Royce's mature use of interpretive musement is startlingly simple, unassumingly powerful, smoothly flexible, and deeply probing. From sign-sender A, through interpreter B, to sign-receiver C, the simple unidirectional (asymmetrical) relation in symbolic logic provides the simple dynamic flow of this musement in community while each member's *epsilon* relation of belonging to the community creates the basic indispensable structure for any community of interpretation. Such a community is empowered by the passional logic of minds whose third attitude of will has brought them into both a love for the whole processing universe and a searching for the still fuller story.[34]

Four tightly cooperative functions interact to harness and intensify the power of the lived logic within musement. This logic first calls the one serving as "spirit of the community" to compare and contrast signs in search of a new mediating third idea. This first function aims to bring minds into unity. Secondly, interpretive musement "discerns things of the spirit." It detects the spirit of genuine loyalty as well as spirits indifferent or hostile to universal loyalty. Thirdly, interpretive musement also keeps affirming as its cause the fuller life of communities—both particular and universal. Finally, interpretive musement requires that the selves involved form a dialoguing companionship, that is, a community.

Interpretive musement has distinctive marks. Its step-by-step search along the way makes it always tentative and flexible. In its pathfinding endeavors, interpretive musement employs a variety of tactics. It reformulates ideas serially, recombines them in enriching spirals and creates provisional syntheses along its way. But all of these moves serve its aim to articulate ever more clearly the deepest principles and ideas of life.[35]

This abstract summary description of interpretive musement pales when one enters into Royce's actual practice of his overall method. For the entry requires one to recognize that for Royce experience deals primarily with the temporal process of human emotions and purposes, not primarily with that of space and its contents. Full human life has its own logic—a distinctive logic that a human minded being must discover if it is to order its own personal and social life. Through the discovery of this concrete lived logic, one discovers a deep unity within all conscious life, howsoever one labels this unity.[36] But according to Royce's second maximal insight into individuality, this unity has as its vital purpose to further individualize the self even as it integrates it further into community. This unity of life also requires that each finite individual direct itself by means both of its instincts and needs and the guidance within the universal communal process. In this way, leaning more toward Peirce than Hegel, Royce countered both collectivism and detached individualism.

Royce's Own Late Cameo of Interpretive Musement

Overall, we can grasp how Royce viewed his general method of interpretive musement by listening to his description of it in one of his last classes on metaphysics. It lies in that "activity of mind" described by Aristotle, "full of interest in the concrete and in natural history" and interacting with the historical process. As Royce continued:

> It is precisely in such commerce...with that sort of variety...that genuine interpretation consists. When the understanding of life takes the form of a *process*, a process every stage of which is irrevocable and at the same time constitutes a progress beyond that which has been already attained, a process guided by the chronosynoptic vision of the whole, then you are dealing with that which is beyond mysticism and that which is at the same time the fulfillment of mysticism, the union of satiety and activity, of triumph and peace in triumph, the kind of union which Paul depicts in I Cor 13. (For now we see through a glass, darkly; but then face to face. Now I know in part; but then shall I know even as also I am known.)[37]

In final summary, then, it is not surprising that Royce continued his overall method of *interpretive musement* that he had employed so successfully in the *Problem* three years earlier. Nor is it surprising that within such musement he continued to use a pair of subordinate methods. He applied his *empirico-historical method* when examining the factual moral development of individuals or communities, or the unique stories of their ethical living— whether progressive or degenerative. He applied his *properly ethical method* when his target became a norm or a series of norms or what fitted in with a norm. Within the dynamics of this one overall method and two subordinate methods, Royce employed his social and logical approaches, as well as his various strategies and techniques.

8. Royce's Mature Art of Loyalty

DEVELOPMENT OF AN "ARTIST IN LOYALTY"

Despite his disagreements with the author of *Zarathustra*, Royce remained deeply impressed by Nietzsche's call for the "transvaluation of all values."[1] In the *Problem*, after he had identified a human self's three most fundamental "attitudes of will," Royce began to attend to the temporal evolution of these attitudes.[2]

Royce's close study of the neighborhood boy in Berkeley also illustrated this evolution of basic attitudes. In his impulsive act of killing the kittens, the child displayed the first attitude of will: the aggressive will to his own life, its way and power. Later, confronted with the problem of evil in his otherwise generally good past life, the child, who is not yet a moral self, does what no moral self may do. He cuts himself off from part of his past and from his society, as if they were less real than his own present self. He slips into the second attitude of will: to withdraw from full life—as found in his past and in society. Yet his moral self depends for its moral worth on his accepting what he has done as well as on what he is now doing. His moral worth also depends on his accepting the genuine grounds for regretting some of his past deeds. Still later, in the light of his generally good past, of his present desires, and of his regrettable deed(s), the youth adopts a coherent plan of life, one based on his resolve to never again kill kittens. By defining himself through this life-plan, he has gained a personal ideal, a cause. He has developed the third attitude of will: being loyal to his more genuine, his more rational self.

Having become a personally individualized and socialized self, and thus a "community of interpretation," this young adult integrates his past, present, and future selves and vitally bonds himself to other similarly committed selves. His cause and its community lie deeper than either his merely impulsive self or his isolated withdrawn self. For his cause and its community direct him to become consistently reasonable and genuinely loyal to the cause of his chosen life-plan. This third attitude tends to deepen and expand into broader communities, with more urgent moral causes. In this way, then, the child grows from a pre-moral state, through the initial moral reflections of a youth, into becoming a moral adult, called to further purify and harmonize his causes.

The individual self needs to grow through the first two attitudes—aggressiveness and withdrawal—and discover experientially their large areas of unwisdom. Only then can one become prepared to commit oneself to the third attitude, the real falling in love both with one's truer self—discovered through one's chosen life-plan—and eventually with a series of communities open to the whole universe. As this third attitude of will gradually becomes dominant, it brings into itself in increasingly purified ways the valid elements of self-assertiveness and self-denial that marked the two earlier attitudes.

Already in this embryonic moral self, then, a "transvaluation of values" has occurred. The moral adult cannot escape wanting a "harmony of wills" with that community of his own past, present, and future selves, as well as with the communities within one's own sphere.

This serial development of the embryonic moral self into a self that is committed to a human community and eventually to the Universal Community involves a serial purification of these three attitudes of will. The purification operates progressively in ever-widening circles of social relatedness—from family, through neighborhood, to nation and universe. In 1916 Royce portrayed this continuous, always tentative development in moral awareness:

> Loyalty, if it is anything, is or ought to be in all of us a growing doctrine of life, *and* a growing method of trying to solve the problems of life. . . . [W]hat one means by loyal conduct can be defined only through a continual effort to readjust the problems of life to an ideal, which, just because it is always living and growing, involves a willingness to reinterpret the situations which arise; to reconsider the solution which we have thus far attempted.[3]

The need for a "harmony of wills"—in the life of the individual and in that of the human community—thus requires a progressive purification of one's ideal, one's attitudes, and one's further approaches to that ideal through an ongoing grappling with life's problems. This need gradually gives birth to Royce's highest ideal: becoming loyal to the promotion of genuine loyalty in all members of the Universal Community. The Universal Community needs the multi-leveled harmony of its logical signs in System Sigma, of its "three leading ethical ideas," of its three normative Signs of Peirce's *Uberty*-ideal (the integrated realm of Truth, Duty, and Beauty), and especially, of all human wills called to the Great Community by the Interpreter Spirit of the Universal Community. This increasing commitment to "harmony of wills" presupposes the ever-deepening conversion of human selves to the "third attitude of will." Human selves are called to reaffirm this attitude in a series of choices that test the depth of their genuine loyalty.

The genuinely loyal self needs to keep rooted in its own divine spark and to reach out effectively to its particular community and affectively to the Universal Community. The self-possessed loyalist wills, at least in theory, to manifest the unity-promotive will of the Logos-Spirit, even when encountering obstacles and tragedies. Although becoming a divine channel to others in a stoic or Spinozistic way is still inadequate for the full art of loyalty, it surely is part of it. The mature Royce, for instance, quoted approvingly a saying he believed originated with Eckhart:

> "That a man has a restful and peaceful life in God is good. That a man endures a painful life with patience, that is better. But that a man has his rest in the midst of (and through) a painful life, that is best of all."

> Our will surrenders itself, then God acts on us—in us and through us, and that is why this is no quietism. The divine life as thus expressed appears very active indeed.[4]

The tests and tragedies of life, then, call human selves to turn their sufferings and "lost causes" into "religious sorrows." Thereby each person discerns ever more fittingly just "who I really am and what I really want to become" as a genuine individual.[5] Governed by the third attitude of will, this moral development contrasts sharply with the types of pseudo-individualisms and disordered loyalties that sprout from merely the first and second attitudes of will.[6]

DIRECTIVES AND PRINCIPLES
FOR THE ART OF LOYALTY

In early 1916 Royce spoke repeatedly of the principles of the art of loyalty. He distinguished these from the principles of his doctrine of loyalty, yet he viewed both as indispensable to his overall philosophy of loyalty. Almost a decade earlier he had begun balancing his doctrine of loyalty with its art.[7] In his *Philosophy of Loyalty* he gave directives for children's pre-moral development, for adolescents in their period of rapid moral formation, and for the "constant training in the art of loyalty" that mature adults need.[8] To learn this art, adults must find and adopt their moral leaders. For this their range of selection must expand in circles of solidarity—from friends, through strangers, to obscure, humble, loyal folk, and even to loyal opponents (286–288).

The "constant training" in the art of loyalty calls adults to take part in the significant process of idealizing their causes (269). To this end they are to use direct and indirect means, as well as "the history of lost causes . . . whose worldly fortunes seem lost, but whose vitality may outlast centuries"—like the lost national causes of the Irish and the Poles. "[O]ne of the most potent influences of human history, . . . the [lost] cause comes to be idealized through its very failure to win temporary and visible success" (280). If one's loyalty to a lost cause holds glorious memories and deep pathos, the ideals it contains become universalized and intensified (279).

For instance, a millennium before Christ, David and Solomon sought a national political kingdom as their cause. It was lost through Israel's later subjugations. Yet the prophets of Israel purified and universalized this ideal into a "theory of the divine government of human affairs." Still later, Jesus and his disciples adopted the kingdom of God as their cause. When Jesus was executed on the cross, however, this seemed a lost cause. Still later, when Christians came to believe that the resurrected Jesus is that present Spirit-sending reality who frees all people from their ultimate fear of death, they concretely idealized the cause of the kingdom of God in a way still more incarnate yet mysterious. For in the Holy One's new Universal Community (Kingdom), the Logos-Spirit's largely unfathomable governance of people's bodily life moved them into a community of embodied members being glorified by the risen Son of David (278).

In order to idealize a cause, therefore, the art of loyalty must employ two comrades: grief and imagination. It must grieve the causes it loses but it must also use imagination "to see in them whatever most serves to link them to the cause of universal loyalty" (288). For loyalty directs its deeds through the practically oriented visions which imagination forms by finding the living flame at the core of any darkened cause that is lost.

Besides these directives, which principles did Royce offer to guide this art? About 1910 he had identified as his first principle in the art of loyalty a memory-based type of discernment of spirits:

> Let us dwell upon the loyal spirit itself; let us make clear to ourselves that whatever we are to do it must be done, not capriciously, but loyally. Our first step, then, is to get into the right attitude by remembering what we who have to face these various problems most need in life. The first principle then of the art of Loyalty is: Try to remember what spirit it is in which you are trying to serve your art.
>
> Now what we most need is not a happy fortune, nor a satisfied emotional life, nor a satisfaction of our caprices, nor anything that can be defined in terms of mere sentiment, however lofty—in brief, nothing that can belong to ourselves as mere individuals. What we need is some steadfast and life long loyalty to an absorbing cause. And this cause must be one whose service helps other people to be loyal.[9]

So Royce's first principle of this art was to discern through memory whether the spirit in which one serves the art of loyalty harmonizes with the cause to which one has dedicated one's whole life, a cause that must also help others be loyal.

Near the close of the same lecture Royce formed his summary of "some principles" in the art of loyalty:

> Three principles of the Art of Loyalty have thus been set before you: First the principle: Steadfastly train yourself to the resolve that your various causes shall be harmonized. Secondly the principle: In case of the appearance of conflict, look beneath the superficial conflict to find if possible the deeper common loyalty, and act in the light of that common loyalty. Thirdly the principle: If conflict cannot otherwise be resolved, act in consistency with your prior loyalty, remembering that, if a change of flag may indeed be sometimes required by some transformation of your insight, fickleness itself is never a part of loyalty. Your cause, once chosen, is your larger self. Fickleness, if deep and deliberate, is moral suicide.[10]

Knowledge of principles, however, is vain if one does not know how to apply them and follow them out. Accordingly, Royce resisted the automatic application of ethical principles as fiercely as he resisted the mechanical following out of any conventional rules of thumb.[11] Genuine moral life demanded an in-touchness with the changing situation and an adaptive responsiveness to it. This called for an intelligent searching out of the "fitting third idea" and a creative embodiment of it when once found. Royce summarized the needed, concrete, and masterful synthesizing of these principles, as well as his aversion for the mechanical in ethics, as follows:

> With these three principles in mind we are able, I believe, to solve by individual choice, and by native tact and skill, most of the problems of the conflict of loyalties. The art of loyalty is a long art. It ought to be the art of life in all of us. It is no art to be carried out by rule of thumb. But it has principles, and some of these I have been trying to state.[12]

Four years later, in the first of his 1914 Berkeley Conferences, Royce had a new, more socially sensitized approach to this art, "The art of loyalty consists in the art of choosing the group of which you can speak in the first person plural and of finding out what its will is."[13] The art highlighted the need to discern both a genuine "we" community and its will to promote human unity.

DEMANDS FOR EXERCISING THIS ART.

Of the artist in loyalty the mature Royce demanded three things: (1) integrate your feelings with the other ethical components to create an energizing balance; (2) strive for growth patiently through a step-by-step procedure; and above all, (3) discern the next step that fits the temporally processing self as situated in the series of its communities. The practical import of these demands calls for clarification.

A balanced integration of affective, cognitive, and conative factors is distinctive of Royce's late ethics. Fostered by his continuing taste for the romantic poets, Royce's rhythmic alternation of affects—trust and fear, joy and grief, eagerness for service and rebelliousness against mere uniformity—supplied powerful energies for ethical life. If in opposition to caprice and fickleness, moral commitment required a sense of seriousness, it also required a playful sense of humor proportionate to those felt ignorances, limitations, and lack of full control which mark radically finite human selves.[14]

The wayfarer's inner discontent at not yet reaching home created an urgency to strive wholeheartedly forward and upward. Felt affection within one's family and bondedness within one's larger community gave rise to the idea of duty. Experiencing griefs and exercising one's imagination to further idealize "lost causes" led to deeper moral insight because one's ideals became more refined.[15] When personally embraced, these purified ideals engendered a sense of honor about one's own and others' moral personality. In their ongoing encounter with the bumps and bruises of fortune, moral selves also needed a sense of humor to keep discerning between the accidental "fortune, feeling, hope, fear, joy, sorrow" and the eternal internal meaning that is the inmost life-plan of one's Self.[16]

Besides the integration of affects, memories, hopes, and symbol-laden imagination, Royce called for even more intricate balancings. Against most Americans' tilt into varieties of exaggerated individualism, Royce strove steadily to balance authentic individualism with genuine loyalty.[17] This striving required him not only to scotch the many widespread pseudo-individualisms and various misinterpretations of loyalty, but also to come down with equal insistence on the true forms of individual and communal loyalty and their indispensable complementarity.[18]

This more balanced striving had refined the vigorous but unnuanced attitude, "It is good to strive," which Royce had uttered as a youthful instructor at Berkeley. In his final year, however, he identified in his now more balanced striving two still further refinements: a militant self-discipline and an interior watchfulness.

Upon the pilgrim's path of moral development, there was to be no undue resting at some level already achieved. Although the mature Royce's emphasis on striving did not entail the necessity of military conflict, he knew that only through "a high degree of conflict" within oneself and through competition with others, do "we reach our highest levels of civilization and loyalty."[19]

To promote these moral goals, one's chief concern should not be productivity and efficiency. To avoid a mere "striving in vain," Roycean moral endeavor requires more than observable good works measurable in short-term units. For although "righteousness is an entirely inaccessible goal because of the majesty of righteousness,"[20] still one's questing toward it must be as unending as the interpretive process is of itself. Above all else, one's personal initiative had to keep in touch with and authentically arise from one's innermost divine spark (*Fünkelin*) through interior watchfulness. Or, as Royce put it even more strongly to his students in his final year, "Your righteousness must issue, like the Trinity, from the very Godhead itself; else all your striving is in vain." 21

Asserting another kind of needed balance, Royce wanted no question in ethics to be viewed as a question for individual ethics only or for social ethics only, for both perspectives were integral to each ethical question.[22] Furthermore, Royce's central aim in his final ethics course was to synthesize his "three leading ethical ideas" into one balanced ethical life. The latter was to arise from that vitally tense yet balanced interchange between the two mysteries of the individual self and the Beloved Community.

If walking on the two legs of true individualism and loyalty called for balance, it also called for a step-by-step movement carried out with both initiative and patience. The art of loyalty demanded that the human pilgrim search for more light without foreclosing possibilities.[23] The loyal pathfinder had to think flexibly, avoid "fixing" on the details of needed long-range plans, and patiently accept as "enough" the light needed for the next step.[24] The tactic first needed was to counteract one's impulsively reactive urge to quash quickly any conflict one feels arising from without or within. This demands self-control and patience.

A negative instance of this occurred in an earlier episode that led up to Royce's mother-daughter case. The already alienated son of this mother had previously brought agonizing disgrace upon the family. Reactively, the mother had then upbraided him so sharply that she unwittingly "transformed [their] estrangement into the last long parting" since on leaving her he committed suicide. By not first conquering her impulse to control him, she failed both to maintain the conditions needed for continued dialogue and to "leave open all the possibilities" for the eventual healing of their estranged relationship.[25]

Royce himself illustrated this needed step-by-step procedure by never granting absolutely final status to his so-called "final definitions." Subsequent reflection always required re-interpretation and revision. Even if he drew closer to his goal, and surer of his direction, the pilgrim must remain tentative. Eight years after his "final definition" of loyalty,[26] Royce told his students:

> I have warned you throughout that what one means by loyal conduct can be defined only through a continual effort to readjust the problems of life to an ideal, which, just because it is always living and growing, involves a willingness to reinterpret the situations which arise; to reconsider the solution which we have thus far attempted.[27]

To this "hard saying," Royce added a confession of his own limitations in dealing with this case; namely, that "[I] never shall answer [it] perfectly, so long as I live in this world."

Royce's late insistence on this "one step at a time" requirement[28] and his practice of it reveal how much his awareness of the art of loyalty had developed since his Urbana lectures on loyalty in 1907.

Finally, and perhaps most importantly, the mature Royce's art of loyalty *discerned what fitted* one's unique self *as* devoted to one's particular community(ies) and the Universal Community.[29] Already in his *Philosophy of Loyalty* he had clearly manifested this requirement for discernment. It underwent a quantum leap in 1912 when Royce discerned the "close connection" between Peirce's doctrine of interpretation and what he himself was trying to express in his philosophy of loyalty.[30] It came to a still clearer grasp and usage in his final year.

In touch with Aristotle's finding that the heart of practical wisdom lies in the "right discrimination of the *equitable (tou epikeiou)*,"[31] Royce focused on finding the equitable or the fitting. This is the special kind of discernment required for moral decision making which starts from the viewpoint, not of the individual, but of a community of interacting members.[32]

At the outbreak of World War I in 1914, Royce so desired to "do the fitting thing" for his Berkeley audience that he shelved his prepared address and drafted a completely new one suited to their changed interests. In 1915 he adjusted sensitively to the many complexities involved in the case of Middlebury College. In 1916, aware of his weakened health, he judged it the "fitting thing" to get more rest and also to climb up and down the ladders of the *Esparta* for an hour and a half daily as his way of keeping his body in shape.

Concerning Royce's mature teaching on "finding the fitting,"[33] a caution may help. Some readers of Royce are so impressed by his stress on "being decisive" and "not dilly-dallying,"[34] that they present his doctrine of loyalty as principally voluntaristic and blindly tenacious. They fail to balance the truth in these aspects with Royce's demands for a prior rational investigation. Before he allowed shifting into action, Royce required prior intelligent investigation of possible courses of action and antecedent rational research through a testing of one's various practical interpretations. Even in the rare event when his own searching still provided no rational guide, he chose to "wait until some other light shines for our eyes" rather than launch into a course decided upon unilaterally.[35]

Already in 1907, Royce refused to give primacy to any goal-centered or duty-centered ethics.[36] He counterbalanced these with that idea of fittingness distinctive of a *cathecontic* ethics.[37] Passing over the many clues of such an ethic left by Royce during the intervening years, I focus on his mother-daughter case of 1916, reprinted below in Appendix B.[38] In it I find seven ways in which discernment of the fitting occurred.

First, in his "Comments," Royce asks himself, his students, and the daughter to discern the proper approach to this case. He recommends that the daughter "should begin . . . with a confession and not with a challenge [to her mother]" (60).

Second, discern the most pressing good to be secured in this case. In 1916 Royce held, unlike his earlier misinterpretation, that healing the estrangement between mother and daughter clearly takes precedence over finding out whether the mother has been dishonest, and over the daughter's maintaining her own position of innocence and dignity (46–47).

Third, discern the right order of proceeding. From among "the other various courses of action which are open to the daughter, . . . she ought *first* to ask "How can I best become reconciled to my mother? How can we best and most quickly reach a clear mutual understanding, an attitude of sympathy and of confidence in each other?" (47). The ideal of the best demands the right ordering of one's steps. If the daughter has recognized that their most pressingly needed good is the healing of their estrangement, then she needs to discover whether to start this healing by herself or through some imported mediator. Since this mother-daughter relationship has become heavily strained and very fragile, in so delicate a matter she should discern that successful reconciliation is less likely if she calls in a family relative, a friendly doctor or psychologist, or a lawyer (50–51).

Fourth, discern the presence of the spirit of ideal loyalty. The daughter needs to examine whether she intends the good of this mother-daughter community more than her own good. Hers must be a spirit of loving loyalty for their bond. Such a spirit will move her to "do the best" to win reconciliation. It will rule out every spirit of false individualism and any disloyalty to their bond. As Royce put it, "Until this best has been done, no assertion of independence, no insistence upon the daughter's righteous demands for her freedom from any responsibility for dishonest conduct, no such rebellion can be advisable or successful" (49–50). The daughter needs to stand in loyal love and "starve out" spirits of rebellion, suspicion, judgmentality, and self-righteousness.

Fifth, discern the disorder which one's own limitations insert into the interchange. Moral realist that he was, Royce recognized how the dynamisms of our faults both poison our relationships and prompt us to project guilt and blame upon others rather than ourselves. Royce explained:

> I am including under the word fault all the varied possibilities of error, of folly, of human imperfection, which practically enter into, and which complicate our life, and which, in a given case, may be the source to which, as we can see,

some estrangement is due. A hasty temper, or a lack of experience, an indolent disposition, or even, as in the case of this daughter, an amiable inability, persisting through many years, to call one's soul one's own, may directly or indirectly lead, or may have led to what now constitutes an estrangement. (54)

One is to be sufficiently in-touch with one's own (and others') sinful human situation to counteract one's human tendencies to accept slanted perceptions and to project guilt on others.[39]

Sixth, discern the distinctive ethical idea ruling one's particular relationship and act accordingly. In this case, the relationship was that of mother to daughter, a bond in which the duties of loving maternal guidance and filial obedience should have predominated (58). Being true to this kind of bond requires the daughter not to envision "a just reversal of the normal position of the successive generations" (59). She is not to allow her desires for independence or for a separated happiness to gain the upper hand over her prior responsibility to fulfill as best she can her duty to her mother. A sense of worthiness or unworthiness assists this discernment. The daughter needs to recognize that she may have tempted her mother to take bank funds in order to educate her. So perhaps the latter needs to say, "I am unworthy to be called your daughter [for having tempted you so]." Then will be proven her fidelity to this fundamental bond, to the healthy mother-daughter love that needs to be restored.

Finally, discern whether one's evidence is sufficient to warrant a certain step. Among these just-mentioned seven ways in which discernment occurs, this final Roycean insistence on having adequate evidence before moving, rather than leaping in the dark, may call for the greatest self-control. In the case at hand, the daughter may feel like assuming her mother's guilt, like calling in a doctor, like running away, like standing on her own seeming innocence. Nevertheless, none of these steps are adequately (fittingly) warranted (59). The daughter's ethical task calls her to detect this lack of evidence and accordingly avoid these easier but insufficiently evidenced moves.

Although our analysis of Royce's call to "find the fitting" has focused on only one case he examined in 1916, the reader can see, even from it alone, how manifold is the work of interpretive discernment in Royce's art of loyalty.

9. Doctrinal Content of Royce's Mature Ethics, 1912–1916

ROYCE'S ETHICS IN 1912

In *The Problem of Christianity*, Royce's philosophical grasp of loyalty came of age. He asserted that "the depth and vitality of the ideal of loyalty have become better known to me as I have gone on with my work."[1] But this "ideal" resembled no abstract Platonic form. Rather it was concretized within the directed life streams of social religious experience (40). In the *Problem* he grasped and formulated clearly how genuine loyalty depends upon a specific fundamental orientation (355–357). The genuinely loyal self must adopt a psychic stance that makes it primarily neither self-assertive nor self-effacing, but dedicated to the whole universe. Genuine moral life requires that one devote oneself to the entire processing world by loving it with wholehearted loyalty. This chosen radical orientation is Royce's "third attitude of will."

In the *Problem* the term "transformation" became even more central for Royce (218).[2] He claimed that a transformation of ethical ideas results if one simply recognizes and adequately considers the experiences of the Pauline Christian churches. These first Christians experienced directly a dynamic form of social religious experience. It birthed in them a first full articulation of the "Christian doctrine of life." In this experience and articulation, a superhuman gift that Royce called "grace" unified the three most essential Christian ideas: community, lost state, and atonement. The "highest good of man"—both as individual and as community—lies in a person's or community's *ethical transformation*. This transformation changes one from a form of existence that is merely natural (that is, "morally detached" from any genuine community) into a mode of life that is interpersonally respectful, dedicated to a particular common good, and also in touch with the Universal Community (218). Neither individual nor community can effect this moral conversion unless aided by the Spirit of the Universal Community. Usually this Spirit operates through one of its human representatives, such as an honest banker or a sufferer for unity, like Abraham Lincoln.

In a most striking development, atonement took center stage in the *Problem's* doctrine of loyalty. Royce described atonement as "the function

143

in which the life of the community culminates" (42, 208). In his fifth plan for the *Problem* he had broken through to "a rationalized form of the Atonement doctrine."[3] He could defend this view rationally. With it he could fittingly replace both the merely moral and the substitutionary (scapegoat) versions of that doctrine. By 1912 Royce emphasized the need for an intelligent design of the strategy which makes sense of a suffering atoner's deeds. He made far clearer, too, the atoning role of the whole genuine community, as well as that of any of its particular suffering servants. In this way, Royce penetrated near the heart of Christianity—the sacrificial side of its Paschal Mystery.

Moreover, "the Will to Interpret" functioned in the *Problem* as a fruitful way of viewing the immanent movement of the Spirit of the Community. For this "Will" is another name for the Spirit of the (particular as well as Universal) Community. This Will commits itself to seeking the unity of two minded beings who may merely differ or even stand opposed. Commonplace leaders like trustworthy bankers and sound business agents embody the Will to Interpret. As Pedagogue Sign-Sender, this Spirit guides the historical development of both individuals and nations, developing unity in them only gradually. Royce installed this Will to Interpret at the heart of his interpretive musement, his new method of philosophizing. Within human limits this method participates concretely in the Interpreter Spirit's synoptic vision that integrates our processing experience and world.

Royce's 1913 doctrine of loyalty radiated a striking balance of temporal process and metaphysical mysticism. He saw that our world's ever-accelerating rate of change would gnaw away many of Christianity's formulas, institutions, and outdated practices. Meanwhile, the Spirit of loyalty would lead human selves to focus with increasing intensity upon that living and life-giving "sword of the spirit" which is "the Christian doctrine of life" (215). As far as sign-communication goes, this doctrine is the only central nerve required if Christianity and humanity are to perdure and grow.

But in this semiotic nerve there operates that mystic touch with the divine which had characterized Royce's metaphysical thought since his 1883 religious insight. In 1899 he had refined his "mystical" (or "second") conception of Being and transformed it into his "fourth" and final conception of Being—that of the unique individual as the object of exclusive interest. Thus he retained, critically purified, and emphasized this kind of mystical touch with the divine. How this mystical touch was transformed by his 1912 insight appeared in the *Problem's* teleological bond—or *epsilon* relation—with the Universal Community and its Spirit.[4] This bondedness provides the constancy needed amid the chancy, ever-evolving processes of the universe. In this way, then, Royce carefully balanced the Eternal and the practical, his metaphysical mysticism and temporal agency.

In summary, we find that in the *Problem* Royce had markedly transformed and developed his philosophy of loyalty. By 1913 he had rendered explicit loyalty's relation to the "third attitude of will," to moral conversion, to the centrality of atonement, and to the needed balancing of ongoing change and mysticism. The question then arises whether, during his four final years of 1913–1916, his loyalty doctrine underwent an equally vast development. I think so. Stating it succinctly, Royce's doctrine of loyalty developed and matured *as much* after the *Problem as* it had done between 1908 and 1913.

ROYCE'S ETHICS IN 1914

In 1914 at Berkeley Royce created a new synthesis of his philosophy of loyalty by integrating three theses: (1) that under certain conditions communities are genuine selves, (2) "that the salvation of every individual man depends upon his voluntary devotion to some such living and lovable community," and (3) that in and through and above his commitment to such a community, one "comes into some genuine touch with . . . one and the same live spiritual reality"—a union that constitutes loyalty.[5]

This integrated vision is more significant than any of its parts. Yet Royce's insight into his third thesis lifted him into a pean about loyalty reminiscent of the poetic and mystical expression of Plato when he described his noetic vision of the Forms. But unlike Plato's vision, Royce's insight came through the moral light experienced through one's loving union with and deed-doing service of community—through Royce's voluntary "absolute pragmatism." This became clear when he developed his third and final thesis on loyalty by means of the following periodic crescendo:

Thirdly, that in and through and above all the countless social forms in which we are accustomed to interpret to ourselves our relation to the community which we learn to love—in and through and above a man's love for his country, in and through and above a devout man's love for his church universal, in and through and above our love of the ideal community of all mankind, as we hope that mankind is yet to be realized in the future,—in and through and above all these special forms which the loyal spirit takes, we all, precisely in so far as we are loyal, come into some genuine touch with one and the same reality, with one and the same cause, with one and the same live spiritual reality. To this one cause all the loyal are, according to their lights, faithful. One undivided soul of many a soul, whose life constitutes the divine life, one genuine and universal community there is. To be united in and with this community, to love it as our father and our mother, as our goal and as our fulfillment,—this is loyalty.[6]

One might incline to rest in this 1914 exaltation of loyalty. Royce did the opposite. Although he had created the *Problem's* opening chapters with amazing ease, he labored strenuously to create the opening chapters of his 1915 Extension Course in Ethics.[7] This suggests that in summer 1915 Royce exerted his mental powers to the full to actually integrate the roots of ethical life by delving even deeper than he had done in the *Problem*.

TEMPORAL PROCESS

The self and community are the two mysteries in which Royce planted his rational ethics of 1915–16. Here we need first to notice how temporal process—a key Roycean theme—enters into these two mysteries. Like the human community, each unique and mysterious human self proceeds through definite stages in its self-identification and in its ethical development. In 1915 Royce integrated these stages around the central psychological process of self-identification. For him the question, "Who and what am I?" deepened with time. In the end it became his most central investigative probe into the dialogic interaction between the two mysteries.

When we first ask the question with which "all ethical questions are bound up," namely, "Who and what am I?" we ask it "merely selfishly." But after being bruised by the world, we later ask it in a "narrowly personal" and a "merely private sense." Finally, having committed ourselves to the world and to all its selves, we ask it in a universal sense which is not merely conceptual but interpretively referent to all selves, oneself included. We then ask the question maturely—on behalf of, or "for and in the name of *whatever reasonable moral being* you please." Here Royce suggests how the temporal process penetrates and alters our asking the central question of ethics.

This suggestion also fits his seriation of the "three attitudes of will," identified in the *Problem*. For in his final year Royce found that whenever we recognize reality, we also value or disvalue it.[8] To raise the question "Who and what am I?" implicitly carries the valuational query, "Since I am alive, is my life worth living?"[9] To this latter explicitly ethical question, selves and communities serially generate three answers, insofar as they live by temporal process.

When one first asks personally, "Is my life worth living?" the finite self's first attempted response is "Yes, if I get what I want." This response expresses and solidifies the "first attitude of will"; namely, the will to assert and prefer oneself without bothering about or being bothered by others. After trying out this attitude several times, most finite selves recognize how frustrating it is since it arouses so many social pressures against oneself.

To the basic question, then, an alternate response arises: "No! Interactive life with others and nature is not worthwhile, because I can't become happy simply by asserting my will." One becomes defensive and, viewing others and the world as largely illusory or vain, adopts a second attitude of will: to withdraw from the world and emphasize one's inner life—perhaps in union with a higher reality. This second attitude often adopts a narrow mysticism of supposedly immediate union—a stance which in Royce's view Meister Eckhart and the Southern Buddhists exemplified.[10]

Finally, through the influence of one or more personally loyal persons, the human self finally awakens to the living reality of a Beloved Community. The self's development of consciousness has then reached the threshold of authentic moral life. It enters into that deeper communal level of life if it wholeheartedly and practically dedicates itself to a community and its cause. In this way it discovers that only by cooperating with other members and by loyally promoting the community's common good can it develop its own unique individuality.

Through this temporal process, the human self thus finally attains a loving loyalty to the universe as a whole. This third fundamental attitude of will arises out of an inward, passional, wholehearted response to a genuine community and out of a gift "as from above."[11] It occurs when one has "fallen in love with the universe" and can therefore utter one's overall "Yes" or "Amen" to the processing universe.[12] Unlike the first two attitudes, with the third one trustfully surrenders to and progressively affirms the Interpreter-Spirit's guidance of the universe. Since the two other fundamental attitudes of will have proven self-contradictory in Royce's logic of infinite community as well as in practice, this third attitude of universal loyalty demonstrates itself in both ways as the only authentic basic ethical attitude.[13]

The timeful process does not end once it has led the human self beyond attitudes of individualistic self-aggression and distrustful withdrawal into a wholehearted loyalty to some community open to the universe. Within the third basic attitude of will there are many degrees of deeper bonding with the Universal Community that lead to fuller self-identification, and to that highest form of genuine loyalty: Pauline charity or *caritas*.[14] Meanwhile, along the way, the human self's process of ethical growth will be led to emphasize now one, now another, of such significant basics in ethical life as one of the three leading ethical ideas.[15]

Purgatively, the advance to this third attitude of will has largely uprooted two noxious weeds that prevent ethical maturation. For by falling in love with the universe, the human self becomes fundamentally freed from the many deviant forms of "detached individualism" and "ethical pessimism"— the two basic obstacles to ethical growth.

Royce himself had struggled long with ethical pessimism and also that ethical skepticism which, as a symbiotic companion, nurtures it.[16] He overcame both, more by examining the way morally excellent people lived than by theoretical arguments.[17] Subsequently, he fought against the protean forms of "detached individualism."[18] He also strove to clarify how "individualism" became genuine by being balanced with true loyalty. The human self's commitment to true loyalty worked a basic liberation from these two "weeds." Nevertheless, their time-entwined dominion over the human self left habits which challenged it to a life-long battle against their ever more intimate forms of self-preference and withdrawal.

THE HUMAN SELF AS "A COMMON REASONABLE HUMAN NATURE"

Our investigative trek with Royce leads us into his 1915 view of the human self. He already told us, "all ethical questions are bound up in it" [the fundamental question of 'Who and what is the Self?']. Since Royce's 1915 view of the human self is highly nuanced, the need for accuracy becomes clear here.

First, as a process of interpretation, the human self is to be interpreted historically. It is not a datum, nor any mere concept, but a timeful process that arises when a human person consciously adopts a life-plan. Adopting a life-plan requires one to interpret a cause as one's own chosen goal and the elements from one's past as significant steps toward or away from that goal. Royce said man was defined in terms of "memories, intentions, and plans."[19]

The mature Royce acknowledged refining his view of how the individual self originated. Earlier he had viewed it as a by-product of its ambient society, which is or is not structured by a civilization and its specializations. In that view, his persistent emphasis fell on the resistances and rebellions which the influences of society evoke in the individual. In 1915, however, while still recognizing these alienating effects, Royce stressed the working of society's "highly unifying tendencies" upon the individual self. When an individual member identifies him- or herself with a stable group's "common idealized past events or deeds" and its "common idealized future events and deeds,"[20] society exercises highly unifying influences upon that member as it mediates these "commonalities" to him or her. Insofar as a member affirms, "This [communal item] is part of my life," the individual's self-identification takes on a communalized-identity. Furthermore, through these highly unifying tendencies society conveys the wisdom of its traditions to the self within the communal current of its own individualization.[21]

Because of its timefulness, then, the human self is an interpretive process that synthesizes present, past, and future to fashion the life-plan that gives it meaning and identity. In brief, Royce's human self is fundamentally a unique moral life whose process is found embodied in human individuals and in their communities.

In his 1915 lecture on "The Self," Royce unveiled a three-dimensional approach to the self when he wrote:

> And each of us, as [a] student of ethics, is making the inquiry as if for and in the name of whatever reasonable moral being you please. Thus we ask a *personal* question, namely, "What is the Self"—but we ask it in an *impersonal* and, in the end, in a sort of *superpersonal* sense. . . . [S]uch inquiries are likely to lead both to surprises, and to paradoxes. We shall meet with both in the course of our study of the Self.[22]

The question is *personal.* Yet since as ethicists we ask it "for and in the name of whatever reasonable moral being you please," our question must come as if from any rational moral agent and be *impersonally* representative of the Universal Community of such agents. Furthermore, it will also involve a *superpersonal* sense. Exploring these three dimensions of the Roycean self means winning a rich context that illumines his most mature ethics.

Take as a person, the human self has its kind of autonomy or self-direction. Its own past, its self-constituting choice of a cause, and its consequent life-plan make it unique. These make the self an irreplaceable process of interpretation in the universe. But this personal self is also a mystery.

Taken impersonally, one of the possessions of the human self is "a common reasonable human nature."[23] Or to set this lapidary phrase in the context Royce gave it, ". . . in some sense, the voice of duty must reasonably make an appeal that concerns all of us, precisely in so far as we are indeed in possession of a common reasonable human nature." Precisely because our human nature is both rational and common to all human selves, we share the same mutual concerns to which duty cannot but make a common reasonable appeal.

Royce's "nature," however, is not an ontological being—neither an Aristotelian *phusis* with its own "beingness" nor a Lockean "unknowable substrate." Instead, by the term "nature" Royce indicates a positive moral life of interpretation. Although his term "self" indicates a unique individual, it also points to its possession of a communality with other human individuals. Although uniquely embodied and passional, the Roycean self also possesses rationality for its moral life. The moral self's life works itself out through its embodiment, which, like its rational self-consciousness, has many social and time-filled ingredients.

Besides these aspects, the human self is finite and tends to be alienated. Royce used finitude in the moral sense of being ethically burdened, of tending towards becoming a "detached individual," or of already being such. His "finite self" usually avoids the sense of "limited being" found among Southern Buddhists.[24] Similarly, when Royce calls the human self "alienated," he points primarily to "an ethical estrangement," to an earlier change in the self's moral relationships, rather than merely to a psychological aversion or a resultant physical distancing from others.[25]

Taken as superpersonal, the human self shows even more its mysteriousness. As Royce taught in 1916,[26] the conception of the infinite is linked inescapably to the idea of the human self. For the latter is infinite in its never-ending search to fulfill its internal meaning. It is also infinite in its quest for happiness, its search for that kind of goodness that genuinely completes its inner poverty. Finally, it is infinite as being in its core a *Fünkelin*, or image of God as a "little divine spark."[27]

The idealization process of the human self also reveals its superpersonal and superhuman dimension. Employing its three principal ethical ideas of freedom, goodness, and duty, the self transforms and synthesizes these into its moral ideal–the supremely free, good, and dutiful person it can become. Moreover, the idealization process continues along the lines of the human self's *Fünkelin* nature to fashion some tri-faceted notion of the holy One. One gradually discerns the holy One as a mysteriously free, good, and righteous Ruler, according to the particular traditions of monotheism within one's community.[28]

While acknowledging a sharp contrast between the usual viewpoint of the mystics and that which "ought to be prominent in the treatment of ethics," Royce insisted that "the contrast also involves close relations."[29] By 1915 Royce had further purified his mystical or "second conception of being." He could settle neither for any pretended immediate union with the divine, nor for any mysticism of mere quiet contemplation. The kind of purified mysticism that he brought over into his "fourth and final conception of being" had to be both contemplative yet also actively practical. It is an ever-flowing desire that struggles forward to come ever closer to the divine without ever fully attaining its unfinished union with that Mystery. While refraining from what he considered to be Eckhart's non-mediated union with the divine, the Royce of 1916 highly appreciated Eckhart's tenent that through painful struggle a human self can achieve peace at its core. Through mediated union with the divine life, the human self wins deep peace and a finite participation in the Logos-Spirit's chronosynoptic vision.[30]

When the human self emphasizes this deep union in a way that transcends a mere "me-and-God" polarity, it has reached the stage of its deepest growth in religious consciousness. By requiring this further stage for genuine ethical life, the mature Royce revealed the vital bond between the human self and the divine community—a bond he thought indispensable for authentic morality. He put it this way:

> The world in which the devout person conceives his relations to the Divine merely in those terms that on the one side he sets God's will and on the other

side he sets his own,—this stage of religious consciousness is never the highest. It is only when the pronoun 'we' expresses the relation between God and the self or between God and the world which is in question, it is only at this stage of the religious consciousness that genuine loyalty exists.[31]

When union and deep inner peace reach this stage, the human self needs to and can abandon itself in complete trust to its searched-for "Captain," its "leader of the world."[32] Describing the superhuman and superpersonal dimension of the human self's "I can" response to duty, Royce recognized this dutiful attitude as:

> obviously humble as well as defiant [of "mere destiny"], submissive as well as proud, conscious how ignorant he is about what, after all, is really good for us mortals in the way of mere luck and of chance happening as well as of natural attainment. *The dutiful spirit leaves to what it calls God the art of making the great triumph*, of solving Everyman's problem [of finding the true Good], and of reconciling the poor individual man whose head fortune so often leaves bleeding, to the blows of chance which he is sometimes too weak merely to defy.[33]

In brief, then, all these aspects of the human self—its multiform infinitude, its idealization process, its genuine mysticism, and its total trust—manifest its intimate union with its divine Deliverance. This union constitutes the super-personal and superhuman dimension of human self as a moral reality. When conjoined with its personal and impersonal dimensions, one can appraise something of the treasure house into which the mature Royce's investigation has led us.

DEEP CURRENTS THAT ALIENATE
OR INTEGRATE THE HUMAN SELF

Personal experiences and voracious reading familiarized Royce with the forces of alienation which disorient the human self. As a child he could not help reacting to his mostly absent father and heavily dominant mother. As a psychologist, he knew the rise of resistances to social pressures, the emergent reaction of the anarchic rebel, and the more morbid forms the psyche can take.[34] He was also sociologically alert enough to recognize the deep currents of alienation that flood in upon the individual self. Their swirl and sweep comes from overly centralized institutions and groups too insistent on standardization, as well as from social bodies infected by racism, greed, one-issue feminism, labor mobs, jingoists, and all other "communities of hate," as Royce called them. Intellectually, if one misinterpreted either individualism or loyalty, one fostered other varieties of self-estrangement.[35] Like being pulled into an underground river, the dynamic power of alienation estranged the human self from its own true center as well as from its fellow humans and community. It detached the individual from safe footing in community. It held one in its deadly downdragging whirlpool strongly enough to make one cry out for deliverance. As long as one was swept along by the current of such deadliness, fear-driven conventional morality became the only kind of "morality" possible. It secured the minimum consensus it needed by recognizing and enforcing behaviors requisite for group survival.

Another name for all these turbulent currents of alienation is "the so-called problem of evil."[36] The mature Royce regarded it as "the most important moral aspect of the world" (5/25). For decades it had goaded his reflections and featured prominently in his major works; it also characterized many of his minor publications and unpublished writings.[37] As late as his final class in metaphysics in 1916 he broke course sequence and lectured on the problem of evil. Seemingly he could not bid his last students farewell without calling their attention to it.

Royce's fourfold response to the problem of evil was to face it steadily, to feel and show irritation toward philosophers who dodged it, to indicate some ways of dealing with it rationally, and to avoid pretending he had found an adequate solution. Recourse to his last metaphysical lectures of 1916 allows one to see this fourfold response more clearly.

Royce wanted steadfastly to confront all disteleologies—death, error, sin, misunderstandings, misfortunes, and so forth. All evil clearly had great moral importance because as past it became irrevocable. Thus it freighted its burden into the present and conditioned future possibilities. Royce was convinced that "a person's moral worth depends on what he has done as well as on what he is doing" (5/27).

Secondly, he felt and showed irritation with those who dodged the philosophical problem of evil by reducing it merely to the practical problem of "getting rid of evil." Earlier he had found Dewey an untroubled optimist because he did not face up squarely to sin, death, and other evils.[38] Royce had also criticized Matthew Arnold for recommending that the sinner not brood on his sins. Such counsel no longer channeled Christ's august soul-searching doctrine on the peril of sin, understood as whatever violates wholehearted love and is healed by repentance and willingness to forgive others.[39]

In his final days, Royce was irritated with philosophers like James and Perry, like Mill and Santayana, for taking the problem of evil out of philosophy and shunting it into the practical problem of improving social conditions (5/27). Instead he insisted that the problem of evil is a genuine philosophical problem. He located it as "the problem of the restriction," the incomplete self-expression of the self of him in whose experience the ill appears (1/13). When we ask "Why such confinement of potential?" we show the problem of evil is "forced on everyone as an aspect of life which you don't understand"(1/13). This limitation is part of reality and may not, without philosophical dishonesty, be treated merely as a practical problem.

Thirdly, by musing interpretively upon the problem of evil, the mature Royce uncovered some theoretical light, a practical suggestion, and a hope-filled hint. As for theory, he told his students:

> If the being of the world involves interpretation, then the interpretation of evil will not amount to showing that it is only an apparent evil. It will involve that which for the person who suffers the evil would appear as a reconciling element in his life. (1/15)

For "by virtue of that interpretation [the world's], the problematical side of the world becomes less problematic at each step." Royce sagely noted that if one interprets and reinterprets the evil in one's life, he will create "a reconciling element in his life." Such serial reinterpretation of one's evils may well reveal one's earlier self-preference and correct one into a more universalistic loyalty, one more aligned to the will of the Interpreter-Spirit.

As for practical guidance when confronting their problem of evil, Royce said:

> The practical expression of our metaphysics would be a confidence that to know the world better is to pardon its ills. The contrasts are not removed by interpretations. The evil aspects are comprehended and therefore pardoned. (1/15)

If one asks why one should pardon the evil aspects of the world, Royce would likely respond that we live in a community of interpretation whose central process is reconciliation. Therefore, since we know that the reconciling community will somehow sometime overcome sin, ills, treasons, and so forth, the fitting thing is to pardon these evils and be an instrument of forgiveness. Yet, just as in the *Problem* he abstained from saying *how* love comes into a transformed self and community, so in 1916 he also abstained from saying *how* the power to pardon and forgive arises in a self and community which are traumatized by evils done to and by themselves.

Lastly, in a final line he offered a hopeful hint: "Atonement, if it occurs, is another matter" (5/27). Atonement is not a matter open to metaphysics but to a philosophy of Christian religion. There the mystery of the suffering servant and of the co-atoning members of his body operates in the evil-burdened community of interpretation to heal, free, and elevate it and its members to the Beloved Community's life.

Atoning energy, then, is that other deep countercurrent at work in ways often unnoticed within the mature Royce's moral world. This stream of atonement heals, unifies, and reconciles. It steals mysteriously into the human self and into its communities as from the depths.[40] Perhaps the human self or some community has long been drifting without any overall aim. Yet now it finds welling up within itself the energy to commit itself wholeheartedly to a Beloved Community (or to become one). And any particular Beloved Community will be open to the Universal Beloved Community. This current of deliverance thus frees the self and the community from their futile drifting. It transforms them into the "realm of grace," into genuinely loyal selves and Beloved Communities. Yet the entry of a human self and community into this river of salvation has to be continuously reaffirmed and supported in the ongoing battle between these two currents of alienation and reconciliation.

THE TWO-LEVEL DOCTRINE AS AFFECTING THREE FUNDAMENTAL STRATA

Relying on experience and refining pertinent concepts, Royce finally interpreted reality as an interpretive process going on between two mutually ultimate and interacting levels—a unique individual and a community—as these are found in three Orders.

Level	Order A	Order B	Order C
1st	any embodied but non-minded self	a human Self, a unique embodied minded being	Infinite Spirit of Universal Community.
2nd	physical Nature's process as time-filled community	finite minded communities (in series)	Infinite Universal Community

Royce's ethics of 1915–16 primarily explores the interpretive inter-action between the two interacting *mysteries* of Order B, that is, the vital relation between a unique human individual and its community(-ies). As finite, both are viewed as morally so limited that they need interaction with Order A—physical objects and nature as a whole—as well as healing from Order C—that of infinite Spirit and its Universal Community. Through its organic needs, interests, and motives, the human self and its communities are linked to embodied non-minded selves and to nature as a whole. Both the unique human individual and its communities are also linked to the universal Spirit-Interpreter and its Universal Community—at least through their likenesses as divine sparks (*Fünkelin*).

Part of the world's process of interpretation includes the Sign-influences of the members of Columns A and C upon the members of Column B. That is, from its own organic selfhood and its environing material nature, the finite human minded self is given Signs that suggest the three leading ethical ideas.[41] For example, by experiencing itself as physically separated from others and able to initiate its own local motion, the human self gathers the suggestion that it is a free, albeit limited, individual. Then, from its experience of functioning healthily or sickly as an organism, the reflective self becomes aware of a kind of goodness, similar to, but higher than that of physical health. Moreover, just as human health depends partly on the individual self but partly on things beyond its control, the human self's sense of the happiness connected with moral goodness reflects something that is partly in its control and partly beyond it. Finally, from the human self's encounters with other embodied individuals and groups, and from its experiences of both needing them, depending on them, and being sometimes frustrated by them, there arises a felt need to respond to call. The human self's interpretation of this need as "duty" is more experiential, concrete, and refined than a conception of duty as an effect of a "moral law or force binding the moral universe."

On the other side, from Order C, another kind of Sign-sending enters the human self's receptivity. From the mysterious Spirit of the Universal Community there radiates into the finite human self—with its unique *Fünkelin* resemblance to this Spirit—far more than the "two doctrines" of the *Problem*.[42] For the human self, both as a unique finite internal meaning of the Spirit and as a *Fünkelin* likeness of it, receives Signs of the divine Spirit's three aspects, sketched by Royce in his "Monotheism" article. First, God as ineffable Mystery and Freedom (emphasized by the Indic view of the apophatic God) communicates its reflection to the human self in the latter's radically unique mysteriousness and the living initiative arising therefrom. Secondly, God as the inner Order of the cosmos and its Leader (emphasized by the Hellenic view of God) communicates its reflection to the human self in the latter's teleological aspiration for the good (which includes true happiness). This joy is somehow felt to lie beyond one's human self in something truer, nobler, and more beautiful. Thirdly, God as the holy liberating One (emphasized by the Hebraio-Christian view of God) communicates its reflection as a voice that is quiet yet clear, stern yet gentle—a voice that whispers "you should" in a mysterious way that overrides those louder, more pleasing voices of pleasure, power, and personal success that lead to amoral or immoral choices.

In sum, Royce attested that the two ideas of Community and Spirit had for him kept growing since 1912 and "certainly . . . assumed, in my own mind, a new vitality, and a very much deeper significance than, for me, they ever had before I wrote my *Problem of Christianity*."[43] This growth could not have occurred, however, without the ethical meanings of Spirit and Community penetrating ever more deeply into Royce's late view of the human self.[44] Moreover, since these two complementary ideas structured his late view of God as Interpreter-Spirit and as Community of Interpretation,[45] he also saw the reflected likeness of these two ideas in the *Fünkelin* of the finite human self–that is, as an individual minded spirit and as itself a living temporal community participating in larger human communities.

Accordingly, when the human spirit feels its initiative to direct its own life, albeit within the bonds of community, it experiences its kind of autonomy. When it aspires to the better and in its unique way depends on community to achieve it, it experiences its form of goodness. When it experiences itself as exigently required to find or create its uniquely fitting response to this communally idealized "better," it discovers how duty shows its human face.

To review our progress thus far, we first noticed Royce's sketches of how the human self develops morally according to the "seasons" of its life. Then we descended into the depths of that self, measuring both its uniqueness and its possession of "a common reasonable human nature." We next felt those powerful moral undercurrents of alienation and reconciliation tugging upon the human self. Finally, we arrived at the central stratum of the human individual and the human community—its "two levels"—and found that these were supported and energized by natural and superhuman individuals and communities. The next chapter will reveal how the Royce of 1915–16 began his intellectual mining into the ethical life of this two-leveled human stratum.

10. Doctrinal Content of Royce's 1915–1916 Ethics

THE CENTRAL ETHICAL QUESTION

In autumn 1915 Royce concurred with Schopoenhauer that ultimately the central ethical question is "Who and what am I?" At first this question sounds more theoretical than practical and also too naive to persist as ultimately central. Such an appraisal, however, arises from one who uses language primarily in a conceptual mode rather than using it to guide interpretation. The latter usage presupposes that to grasp being is to estimate it and thus to live in the world of values and ethics. Royce's ultimately central question becomes profoundly ethical:

> [On the one hand] every man inevitably finds himself as apparently occupying the centre of his own universe . . . [and this] inevitable illusion of perspective is, of course, responsible for what is called our natural selfishness. But on the other hand, this illusion is no mere illusion. It suggests, even while it distorts the true nature of things. The real world has a genuine relation to the various personalities that live in it. . . . Values do indeed alter with the point of view. . . . So far as moral values are concerned, it is therefore indeed certain that no ethical doctrine can be right which neglects individuals, and which disregards . . . their duty to centralize their lives, and so their moral universe, about their own purposes.[1]

Within the human self's biased self-centeredness lies a hint of truth concerning its moral universe. Its "inevitable illusion" estranges the self both from its true internal meaning and from interacting healthily with other selves in society. Trying to interpret what its lived world is all about, the human self, as inevitably illuded, is interested psychologically in what it perceives as most central: itself or "I". Hence, when it asks, "Who and what am I?" it probes spontaneously into its own mystery and structure. Nevertheless, the hint of truth found in each self's autonomous creation of its "moral universe" gives this "I" an inescapable moral quality. The self sees that it cannot have a meaningful life unless it adopts its own purposes, and yet it is aware that its meaning will be frustrated unless those purposes somehow *fit in with* the basic purposes of other human selves.[2]

157

In 1915 Royce claimed that the question "'Who and what is the *Self'*...interests all of us...because *all* ethical questions are bound up in it."[3] Phrased in terms of "the Self," the central question necessarily leaves out some of the uniqueness felt in the mysterious personal question, "Who am *I*?" Royce thus moved first to generalize the personal question. Though perhaps others do, he did not lose sight of how logically complex is this quest for self-identification.[4]

Royce's interpretation of his complex starting question not only moved from a personal through an impersonal to a superpersonal sense, as we saw, but also alternated back and forth between the "who" and "what" of the question. Hence, what counted was *how* one mused over this starting question. One was not to ask it in any "merely private" or "merely perceptual" or "merely conceptual" manner but rather in a processive way that was genuinely interpretive, intrinsically unending, and always partly fallible.

Shortly before his death, Royce acknowledged that since writing the *Problem* the ideas of Community and of Spirit had acquired new life and a far deeper meaning for him. This growth could not have occurred without the ethical aspects of these two ideas permeating ever more deeply into Royce's view of the human self and its communities. Moreover, in his maturity these two ideas supplied him with his best approaches to God (as a Community of Interpretation and especially as a Spirit-Interpreter). Accordingly, during his final year, while musing long upon Eckhart's view of the human soul as "a unique glimmer of the godhead," Royce saw the human self as called to the fulfillment, in lived-time and society, of both its unique individuality and its communal nature. Consequently, if the human self concretely feels its freedom to direct its own life uniquely, it also feels its membership in communities. If it aspires to goodness in its own way, it also appreciates fidelity to its community relationships as the only way to achieve this goodness. If it hears the call of duty according to its individuality, it also interprets this call as requiring it to find or create a response that fits in with the central thrust of its communities.

Furthermore, since each genuine community has its own "mind," which is also engaged in a self-identification process, its central question, too, is "Who and what am I?" Hence, the central dynamism of Royce's mature ethics lies in the vitally tense interaction between the two mysteries of finite self and finite community as both further investigate their questions of self-identification. Assisting these parallel quests are the two major influences upon this tense interaction: the community of Nature with its non-human individual selves and especially the Universal Community with its Pedagogue-Spirit of interpretation.

THE MOTIVES AND PROBLEMS OF
THE CENTRAL ETHICAL QUESTION

Having refined the central question of ethics into "Who and what is the Self?" Royce needed to interpret it analytically. He pursued this by using his empirico-historical method. His aim was to extract answers to three questions: (1) What psychological motives lead us to raise the central problem? (2) What subordinate problems are revealed by these motives? and (3) To which ethical values do these psychological motives point?[5]

His analytic interpretation thereupon unearthed the human aspirations for freedom, for the better, and for a dutiful response within a harmonious community. These longings motivated the central question of the Self. But Royce found that these psychological motives are

> [strangely conflictive and] lie at the basis of some of the most ancient of ethical tragedies. Dutifulness and independence of spirit, self-possession and anarchy, fidelity and helplessness, these are names for characters which, in some of their most striking contrasts and conflicts, appear now as virtues and now as vices,—traits which are interwoven in our nature so that their preciousness and their perils are as familiar as they are hard to estimate. We cannot live our moral life without them. But with them we can live only at the expense of inner and outer warfare, until we learn how to harmonize them.[6]

No moral life without these motives and the subordinate problems they generate. Yet the pressing need is somehow to harmonize them. Otherwise, the human self cannot confront its central self-identification problem in a balanced way.[7] A closer study, then, of this start of Royce's empirico-historical method seems in order.

First, when the human self directly experiences its central question, "Who and what am I?" it feels its freedom to ask or not to ask, to focus upon its "who" or "what," or upon its "am," or "was" or "will be." In this way a person finds the inwardly felt freedom energizing the self yet also feels self-constricted by its temporal flow, time-span, social constraints, and its own limited powers. Individually it asks, "In what sense can I, if at all, direct my life?" and "When directing my life in this sense, what kind of initiating yet limited self am I?" One discovers that one's life course is only partly under one's control. In other words, one finds the double truth that one is "master of one's fate" but also caught within the forces of fortune. In this way the human self is challenged to discover by interpretation that humble, liberating truth which lies between the dangerous horns of the basic but exaggerated human dilemma: either complete determinism or complete freedom.

Royce generalizes this first puzzlement as "the problem of the sense in which man can be, if in any sense he truly can be, the director of his own life plan, the captain of his own soul."[8] He called this mixture of felt freedom and constriction "Henley's Problem," after the author of the then-popular lyric poem, "Invictus."[9]

A second motive (interest or concern) that Royce found at work when one asks the central question of ethics was the human self's desire for the good, for the better. Individually a self asks, "Can I attain my true good? And if so, in what sense?" Royce called this "Everyman's Problem." As generalized, this problem asks wherein lies the genuine human good, whether the human self can attain it, and if so, in what sense.[10] Whether asked objectively or subjectively, Everyman's Problem challenges the human self. Objectively, can the human good be found in amoral values alone or must it include moral character and growth? Subjectively, which fundamental attitude alone leads to the true human good—individualistic self-assertion, or individualistic resignation and withdrawal from the world, or a whole-hearted commitment to the universe?

A third basic motive that Royce found at work in the human self was an urgent demand or inescapable call to respond to this desire for the good. One feels a central "ought" or duty. This is the most puzzling of the three motives. Royce concretized it in terms of the rebellious individual who accepts his interests in freedom and goodness but is puzzled by this other motive which suggests an "obligation to follow some will not my own, to obey, to be bound by laws which are not of my own making?"[11] He called it the "Problem of Emerson's Youth" because of Emerson's subtle description of a youth's positive response to the whisper of duty despite the surrounding clamorous voices of pleasure, success, and power.[12]

Generalized to an impersonal level, this problem became: How can a self be a genuine person if also under obligation? Or again, if a human self wants to move freely in certain ways but finds itself duty-bound to move in other directions, what kind of conflictive (estranged) self is being revealed? Commenting that "Emerson himself knew of no conflict between the solution of Henley's problem and the nearness of God to man (which inspired the Youth's answer to Duty,)" Royce uncovered the superpersonal dimension of this third basic problem. Does duty call the human self to respond not only to its own internal meaning and the legitimate calls of society and nature, but also to a divine pedagogy and directive?

ROYCE IDENTIFIES ETHICS'
THREE PRINCIPAL LEADING IDEAS

Since these three psychological motives and their problems reveal cognitive content, Royce detected in them the structures that were directing these motives and problems: namely freedom, goodness, and duty.[13] His emphasis fell on the need of forming a balanced synthesis of these three ideas within the central idea of a genuinely loyal Self who was authentically free, ethically healthy, and fittingly responsible.[14] Specifically, these were:

First, guided by the idea of finite self-direction (or limited autonomy), the human self freely originates the choice of its own cause and, according to its consequent plan of life, directs itself to serve that cause. Without this initiative the self cannot be moral. Some of the limits it experiences, however, lie in its social and timeful relations. Furthermore, it experiences felt tendencies to wholly independent initiatives, without regard for others and for the significance of its own past and future. It also experiences tendencies to withdraw from others, from its temporal nature, and even from its truest self. All these estranging tendencies call the self to emphasize a stronger desire for the good and more steadfast fulfillment of duty. It can, however, effect this balanced synthesis of the three ideas only by being healed and reconciled through the influences offered by a genuine community and its mediators. Royce's two other leading ethical ideas, then, permeate the human self's free self-direction and form a living synthesis with it.

Secondly, enlightened by the idea of the good, one asks, "Does the good lie in the bondedness of the human self to genuine community?" "Can a human self attain the good by itself alone?" "How do happiness and pleasure, unhappiness and pain relate to the true human good?" Royce held that one can discover the true human good only by intelligently committing oneself in loyalty to a genuine community. Thus the genuineness of the human good is doubly conditioned. It must be pursued freely according to one's unique self-direction. That is, it may not be determined either by convention alone or simply by some abstract mathematically balanced calculation of pleasures and pains. Secondly, the human good needs to flower out of the deep root of truth and the straight stock of fairness—that is, out of fulfilling one's call and duty—rather than to arise merely out of some experts' estimate of the "greater good of the greater number."

The mature Royce's criticism of utilitarianism made this clear. In his third lecture, Royce contrasted Bentham's utilitarian creed against Aristotle's nuanced view of that happiness which is the good proper to the human self:

> Happiness depends upon what Aristotle called a certain harmonious activity of the whole nature of the happy man [and] . . . also depends in part upon social conditions [so that he] . . . who has no social order, no ties, no city state in which he feels at home . . . cannot, in Aristotle's opinion, be happy.[15]

By contrast, added Royce, the more one studies Bentham's simplified doctrine of a human good that can be legislated, the more one finds it "increasingly in-applicable" to current socio-economic conditions. For the more one is guided by a comparison of these two views, the more one realizes that Bentham's "greatest sum of pleasures for the greatest number of individuals . . . becomes less and less an adequate definition of that good which a wise man most reasonably pursues."[16] Thus, because of its inadequate emphasis on freedom and duty, Royce found the utilitarian principle a weak guide for finding the proper human good.

Thirdly, human selves experience the idea of duty through their sense of moral obligation. The mature Royce retained much of Kant's view that moral obligation characterizes any finite rational agent. Royce's experiential bent, however, clad duty in a more human dress, as "primarily an idea of helpfulness to those whom we love."[17] For him duty calls for a free fidelity to one's unique internal meaning, to one's set of chosen causes, to one's series of human communities, and to solidarity with the whole human family. For the latter urgently needs a "new wise provincialism" to withstand the attitudes, practices, and institutions of larger societies that collectivize and standardize the smaller communities of the human family. Only by a dutiful respect for the unique individuality of these "provinces" can the human good be approached effectively. And it is towards this vision of the good that Royce's multi-faceted ideas of duty and freedom are directed, thanks to the exigent call and influence of the Spirit-Interpreter of the Universal Community.

In sum, then, Royce started ethics from its central question, "Who and what is the Self?" In it and its connected subordinate questions, he identified the interests and problems experienced psychologically by the human self who asks these questions. Within them he found the "three leading ethical ideas." Empowered by them, he began to catch sight in his final year of some key ethical insights—some of secondary magnitude, and others of still greater significance.

SECOND MAGNITUDE INSIGHTS

By 1915 Royce was placing noticeable emphasis on that basic community reality: the *family*. His own experience of family, especially during his final decade of familial suffering and tragedy, intensified his appreciation of how central to his late ethics of loyalty was the family community.

As we saw, Royce's centering upon the family became noticeable in 1901. He had then pictured a madonna and child as the vital center and goal of the whole evolutionary process. Other humans and societies, non-human animals and the plants, and all nature have evolved in concentric circles of supportive and protective presence around this central family pair. Then in 1907, Royce's Urbana Lectures and Lowell Lectures took notice of family re-lationships. In the *Problem*, studying the biblical story of Jacob's family with a detail that on first reading may seem excessive, Royce centered his attention on the familial estrangement and reconciliation of Joseph and his brothers.[18] After 1913 Royce's focus on family became far more evident, particularly in *War and Insurance* and in his Last Lectures on Metaphysics. He used his theory of a "community of interpretation" to allow father, mother, and child to play the role of mediator serially. He used the family's three basic relationships to identify three species of loyalty.[19] In his final year, Royce saw the family as the original community, the formative crucible, and the basic symbol of ethical life—in its ups and downs as well as in its central relationships.

By 1916 the role of family in ethical life had fostered Royce's "supersexual insight," as he called it.[20] Describing the kind of loyalty proper to siblings, Royce found that Sophocles "suggests to us the ideal human being" in his tragedy, *Antigone*. This Greek heroine, moving in "her world of the patriarchal family and of the gods of the underworld," showed "the wisdom of Athene . . . [and] the weakness of a mortal woman." Her Hellenic culture subordinated woman to man in a "dangerous pair relationship" and did "not encourage a woman to assert herself." Yet against the command of her uncle the king, Antigone personally buried her brother slain in a battle against the king. Clinging rather to the gods' eternal law that required her to bury her brother, Antigone displayed a feminine compassion for her brother, a masculine independence from the king, and a religious fidelity toward the gods. In Antigone's choice to bury her brother and to endure bodily death as punishment from the king, Royce found in her an ideal synthesis of the masculine and feminine traits, charged with sexual energy, yet ranking with the angels in her moral excellence. As he put it:

> Antigone, in her realm of tragedy, suggests to us the ideal human being—that being who is neither man alone nor woman alone, and still less a neutral being devoid of sex, but a being of angelic rank, above the level that divides man and woman, and that makes them a Dangerous Pair, mediating their contrasts and opposition, artistically justifying their very blindness, and their vanity, showing us what, Ideally speaking, human nature might be intended to be, were it not for the division of the sexes, and what the angels of light might be, in a world where they are neither married nor given in marriage.[21]

Antigone's embodied integration of the strengths of man and woman and her living synthesis of independence, goodness, and duty in a wise, wholehearted, religious loyalty signaled what human selves can and should become.

Secondly, in his final years Royce used the term *solidarity* with increasing frequency.[22] He did so to point up how concretely rich and thick communal life really is and how intact it must remain. Perhaps his growing conviction about and practice of close-bondedness in family led him to stress solidarity within and between all communities.

One instance of this arose in his increasing insistence on the need for a "new and wise provincialism," distinctive of each region and able to withstand the trends to mass culture and centralization.[23] A second instance lay in Royce's increasing emphasis on the "cult of the dead," a bonding with the community of those now gone who have supported us by care, love, example, and wisdom.[24] A final instance of solidarity appeared in Royce's plan for a mutual international reinsurance against war and other tragedies.[25] Individual nations have already supported private insurance corporations against unexpected risks and losses—that is, reinsured them. As a next step, a neutral international treaty company could be formed, financed at first by the indemnity payments from the war and then by the premium of participating countries (large and small, victors and vanquished). This international company would offer subsidiary help to nations that meet unexpected risks and losses arising from natural calamities, economic crises, and future war. This reinsurance company, directed by a neutral international board, would exercise a preponderant peace-keeping effect. As Royce insisted, "There can be no true international life unless the nations remain to possess it."[26] Here, again, Royce insisted that just as each solidaristic community requires its uniquely individual members, so too at the higher level, the international family requires its member-nations that are "wise provinces," each with its own unique solidarity and cooperation. Towards securing this, Royce esteemed political means as less important than business, science, and art—especially the social arts—and genuine loyalty, or Pauline charity, as most important.[27]

Thirdly, from 1914 onwards, Royce focused on and purified the notion of *mediation* or agency.[28] He saw how indispensably and fruitfully mediation works in corporate institutions (including businesses and the church). So he stated his radical conviction, "Without some form of institution that embodies such offices [of mediation or agency] civilization could not exist."[29] He distinguished between adversarial and non-adversarial forms of mediation, which he called, respectively, its "forensic" and "non-forensic" forms. He saw that the "best forms of mediation in the practical world are not forensic [adversarial, but those processes which] . . . prevent disputes from arising"(9).

Preferring Peirce's non-adversarial triadic community of interpretation as more general than the inherently hostile dialectic of Hegel and Marx, Royce gained a position that would forestall the rise of quarrels (11). To do so he criticized that basically adversarial ("forensic") form of the idea of mediation which is popular in everyday life, traditional in most theologies, and distinctive of the philosophies of Hegel and Marx. The aversion or even hostility in their "dangerous dyads" enters the mediator relationship as an addition or accident and reveals its moral weakness.

Instead, taught Royce, emphasize as primary the cooperative (non-forensic) form of mediation. Insist that each member of a triadic community of interpretation possess a positive "will to interpret. . . [and] to promote unity." Call its mediator to his proper role of empathetic and creative leadership. Loving loyalty calls for such discipline in community members.

Accordingly, Royce was led to conclude, "I believe that we are only beginning to realize what type of mediation promises most for the future both of philosophy and of the social order" (11). In the mature Royce, then, mediation involves elements of the Art of Loyalty, union with a superhuman Spirit of interpretation, and the distinctive marks of play, hospitality, and the Peircean intent of *Uberty* in reasoning. The latter requires that the mediator search persistently for a unifying interpretation that further exalts "beauty, duty, or truth."

Two of Royce's applications of this transformed and purified notion of mediation deserve notice. He applied his non-forensic form of mediation to the philosophy of religion. Here Royce removed the hindering image of the "hostile divine One." Traditionally, most theologies have used forensic mediation to explain the phrase that describes Christ as "Mediator between God and man."[30] So following St. Anselm, they had tended to present God as irritated and angered by our human disobedience and thus in need of being appeased.[31] Many theologians assumed, then, that to think about the mystery of redemption they had to view God as needing to be placated, as, in short, the "hostile One." Yet not all redemptive theologies fell into the bizarre popular extremes of turning Christ as Mediator into a substitute victim (of a punitive King) or a sin-laden scapegoat. Even the more restrained theologies of redemption, however, frequently still employed a notion of forensic mediation that forced them to perceive God as the hostile One.[32]

Royce saw the current pressing need, then, to use a non-forensic version of mediation to explicate *redemption*. To start talk about redemption by saying sin had made people into God's enemies only too easily makes people think of God as offended or even hostile toward sinful human selves. Upon reflection, one can detect how anthropomorphism oppresses this view of God. Not many people, however, take time enough to reflect accurately that from their sense of guilt as sinners they are projecting upon God a hostile attitude toward themselves. Nothing is more human; nothing more misleading regarding God. Thus the warped image of a hostile God damages their relation with the mysterious holy One.

On the other hand, if the Interpreter-Spirit of the Universal Community is really a Spirit of loving loyalty toward human selves, she can never be other than understanding, patient, and ever-merciful toward human sinners. All throughout human history, she can only be inviting sinners to convert into ways more open to further union or reunion. From her side, no adversarial relation can exist. Thus from the human side, there really is no war, only a misperception of the Holy Spirit as the hostile Other.[33] If people become genuinely loyal, however, they will instead fashion a fitting response to the friendly divine Spirit by an "unearthly confidence" which, with radical trust, "leaves to what it calls God the art of making the great triumph."[34] To me this Roycean application of his purified notion of mediation to the philosophy of religion seems particularly fruitful.

Royce also applied this non-forensic notion of mediator to those who animate the business world's morally sound "communities of interpretation." He identified a threefold criterion for testing the moral soundness of various economic investments (10–12, 29–35).[35] In brief, he asked whether bankers and other investors (1) desire to continue a successful business enterprise more than maximizing profits; (2) prefer the functional common good of their community of interests over their individual advantages; and (3) really intend that their investments somehow benefit materially every member of the human family. That is, does this realistic catholic intent prevail over the frequent tendency to restrict their benefits to a closed group, such as stockholders, a family firm, one's nation, or a bloc of nations? Since a closer look at this "new moral idea" about investment ethics seems needed, we will first look with Royce at the moral climate found in the banking and investment industry, then describe his "moral idea" of investment, and finally close with an evaluation.

The importance of the banker (investor) as mediator lies in his being the intermediary "third" between lender and borrower. Thus the banker elevates the usual one-to-one social interactions which, as dyads, are fraught with many blindnesses and accidents. Many passions darken persons' dyadic relationships. These often become tense or even hostile simply by the efforts of one or both members to make clear how their individual attitudes and intents differ. Such dyadic relations "constitute what one may call the original sin of man the social animal" (20). Royce found this the basis of the "lost state of natural man." He found that "Kant once well characterized [it] by saying that an individual man can by nature neither abide the presence of his fellow man, nor yet do without him."[36] Royce clarified:

> In any case man may be defined as the animal who, being rational needs to understand his mate, but who, in his dual social relations fails to understand. The greatest evil of human social life lies not in the elemental greed, the selfishness of men, but in their failure to understand one another. Remember your own controversies and estrangements—the tragic failures of your own life as friend, as winner of your fellowman's confidence, if you wish to understand to what I here refer. (20)

In contrast to these negative spirits, Royce believed that the modern mind has penetrated to a new moral insight. Unlike the ancient and medieval mind that said loaning on interest was usurious, the modern mind has detected interest-bearing loans as just. Modern banking and insurance have partially expressed these motives but ethicists have only imperfectly studied "the source of their moral importance as elevating and ennobling influences in human life" (26). The modern mind thus shows working in it "certain moral motives, certain springs of action" (27). Disclaiming any technical expertise in banking and insurance, Royce viewed "these newer social motives" as "amongst the best of our guides" and called Americans to grasp them more adequately since they "may help us to know the moral core . . . of the civilization in which these modern forms of financial activity have found their place" (28).

Striving toward this more adequate grasp, Royce identified four moral insights that have arisen since the modern mind discovered that loaning money at interest within reasonable limits constitutes an ethical source of more money. The modern economy: (a) rests upon a system of credit that calls for real yet critical trust, (b) is animated by future prospects and a pioneering spirit, (c) is held together by the mutual moral commitments it requires (e.g., promises and contracts), and (d) is propelled by the hopes of future profit and of enhancing the lives of many people (28–30). Yet all these moral relationships of trust, hope, promise, and commitment are likely to be *misused* because all human selves are so deeply tainted with the "original sin" described above (31). Hence, the work of the commercial or financial "agent," as the wise spirit of the economic community, is:

> to make this community of three [lender-investor, borrower-recipient, and banker] act, in certain respects as if it were one man. It is therefore not merely his principal [the lender-investor] whom the agent serves. He serves the threefold personality of his community. For only through such service can he hold this community together. And unless he holds this community of three together, he cannot accomplish the purpose of his principal, nor yet succeed as an agent. He does not merely live in his little community of three. He is the inspirer and creator of its own life and of its unity. (22–23)

To these generalities of business ethics the mature Royce added some new specifics. He identified the "spirit of the [modern economic] community" with the

> moral idea which has most informed the modern system of credit, which has also done most to hold great masses of investors and of producers together, and which has thus rendered the loaning of money at interest not only a legitimate but a constantly advancing function of modern business. (28–29)

This idea requires that a triadic relation be created by inserting a financial mediator (e.g., a banker) into the so easily alienated dyadic relationship between lender and borrower. Furthermore, it requires that this mediating agent inspire and create the following interests in his or her triadic community:

> that neither the borrower nor the lender shall, when the day of reckoning comes, regret the loan, but that both of them shall desire to continue, through the banker's aid and under his advice, similar transactions. . . . In this community the greed that deceives or despoils may indeed continue to exist; but it will have no necessary place. It will at least tend to disappear [because of, e.g., the banker's role as guide and advisor]. (32)

In brief, the agent's interest that is most vital in the modern system of credit is not the maximization of profit but the enduring satisfaction of borrower and lender so that they continue their transactions. For this latter purpose, he must prevent both lender and borrower from regretting the loan already made and he must animate them, through his aid and advice as a banker, to keep initiating similar transactions in the future. In this way the banker, as "spirit of the [economic] community," will actually tend to reduce the dangerous dyads of "original sin"—expressed in economic shortsightedness, greed, and cheating.

Royce's "new moral idea" deserves scrutiny. We first examine a banker's community; then apply this idea to any moral community. Let the banker's community be symbolized thus:

A = Lender; B = Banker; C = Borrower. (See figure 2.)

Figure 2

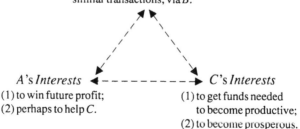

B's Interests
(1) to avoid future regrets in A, B, and C;
(2) to evoke A and C to desire to continue similar transactions, via B.

A's Interests
(1) to win future profit;
(2) perhaps to help C.

C's Interests
(1) to get funds needed to become productive;
(2) to become prosperous.

One needs to notice that all these interests, hopes, promises, and prospects are likely to be misunderstood or misused by one or more of the three members. Yet A, B, and C are each interested in a successful outcome of their interaction. This intent forms their *basic common interest* which mediates between any of their misleading ideas, attitudes, or practices, encourages a self-corrective critique within their interpretive process, and draws them into a unity of shared life and activity.

When evaluating this "new moral idea," late twentieth-century business ethicists might wish more detail. Just how does Royce's community of interpretation, animated by its mediating "banker," distinguish between honest profit making and greed? Just how would such a community and its "spirit" reduce the moral deviancies of business people? Such needed insistence on detail, however, can blind critics from seeing the fecund triad of lights within Royce's "new moral idea."

First, he showed how timefulness was relevant to business endeavors. That is, he clarified how important his notions of "community of memory" and "community of hope" are for any business enterprise. The financial officer must create and inspire—in himself and in the other two members of his business community—both an interest in expecting a happy memory of their mutually sustained risks and benefits, and also an expectation of continuing the "constantly advancing" satisfaction and success of this community into the future indefinitely.

Second, this satisfaction and successful profit making must be "universal." That is, beyond its three immediate participants (say stockholders, producers, and bankers), it must also somehow benefit every member of the Great Community of humankind. For Royce's norm of genuine loyalty demands that its every deed enhance effectively, even if slightly, the living situation of the whole human family. Concretely, if the business community restricted its benefits to an enclosed group only, it would turn itself into a "community of hate" towards the rest of humankind.[37]

Third, Royce has defined these participants' community of interests in terms of a dynamic common good that grows through the members' functional union of interests. Beyond these three "lights" in his "moral insight," moreover, there is the symbolic value of Royce's economic community of interpretation, which sets a model for the moral life of a responsible self.[38]

FIRST MAGNITUDE INSIGHTS

Climbing beyond the nearer range of Royce's three secondary insights, we now find rising before us, the main range of Royce's most mature ethics. There I discern four pinnacles that arose after Royce wrote the *Problem*: (1) he synthesized ethics' "three principal ideas"; (2) he recognized three kinds of genuine loyalty within humankind's three, family-based, interpersonal relationships; (3) he pioneered in creating "an ethics of the fitting";

and (4) he explicated genuine hope as an indispensable dynamic within true loyalty.[39]

Concerning his first major achievement, Royce identified and synthesized in 1915 three principal ideas in ethics. He did so by using the integrative power of loyalty when he told his students:

> Loyalty, as you remember, is an effort to bring into union, into a sort of synthesis and cooperation, the three leading ethical ideas: the idea of independence, the idea of the good, and the idea of duty.[40]

By 1915 Royce was very familiar with the history of ethical thought-systems. From them he extracted "three leading ethical ideas," around which he chose to organize his 1915–16 Extension Course on Ethics. The autonomous free initiation of ethical choices, primarily from one's own unique personhood expressed the idea of independence or free self-direction. The generally successful quest for becoming humanly happier revealed our meaning of the good. And if one accepted the equality and diversity intrinsic to any human community (as well as its consequent bonds of mutuality, justice, and other exigencies that the linkage of members and communities requires), then he or she lives under duty or obligation.[41] In what became his final quest in ethics, Royce used the interpretive process in order to weave together these leading ethical ideas of personal freedom, happiness, and duty. He braided them so artfully that their synthesis worked a major transformation of his mature ethics, giving it a new symmetry and far more nuance.

In Royce's second major insight, we discover three fundamental kinds of genuine loyalty identified by Royce in 1915. Even after publishing the *Problem*, he kept interpreting loyalty and disloyalty ever more profoundly. Attracted to the family as humankind's most basic community and guided by his three leading ethical ideas, Royce zeroed in on the family's three most basic relationships: those between siblings; between friends, spouses, or lovers; and between parent and child. He recognized further that, as healthy or estranged, these relationships deeply affect the other forms of communal life.

Discerning three forms of estrangement that endanger these three relations, he named them "(1) the lovers' quarrel, (2) the fraternal strife, (3) the conflict of the successive generations."[42] Pair relationships, though seemingly wholesome, contain a "dangerous dyad" that causes alienation or even tragic hostility.[43]

In general, then, if someone fittingly emphasized that particular "leading ethical idea" most characteristic of the particular relationship in question, then the distinctive type of fundamental loyalty proper to the particular relationship would arise. Hence, to deal insightfully and remedially with these three family relations, Royce needed to identify which leading ethical idea should be emphasized most in each case. Without violating his central synthesis of the three principal ethical ideas, he would in a particular instance focus on one idea while allowing the other two ideas to play their indispensable, and in this instance less central, role. Thus each idea would in its turn nourish a distinct kind of loyalty—one most suited for a particular basic family relation.

To be specific, in the case of siblings, each brother or sister is called to emphasize the other's equal freedom and autonomy, according to the first leading ethical idea.[44] If each sibling does so, increased union will arise— perhaps even reconciliation and a healing of a past alienation. If a brother or sister respects most of all the independence of the other sibling, both will enjoy physical and psychological "free space." Both need this if each one's self-development is not to be interfered with or diminished by one's sibling. Sibling-loyalty, then, respectfully creates the adequate "free space" needed by the other.

Secondly, Royce saw that the interpersonal bond between friends, spouses, or lovers centers primarily on the second leading ethical idea, goodness. Friends, spouses, and lovers fulfill their basic need when they share happiness continuously. Nevertheless, this kind of goodness can arise only if their love either grows constantly without estrangement or overcomes estrangements that arise. Studying this kind of goodness, Royce came to the conviction that if spousal love is to grow enduringly, it must, like joy, be "born a triplet." That is, since the goodness distinctive of friends, spouses, and lovers tends to be fruitful, these lovers must in some way tend to generate their kind of loving loyalty if they are to attain a happiness that perdures.

Finally, in the parent-child kind of loyalty, Royce saw the need for a primary emphasis on duty if successive generations are to be bonded together fittingly. Parents must transmit, and children need to receive, life in all its levels. Involved here is the communication of physical, affective, socio-cultural, intellectual, moral, and religious life, as well as a transmission of that refined wisdom which previous generations have purified from received traditions. Parents are called to hand on to the next generation all this life and wisdom, not only undiminished but hopefully enhanced. This requires in both the senders and receivers within each familial community of interpretation a clear recognition and faithful observance of each one's duties.

In brief, then, by 1916 Royce had worked out a significant development of his doctrine of loyalty and its art. His doctrine of loyalty now explicitly integrated three leading ethical ideas. He had found that each of these was a more suitable principal interpreter than the other two in loyalty's three specific kinds: sibling loyalty, friendship loyalty, and parent-child loyalty.

Royce's "ethics of the fitting," or *cathecontic* ethics, constitutes the third major peak in his most mature morality.[45] That is, to make the right ethical choice, one had to find by interpretation "the fitting thing" in the overall situation. As we saw, Royce insisted that for genuine ethical life his three leading ethical ideas had to be integrated appropriately. This kind of apt integration occupied more of his ethical heartland than did the pragmatic fittingness of the utilitarians—although theirs too had its place. Besides calculating consequences, the genuine loyalist also had to be effectively committed to the common good, to keeping promises faithfully, and to treating all persons respectfully and without manipulation.

Royce extended this norm of the fitting into other areas beyond both his apt synthesis of the three leading ethical ideas and his adequate balancing of practical consequences. A moral agent should make her present decision dovetail with both her chosen life-plan and her future hope.[46] As a thinker, she is to search for that question which next suited her inquiry.[47] Any "agent" in a secular community—of business, banking, insurance, legislation, or counselling, for example—has the duty of choosing what "fits" both her principal and her client.[48] Above all, any human self (X) who tries to relate ethically to another human self or selves (Z) within the processing context of an interpretive community (Y) should search for and be guided by a "third idea" that fits all three.

In the paradigmatic ethical situation just indicated, a similar interpretive "finding of the fitting" is needed to create and build a fundamental ethical relationship. X lives with her partly unique and partly shared memories, hopes, freedom, interests, and promises. So, too, do other selves (Z) live with their partly unique and partly shared memories, hopes, freedom, interests, and promises. The problem becomes how to unite these two without violating either. The interpretive process operating in their community (Y) leads towards a wise reasonableness that inserts self-correction. For this reason it tries to discern a "fitting" way either to overcome alienation between X and Z or to further unite them. Thus, only through the influence of the life and agency of this Community of Interpretation, will X's individual human self be led to *prefer what is better* for the whole community, for herself, and for the other members who comprise the communities involved—local, national, or global. This community's interpretive process operates through its language, customs, religion, discoveries, and hopes. Thus it leads the individual self X to find or invent that mediating "third idea" which fits in better with the long-range consequences. While leaving the personal decision making to X's own autonomy, the communal process calls her to this mode of action rather than any other.

Bold hope emerges as the fourth and final peak in Royce's most mature ethical growth.[49] He experienced it during his final dark years and expressed it especially in his *Hope of the Great Community* (1916). Here within genuine loyalty he identified foundational hope as an affect indispensable for ethical life. Basic pessimism stifles such hope. Popular "ethical individualism" with its disregard of the universal common good overwhelms such hope. Royce's decades-long struggle against these two "spoilers of mankind" reached fruition in his *Hope of the Great Community*. Here, as if sketching a lofty pinnacle in the Sierra, he first identified the massive bulk of genuine hope. Above this he limned the highland-like attitudes leading to a symmetrical peak. Thereupon, in the rich soils of human life he traced out the rugged base that sustains this kind of hope.

Like a mountainous bulk that sustains crest upon crest, the core of Royce's critically honed hope supports that other hope which must operate in his "communities of expectation."[50] Nevertheless, because attached to the Spirit's immortal and dynamically most central intent, Royce's basic hope lies in human selves' commitment to the ideal of the Universal Community. This ideal has "to do not merely with the sentimental and romantic aspirations of humanity,"[51] but with the basic intent of the Spirit of the Universal Community. Human selves' commitment to this ideal rests on an "unearthly confidence that, beyond all sorrow, all shall be, for the dutiful, somehow good."[52] Thus Royce's animating hope lifts up the heart in a way that only genuine loyalty can. It relies ultimately on the love, direction, and pedagogy of the Spirit-Interpreter of the Universal Community.

Roycean commitment to this ideal opens up a middle path, whereby one escapes both from radical pessimism and from the corrosive forms of ethical individualism. Lacking this commitment, some Americans caught today in consumerism and a merely functional existence reveal faces etched with pessimism.[53] Or, at the other extreme, ethical individualists seek their own personal or collective aggrandizement so impetuously or shrewdly that they kill genuine hope in others and even in themselves.[54]

In contrast to these affective attitudes, Royce positively delineated a third attitude: the kind of hope that fits genuine loyalty. It is found only in the genuinely loyal, for they alone have been ethically and religiously transformed by their commitment. Royce described them as persons who "walk not after the flesh, but after the spirit" of the Universal Community, and who live by genuine Pauline charity.[55] They form that consciously unified community which alone can offer salvation to distracted humanity and to alienated individuals.

Upon the massive bulk of this mountain rose the many highlands and crests heading towards the peak of Roycean hope and assuring its balance. These included a sense of fallibility, a contrast of humility and humor, a critical wisdom, and a whole-hearted practical commitment to further promote the coming of the Universal Community. Roycean hope clearly did not rest on any Polyannaish daydream that humankind's Great Community would inevitably be realized or even that our human race would surely survive on this planet. He clearly foresaw, among other future possibilities, that unchecked destructive forces might extinguish the whole human race as completely as similar forces had rendered the saber-toothed tiger extinct (28). He also foresaw that some fanatic's dream of worldwide conquest—military, economic, religious, or other—would only lead to a "more or less universal community of hate" (53). Unlike many "pragmatists of the short range" who dodged talk of human death, ultimate tragedy, and nature's overwhelming calamities, but very much like William James's facing his own "going down in the wreck," Royce confronted head-on these dread issues that seem irredeemably hopeless.

He located the mountainous base of his central hope less in political structures and more in science, art, philosophy, and the humanities, in economics, ethics, and religion. Philosophically, Kant's third basic question, "What may we hope for?" impressed Royce deeply. So, too, did Kant's postulate of immortality as a requisite for any rational ethics. Convinced by these insights, the mature Royce held as a vital nerve of philosophical ethics that if justice were permanently wrecked here on earth, then human life would be utterly worthless and therefore at bottom hopeless.[56]

Besides this philosophical basis for hope, Royce found indispensable the vision of the Great Community proposed by our poets and prophets. Although political processes may supply some support for this hope (57), greater sustenance will come from the progress achieved during the nineteenth and twentieth centuries in art, industry, science, and social development (38–39). Humankind's slowly growing social arts foster this hope and fashion interpretations that fit pluralistic communities and selves. When agents in insurance, banking, counselling, and other forms of non-forensic mediation exercise these social arts, they promote humankind's Great Community by generating that "ideal significance" to which prophets and poets first awaken us (59). As an example of this secular stimulation of hope, Royce proposed, as wholly novel, the creation of an international board of trustees who would reinsure the nations' own insurance policies against war. The leaven-like effect of this board would gradually make all people aware of the Great Community of the future and thus increase their hope (69).

Beyond philosophical, scientific, cultural, economic, and some political warrants for his hope, Royce emphasized, above all, the ethico-religious basis for hope. As mentioned, the divine side of this basis lay in the love, direction, and pedagogy of the Spirit of the Universe. Its human side lay in "this salvation of a community through an human transformation that is universally significant" (35). Little wonder, then, that the mature Royce viewed such hope as supremely important. For the heart of this hope lies within that transformed life of loyalty, within some genuine community that promotes the Great Community, or as Royce sometimes called it, "the church universal" (33). Ethico-religious transformation (or "salvation") radiates from the Great

Community, which is missioned to hold the ideal of human community before the eyes of all people so that this vision keeps hope alive in human hearts struggling amid tragedy.

Besides this sketch of the massive bulk, the highland crests, and the deep base of Royce's mountain of hope, we find in some of his final deeds a concluding witness to what his basic hope prompts a person to do.[57] This hope energized Royce in his Tremont Temple and Lusitania addresses of 1914–1915. While Prussian troops invaded Belgium without provocation and while German U-boats torpedoed innocents, his fellow Americans were still slumbering. So Royce proclaimed those prophetic, biblical, clarion-calls to the consciences of fellow citizens. He hoped in an operative Community of Interpretation which would be embodied in an "International Mutual Insurance Corporation."[58] His strong hope led him, in the face of many objections but with the support of financial experts, to publish his plan for the reinsurance of the nations against war.[59] At his sixtieth birthday celebration in December 1915, Royce confidently closed his autobiographical sketch with a quote from Swinburne's hopefilled "Watchman, What of the Night?"[60] Finally, Royce counterbalanced his frustration and grief over the war with his final collection of essays, appropriately entitled, *The Hope of the Great Community*.

In summary, then, of Royce's ethical insights of the first magnitude, we glimpse four pinnacles of Royce's most mature development in ethics. He integrated a triad of three principal ethical ideas. He identified three kinds of genuine loyalty. He pioneered in developing an "ethics of the fitting." He both taught and practiced that bold hope which is the inseparable companion of genuine loyalty.

11. Some Dialogue-Partners Forming Royce's Mature Ethics

The recently discovered Royce family correspondence reveals Josiah during his final decade in the midst of domestic problems and tragedies. He stood steadfastly encouraging, surprisingly hopeful, and domestically intimate. This unexpected evidence unveils a powerful influence that purified, deepened, and nuanced Royce's mature ethics. Here, however, we examine some philosphical influences upon his late moral thought—some of which may surprise many Royce scholars and historians of philosophy.

Royce's senior by almost fourteen years was William James. For thirty-five years these two intellectual giants interacted in an ever-deepening friendship, marked by interchange of ideas and growing philosophical opposition yet also by an increasing mutual respect. Hence, students of Royce have emphasized the dominant presence of William James as a major dialogue-partner in forming Royce's mind. Few of them, however, portray this influence as peaking after James's death in 1910. These students recognize, moreover, that in his final years Royce's growing insight into the method and basic "simple ideas" of Charles Sanders Peirce transformed Royce's thought after mid-1912. Some of them are even beginning to take into account the effect which this Peircean transformation worked upon Royce's late ethics of loyalty.[1]

Most Roycean scholars, however, have not pointed out that the Apostle Paul exercised a presence in Royce's late ethics as strong and transformative as that of Peirce. This oversight is all the more surprising when one recalls that the late Royce claimed to be a "Christian metaphysician" who highly treasured St. Paul.[2]

Royce acknowledged the thinkers to whom he was indebted and often indicated the degree of his indebtedness.[3] Royce's testimonies are often confirmed by scholars who have studied him in depth. These indices allow one to estimate which thinkers have influenced Royce's philosophical growth with varying degrees of impact. Guided by these signs and my own experience, then, I venture to construct the following table to indicate—albeit tentatively—the degree of impact which great thinkers exerted upon the *mature* Royce.[4] Except for Peirce and Russell, I place in a separate division the logicians and philosophers of science with whom Royce was in dialogue at various times in his life.[5] Similarly, I indicate in another sperate division the chief religious writers, literary figures, and musicians who deeply enriched Royce's psyche.[6]

How much Royce's own genius accounted for his mature creations needs to be placed on the opposite pan of the scales. If this is done, I surmise that the tip of the balance will favor Royce's originality. Table 1 presents Royce's dialogue-partners during his mature period and is based on how closely and deeply they affected him. The three columns attempt to identify who, beyond most logicians, were the maximal, who the major,[7] and who the simply significant members within that "community of interpretation" which formed the mature Royce's philosophical thought-world. Asterisks [*] indicate dialgue-partners somewhat surprising to some Royce scholars.

MAXIMAL	MAJOR	SIGNIFICANT
C. S. Peirce	1. Plato	Aquinas
the Apostle Paul*	2. Schopenhauer	Aristotle
William James	3. Fichte	Henri Bergson
Immanuel Kant	4. J. S. Mill	John Eckhart
	5. Hegel	Percy Gardner
	6. B. Russell	George Santayana
	7. Spinoza*	Ernst Troeltsch
	8. Nietzsche*	Wilhelm Wundt

The mature Royce increasingly practiced his "cult of the dead." By 1915 it included communing with such thinkers as Kant, Peirce, William James, as well as with the Apostle Paul, Spinoza, and Nietzsche. We begin our study, then, by examining briefly Royce's expected dialogue-partners—Kant, Peirce, and William James. Then we turn to investigate at greater length Royce's dialogue with partners unmentioned in most studies: the Apostle Paul, Spinoza, and Nietzsche. We conclude by focusing upon Royce's dialogue with life itself, a maximal influence upon him during his final years.

THE EXPECTED DIALOGUE-PARTNERS

Immanuel Kant

The mature Royce reinterpreted the three ethical postulates of freedom, immortality, and God, proposed by "old father Kant." Out of the unique "internal meaning" of each individual human self arose three radical Signs calling for interpretation. The first Sign, that of human *self-direction* (or rational freedom), arose from a human self's inmost initiative as guided in part by its common rational nature. Such autonomy was limited concretely by each self's past and future, by its societal conditions, by its biological base, and by its psychological time-span, ignorances, and habits.

To fulfill the human self's internal meaning, a second Sign was required, that of an *endless series of deeds*. The human self's time-form had to be unending because no purposeful finite will can ever carry out its inmost mission short of an infinity of deeds.[8]

Finally, hope of the Great Community characterized the internal meaning of each finite human self. For a saving *Interpreter Spirit* of the Universal Community mediates artistically the self's own interpretive processes and those of humankind. This Spirit, however, does not function primarily to restore the balance of the moral order by rewards and punishments, as does Kant's postulated deity. Instead, Royce's Interpreter Spirit restores the moral order primarily by reconciling atonement.

In these ways, then, the mature Royce had not forgotten the important role played by Kant's three postulates for integrating ethics. Yet to integrate his own ethics, Royce found three concrete Signs: self-direction, endless series, and Interpreter Spirit. He owed this discovery to his application of Peirce's doctrine of Signs to the three dynamisms that Royce experienced within the process of human ethical interpretation.

Charles Sanders Peirce

As indicated, Peirce's impact upon Royce in his final years was immense. Royce's most significant and gradually deepening insight into Peirce took place in 1912. In mid-1913, Royce received a "deeply prized" last letter from Peirce. In 1915–16, Royce spent many hours sifting through and studying Peirce's unpublished papers, which then lay piled about in his office in Emerson Hall. This gradual insight of 1912, the 1913 letter, and his later musings over the papers of Peirce exerted increasing influence upon Royce in 1915–16.

Little wonder, then, that in 1915 Royce employed Peirce's doctrines of interpretation and of Signs even more than he had done in the *Problem*.[10] The movement from doubt to belief in Peirce's process of inquiry also colored Royce's final reflections. So, too, did Peirce's fallibilism and tentativity.

Moreover, because of his deep prizing of Peirce's last letter to him, Royce came eventually to express a pair of ideas found in it: *Uberty* (or full-breasted richness) and *abduction* (or the rational discovery of an hypothesis). He found that Uberty—the mounting fullness of beauty, duty, and truth—constitutes that good which calls for the "progressive interpretation and progressive realization [of the community of humankind and of each member self in it]."[11]

In the letter of 1913, Peirce had also insisted that "the art of making explanatory hypotheses is the supreme branch of logic." This led Royce, I believe, to search for, and by abduction to find, an explanatory hypothesis that integrated ethical life in a novel way. Having identified the three most fundamental ethical ideas, he reached two hypotheses by abduction. First, integral ethical life lies in the practical synthesis of these three ideas. And second, the genesis of these ideas lies in the ongoing interpretive process of inquiry into the mysteries of the individual self and of its community.

William James

From the death of William James in 1910 to Royce's death in 1916, James's titanic shade hovered over Royce's mature reflections. During these six years, the pages of Royce's writings again and again reveal the figure of James arising like some haunting memory for Royce. This occurs in his articles and major works like *Sources* and the *Problem*, in his Berkeley Conferences of 1914, and in his final academic courses. Little else should reasonably be expected, however, since for thirty-five years Royce had known William James personally as his nearest philosophical dialogue-partner and as his closest friend beyond his own family.

When still a teenager, Royce had his first meeting with James in Cambridge.[12] Soon, at the Hopkins, Royce was impressed by James's visiting lecture on the radical role of instinct in psychic activity and on the purposive nature of ideas.[13] Thereafter, they interacted increasingly, exchanging ideas, criticisms, and encouragements as their friendship developed in the late 1870s and 1880s. In the 1890s the bond between them was strong enough to endure intense argument. For then, at the gate of one of their Irving Street homes, they would stand for hours exchanging views and probing each other's mind. All this shared life had to make William James part of Royce's soul and at least among the predominant dialogue-partners in Royce's late musings on ethics.

After James's death in September 1910, signs of his presence in Royce's thought and affection are far more numerous than those found in Royce's well-known addresses that honor and appraise James as a man and philosopher.[14] After 1910, in many of Royce's courses and writings, James served as a source of inspiration and opposition. For example, Royce's Philosophy of Religion course at Yale in 1910–11 compared and contrasted James's position with his own on many different aspects of religious experience and religion.[15] James's presence is dominant in both *Sources* and *Problem*, the major works that Royce produced after James's death. Similarly, James is present in many of Royce's lesser post-1910 writings, even where one would not at first expect James to appear.[16] Strangely enough, however, when in his "Nietzsche" article Royce offered his list of titanic ethical individualists, he did not include James in whom he had found even more "titanic features" than James's portrait-painter had reproduced.[17] Was it Royce's reverence for James's uniqueness that kept him from "classifying" his friend?

Despite the vast philosophical differences between these two intellectual giants, how did James affect Royce's late interpretation of ethical life? Which ideas did he adopt from James and which did he reject? A brief survey reveals the following identifiably Jamesian elements central to Royce's late ethics.

Royce noticed carefully how James's psychology of "the stream of consciousness" had deepened during the decades into a metaphysics of "radical empiricism." James's primal stuff of our universe was a profound, pre-articulated, forward flow of pure perceptual process. Something of a parallel lies in the late Royce's basic, forward-thrusting, hermeneutic process of the Universal Community of interpretation. Admittedly, Royce avoided the "irrational" or anti-intellectualist tone present in James's radical empiricism. The Logos-Spirit guided Royce's process of triadic interpretation towards an intelligible Universal Community. James's final considerations about the "interpenetration of consciousness" and the "compounding of a larger self" likely approached Royce's late view of a community of interpretation.[18] But James never accepted Paul's idea of "the Spirit in the church" with its consequent teleology of spirits and the basic structure of the processing universe that Royce advocated.

From James's *Principles*, the chapter on "Habit"—itself influenced by Peirce's idea of habit—exercised a great impact on Royce's theory of an individual self. For Royce's "psychic extensions" had to become habitual if his kind of human self were to develop any coherence and thus any sense of its own identity. Furthermore, Royce employed habit for human selves' mutual appropriation of common past or future events and deeds. By this mutual appropriation people united consciously and constructed a "community of memory" or a "community of hope." In addition, the constancies needed for reliable interpretation throughout the whole Roycean universe of interpretation echo James's and Peirce's stress on habit.

For James, instinct is the basis for whatever emerges into consciousness. As early as 1878 at the Johns Hopkins, young Royce had heard James lecture on instinctual responses arising from reflex arcs that link the senses and brain of an animal.[19] Upon this primacy of the instinctual, Royce built his empirico-historical method which he employed in both the *Sources* and the *Problem*. The role of instinct was also the basis for his memorable response to Arthur Lovejoy concerning the task of philosophers to plumb accurately the deep and meaningful popular mind.[20]

James's stress on the uniquely personal individual became one corner-stone for Royce's late ethics. It must be granted, however, that Royce felt a need to counterbalance this stress on the individual by emphasizing his own "second level" of reality—the community that James left in silence. Nonetheless, he agreed with James in insisting on the need for a personal decisiveness that had to deepen serially if one's genuine self were to be further individuated. In this way Royce concurred with James in his emphasis on genuine self-determination, even while he disagreed with certain Jamesians who exaggerated this tenet into excessive individualisms.[21] Moreover, when one studies these distortions of the individualization process, many parallels can be found between Royce's "detached individual" and James's "sick-souled self."

Royce's individual self shows a voluntarism that often reflects James's "Will to Believe." This will is found in Royce's postulates, in his final definition of loyalty, and in the role he assigns both to his modes of action and to his "three attitudes of will."

Finally, James's priority on subjectivity led Royce to escape a mere copy-theory of knowledge and to define an idea as an internal meaning seeking fulfillment. This became the radical starting point for Royce's *The World and the Individual*. In his final year, Royce gratefully recalled how James, as a visitor at John Hopkins University in 1878, had opened his lecture series with such words as these concerning the problem of knowledge:

> I call your attention to the fact that our minds are never engaged in merely copying objects. We are always reacting, responding, making over our world. It is our response to the world about us that constitutes our consciousness of it. And if you define the mind in terms of the responses in question, you will understand it better.[22]

The central thesis of pragmatism—that an idea is a subject's plan of action—arises from this priority on the subject. James's insight is indispensable for all forms of pragmatism, including Royce's. The "internal meaning" of his middle period is a plan of action, as is also the "will to interpret" of his final period. Royce's "absolute pragmatism," however, prevents any of these individual "plans of action" from being hermetically sealed off from each other. It calls for their "belonging" to the absolute life of the all-knowing Universal Community.

Nonetheless, despite this massive debt to James, Royce found that his own original insights forced him to resist James in many areas. Royce saw keenly, especially after 1913, that James's version of pragmatism was shortchanging Peirce's version of it. Royce was convinced that when James accepted an idea's "workings" of *any* kind, he distracted people from Peirce's more inventive kind of pragmatism. Peirce opened up people's minds to the world of possibilities by insisting on "working out" logically *all* the *"conceivable* consequences" of an idea (rather than merely the effects of the idea which were currently open to our experience).[23] Thus, because the Jamesian pragmatist was too eager to seize upon something found in present experience, he omitted and even foreclosed any discovery of the world's many "would-be's." Yet each member-self and its community of interpretation needed to consider these latter possibilities for wiser choices both in moral and other practical matters.

Royce exemplified this in-depth critique of James by focusing on the role of genuine deduction in an ethics of toleration.[24] Unlike the boring textbook examples of spurious deduction (wherein one concludes by pulling the cat out of the animal bag after having first put it there), genuine deduction exhibits amazing fecundity. Because James simply accepted belief or non-belief as the "working-out" of a certain idea or proposition, Royce criticized him for shortcircuiting the fecundity of Peircean deduction. Royce wrote:

> So long as it is supposed [as James and other popular pragmatists suppose] that the main purpose of deduction is to produce belief in the conclusions, the psychology of certain of the most important human thinking processes must be lost. . . . [For instance,] a great deal of toleration depends upon seeing how my opponent's conclusions are related to his premises, although I may have no belief either in his premises or in his conclusions. The process of deduction, in case of a practical deliberation concerning what it is best to do, helps us because we thereby learn in advance what *would* be the case *if* so and so were done, even if we ourselves have no tendency whatever as yet to decide in favor of the hypothetical course of procedure.[25]

Here Royce echoed Peirce's emphasis on *would-be's* to work out conceivable consequences in a fruitful way. He refused to focus simply upon some belief or non-belief that follows factually from some idea. For if preoccupied this way, one's mind would not discover the many other possible courses of action—perhaps far better ones—which Peirce and Royce strove to bring to awareness.

Royce also appreciated the "axiom of skipped intermediaries," found in James's *Principles*.[26] He often referred to it to illustrate deductive sequences. Nevertheless, Royce found James quite short on most of formal logic, particularly its recent advances into the "new logic." Thus James missed those unique truths which are absolute because any attempt to deny them reinstates them.[27]

As mentioned, James's radical empiricism finds some parallel in the future-facing interpretive process of Royce's community of interpretation. Nonetheless, Royce strenuously resisted James's use of radical empiricism to suggest that our knowledge of other minds arises mainly "by analogy."[28] This led into the Jamesian thesis that any religious experience occurring in a church had to be "conventional" and therefore shallow and insincere—an opinion that struck Royce as "a profound and a momentous error."[29] Royce knew that deep communal experience was the matrix of the religious energy at the heart of genuine loyalty.

James's pure individualism, mitigated neither by community nor by its Spirit, appalled Royce. He followed James's final developments towards sociality with expectation for he saw them leading eventually and unavoidably into a kind of communal consciousness that resembled Fechner's "compounding of consciousness."[30] James's death, however, cut short this growth and frustrated this hope in Royce. Yet, since behind this image of "compounding" lay James's pluralistic universe, Royce disagreed with the irrational ground and unstable tone of such a "community." In it Royce discerned a potentially non-convergible pluriverse that ultimately lacked both Logos-Spirit and intelligibility. James had borrowed the fluxing stream of Heraclitus without including the latter's ever-constant Logos. This Logos, transformed into the Logos-Spirit by the Apostle Paul, his fellow Christians, and Royce, operates through a "fluent quest" that gives unity, intelligibility, and general direction to the world.[31]

UNEXPECTED DIALOGUE-PARTNERS

The Apostle Paul

From his boyhood days in Grass Valley, Royce was familiar with St. Paul's letters. In his Berkeley writing of 1879, he used Paul as an example of a reformer.[32] In his article on Tolstoy's ethics (1893), Royce proposed Paul as a loyalist to an unseen moral order, as one reminding us of absolute moral demands and radiating the spirit of prophecy into moral discourse.[33] In his mid-fifties, when preparing for his philosophy of religion class at Yale, he "look[ed] up afresh Paul on the subject of spiritual gifts."[34] Royce soon brought Paul forward to front stage at the climax of his *Sources*.[35] A year later, his drafting of the *Problem* included many references to Paul's letters to the Corinthians, Ephesians, Romans, and Thessalonians, as well as to the Gospel of John. Royce also reported owing much to the English theologian, Percy Gardner, and to his studies of Paul, particularly to his latest work, *The Religious Experience of the Apostle Paul*.[36]

In his late fifties, then, Royce regarded Paul as a hero and highly esteemed many of his teachings. For instance, he spoke of the "eternally true teaching of St. Paul regarding spiritual gifts."[37] Regarding the essence of Pauline Christianity and the actual life of the Pauline churches, Royce judged that we have in the "Pauline epistles, information which is priceless, which reveals to us the religion of loyalty in its classic and universal form."[38]

For Royce this information was priceless because it put him and others in touch with the actual experience of some early Christian communities. The latter had felt and known the saving presence of the Logos-Spirit at work in their midst.[39] This experience revealed the universal form of any genuinely loyal community—a form constituted by the three "most essential Christian ideas" (community, sin, atonement) which were integrated by the more general idea of grace. Wherever such experience occurred, the essence of Pauline Christianity became manifest.

Royce inferred that a transformation of ethical ideas would follow if anyone reached an "adequate recognition of these simple considerations" concerning the information in Paul's letters and concerning the need to tread a middle path between orthodox and liberal Christianity.[40] Royce believed that, thanks to Paul and Peirce as well as to his own designs of the "logical and social approaches" to ethics, he had achieved this transvaluation of ethical values.

How, then, was the Apostle Paul present in this transformation? Alerted by Paul's governing figure of "the Body and its members enlivened by the Logos-Spirit,"[41] Royce prioritized community as his leading category and Spirit as his leading dynamism, even while maintaining emphasis on the uniquely individual member-selves.[42] In line with Paul's teaching,[43] Royce saw that both individuals and communities were burdened by their deafness to the divine Spirit and thus by inner and outer conflicts. This non-responsiveness to the Spirit turned people into "lost individuals" or even "traitors" and groups into "communities of hate."[44]

Nevertheless, both Paul and Royce viewed communities and individuals as called to a new life, as being raised up to graced life by the life-giving Spirit.[45] So a transformative process was at work whereby both communities and individuals became a "new creation."[46] This profound and cyclic passage "from dying to rising" reproduced serially the pattern of the master's Paschal mystery in each community and in every transformed member. It also revealed a new level of communal life in the Spirit. Through this passage one escaped from the captivity of merely conventional ethics and entered into genuine ethics.

Finding in Paul's letters the universal social form of the loyal community, Royce was led to focus upon the members' indispensable activities of interpretation, communication, and cooperation whereby the early Christians built up their "community of memory" and "community of hope."[47] In 1916 Royce tentatively identified the vital energy and integrating order of the unique individuals who constitute these loyal communities of interpretation:

> Possibly the law of heaven may be, as St. Paul maintained, the law of charity. But the order of heaven will then be the order of the concrete individuals whose

spiritual unity, with one another and with their Lord, the Apostle so eloquently characterizes.[48]

The charity-based unity of interpretive life relies upon the peculiar adaptation which the ideas of the Individual and the Community possess for interpreting each other. This unique adaptation grounds Royce's social and logical approaches to interpretive musement. Little doubt, then, that the central life of a Pauline community is charity (which includes faith and hope) and that such an integrating life-energy gave Royce the idea that in the ethical life self-reflective loyalty is the "form of all forms" and the source of love and justice.[49] Again in his final year, Royce wrote:

> In the general history of civilization, loyalty, which is identical with the practically effective love of communities as persons that represent mind on a level higher than that of the individual, is, like the Pauline charity (which is explicitly a love for the Church universal and for its spirit), the chief and the soul of the humanizing virtues—that virtue without which all the others are but "sounding brass or a tinkling cymbal."[50]

This charity-like loyalty empowers members with responsibility not only for promoting the interpretive process by mutual communication and cooperation, but also for reconciling estranged selves and channeling forgiveness to those who have grieved or stifled the Spirit of the community.[51]

The central activity that directs the life of the community of genuine loyalty is a discerning interpretation. The Pauline roots of discernment (or "testing the spirits") were plainly visible already in the Royce of 1899 who advised his fellow Americans to "prove all things . . . hold fast that which is good."[52] In *Sources* and the *Problem* his call for "discerning the spirits" became far more explicit.[53] To avoid misinterpretations, some lived union with the Spirit of the Universal Community is required. Such union with this Spirit (sometimes called "the Will to Interpret") requires that one grasp the ideals of interpretation both of the Universal Community and of God the Interpreter. Pointing up the consequent requirement to pray for the spiritual gift of interpretation, Royce went on:

> These ideals, however, are grasped and loved whenever one first learns fully to comprehend what Paul meant when he said: "Wherefore let him that speaketh with tongues pray that he may interpret." This word is but a small part of Paul's advice. But in germ it contains the whole meaning of the office, both of philosophy and of religion.[54]

This text may strike secularists as odd. Royce meant by it, however, that Spirit-guided interpretation is the vital source of responsible philosophy and religion. Furthermore, he meant that one must pray for the gift of discerning interpretation if one wants to be either authentically philosophical or religious.

When Paul says "Whatever you do, do all for the glory of God,"[55] and when the mature Royce recommends that each person use the test: "Does this [action, attitude, etc.] help towards the coming of the universal community?"[56] both teach an eschatology of the present moment. That is, both find in every deed, in every now, the central presence of the Logos-Spirit (or Absolute). This is the Eternal or present Ultimate (= *Eschaton*) with which each human choice is to be united and which every present choice should manifest.[57] As Royce had said in 1911, this Eschaton or Absolute is "the most pervasive and omnipresent and practical, as it is also the most inclusive of beings."[58]

The ethical teachings of Paul and Royce are often strikingly parallel. Paul models one who "runs the race, fights the good fight, holds the faith."[59] Royce insists on striving for ethical growth. Paul requires labor of those who would eat and Royce predicts woe "to those at ease in Zion." Like Paul, Royce insists that without wholehearted works, any divinely initiated faith is vain.[60] Like Paul recommending patient endurance, Royce lived and taught the importance of such courage as shows itself distinctively in finding a religious mission within sorrows and in bearing them patiently.[61] Like Paul recommending that his Roman Christians work for peace, so Royce aimed at preventing future war through his late works on insurance and reinsurance.[62] Like Paul, insisting with his Corinthians on the need for order in their community, Royce stressed how indispensable order was to community life. He challenged Americans who instinctively oppose "big corporations" without weighing the goods and services these generate. Instead, Royce saw these institutions as the mixed goods they are and, like Paul, insisted on fitting obedience to those in positions of authority for the sake of good order.[63]

These parallels, then, and likely many others, show that the mature Royce often re-read the Apostle Paul and reflected profoundly on his insights. Thus he let Paul play as prominent a role in his late interpretive musements as did Peirce and James.[64]

Benedict Spinoza

In his introduction to Royce's writings on logic and methodology, John J. McDermott notes insightfully:

> The persistence of this problem in the thought of Royce [of reconciling free finite individuals with the Absolute] is an indication that his early fascination with Spinoza left its mark, perhaps more extensively than that left by the work of Hegel.[65]

McDermott's remark may surprise those who classify Royce as a Hegelian. It calls for someone to inventory the cues Royce took in from Spinoza and

Hegel, as a basis for comparison. Here we can only briefly survey Spinoza's impact on Royce.

After twenty-year-old Royce had studied Spinoza's work in its Latin original, he offered two addresses on Spinoza at the Johns Hopkins and soon described Spinoza's work as "one of the profoundest of the products of the human intellect."[66] In *The Spirit of Modern Philosophy* Royce showed originality by starting the story, not from the *cogito* of Descartes, but from Spinoza. He identified the latter as "the man who was in many respects the deepest speculator of that whole [early modern] age."[67] Parallels abound between the Absolutes of Spinoza and of the early and middle Royce.

In his middle period, Royce reaffirmed Spinoza's themes that those who seek after power are vulnerable to external forces and that when a seeker after power "ceases to suffer, he ceases also to be."[68] Royce published an article "Benedict Spinoza" and called for a genetic account of Spinoza's thought growth.[69] Far more significantly, in his middle-period masterpiece, *The World and the Individual*, Royce often referred to Spinoza. Yet Royce moved beyond Spinoza's mixture of realistic mysticism, just as he also moved beyond that "really marvelous vacillation of Spinoza, as regards the central importance of self-consciousness in the whole life of man and of the universe."[70]

In the thought of Royce's mature period, Spinoza keeps revealing his presence. In 1912 Royce chose Spinoza as the model of all those philosophers who attempt to comprehend reality within the scope of a single master concept.[71] In late 1915, in his article "Negation," reiterating the Spinozistic theme "*Omnis Determinatio est Negatio*," Royce founded the very possibility of a limited universe of discourse upon negation. Hence, without such a universe, neither logic was possible nor any of those "unsymmetrical distinctions of value, of preciousness, of grades of being, and of processes of emanation."[72] In Royce's 1916 article "Monotheism," he found Spinoza's God to be of the Indic type and in his article "Mind" he proposed Spinoza's purely intellectual insight of "substance" as an ideal of *conceptual* [= preinterpretational] knowing.[73]

In his last course in metaphysics Royce dedicated two entire lectures to clarify how Spinoza the mystic had taught that "Blessedness is not the reward of virtue, but is virtue itself."[74] He regarded Spinoza's essay "On the Improvement of the Understanding" as "a monument of the kind of philosophizing in question" since Spinoza defined "a spiritual success which is more than efficiency."[75]

The heart of Royce's late ethics, consistent with his logical System Sigma, lay in the genuine loyalist's union with the Beloved Community—a union that is blessedness. Spinoza had directed future sages to free their minds from needless dependence on external powers and images for unswerving union with God. Similarly, the mature Royce called truth-seekers to free themselves from excessive dependence on worldly powers and merely natural communities so that theirs could be the blessedness of a genuinely loyal life in the unity of the Logos-Spirit and its Beloved Community. Such a doctrine bore a striking resemblance to that of Spinoza, whom Royce had long since found to be a "cool-headed lover of formulas and of mathematics; but . . . none the less a true mystic."[76]

Friedrich Nietzsche

Royce's published references to Nietzsche seem to have started around 1900.[77] They became more frequent in 1908, occurring both in *The Philosophy of Loyalty* and his "Problem of Truth" article. In the latter, Royce concentrated on Nietzsche's insightful contributions yet criticized his excessive individualism. Royce found that Nietzsche's impoverished idea of community affected his theory of truth.[78] In 1910 at Smith College Royce briefly instructed undergraduate women objectively yet briefly on the "goods and evils" of Nietzsche's thought.[79] Thereafter, Royce's references to Nietzsche, particularly in his article posthumously published in *Atlantic Monthly*, reveal his deepening interest and closer study of Nietzsche.[80] To Royce, this enigmatic "writer of aphorisms" (321) seemed a new star that, despite its fitfulness, radiated novel rays and bold insights, especially in ethics.

After some initial casting about,[81] Royce aimed in his late "Nietzsche" article to analyze the heart of the ethical teachings found in *Thus Spoke Zarathustra, Beyond Good and Evil, Genealogy of Morals*, and *Anti-Christ*. Here Royce judiciously interwove long salient quotations from Nietzsche into a continuous exposition of his ethics. This bold pioneer effort produced a generally accurate interpretation and placed Royce among the first Americans to call public attention to the importance of Nietzsche.

Ethics studies how a human self should direct its personal energy within our fluxing universe. For this study, Nietzsche had identified, as Royce's posthumous article put it, one presupposition and three inquiries into the human self's personal energy (322–23). He presupposed that conventional (or "herd") morality failed to meet the required standard. For the life of authentic ethics has to lie primarily, not in conformism, but in autonomous decision making. Thus Nietzsche brought ethics back home to its true inner sanctum, rather than letting it continue its deadening search outside for group approval, customary behavior, mere rules, and principles.

Within this authentic abode of ethics, Nietzsche identified three basic quandaries that need increasingly personal and authentic answers if decision making is to be genuine. Royce expressed these three struts of Nietzsche's ethics in a trio of questions—each one phrased alternately to enhance its meaning by complementarity. (1) Who am I and what do I want? (2) "What does this will that seeks power genuinely desire? [and] What is the power that is worthy to be mine?" (322). (3) How, then, should a noble self that seeks perfection relate to the fluxing universe around it? And who will have the courage and stamina to endure the "eternal return"? Some clarification of these questions seems in order.

(1) By his first paired question, "Who am I and what do I want?" Nietzsche searched for his own identity by investigating the taproot of his will. Here Nietzsche found, according to Royce, "that his own will is, above all, what he calls the will for power" (322). As regards how to direct that power, Nietzsche's concern pressed far more upon its inward use, however outwardly it may also need to be used.

(2) Accordingly, "What does this will that seeks power genuinely desire? What is the power that is worthy to be mine?" (322). Clearly such a reflectively questioning self has come to treasure its power to determine itself, that "flame and fuel" of its own life-energy. It so senses its interior power and appreciates its ideal of becoming the perfect self (the future human or *Uebermensch*) that it treasures its own uniqueness and dignity. Thus it must always strive to approach this ideal and must contemn all mediocrity, all living that is "merely moderate."

(3) When once a self is equipped with a sense of its own nobility and strives for its own perfection, how ought such a self relate to the universal flux around it? In this third ethical problematic of Nietzsche, his initially vague probe rested on two assumptions. They needed to be recognized before this probe could be brought into a focus sharp enough for founding Nietzschean ethics. First, the human self must inquire what significance this processing universe has *if* one accepts Nietzsche's "mystical intuition" that the universe is structured by an "eternal return." Consequently, the self must recognize, that such a universe and every self in it can have no external term that fulfills all its strivings and processes. For, as Royce put it, "neither heavenly joys nor the will of the gods, neither Nirvana nor the beatific vision, can be admitted into the [Nietzschean] doctrine to give purpose to life" (325). Hence, the "deepest problem of life becomes the attainment of sufficient courage to endure the hardships of the world-cycle, knowing that by just this series of struggles the complete life has to be expressed" (327).

The human self, then, faced with reality's eternal return and perhaps in horror or terror before it, finds that ultimately its third and most pressing ethical question becomes: (3) Who has the courage and absolute endurance to accept this eternal return? (327). Nietzsche found such courage only in those who remember that the closed cycle makes struggling itself meaningful; or, as his answer was rephrased by Royce:

The reaction from this terror at the haunted way of life [that all this has happened before and will happen again] comes when one remembers that the closed circle of eternal life is one of significant striving and that therefore the very closing of the circle involves the completion of the striving. (326)[82]

The human self translates this meaningfulness into courageous action if it follows another of Nietzsche's recommendations. Each striving self must embrace both its weaknesses and the evils it feels inside and outside itself. It must win these over to the service of its own perfection, even by fearlessly accepting them, working them out, and thereby conquering them (327).

Is it probable, then, that Royce's version of Nietzsche's three questions for starting ethics is linked to his own late ethical inquiries? A cluster of facts suggests so. Royce seems to have written this "Nietzsche" article in his final years. In his 1915–1916 Extension Course on Ethics, Royce found that Nietzsche's first question, "Who am I?" echoed the seemingly eccentric puzzlement of Schopenhauer. This question also identified the fundamental musement out of which Royce fashioned the triad of questions for starting his own maturest ethics. Moreover, in the same course, Royce referred explicitly to Nietzsche as advocating that one be "captain of one's soul" in a totally self-determined way.[83] Finally, when Royce started his 1915–16 ethics from three questions, in many ways he paralleled his own late portrayal of the Nietzsche who started his ethics from three questions. We listed Nietzsche's three questions above. Royce's three questions to start his 1915–16 ethics, were partly different yet partly parallel: (1) In what sense can a person truly be director of his own life plan, or "captain of his soul"? (2) What is the human good that everyone seeks (in some form)? and (3) What is my duty, or what is this "obligation to follow some will not my own, to obey, to be bound by laws which are not of my own making"? Clearly these two sets of initial questions show sharp contrasts but also many striking parallels. Both Nietzsche and Royce start from a trio of questions; both focus on self-identity and autonomy; and both try to integrate aright the thrusts of their three questions.

Turning from methodologies at the start of ethics, we find further startling parallels between Nietzsche and Royce in some of their basic ethical positions. Their voluntarisms provide an initial point of comparison. Royce defined his absolute voluntarism as "a theory of the way in which our activities must go on if they are to go on at all."[84] His focus on the will and its modes of action zeroed in upon that same "will to become self-possessed," the heart of Nietzsche's "will to power."[85] Furthermore, Royce's "Nietzsche" article offered some clues (322, 330) that Royce may have used Nietzsche's contrast between the moralities of nobles and slaves as an unacknowledged source for his distinction in the *Problem of Christianity* between at least the first two of his three fundamental "attitudes of will" (self-assertion, self-negation, and genuine loyalty).[86] Just as Nietzsche's morality of nobles is marked by a triumphant affirmation of oneself and by a spontaneity of valuation, so too, Royce's "first attitude of will" operates as the will of self-assertion and affirmation. Then, too, just as Nietzsche's slave morality always first needs a hostile external world and rises essentially from an angry irritation—which Nietzsche calls *ressentiment*—so, too, Royce's "second attitude of will," the will of self-denial, says "No" from the outset to what is outside, to what is different, to what is not itself.

Royce included Nietzsche among his vast constellation of individualists, e.g., Emerson, Whitman, Byron, Goethe, Faust, Cain, Manfred, and still others (321–322). Yet voluntarist Royce beheld "the star of Nietzsche" as "very original" since his doctrines of *Uebermensch* and of the eternal return rendered his kind of "ethical Titanism" unique indeed. If one were awakened by Zarathustra's call to realize the "emergent future human" in oneself and responded by giving oneself to the internal striving this realization required, one would have to "transvalue all values."[87] Negatively, one would have to "escape from lower ideals" and not "tolerate . . . commonplaceness, vulgarity, or mere content with convention, with tradition, with circumstance" (325). Positively, one's noble aristocratic soul would have to attain "sufficient courage to endure the hardships of the world-cycle, knowing that by just this series of struggle the complete life has to be expressed" (327).

Having summarized Royce's exposition of Nietzsche, we ask in what ways does Royce's mature ethics parallel Nietzsche's and also diverge from it? Royce delighted in Nietzsche's individualism because he himself increasingly emphasized the individualization of the self. This emphasis is often overlooked because of some Roycean scholars' one-sided stress on community. Then, too, Royce's ethical theme, "It is good to strive" certainly paralleled that of Nietzsche. Royce echoed Nietzschean themes by his stricture against "those at ease in Zion" and by his insistence on the "courage and absolute endurance" needed to bear life's tragedies and to endure the ostracism and downdrag of the "herd." Royce's suspicion of Schopenhauerean "pity" probably derived from Nietzsche. Again, Royce so purified loyalty into "genuine loyalty" and even into "Spirit-led graced loyalty" that he focused his ethics directly on only the few authentically moral selves. By thus placing beyond the pale of genuine morality all the people incapable of it, Royce's ethics approached the ethics of the *Uebermensch*. In it, Nietzsche had found that *the* "moral problem concerns the perfection, not of society, not of the mass of men, but of the great individual" (322).

Nevertheless, in many ways Royce diverged from Nietzsche's ethic. Although past experience and traditions had to be sifted to find their core of wisdom, as a historian Royce appreciated the richness of one's personal and cultural past too much to concur with Nietzsche's "greatest thing ye can experience . . . [your] hour of great contempt" for your past happiness, virtues, reasoning, and conventional moderation.

Secondly, Royce placed each human self in communities and held that their universal processing is guided by a pathfinding Spirit of Interpretation—not a Nietzschean "dead God" but an immanent and transcendent Spirit of the Universal Community. Royce recognized that Nietzsche had not fairly appreciated Christianity, especially in its early forms (330). Just as Royce opposed James's pluriverse, so he could not accept Nietzsche's world of minded beings all heading off in their own ultimately capricious directions. Nietzsche's view presupposed that the thirst in human wills for a complete and conscious self-possession and fulfillment did not constitute an immanent teleology in all of them (325). For Royce the "service of mankind" (which Zarathustra condemns) is indeed not to be "slavish" (325) but instead a genuine service that is wholehearted, practical, and dedicated to promote the coming of the Universal Community.

Again, the Roycean "Eternal" partook of the Spirit's knowledge and presence; its eschatology knew nothing of Nietzsche's "eternal return," which Royce regarded as a "purely fantastic freak of the imagination" (325). Instead, whereas Nietzsche's "wanderer in life's wilderness sees no shining light of an eternal city beyond him" (326–327), Royce's pilgrim self certainly does.

Finally, unlike the fundamental hostility operating between Nietzsche's nobles and slaves, Royce's genuinely loyal selves must love and promote every human self—both in its uniqueness and in its bondedness with community. As Royce put it:

> Nietzsche appears as entirely failing to see the organic character of the true life of cooperating individuals. . . .[In his omission of the] great problem of reconciling the unique individual with the world-order. . . .lies his perfectly obvious limitation. (327–328)

Consequently, we find that Nietzsche played a considerable role as dialogue-partner with Royce in the latter's final decade of thought. Few have recognized this role. Yet Royce treasured Nietzsche at least for this, that "no one has better expressed in recent times than he [Nietzsche] the ideal of the search for a consciousness of perfection" (331).

LIFE ITSELF AS A DIALOGUE-PARTNER

Around the turn of the century, Royce chose to identify with the "philosophy of life" movement.[88] At that time Bergson and James spearheaded the movement. Before then, however, some favorite poets of Royce, like Sill and Emerson, Wordsworth and Tennyson, Goethe and Schiller, had also gone to life itself as the source of their wisdom. Life in all its richness exceeded the realm of percept or concept or even any union of the two. Life was too deep and rich to be exhaustively handled primarily either by reason (with its judgments and inferences), or by one's affective life of feelings, or even by personal freedom (with its initiatives and appreciations). However requisite these component dynamisms were for human life, they could not claim identity with life itself. For the latter consisted in that total process of interactions between those mysterious ultimates of selves and communities. Affecting these interactions, selves had their types of fundamental "attitudes of will" while communities had these and their basic societal and institutional structures.

Accordingly, the mature Royce committed himself to become an interpreter of this deeply experienced life. Even if confusedly, common sense knows such life and offers this knowledge to philosophers as an inexhaustible well-spring for their reflection. Commonsense knowledge and life also challenge philosophers to fashion their assertions about life in an adequately balanced way.[89]

In 1908, Royce clearly evinced his commitment to philosophize in life and on life.[90] This led him to investigate the religious aspect of life in 1911–12. As the tragedies of his homelife, career, and World War I swirled around him more fiercely from 1910 to 1916, his philosophy of life developed into a philosophy of winning more life through dyings. That is, he examined how to find life-giving ethical energies at the heart of "lost causes," lost campaigns, and lost friends. This increase of interior life deserves notice.

The mature Royce's philosophy of gaining more life through dyings had to include human energies and purposeful initiatives much richer than mere concepts. For Royce, the "rich stuff" of human moral life synthesizes temporal process, passional attachments, deeply personal alienations and reconciliations, along with the mysteries of selves and communities in their historical processes. Here lies the deep spring of experienced human life. From it philosophers must draw their ideas and theories—their pale and frail reflections of reality lived interpersonally.[91]

Within Royce's genuine loyalty a living logic directed his philosophy of life and dying. This passionate logic shows itself as a "passover logic," leading from life through death to more life. It arises from passionate interests that are deeply practical.[92] As fruit of these practical interests, an idea (or Sign) calls the one who receives it to focus more on "taking up the same attitude toward things that he [the sign-sender] takes" and less on its object—although this secondary focus is also needed.[93]

Scholars need, therefore, to counterbalance the recent stress on Royce's formal (symbolic) logic—dominant as such logic is in Royce's thought!—by increasing studies of Royce's "logic of life." His increasing stress on the latter stands out in both his 1913–14 Seminar and his 1915–16 Extension Course on Ethics. Hocking, the colleague who arguably best knew the mature Royce's philosophy, testified to this centrality of passional logic in the mature Royce.[94]

In his letter of March 20, 1916, to Mary Whiton Calkins,[95] Royce described his intellectual development since 1912. He acknowledged that the experiences of, and reflections on the ideas of Community and of Spirit which led him to write the *Problem* "have been working on my mind daily more and more, ever since I wrote that book." In this letter he further declared that in 1916 he interpreted a true community to be just as much a person (in his ethical sense of the term "person")[96] as was any individual human self. Royce wrote:

> For me, at present, a genuinely and loyally united community, which lives a coherent life, is, in a perfectly [literal] sense, a person. Such a person, for Paul, the Church of Christ was.[97]

Royce found loyally united communities to be genuine persons, in his ethical sense. Besides this, he found that to offset the effects of disloyalties in such communities, the Logos-Spirit animates many of their members to acts of atonement. The Spirit gathers these atoning deeds into a communal energy more effective even than reconciling words. Through atoning deeds the Spirit flashes a signal into the whole world of interpreting minds in such a way that corresponding deeds of highest loyalty are called forth. For example, in their heroic defense of Verdun, French soldiers were then offering their atoning deeds and thus calling the world to similar heroic actions to discipline a unilaterally aggressive nationalism. In brief, then, Royce's letter to Calkins identified some ideas and energies which had deepened and broadened Royce's mature ethics since his writing of the *Problem*.

Under the influence of Peirce's triadism, the mature Royce had in 1912 searched for Christianity's three "most essential" ideas. Little surprise, then, that in 1915 Royce should go searching for the three principal ideas of ethical life—even if it constituted a novel enterprise.

To appreciate this move in Royce's final ethics, it helps to survey other triads of notions fundamental to ethical life. Why was Royce drawn to the one he considered as *the* most fundamental triad of leading ethical ideas? Ancient and medieval philosophers had emphasized happiness, human excellence, and friendship. Scottish and Kantian ethicists had focused on moral sense (sympathy), respect for persons, and a natural moral order or law. Later British and American moralists built upon instinctual appetites and needs, pleasure and pain, and calculable consequences.

In his youth, Royce had already shown himself in touch with the key requirement for ethical life in communities. In his history of California, his study of the life of miners there had identified its critical disease: a "lack of reverence for the relations of life."[98] This diagnosis helped him later to identify both the basic relations needed for healthy communal life and the fundamental ideas guiding such life.

In 1912 Royce acknowledged that he had looked back over "the [five-year] course of my study of what loyalty means."[98] Three years later, his continuing investigation of the meaning of loyalty had deepened. For in 1915–16, by employing his social approach to ethical life, he mused upon "the form of social *moral* experience."[100] His interpretation showed him that, although the meaning of loyalty embraced the other triads of ethical ideas just mentioned, nevertheless, autonomy, goodness, and duty constituted the ideas *most* central to ethical life.

In the *Problem* he had found that genuine loyalty depended upon "a form of social *religious* experience."[101] Similarly, in 1915 he discovered that the genuinely moral life depends at least as much upon the ideas most responsible for the passional logic of loyalty, upon the ideas that constituted "a form of social *moral* experience." A genuinely loyal willingness to serve a common good was simply inconceivable without a free yet dutiful self-direction towards moral goodness. In 1915–16, then, Royce intended to investigate the basic form that social moral experience takes when marked by either communally shared life or alienation.

As we have seen, Royce recognized the family as the basic unit in human life and each of its members as "belonging" to the family's communal life. Moreover, in mid-1913 Royce's letter from Peirce included a paragraph on the irreducibility of 3 to 1 or 2. I suspect that the combination of this paragraph and his ideas on family suggested to Royce how three basic relationships arise out of each member's different way of "belonging" to the family. That is, the *good* of love arises in the 1–2 relation of conjugal friendship. *Duty* arises in the 1–2–3 relationship between parents-and-child. Finally, upon these bases, *equal autonomy* between siblings arise in a 3–4–...n relationship, with its corresponding demand for respect for the freedom of each brother or sister. Through all these ways and means, then, Royce was dialoguing with life itself, especially with ethical life.

In 1912 Royce acknowledged that, as part of his philosophy of life, his "philosophy of loyalty" had been growing since his early published effort of 1908. Looking back on this growth, Royce recognized that his insight of 1912 into Peirce's doctrine of signs and of interpretation had given his philosophy of loyalty "a new concreteness, [and] a new significance."[102] In brief, although Royce's ethics had developed greatly between 1908 and 1912, his philosophy of loyalty grew even more after the *Problem* up until his death.

In this chapter, then, we have called attention to the persistent presence of Kant, Peirce, and William James in Royce's musings after James's death. Then we traced the major influence of the Apostle Paul, Spinoza, and

Nietzsche upon Royce in his mature period. These three unexpected dialogue-partners also serve to symbolize how diversely Royce reflected upon ethics from 1912 to 1916.

In his recent Gifford Lectures, Alasdair MacIntyre discussed three diverse, even antagonistic paths of ethical inquiry—the ways of tradition, encyclopaedia, and genealogy.[103] Long before this, Royce's use of Paul symbolized his use of tradition in his ethical reflection. Tradition was to be critically purified and revised but always appreciated for the seeds of time-tested commonsense wisdom it contained. Royce's attachment to Spinoza may symbolize the mature Royce's insistence on the role of the Eternal in ethics. Possessing a chronosynoptic (*sub specie aeternitatis*) viewpoint, the Eternal Logos forms the central axis guiding the encyclopaedic swirl of right and wrong finite choices towards the home of the Universal Community. Finally, Royce's appreciation of Nietzsche may symbolize Royce's use of the genealogical approach to ethics and the need of a transformation from conventional to authentic morality. Fortunately, Royce's use of alternation and especially his general method of interpretive musement overcame the clashings of these approaches and wove them into one significant fabric of many strands.

To sum up, then, this chapter has simply surveyed how some of Royce's dialogue-partners influenced his post-1911 musements about ethics. To set these influences in their proper context, we must take into account the key ideas Royce drew from those other thinkers with whom he also dialogued: Plato, Schopenhauer, Fichte, Hegel, the "new logicians," and many others. We must add to this the concrete ethical experiences of his diverse encounters with life as he found it overall and especially in his home with Katharine, his sons, and in-laws—a life whose colors have recently come to light in the Crystal Falls Collection. Finally, we need to weigh the role of Royce's own genius for original ethical insights, as a powerful counterbalance to the input exercised by these three sets of dialogue-partners. Is it any wonder, then, that the mind of the mature Royce was almost overwhelmed by the riches of such profound and diverse ideas? Before he spoke of the law of the "fecundity of aggregation," he had experienced how fecund this rich aggregate of ideas was and had detected their "tendency to orderly cooperation."[104]

12. Comparison and Contrast with the Ethics of Other Philosophers: Utilitarians, Naturalists, and "Responsibilists"

To compare and contrast Royce's mature moral philosophy thoroughly with the methods and doctrines of other ethicists would require dissertations. A merely initial essay in this direction, however, may provide instructive context and light. The present venture, then, aims simply to highlight Royce's attitude and tone in relation to some other philosophers. So general a sketch, then, cannot claim to be rigorously fair to the ethicists selected. Before comparing and contrasting the ethics of the mature Royce with those of John Stuart Mill, John Dewey, and H. Richard Niebuhr, some notice of its relations with the ethics of Kant, Hegel, and some European contemporaries of Royce seems a needed background.

Compared to his "old Father Kant," Royce also took the "transcendental turn" and became a cognitive phenomenist, at least until his Peircean insight of 1912. Nevertheless, as an instructor at Berkeley, Royce already realized how deeply evolutionary change had affected human consciousness. So he already doubted the purported unchangeableness of Kant's categories and in the end adopted Peirce's new list of categories. Three decades later, Royce had become far more experiential, fallible, and phenomenological than Kant. Unlike the latter, Royce allowed the idea of duty no more of a leading role than he granted to the ideas of autonomy and of the good. And he subordinated all three ideas to that loyal communal life enjoyed by those who have committed themselves to the Universal Community. More humble in his final years than in earlier ones, the mature Royce spoke easily of the growth of his cause, of his ideal, and of his consciousness. He also felt he needed to re-interpret ideas without fixing upon any one interpretation of them. He worked up from experienced cases and, while using principles, insisted on a case-by-case fashioning of directives for individual selves. This empiricism sounds startlingly different from themes characteristic of Kant, who started with any finite rational agent,

199

deduced consistent *a priori* principles, and stressed a formal universalizability throughout his ethics.

By contrast, the mature Royce generalized within a cyclic pattern of interpretation. That is, he started from his phenomenology of a consciousness developing ethically. In this phase he kneaded data from sociology and insurance theory, from individual and group psychology into his late moral philosophy to generate an ethical phenomenology. His concern was how the human self and its conscience grows within society, just what impedes this growth, and how the self is freed from estrangements. Next, he uncovered the centrality in consciousness of certain undeniable and inescapable self-reinstating structures—e.g., his three leading ethical ideas. Then, using interpretation to unite these principles and his empirical data, Royce created a normative ethics that offered general direction to any human self. Yet to win a directive appropriate to one or another individual, Royce had to complete the cycle. This demand made him interpret his general directives through the mediating lenses of various cases and the unique situation of the individual involved. In brief, unlike Kant, Royce relied far more on experience and the contributions of the positive sciences.

Royce's interpretive method contrasted with Kant's primarily conceptual method. Royce employed data from sociology and psychology far more than Kant did. Concerning the relation of ethics and religion, Royce did not wall off his ethics from the superhuman, as Kant did, by requiring a "religion within the limits of reason *alone*." For, even though, as a moral philosopher, Royce confined himself to study ethics "from the human side" only, nevertheless his ethics opened itself to the possibility of a religion initiated "from the divine side."

Still, Royce's late moral philosophy lay closer to Kant's than to Hegel's. Royce himself and some Roycean scholars have pointed this out.[1] The German idealists, including Hegel, clearly influenced Royce and he derived many of his cues from Hegel's *Phenomenology of Spirit*. Yet he came to criticize the narrowness of Hegel's idea of rational mediation. It needed the plasticity and fruitfulness (*ubertas*) that Royce found in Peirce's method of interpretation.[2] Royce soon pointed out his ground for this criticism: Hegel "treats the idea of negation at length, but [he] does not clearly see in what relations negation stands to order."[3]

Despite these differences, however, a first reading of Royce may suggest a near identity between the triadic element in Roycean interpretation and that of the Hegelian dialectic. Vincent C. Punzo of St. Louis University, however, has pointed out the essential difference.[4] Unlike Hegel, Royce did not maintain that interpretation enabled a person to follow the unfolding of the whole of reality. By contrast with Hegel's dialectical method, Royce's interpretive method was much more limited and restrained. Royce distinguished clearly between interpretation as a method for human truth-seekers in their dealing with reality, and interpretation as the communal process that is reality. Hegel does not seem to have drawn a similar distinction within his own dialectical process.[5]

Finally, whereas Hegel chose a primarily noetic Logos as his base, Royce, in a move closer to Fichte's, built his philosophy on the primarily ethical, volitional, and striving character of the self—first, of the human self-community, and only later and inferentially, of the divine Self-Community. A realistic element thus marks the mature metaphysics and ethics of the Royce who in 1916 told his students:

> Let us insist that the world of fact is certainly in some sense precisely that which is independent of us. For what we want to know when we undertake to know is precisely that which is independent of us. . . .
>
> The whole intention with which we approach our idealism is the intention to be as realistic as we can. . . . The idealist faces the problem of objectivity, the problem of truth, the problem of that to which one submits his mind whenever one is seeking for fact as fact.[6]

This realism appears both in his full-hearted dedication to a real unique Other and in the primacy he set on freedom and subjectivity rather than on an intellect that is dominated principally by objects.[7]

Against this background, attention can now focus on some ethicists more contemporary with Royce. Scanning a few of these influences on Royce can serve as prelude to selecting a particularly significant thinker with whom to compare and contrast the mature Royce.

The basic tone of Schopenhauer's philosophy is pessimism. Royce's mature ethics, although created within a context of tragedy, avoided pessimism because the human self's truth-seeking intelligence leads one's will. Through this rational will, a human self is called to fall in love with the universe.

Henri Bergson, the advocate of pure intuition, was another European whom Royce believed he had surpassed.[8] Royce judged that ethics needed more than an immersion in the immediate *durée*. The interpretive mode of ethical knowing needed to be more patient, mediated, and serial, so as to cumulate eventually into a synoptic view of the overall meaning of one's own life. Within the context of its overall meaning, the Roycean self can, through its life of interpretation, make a moral decision more fittingly than can be done by an immediate intuition of the *durée*.

After this brief scan of European influences upon Royce—Kant and Hegel, Schopenhauer and Bergson—we turn to England to examine the relations between Royce and John Stuart Mill. For Mill seems to be the British thinker who most influenced Royce.

MILL AND ROYCE

William James's dependence on John Stuart Mill lies publicized in the well-known dedication to Mill of James's *Pragmatism*. Although Royce's relation to Mill is less well known, it began in the early 1870s. Before Royce invested one year to studies in Germany, he had eagerly read Mill and largely agreed with him.[9] How much Mill influenced Royce becomes clear from an autobiographical confession Royce made in his final year:

> I began the study of philosophy before I ever read any German idealism, which was quite unknown to me until I had become acquainted with Mill. I was especially influenced by Mill's examination of the philosophy of Sir William Hamilton. Over against the influence of Mill stood for me the influence of Herbert Spencer. Mill was a critical empiricist, on the whole accepting a Berkeleyan account of the world, though altogether deprived of the theological elements of Berkeley's doctrine. For Mill, the world is known to us through experience, the experience of the outer senses and the inner experience, a world of data of sense or feeling; and all that we can say about it is that these data are such. . . . Mill's chapter "The psychological theory of the external world" is one of the most important philosophical productions of English thought of the last century.
>
> I became through Mill's influence a decidedly skeptical critical empiricist, with this result: . . . [any intuited] "necessary" or "fundamental truths" must fail as the basis of thinking.[10]

Mill's influence upon Royce before mid-1875 affected this young Californian's ideas of utility, liberty, and religion.

Yet it seems misleading to infer that Mill's immediate influence on Royce directly affected the latter's practical philosophy. Rather, Mill's style of thinking and theory of knowledge principally affected Royce's speculative outlook.[11] Mill bequeathed to Royce a spirit of anti-fundamentalism and a spirit of anti-dogmatism (along with its suspicion of the pernicious effects of universal metaphysical statements).[12] Royce often referred approvingly to Mill's definition of matter as a mass of "permanent possibilities of experience." Concerning the non-intuition of any fundamental truths or supposedly self-evident first principles, Mill's influence on Royce was buttressed by that of C. S. Peirce, whom Royce read when he returned to Berkeley.

By way of contrast, Mill's system involved a conceptualistic rationalism that knew not interpretive musement. Its basis lay in atomized empirical data detached from any unitive communal life and its process. It arose from a will to be self-assertive and knew no primacy of universal loyalty. By reading Mill, the early Royce became, as he later acknowledged, a "decidedly skeptical critical empiricist." During those early years of 1872 to 1882, Royce's personal experiences of radical doubt and pessimism led him eventually to see that ethical skepticism and relativism were the direct results of Mill's epistemology and utilitariansism.

As for speculative philosophy, then, Royce admired Mill's conceptual rigor and his logical acuity.[13] Yet Royce judged that "Mill left you to the data of sense, to the endlessly shifting variety of the fortunes of experience."[14] Within the nature of the self with its irrevocable past and its unavoidable bearing into the future, Royce found certain undeniable self-reinstating truths which needed to be recognized. Hence, the merely prudential calculations of the strict utilitarian were an inadequate substitute for Royce's wise love of the whole universe and his consequent modes of loyal action. He felt that Mill missed the kind of loyal commitment to the Great Community of humankind that generates a synoptic wisdom. The latter provides a sense of overall direction to the integral life of both a human self and its series of communities.

As for practical philosophy, although Royce found mixed blessings in Mill's *On Liberty* and *Utilitarianism*, nevertheless, with the passing years he came to regard these works, too, as inadequate overall. They succeeded in stressing the autonomous and the teleological dimensions of ethics—ones that Royce made central to his doctrine of self-constitution. Royce endorsed enough of Mill's liberal tradition to require that one avoid interfering with others' freely chosen different loyalties if one wanted to be loyal to loyalty. Mill seems to have inspired much of Royce's passion for academic freedom. Yet Royce disagreed radically with Mill's views that reality ultimately consisted of only atomized individuals and that the goal of human life lay in the greatest sum of the painless and agreeable.

Instead, Royce believed that since communities were logically and existentially correlative with individuals, communities were just as basic to the universe as were individuals. He also believed that the goal of human life lay in such interpretive, mediating, and atoning activities as lead communities and individuals to a transformed life. Not the self-assertion of primarily self-interested atomized individuals, but the commitment to serve communities and thus develop the self through atoning deeds was Royce's non-Millsian way.

Turning to the American scene, we find in Royce's late ethics several traits common to the ethics of many other American philosophers. I believe that Royce's late thought reveals a hierarchy of ideals—rising from the logical, through the ethical, to the aesthetic ideal. A parallel hierarchy of ideals is evident in Peirce, and possibly in Whitehead and Dewey. For Royce, the aesthetic ideal leads clearly to the religious.

As already mentioned, the mature Royce tended to a kind of realism because of his "will to interpret" the Other and because of his adoption of Peirce's interpretive process. Royce's continuing interest in, and use of physiological and psychological research in his ethics permeated it with American experientialism. Royce's late ethics has the built-in demand of adjusting to the experienced real as changing. Although it starts from and returns to this experienced real, Royce's late ethics also demands that this cycle be mediated by genuine logical inferences of various kinds. Certainly Royce's success as an interpreter of scientists during his seminars on scientific methodology revealed the fecundity of his late logic for the philosophy of science and the power of his late ethics to generate a community of cooperating scientists. One may recall, furthermore, the initiating role Royce assigned, even from his early days, to instincts, spontaneous interests, and impulses. This remembrance leads one easily to wonder whether Royce and James were not, after Hume, significant sources for those "springs of action" which mark the later ethics of Dewey and Santayana.

Although Royce's mature moral philosophy shows some themes and ideas common to other classical American philosophers, it clearly distinguishes itself in many ways. Dedication to a cause and thus to the Other to whom one gives oneself characterizes Roycean ethics—especially insofar as one views the cause as a unique individual Self-Community (finite or infinite). Although Royce shares with James an emphasis on every person's need to be saved, yet he uses the themes of salvation, lost state, and atonement in a distinctive way. For Royce, no one can be saved without opening oneself to the influences of the community. In order for one separated from community to enter it, mediation by some suffering servant is required. For union can be restored only through this process of atoning reconciliation. Roycean ethics culminates in this distinctive theme. Then, too, no other classical American philosopher has studied the problem of evil—both physical and moral—so directly as Royce. Unique indeed, then, was the "ethical house" Royce built in his maturity.

As we saw, Royce's ethics employed scientific findings—specifically, those from biology and physiology, sociology and psychology. Yet unlike others, he did not wholly "biologize" his ethics. Royce emphasized an ethics oriented to the formation of an ethical individual's true self through genuine loyalty to an authentic community. He did not reorient that self primarily back into the physical universe. Such a primary destiny would follow if one held a truncated view of the human person as primarily an animal adapting to its environment. Instead, the late Royce gave priority of focus to human minded beings, embodied in organisms and communities. Such selves signal loyalty and truth to their peers mainly to draw them to further holistic human development. The dedicated services of such selves enhance the Great Community's culture which is properly human and humane. Royce's mature ethics, then, pointed beyond the biological into the unending holistic development of each unique conscious human self and of its communities.

Unlike many other American ethics, then, Royce's is not exclusively "this worldly." Because of its unique way of relating to the Other, the Roycean ethical self is already an individual yet must ever strive to achieve its yet fuller individualization. Hence, Royce's mature ethics demands greater present striving to enhance the quality of existing human communities than any other classical American ethics.

The vital impulse within the individual self's relation to the Other swings rhythmically to its different relata—to its true *ego*, to its *alter*, and to its community. Similarly, the vital impulse within the life of the community swings rhythmically to this or that individual insofar as one, being a service-provider or indigent receiver or interpreter, offers one's distinctive gift (contribution or need) to the community.

Again for Royce, the individual human self serially emphasizes the three leading ethical ideas according to its present particular interaction as a member within its community. Similarly, the whole community's ethical life highlights serially, sometimes the community's good, then its common duty (or responsibility) amid other communities, and later its autonomy (or unique self-direction). In both of these temporal dialectical processes, the ethical consciousness of the self and of the community is being called to more balance.

Therefore, Royce's mature ethics is unique. Upon self and community it sets coequal ultimacy. Within loyalty it synthesizes experiential impulses and the three leading ethical ideas. It lives by the process of a mediating interpretation that alternates its consideration rhythmically and approaches its questions individually and socially. Royce's mature ethics, then, contributes its distinct treasure to American thought.

ROYCE AND DEWEY

To better understand the claim just made, we turn to compare and contrast Royce's ethics with that of John Dewey. Royce admired Dewey as a brilliant, clear, and confident thinker whose style was rugged and incisive.[15] If we search for similarities between these two thinkers, we uncover many— for instance, their emphasis on intelligence and on creating harmony. Like Royce, Dewey also regarded philosophy as "inherently criticism."[16] Like Royce, Dewey discerned between projected ends that are truly good and those that are merely transitory. Like Royce, Dewey strove to harmonize the multiplicity of human desires and needs. Like Royce, Dewey also tried to free philosophy "from too intimate and exclusive attachment to traditional problems."[17]

Despite these general lines of similarity, differences abound. In their shared notion of philosophy as a liberation from rut-like traditions, the different way in which these two interpreted freedom became almost explicit. For Dewey, human freedom is initially and radically a freedom within the natural human community, a community from which any intimately operating divine Will to Interpret has been excluded *a priori.* For Royce, human freedom comes about only through a freedom for others, a freedom through commitment to and union with the divine Will to Interpret the human community.

Royce's early critique of Dewey perdured. In Royce's eyes, Dewey remained too optimistic, too unaffected by the problem of evil, insufficiently engaged with the tragedy of malice and ill fortune. Because of this Royce would regard Dewey's ethics as an ethics of the strong, not of the oppressed, or in current speech, an ethics for the First World people who are "on top," not an ethics for the downtrodden Third World.

Dewey constructed the moral good without any real pre-existing Will that serves as a moral norm. He rejected the view that prior to here-and-now experience one can know what is right or wrong for an individual in a particular situation. Instead he thought the moral situation arises out of a conflict of obligations and loyalties. In these conflicts the agent faces the constrictive duty of working out the right decision.[18]

Similarly, the mature Royce was strongly opposed to any prefabricated individual moral decisions. He called for intelligent probing into the details of the situation in order to come to see what is appropriate, right, and preferable. Yet, while thus stressing the human construction of the moral good, Royce set this activity within the context of a pre-existing Spirit of the Universal Community. Its Will is to teach and save the Universal Community. This Will sets the target which human choices either hit or miss. As Royce said in 1915:

> The dutiful spirit leaves to what it calls God the art of making the great triumph, of solving Everyman's problem [of identifying where genuine goodness lies] and of reconciling the poor individual man whose head fortune so often leaves bleeding, to the blows of chance which he is sometimes too weak merely to defy.[19]

God-talk like this may evoke memories of Dewey's critique of "ultimate ends." Royce, however, saw ambiguity in talk about any "ultimate." For him, "ultimate" sometimes meant the last chronologically. Such an ultimate is impossible for a finite human spirit called indefinitely to find its further identity. But sometimes "ultimate" meant the supreme in value. So when Royce talked about ends in view, as he did, he recognized the developmental series of means and ends. Yet he also recognized that this serial process is called to respond to the Logos-Spirit's Will to Interpret the universe in a way that enhances the human world through community and atonement.

Whereas both Dewey and Royce emphasized the role of intelligence in the human project, they viewed intelligence in contrasting ways. Dewey stressed creative intelligence. It is called both to interpret a problematic situation actively and to solve its way of construing the situation by raising questions, forming hypotheses, testing them, and achieving a settled belief. Although Roycean intelligence is just as committed to creative inquiry, it also honors the receptive side of minded being—its openness to the effects of our limitations, to paradoxes to be mused upon, and to mysteries. For Royce, reality is more than a set of problems and mind is more than a problem-solver. For Royce, although the human mind must strive in its own creative inquiry, it is called to openness to grace "as from above." It is also open to that hope-filled gratitude for love which enables one to confront dire tragedy, to atone, and to reach fuller life for oneself and one's community.

Finally, perhaps the most radical difference between Dewey and Royce—one that produces all the differences just mentioned—lies in their different views of the human person. This divergence is brought to focus in the question: Is the evolving human animal equipped with a "divine spark," a *Fünkelin*-center?

Evolutionary theory impacted heavily upon both Royce and Dewey. Both spoke of instinctive energies and impulses, of the evolution of humans from the animal kingdom, and of stages of physical and psychic development. Yet Royce's view of the human self seems more richly and specifically religious than Dewey's.

Dewey deftly portrays "a sense of the whole" that is religious in several culminating passages of his works.[20] One can assert accurately that within the community of humanly enhanced nature Dewey naturalized the divine spark and found in individual human member-selves the potential of sometimes sensing that communal bonding of selves which "claims and dignifies them."[21]

Within Royce's community of interpretation lies a threefold religious spark. The finite human self has a *Fünkelin*-center which I do not find in Dewey. This divine spark empowers the human self to recognize its Deliverance coming to it.[22] Deriving from the Spirit, this spark also constitutes the human self's internal meaning. The latter is so divinely stamped that it cannot rest until it is united teleologically with the divine itself. Moreover, Royce's Universal Community mediates to finite human selves the Interpreter-Spirit's "doctrine of signs" and "Christian doctrine of life." Thus, we not only partake of specific leading ideas but also, as Royce put it,

> we conceive of the whole nature of things as somehow interested in us and in our salvation, . . . [and] we call this nature of things divine, in a very familiar sense of that word.[23]

Finally, this pedagogue Logos-Spirit is source and term of finite selves and communities and hence more of a "divine sun" than simply a spark.

In sum, then, in and around the human self the religious is thicker and deeper in Royce than in Dewey. Royce's internal meaning is related to the divine and called to concur with the Will to Interpret the universe. For all its limitations and illusions, the Roycean human minded being is not simply a significantly higher degree of development on the evolutionary tree. Instead, as an animal that interprets, it is called, in its own autonomy, to sense that the whole is interested in us and in our salvation, to resonate with "whatever intercourse there may be between the divine and the human,"[24] to cooperate with the Will of the Spirit of the Community, and to find warrants for hoping that it will find what it values supremely.

ROYCE AND H. RICHARD NIEBUHR

As our third and final thinker, we select the American ethicist, H. Richard Niebuhr (1896–1962), because he derived much of his inspiration from Royce. Comparing and contrasting Niebuhr's work with that of the late Royce shows that Niebuhr only partially utilized the potential of Royce's mature ethics. Through this comparison and contrast, the scale of Royce's contribution to American moral philosophy may stand out.

In 1915–16, when Royce selected and synthesized his three leading ethical ideas, he antedated Niebuhr's main ethical work by nearly half a century. Niebuhr made his significant contribution to ethics chiefly in his ground-breaking work, *The Responsible Self* (1963). Yet he seems never to have studied Royce's unpublished papers, especially those of his final years.

Granting the importance of Royce's doctrine of loyalty, Niebuhr analyzed it to uncover Royce's "triadic structure of responsibility in social existence in general."[25] In the area of responsibility theory, Niebuhr clearly developed, deepened, and nuanced Royce's key ideas of the call-response dynamism and of "the fitting." Concurring with Royce's view that interpretations arising from genuine loyalty are "especially adapted for application to our moral life in particular,"[26] Niebuhr also took Royce's theory of interpretation and reinterpretation and adapted it to his project.[27] Yet Royce emphasized more explicitly than Niebuhr that we fittingly know the chief ethical ideas of freedom, good, and duty only by interpretation, not by perception, conception, or some combination of these.

Concerning these three central ideas of ethics, Niebuhr sifted various historical theories according to the classical dichotomy between goal-centered and duty-centered ethics. To this bi-polar scheme, which rested on the ideas of the good and duty, Niebuhr added the idea of responsibility. It reached concrete embodiment in his responsible self in community. This move, however, seems to have reduced the idea of autonomy (freedom of self-direction) to less than a principal ethical idea. For when Niebuhr equated freedom to one aspect of the human ability to inquire, he seems to have accepted this consequence.[28] For Royce, however, free self-direction remained a principal ethical idea. And he found this autonomy not only in the inquirer but also in the selves who give themselves to loyalty and in those who refuse to do so, in the recipients of interpretation, and in all communities, good and evil, that operate within the Universal Community.

By selecting three principal ethical ideas, Royce suggested three irreducible centers of ethical life and theory. He synthesized these concretely in the human self who is genuinely loyal only if he is responsible in deed to some particular community that is open to the Universal Community. As Royce had taught the 1915—16 students of his Extension Course on Ethics through a central passage already analyzed:

> The question: "Who am I?" is inevitably and closely related to each of the [three] ethical questions that we have so far faced in these lectures. If I am to know what is meant by my independence, or by my good, or by my duty, I must know who I am.[29]

Thus Royce made in-touchness with one's unique identity the indispensable condition for grasping the meaning of the three chief ethical ideas. And the more one grows in interpreting oneself truly, the closer one approaches a fairer understanding of these ideas.

Furthermore, Royce's 1915 way of synthesizing his three chief ideas within "the loyal servant of the Community" seems even more enlightening and fecund than Niebuhr's valuable ethical synthesis in the ideal of the responsible self. For Royce's way seems more tailored to how moral consciousness grows, resonates biblically with the "suffering servant of Yahweh," and points more realistically to the self's call to atonement.[30]

In Royce's 1916 "Comments" on the mother-daughter case, he taught, as we saw, that parties in dialogue should interpret empathetically the mind of the other. They should intend and bring about openness in interpersonal relations. They should first emphasize the good of their shared life. They should avoid whatever their opposite number will interpret as a threat—such as blaming others, calling them to account, challenging them, insisting first upon one's right before focusing on the common good to be developed. Moreover, in his article "Order," of the same final year, Royce taught that drawing conclusions is essential to loyalty.[31]

It follows, then, that a person lacks loyalty—or is irresponsible—if he fails to infer the probable responses of others to his own action. Similarly, one would fail in loyalty and responsibility if he failed to examine whether one's intended action threatened another person inappropriately. One's intended action might, for example, project suspicion or guilt, overlook a primary emphasis on the common good of the shared life, disregard a common sense of human fallibility, or demand an immediate fulfillment of a specific rights-claim. How different are these responses from that which Royce recommended the daughter offer to her mother: a sincere confession of the burdens one brings to any community of interpretation! In the light of Niebuhr's later work on responsibility, then, Royce's directive seems prophetic that the genuinely loyal agent should foresee both the inner interpretations which others will make of one's action towards them and the future orientations that others will take towards oneself.[32]

In sum, Niebuhr fortunately found much in Royce: the triadic structure of social responsibility, an ethics of the fitting, and a recognition that our idea of the divine becomes warped unless it is purified by the idea of non-forensic mediation. Nevertheless, other late Roycean emphases—on the family, solidarity, economic mediation, and on an Antigone-like supersexual humanness—apparently escaped Niebuhr's notice. So, too, did some of the mature Royce's insights of prime importance—his identification of three leading ethical ideas, his recognition of the important role of the diverse species of loyalty, and his rooting of bold hope in the Spirit of the Universal Community.

From this evidence, then, something of Royce's stature as a moral philosopher comes to light. Yet surprisingly, in the past Royce has been much overlooked and "shelved." This happened partly because later currents of pragmatism, naturalism, and analysis became dominant in twentieth-century American philosophy. But Royce's own attempts to popularize his view and keep them simple, along with his garrulity, also contributed to his subsequent ostracism.

When sixty-year-old Royce offered his "Introduction to Ethics" course at Boston University in 1915–16, it resembled an elderly Isaac Newton or Albert Einstein offering an "Introduction to Physics" course to an evening college class. Offering ideas of such ethical penetration to tyros in moral philosophy was enriching even to them[33] and much more to later researchers. Yet it was self-concealing for Royce—just as parallel introductory courses would have been for a Newton or Einstein. Paradoxically, when Royce, the frail "Socrates of Irving Street," commented on ethics in 1916 from his Boston University podium, he concealed his true stature as an ethicist.

Fortunately, a far apter symbol of his achievement in ethical thought lies in the towering Sierras of his native state. For in those mountains, a California peak has fittingly been named "Mt. Royce" in honor of Josiah. The synoptic vision that Royce generated is so broad and high that it takes years even to approach and survey that gigantic range of mental Sierras which his mind pushed heavenward. He filled it with a treasure that to a large extent still remains buried.

A trend is developing, however, to recognize Royce as a complex giant of extremely intricate and profound insight—a trend promoted by Gabriel Marcel, John Smith, John Clendenning, and many others. What is needed practically is a careful reexamination and reinterpretation of all of Royce's ethical contributions. Through such a scrutiny, those things which Royce simply presented in a popular way will be sifted away from those more refined and disciplined insights and clues which form the treasure of Royce's mature moral philosophy.

13. Strengths and Weaknesses in Royce's Mature Ethics

Several misinterpretations have hindered a fair evaluation of Royce's mature ethics. Some of these have perdured through many decades. Paradoxically, if one associates Royce uncritically with "loyalty," one occasions several of these misinterpretations.

Some think loyalty calls for a blind devotion that approaches fanaticism. This is exactly what Royce countered with his intelligent rational loyalty of reinterpretation. Others take loyalty simplistically as the pure undifferentiated center of Roycean ethics. As a result they fail to notice that if Roycean loyalty is to become and remain genuine, it requires certain compensatory dynamisms. These include a coequal emphasis on authentic individualism and loyalty, on justice and benevolence, on principles and situation, on persistent inquiry and a Christian mystic's openness to grace, on courageous whole-hearted endeavors and an ultimate trust in the Spirit.

Still others think that Royce shifted the center of moral life from love to loyalty and thus diminished the importance of love. Through genuine loyalty, however, Royce required more love in moral life.[1] He required not only devotion to one's chosen beloveds and every individual human person, but also loving commitment to some particular community, to the universal church, to the human race, to the finite universe, and to the Universal Community.

Furthermore, when evaluating Royce, some people forget his setting. They project end-of-century expectations back upon a start-of-century thinker. Then they are disappointed that Royce's mature ethics has precious little to say about feminism, nuclear deterrence, media domination of public opinion, non-violence, and imperialistic capitalism. Unrealistic expectations, such as the foregoing, need not detain us.

Other appraisers of Royce easily overlook the balance between the rational and nonrational aspects of his late moral philosophy. Some resemble William James when he viewed Royce as "the Rubens of philosophy." They judge that because of his impulsive voluntarism Royce was an anti-intellectualist who lacked careful logic and rigorous argumentation. On the other hand, others resemble William James when he viewed Royce as the intellectualistic builder of a block-universe. They picture him as so much of a logical thinker, rational interpreter, and dialectical philosopher, that they lose sight of how he integrated feeling and freedom, creativity and intuition into his late ethics.

A fairer understanding of Royce's mature moral philosophy, then, requires a balanced interpretation of its rational and nonrational elements. The latter include the powerful vital processes underlying human reason. For the hidden persuaders of reason include that human flow of habitual tendencies and shared moods, of affections and memories, of images, myths, and creative fancies. Also deserving notice is that prerational "union of minds and of hearts" which most people, including philosophers, usually feel, simply because they happen to find themselves existing together in the same boat of life.[2]

Royce's sense of fidelity to the wisdom of common folk required him to keep in touch with their traditions and myths. This called him to purify their lore from superstitions and merely legendary factors. Only if it were purified carefully, could ordinary people easily imbibe from their community's wellspring of values. Only if the myths and traditions of their culture were thus criticized, could they harken to its genuine message.

To summarize in contemporary terms, Royce balanced the right and left side of the brain, its masculine and feminine contributions. In fairness, then, evaluators of Royce are called to aim at an equal balance. Having noticed these unbalancing misinterpretations, we may approach a fairer evaluation of Royce's mature ethics. First, we will respond to six probing questions about him. Then we will start to identify some of his weaknesses and strengths.

SIX QUESTIONS ABOUT ROYCE

First, did Royce found a new type of moral philosophy? Perhaps, as Stroh says, not "as a rationalist and idealist."[3] But as an interpreter of what simultaneously fits one's particular community and the Universal Community, the mature Royce created a new type of moral philosophy, a *cathecontic* ethics. Later ethicists, like Paul Ramsey, H. Richard Niebuhr, James Gustafson, William Spohn, and others have used and developed Royce's new way.

Secondly, is self-realization a faithful and accurate way of focusing on the center of Roycean ethics? Although Peter Fuss thought so,[4] I cannot concur, judging from the evidence I have reflected on. For the language of self-realization tends to make Royce into more of a psychologist than a philosopher. More tellingly, to center on self-realization violates Royce's caution against shifting the focus off of the "community to be served by loyalty" onto the individual self. One thus intensifies the illusion of self-centeredness against which Royce battled all his life. For example, after insisting that "being loyal to loyalty" requires the highest personal cultivation, Royce added significantly, "But self-cultivation which is not related to loyalty is worthless."[5]

Thirdly, is the problem of evil the capital issue in Royce's philosophy, as Duron and McDermott say?[6] I agree with this interpretation provided that one takes the term "evil" broadly and triadically. Viewed broadly, evil includes error, ignorance, and natural misfortunes like sickness and death, as well as such moral evils as sin, negligence, stubborn resistance to community, and treason. Viewed triadically, evil is inescapably related both to a finite good from which it derives and to the infinite good which is its norm.

Fourthly, is Royce the most Calvinistic, or perhaps the most Puritan, of the classic American philosophers? Here one first needs to clarify the question. Originally Royce's parents were Baptist and later became Disciples of Christ. This exposed Royce the boy and youth to elements of the evangelical and Reformed traditions. Later, through life in Cambridge he imbibed the Puritan mind still influential in nineteenth- and early twentieth-century New England. Insofar as these attitudes, moods, and doctrines featured in Royce's psyche more than in those of Peirce, James, and Dewey, I lean towards a positive response to the question. Nevertheless, many qualifications are needed.

For instance, I cannot agree with the type of Calvinist into which George Santayana painted Royce when classifying him as "philosophically, [a] perfect Calvinist."[7] First, Santayana did not distinguish between the young Royce who taught him, the middle Royce whose colleague he was, and the mature Royce whom he neither met nor understood. Moreover, the mature Royce did not show the distinctive marks that, according to Santayana, made one a Calvinist; namely, one who feels an "agonized conscience," "a fierce pleasure in the existence of misery, especially of one's own," and that "human nature . . . is totally depraved."[8]

Taking up the suitability of the term "Puritan" for the mature Royce, we again need some clarifications. If interpreted negatively, with its popular emphasis on sexual morals, then "Puritan" does not fit Royce in the sense of being prudish, but only insofar as he, like William James and Woodrow Wilson, shared the mentality of their Victorian Age. Taken for its positive strengths, "Puritan" fits Royce insofar as he and the Puritans held points in common. Both defined individuality socially. Both stressed the moral requirement to participate in public life. Both stressed responsibility and its inescapable role in moral life.

Perhaps this fourth question is better sharpened by asking whether among classical American philosophers Royce is the one most akin to the

Puritan philosopher, Jonathan Edwards. Although I have not found evidence that Royce studied Edwards directly,[9] interesting parallels connect the two. They both were idealists and skillfully employed the logic they knew. Edwards's emphasis on governments by covenant finds some parallel in Royce's communal commitment to the ideal of the Beloved Community. Edwards's concern for "excellency" parallels Royce's concern for a "universal cause." For Edwards, virtue was a response to the excellency of Being in general, and for Royce, genuine loyalty was a response to the universal cause embodied in the Universal Community.

Nevertheless, significant differences separate Edwards from Royce. To the former, a Darwinian worldview was unknown but well known to the latter. Edwards knew nothing of the "new logic" of the late nineteenth century but Royce let it guide his interpretations. Edwards used philosophy as a handmaiden to theology whereas Royce employed philosophy as an autonomous discipline and eschewed the name of theologian. In sum, then, although Royce seems the closest of classic American thinkers to Jonathan Edwards, this statement needs prompt counterbalance to reach a "fairer understanding" of these two great American philosophers.

Fifthly, did the mature Royce, as Duron claims, package all the virtues and duties into loyalty beforehand so that his derivation of them from loyalty became a foregone conclusion?[10] Stated otherwise, did Royce lose sight of the objective formal differences of the virtues when lauding loyalty as "the heart of all the virtues"? In response, it seems that the usually accurate Duron nodded here when he read Royce. For even in his late middle period Royce nuanced his claim in two ways which Duron seems to have overlooked. Royce designated "the *spirit* of loyalty" or "loyalty, as properly defined"— not simply loyalty—as "the heart of all the virtues." He wrote that loyalty

> . . . in its inmost spirit . . . really is the heart of all the virtues, the central duty amongst all duties . . . [that] the spirit of loyalty [w]as the central spirit of the moral and reasonable life of man. . . . *In loyalty, when loyalty is properly defined, is the fulfilment of the whole moral law.*[11]

In 1916 Royce clarified that "spirit" is often to be understood in the light of the social order.

> By the spirit in human life one doesn't mean the esthetically beautiful or what is meant by the "higher emotions," but *whatever brings us into union with the community.*[12]

Whether through persuasion or some dialectic of opposition, any spirit that promotes unity tends towards the Universal Community. If over long periods a spirit moves in this way, it is the spirit of genuine loyalty. Because in Royce's opening definition of loyalty this spirit was only implicit, he regarded that definition as not yet proper.[13] It reached final and appropriate form only at the close of *The Philosophy of Loyalty* when he interpretively identified the "inmost spirit" of loyalty as *"the will to manifest... the conscious and superhuman unity of life....* in and through the deeds of individual selves."[14]

Moreover, the spirit of loyalty is found only in a transformed genuine loyalty. The latter requires a devotion to individuals and communities, a dedication to some particular community, and an openness to the Universal Community. In a transformed genuine loyalty this multiplex balance of commitments gives rise both to the three species of loyalty (Roycean benevolence), specified by the three different kinds of family-like bonds, and to justice, specified by different kinds of contractual obligation. From benevolence and justice, as integrated by the spirit of loyalty, flows the panoply of Royce's virtue ethics. And loyalty's balance of one's manifold commitments also supplies the power needed for the delicate settling of conflicts of loyalty.

Duron's misperception, then, may have been occasioned in part by his translating "loyalty," not as *loyauté*, but as *loyalisme*. He thus made Roycean moral life sound even more abstract and conceptualistic than it did in the "loyalty" of its English original. By contrast, Royce felt eventually that he had to caution readers explicitly against turning the vital ethical energy of transformative genuine loyalty into an "artificial abstraction."[15]

Sixthly and lastly, is Royce's mature ethics vulnerable to the attacks of contemporary deconstructionists? Does Royce build upon a purported foundation whose relativity relativizes his mature philosophy? We can await the eventual overall outcome of the often pyrotechnical debate between foundationalists and anti-foundationalists.[16] Amazingly, by employing both strands of thought, Royce achieved a balance in process. His basic logical system (*Sigma*) starts both from freedom and a Self-determination whose every subsequent step is marked by further freedom and further self-individualizing steps. His mature metaphysics centers on Community and Spirit in Process through fallible interpretations drawn closer to the intent of the Logos-Spirit. His mature ethics arises out of his "third attitude of will" but dialectically embraces the first and second attitudes through reconciling atonement. However foundationalist was the Absolute of Royce's early and middle periods, the mature Royce, transformed by his Peircean insight, proposed the Logos-Spirit of the Universal Community as respectively, the living center and field of his process philosophy, as the truth-knowing-and-generating dynamism at work in his vitalized communal structure. This Spirit exhibits great fluidity of embodiment, is affected by the deeds of the partly blind yet beloved member-selves of the Universal Community, and encounters the various evils impeding finite selves and communities with its fiercely constant and reconciling intent. Consequently, the image of the temporally expanding helix, rather than of a foundation, more aptly indicates Royce's mature philosophy and ethics.

WEAKNESSES OF ROYCE'S MATURE ETHICS

First, we spoke earlier of the nexus of Royce's ethics with his metaphysics and epistemology. If this latter pair reveal a weakness, it affects Royce's late ethics.

Linguistically, Royce needed to insert into his "ontological vocabulary" the actuality of being; that is, its "to be" or *esse*, which is different from what he meant by "existence." In 1916 his ontological vocabulary included "being" (any object thought of), "existence" (what any being in space-time has, whereas numbers lack existence but have being),[17] and "reality" (a teleological holistic dimension possessed by an object that has a meaning, a significance, a totality, such as the world).[18] Had Royce added *esse* to this vocabulary, he would have, when commenting on Santayana's four meanings of "is," transcended to a fifth and primary sense of "is"—its meaning in such judgments as "God *is*" or "A centaur *isn't*."[19]

Metaphysically, then, since Royce restricted causality to events in space-time, he denied that the Absolute (or God) causally creates finite beings.[20] Idealist Royce looked on a finite individual rather as a divine idea or Sign than as a finite being possessed of its proper actuality and structure.[21] Royce's finite individual became primarily a manifestation of the divine rather than an integral whole equipped, as Thomists would say, with its own to be (or *esse*) and intrinsic essence. In this Royce was more Platonic than Aristotelian, more Augustinian than Thomistic.

In other words, Royce needed to face head on Heidegger's starting question for metaphysics, "Why should there be anything at all, and not nothingness?" He needed to explicate a metaphysical interpretation of *esse* as the actuality of being, or, to put it negatively, as the "not being nothingness" of any self and of the world. In brief, Royce needed to balance the being of signifying with the being of actuality.

Epistemologically and to his credit, Royce made *life* an even more ultimate source of interpretability than order (or coherence). Yet, although he used Anselm, Suarez, and Kant to witness the difference between *esse in re* and *esse in intellectu* and thus grasped real *esse*,[22] he did not add *esse* to what he called his "ontological vocabulary." Yet human minded beings can find the actuality of being either in or out of matter, space, and time.[23] One's experience of full self-reflection evinces this truth. It is supported indirectly by a performatory contradiction involving a *reductio ad absurdum*.

Perhaps a contract with Gilson's interpretation of Aquinas may clarify. Gilson based his interpretation of Aquinas's doctrine of *esse* upon one interpretation of Genesis 3:11–20.[24] On this basis, Gilson highlighted the actuality of the divine "to be" and generated a strict analogy of being (through causal proportion) whereby he partly explained the divine creation of finite beings. Gilson's exegesis of God's *esse*, however, hardly conveys a sense of the "Mystery of Being," as Marcel witnesses. Nor did Gilson's emphasis on *esse* convey the dynamism in God's creative concurrence with the world's process. Furthermore, given the unique kind of "production" that divine creation has to be, the term "causality" may first need to be expanded to include another kind of causal efficacy—beyond Aristotle's four kinds—to one that may be called "emanative causality" (which is found experientially in a human self's "production" of a new idea).

If the foregoing remarks are basically on target, then the metaphysical positions of both Royce and Gilson seem in need of being reinterpreted and clarified further so as to be brought into a more intelligible higher synthesis. This first weakness in Royce and Gilson, then, invalidates the thought of neither. And given the mature Royce's deep sense of fallibility, one would expect him to delight in admitting this shortcoming regarding *esse* so that he might strive to achieve a still fairer interpretation of reality.

Secondly, Royce recommended that one should decide rather than procrastinate when, after thoroughly investigating the facts, a person still wondered whether to prefer one or another cause.[25] Effective action requires decisiveness, of course, yet a tough decision carries with it the danger of anchoring the decider too fixedly in one's chosen course. The decider may then become impervious to later accumulating evidence which calls one to reconsider whether or not one should continue on one's chosen course.

In decisions about persons, this danger becomes acute. In his mature period Royce tried to restrain his judgments about others. Nevertheless, his "fondness for articulating, for defining"[26] seems to have led him, especially as World War I grew fiercer, to brand people as enemies, to move towards aggressive steps to stop a foe. He claimed to be trying to avoid contention, but towards the German-Americans in the United States, he held that "America will teach them . . . peacefully if we can, but authoritatively if we must" not to sow dissension in this country.[27] He called the Kaiser an "enemy of the human race" and saw the Prussians as branded with "the mark of Cain."[28] Did such talk show Royce allowing the need for decisiveness to trap him into belligerence towards those who disagreed with him? He confessed that his sense of deep elemental rebelliousness led him to imagine himself standing cheerfully in the guard around the scaffold at the hoped-for hanging of the Kaiser.[29] When thrust into emergency situations, then, Royce sometimes became aggressive, like a mother bear when her cubs are threatened. One can recall his decision in 1916 to charge physically down the icey duckboards of the Harvard yard against an advancing Professor Munsterberg.

Of course, to argue from a philosopher's questionable behavior to a flaw in his ethical doctrine is illegitimate. But his behavior may occasion a question about that doctrine. Did Royce's ethics, then, lack that stress on nonviolence which we find in a Ghandi, a Martin Luther King, Jr., and a Thomas Merton? Few indeed can practice Ghandian nonviolence genuinely. For only a few can fulfill Ghandi's requirements that genuinely nonviolent persons deliberately embrace their vulnerability and maintain inner restraint when being wounded. On the positive side, however, Royce's tone of an inflexible decisiveness in emergency situations, may evidence, among other things, that he designed his ethics, not for a Ghandian-type elite, but for the more common and ordinary folk.

Thirdly, the lack of sexual and political ethics in the doctrine of the mature Royce may disappoint present-day readers. It must be noted, however, that since Royce only divided ethics into "individual and social ethics," the specialized branches of business, medical, legal, sexual, and political ethics seem to have not yet arisen. Moreover, Royce's usual reticence about sexual ethics needs to be set within the context of the kind of response that academics then gave to sex and sexuality. For instance, sexual psychology is practically a non-entity in William James's *Principles of Psychology* of 1890.[30] Twenty years later Freud's seminal lectures on psychotherapy at Clark University evoked little stir—certainly nothing like the reaction that about fifty years earlier Darwin's *Origin of Species* had generated in English universities. Freud's lectures at Clark certainly did not generate in Royce's lifetime the sexual revolution of later decades. Rather, Royce adopted those polite Victorian mental habits of academe which succeeded in maintaining a general silence on the topic of pre-adolescent sexuality.[31] Since the time for sexual ethics had not yet ripened in the New England of 1910–1916, Royce's general silence on this topic becomes more understandable. Hence, within the Victorian ambiance then dominant at Harvard, Royce's "supersexual insight," described above, seems all the more remarkable.

STRENGTHS IN ROYCE'S MATURE ETHICS

In this section we will first survey in general some strengths in Royce's final ethics and then turn to its relation to American philosophical ethics. Thereupon, we will focus on the strengths in his mature analysis of ethical life and in the relations he saw between ethics and religion, biblical traditions, and Christianity. The chapter will close with the broaching of some questions not resolved in this evaluation.

A General Survey of Strengths in Royce's Mature Ethics

An initial survey that catalogues some strengths in Royce's mature ethics may serve either to index topics already elaborated or to provide a check-list of topics needing future study. The way Royce interwove the ideas of Spirit, Community, and Process into his late ethical thought certainly constitutes one of his great contributions to ethical thought. This integration is rooted in his mature doctrine, mentioned above, of the "relational form of the ontological argument."[32]

Secondly, nominalism holds that individuals are the only ultimate realities, simple units related only externally. Much as Peirce saw nominalism as the bane of modern philosophy, especially in its British versions, so, too, did Royce mount a much needed critique of nominalism, running from his *Primer of Logical Analysis* (1881) to the *Hope of the Great Community* (1916). For instance, many readers of *The World and the Individual* regarded its exposition and critique of "Realism" as strange and exaggerated. They failed to recognize in it a logically based critique of the very nominalism that their position presupposed.

Another quite significant contribution was Royce's focus on the "three attitudes of will." He showed that only the third attitude avoided performative self-contradiction. When he tried to deny the third attitude, it re-established itself and reinstated his positive loyal embrace of the universe as a whole.

With his stress on fidelity to experiences and on the need to accept the proven results of scientific investigation, Royce developed a well-balanced ethics that avoided two extremes. It was neither so prefabricated that it rested mainly on *a priori* principles and an Absolute. Nor was it so situational that it required no fidelity to further intellectual searching or to the constant bearing of self-reinstating principles. One may even look for parallels between Royce's mature ethics, with its experiential scientific interpretational method, and recently revised versions of natural law ethics.[33]

The strengths of Royce's general and subordinate methods in his late ethics, of his art of loyalty, and of the contentual insights of first and second magnitude are too significant to detail here. Nevertheless, some summary remarks on these strengths need to be made.

Royce's empirico-historical method witnesses to how, in his final decade, he increasingly used the data from illuminating cases and the positive sciences to initiate and enrich his ethical reflections. Further research into this special method confirms how correctly W. E. Hocking had testified in 1916 to Royce's empiricism.[34] Again, as a historian of philosophy, Royce also applied, almost by second nature, his habit of viewing things historically, to the study of moral development, especially during his final decade.

His special ethical method called for a distinctive kind of interpretation —one animated by genuine loyalty—and for a normative investigation of ideals and problems. Stimulated by the dying Peirce's letter of mid-1913, Royce pondered why there occurs in us an "exaltation of beauty, duty, or truth." He employed his three leading ideas of freedom, duty, and goodness to carry out serially his reconsideration of ethical ideals and problems.

Keeping in touch with current world problems was also a demand he made of himself during his late investigation of moral life. For instance, he insisted that each nation is subordinate to the "principles of international morality" and contemned any State that rejected international duty by claiming, as he saw Germany doing, "that there is no moral authority on earth which ranks superior to the will of the State."[35]

He advanced his ethical investigation dialectically by alternating his "social and logical approaches." He focused his special ethical musement upon the question, "Who and What am I?"—a problem that led into the paradox and mystery of self-identification.

Royce's general method of interpretive musement presupposed in the interpreter the third attitude of will and a union-promoting "will to interpret." This general method mused over possibilities, proceeded fallibly, depended on other minded beings, and tested proposals for furthering union. Through its teleological impetus and the mediated guidance of the Spirit of the Universal Community, it corrected itself as it proceeded into the future.

In his final years Royce emphasized the art of loyalty as much as its principles. For his was a philosophy of life that also required him to focus on how to live the moral life. The art of loyalty meant idealizing one's causes by the use of both grief and imagination and by training oneself to harmonize one's causes. When the artist of loyalty encounters a seeming conflict of causes, she searches for the common ground both share. Amid life's ups and downs, she does not forget her ideals but harnesses life-problems to her ideals. With the light of the latter, she endeavors to discern the fitting response in an ongoing reinterpretation of her situation, of her past, and of possible future responses.

Regarding content, Royce's late emphases on family, solidarity, and mediation are today clearly needed for an ethical entry into the twenty-first century. So, too, does humankind today need loyalty to the Great Community of the whole human family, if exaggerated nationalism, ethnic hubris, and environmental neglect are to be overcome. In the frequent conflicts within interpersonal relationships—whether at the familial, local, national, or global levels—people also need to identify which species of loyalty needs to be emphasized.

Furthermore, to acknowledge frankly with Royce that human selves live amid currents of sin and salvation will enable people to recognize that

Royce's mature ethics suits their actual situation realistically. Any *merely* rational ethics will surely prove unsuited, for it knows nothing of the role of affectivity and commitment in moral life and scarcely faces up to human weakness of will, sin, and tragedy. Instead, the wiser purchase seems an ethics, like that of the mature Royce, which takes all these factors into account and confronts directly the human situation as saturated with energies both sinful and salvific. Such an ethic enables contemporaries to use "the fitting" as a normative guide on life's journey of ever greater moral development. Such an ethic leads through the rough spots of isolation and tragedy onto the higher paths where people can even generate the reconciling energies so needed for those still caught in the swamps of alienation, arrogance, and cynicism. Amid the widespread psychic moods of failure and discouragement, of frustration and guilt, few inner dynamisms are more needed than the bold radical hope that Royce emphasized. It is a hope founded ultimately on the Universal Community and its Spirit.

The will of the Universal Community's Spirit initiates and sustains an objective moral order, even if finite individual wills must respond to it through their own perspectives. This order is reflected in Royce's few formal principles "that predetermine all of our concrete activities."[36] These universal principles are found to be absolute since the effort to deny them only reinstates them performatively. The objective moral order is also reflected in Royce's absolute modes of action—for example, in his third attitude of will, or his devotion to universal loyalty, or his respectful estimate of minded being in himself and others. Royce's self-reinstating principles and his absolute modes of action are validly interpreted, then, as "expressing a will which . . . has an universal absolute nature,—the same in all of us."[37]

Metaphysically, Royce contextualized his mature ethics within a processing universe that was teleologically directed, via a "wise provincialism," towards eventual union of member individuals and member communities, within the Universal Community. Despite all this process and change, however, Royce's pluralistic universe did not flow into a possibly non-convergible multi-verse, as James's world did.

Epistemologically, Royce synthesized and balanced the three motives of pragmatism, personalism, and objectivity within his modern theory of truth. Since this critically pragmatic theory governed the generation of true interpretations, it served as a fitting basis for his late ethics.[38] Similarly, in his ethics Royce was clearly a cognitivist and in no way a mere emotivist.[39]

Again, Royce taught that people need the experience of "lost causes." For such losses can bring home to illuded human selves the true site and nature of spiritual fulfillment. Such losses can purify human selves from the illusion of equating the events of human history with the authentic cause of human selves.[40]

Furthermore, Royce's insight of May 1916, that "the very recognition of Being is itself an estimate" seems profoundly significant.[41] By avoiding an inference, he here circumvented the so-called naturalistic fallacy in which one tries illogically to infer an "ought" from an "is."[42] Although percepts and concepts cannot recognize Being as a value or disvalue, interpretation can. Thus, interpretative knowing became indispensable for Royce's experientially rooted ethics.

Then, too, after 1916 the moral cancer of ethical relativism clearly metastasized among Americans. But Royce had erected a bulwark against ethical relativism with his anti-nominalism, his tenet of a "common rational human nature," and his self-reinstating principles. The ground for his self-reinstating principles lay in the experience of trying to deny them. The attempted denial created a performative contradiction and only served to highlight the undeniable fact that such principles are used unavoidably. Some of these principles are speculative; e.g., the past cannot be revoked; the future cannot be avoided. Some are practical; e.g., be loyal to universal loyalty; respect humanity equally in yourself and other persons. Such undeniable principles, of course, still need to be embodied in decisions that are tentative, situationally conditioned, and relative to one's will. Nevertheless, such principles insert enough of the absolute into one's consciousness to limit the valid range of ethical relativism and to hold one accountable to absolute standards.

Strengths in Relation to American Ethical Thought

Royce described his pragmatism as an "Absolute Pragmatism" since inescapably "all search for truth is a practical activity, with an ethical purpose."[43] Since this ethical goal of truth-seeking is knowable, at least in general, Royce could not and would not tolerate the narrow kind of pragmatism that did not know its overall purpose of truth-seeking and ethical growth. For if human selves simply settled for an accurate solution of some particular life-problem without caring to fit their solution into the overall direction of their lives, they became dehumanized. For this reason Royce required a person to have some synoptic vision for ethical life—that one view it, namely, through the ideas of the community *and* the individual, through the lenses of concrete social dynamics *and* logical implications. He also required that one adopt some wise and at least general view within which to direct and carry out one's life choices.

Royce served American ethics well by calling attention to a more authentic "translation" of C. S. Peirce's pragmatism than William James had offered. Whereas James had called people simply to live in the light of actual consequences, Royce told his audience to live in the light of all possible consequences. The latter directive not only contained more fecundity and innovation,[44] but also drew attention to Peirce's profounder meaning of pragmatism. In sum, Royce's correction of James's interpretation of Peirce's pragmatism may have saved discerning American thought from getting caught in too narrow a view of pragmatism.

Then, too, according to James's description, a "tough-minded" thinker is empiricist, materialistic, irreligious, and pluralist.[45] The mature Royce, however, showed he could be empiricist and rational, idealist and realist, artistic and scientific, religious and secular, and so monistically communitarian that he was open to a pluralism of interacting individuals and communities. He showed that one could be "tough-minded" and "tender-minded" in different areas at the same time. Royce thus seems to have become himself an example of a "third way" lying between James's dichotomy of the "tender-minded" and "tough-minded."

Strengths within Royce's Analysis of Ethical Life

We start by viewing Royce's analysis in general. Royce's lifelong wrestling with the problem of evil is a commonplace. The reverse side of his ubiquitous encounter with the problem of evil, however, receives less attention; namely, Royce's *struggle with the problem of the better*. He found that the human self's wrestlings with various conflicts of loyalties occasion vital challenges for moral development. Not that, *pace* Dewey, all moral life consists in nothing but a series of conflicts. For there are non-conflictive reaffirmations of morally good habitual tendencies.[46] Nevertheless, moral life also brings its conflicts of loyalties, as Royce knew. These may arise between general loyalties (such as motherhood or professional career), or between inadequate and fully human living (such as a student's mostly passive presence in a classroom or raising questions about the teacher's presentation) or between acting on one's own and with competent consultation (such as driving a carriage by one's felt skills alone or by also taking judicious account of the other passengers' remarks about traffic). Concerning the last mentioned type of conflict, Royce said in 1914:

> Nothing is more disastrous in human life than the effort to think of our moral problems in terms of our conflicting interests as detached individuals. . . . But when friendship and common human activities have made of us something which is of the nature of the community, then we can speak of this community in the first person plural. And the effort to interpret this will ["our common interest"] is not a hopeless effort.[47]

When these various conflicts of loyalty arise, they call one to do more than simply follow an already established habit or a previously determined intention. They call one to actualize a decision in the present, to make a moral choice for better or worse. They confront one with decisions: Shall

I adopt the third attitude of will or slip back into the easier first or second attitudes? Shall I discern or not discern an intelligent way of greater service to my community and to all people?

In interpersonal relationships conflicts often arise from an unfitting use of power. The question arises, then, whether Royce developed an ethics of power within his ethics of a community of interpretation. To my knowledge, Royce never dedicated a lecture or chapter explicitly to an ethics of power. Yet he showed clearly his recognition that in this area the burning question was *how* power should be used.

On this issue, I find Royce subtle and adroit, as shown in his treatment of the three species of loyalty. According to that doctrine, the best use of power between friends becomes truth-seeking love. The best use of power between siblings (or their corporate and national equivalents) is insistence on equality. Then, too, various kinds of "generational gaps" arise because of different lengths of experience in technology, nationhood, religion, art, and so forth. In these situations, which resemble the parent-child relationship, the best use of power becomes an honest mutual recognition of the different positions of the "two sides," of their diverse yet complementary responsibilities to each other, and of the guidance of both human and superhuman "spirits of the community."

Then, too, because he had often reconsidered the long history of ethics in the West, Royce did not allow himself to accept the traditional dichotomy between teleology and deontology. Instead, he transcended this either/or split by focusing on the moral life of genuine loyalty. That life needs to integrate harmoniously the three leading ethical ideas—freedom, goodness, and duty.

But this life must arise from the third attitude of will. Royce's mature analysis of moral life identified this attitude as the only valid one constitutive of genuine ethical life and necessary for maintaining it. The third attitude effected the vital balance needed between an authentic individualism and a genuine loyalty devoted to a particular community yet open to the Universal Community.

Mention of balance suggests that we shift the focus from the general features of the mature Royce's moral analysis to his increasing concern for balance and harmony. His mature sense of the inadequacy of any one position[48] led him to emphasize the need of a process of complementarity. Each insight needed to be counterbalanced and set within the enriching dynamism of the interpretive process. By such a dialectic he could reach a fuller and fairer understanding.

For instance, when he sketched Emerson's view of the youth's call to patriotic duty, Royce felt he had to raise several objections to this view. Only thus could he portray a more complete view of duty. Again, despite the numerous signs of both teleology and deontology in Royce's late ethics, he would not permit a primacy of place to these ideas. Rather, he insisted on integrating them with that third "great and fundamental idea"—free self-direction. Then he harmonized all three principal ethical ideas within the concrete operation of the life of loyalty. In this operation the loyal life and its normative ideas were adapted appropriately to one situation after another.

Other instances of balance deserve notice. Royce effected a strong union of reason, emotion, and will in his ethics. Each factor in this triad had to affect the other two and all had to be directed harmoniously. Royce's mature ethics was marked by a similarly strong and wise balance of memory and hope, both in the individual and the community. This contrasted with a naturalistic ethic that so overrates the future that the past is likely to be disregarded. Thus, such a naturalistic ethic, claiming to be prospective rather than descriptive or normative, tends to overlook the wisdom purified from humankind's past successes and failures. A final instance of the balance Royce created appeared, as we saw, in the way he harmonized method, art, and content to generate his late ethics. None of these three factors was adequate by itself; only their synthesis could foster a fairer understanding of ethical life.

Strengths within Royce's Relation of Ethics and Religion

Royce's "appreciative sense of the more vital" enabled him to scent the human danger in a merely self-enclosed human ethic.[49] This sense led Royce to create, as early as 1883, a philosophical ethic open to the divine. He succeeded in maintaining the philosopher's perspective of studying ethics simply "from the human side." Yet, by putting it this way in the *Problem*, he also called for a complementary view "from the divine side." From this latter side, an ethics would employ a specific faith-held revelation from God about his willed intent for a humankind that struggles in a sin-filled yet salvific situation and about human persons' fitting use of their freedom in response to this will of God. Such a discipline is called "moral theology" and complements a religiously animated philosophical ethics.

Royce showed this openness to the divine when he allowed the "three Christian ideas" of the *Problem* to influence his ethics. Many Americans operate out of an isolated individualism, or a self-touted psychic healthiness, or a yen for the pleasant and comfortable. Royce criticized such self-centered individualisms and hedonisms by emphasizing the counterbalancing ideas of community, our situation of natural alienation, and the need for medicinal atonement. He held that this latter triad of Christian ideas was more needed by, and better suited to, Americans' way of actually living than was the former hedonistic triad which marked the "detached individual."

American naturalists propose a methodological atheism—such as appears in their "Humanist Manifesto." They may reconstruct the term "God" to mean the lure of the ideal to the better. Such redefinition does not coincide adequately with the holy mysterious One whom Christians address as the "God and Father of our Lord Jesus Christ."

By contrast to the naturalists, Royce kept his ethics open to the Christian divine in the following ways. More than any other classical American philosopher, Royce employed biblical language, which he and the Apostle Paul called the "sword of the Spirit," which is believed to carry the effective Word of God. He also concurred with Wordsworth in viewing duty as the "daughter of the Most High." In some real sense, then, he made conscience, as the mouthpiece of duty, a fallible yet actual expression of "the voice of God." Moreover, Royce's human self was open to the divine since, by becoming a loyal finite self in a genuine community, it thus encountered the direction of the Logos-Spirit of the Universal Community. But to sift between such direction and those other directions being inserted by self-centered assertiveness or withdrawal, Royce insisted that the genuinely loyal self must keep "discerning the spirits," a gift won by praying to interpret. In these and other ways the mature Royce indicated that people's moral and religious interests cohere.

Biblically, Royce drew upon the Hebraic view of God as the "righteous Ruler of the world."[50] This God summons human selves to follow their inner divine spark (*Fünkelin*) and become doers of what is right, like God himself. It is at least psychologically problematic whether a human self can have a positive self-image if he or she lacks a sense of being a divine spark, an image of God. But, according to Royce, a human self, through its basic *epsilon* relationship, enjoys the powerful embodiment of "belonging" to the righteous pedagogue Spirit-Interpreter. Naturalist ethicists lack this resource.

Through his doctrine of *epsilon* embodied in the *Fünkelin*, Royce echoed much of the ethical view of his beloved Jewish-Christian, the Apostle Paul. For both held that the Logos-Spirit intends to heal and restore alienated humankind into her company. Both men thought that this Spirit exercises a dynamic influence by leading human selves toward righteousness, transforming them into it, and when once attained, by enhancing them in it. For this righteousness wells up from the Trinity and from it borrows its majesty. One's righteousness does not consist in success or efficiency, but in the blessedness of this union with the divine.[51]

Beyond the idea of God as righteous Ruler, the Hebrew scriptures also confirmed Royce's mature ethics with their idea of covenant and its product: a covenanted people. According to this traditional biblical idea, God, his people, and its individual members are all required to be faithful (loyal) to the covenant. Since Royce's idea of loyalty can therefore be traced back to God's covenants with Abraham and Moses, its historical roots reach back much farther than the "federal theology" of the Puritans, or the oaths of

Japanese Samurai, or Calvin's doctrine of the covenant, or the mutual pledge of a medieval knight and his lord, or the new covenant of Jesus in his blood.

Sharpening our focus, we can investigate the strengths found in Royce's mature ethics, considered as a Christian ethic. Is there, for instance, a specifically Christian tone to Royce's "three principal ethical ideas"? His first idea of freedom became genuine only when it operated in a human self who belonged to—was in *epsilon* relation with—the Logos-Spirit of the Fourth Gospel.[52] The uniqueness of such freedom is seen in its Christ-like commitment to serve others—sometimes even in an atoning way—by serving the cause of a particular community that is open to the Universal Community.

Another basic idea of Royce was duty. Within the actual human situation, marked by both sinful and salvific energies, duty transcends merely rational guidelines. Royce spoke of a higher or "genuinely rational attitude" which consisted in "the consideration of the true good which comes from seeing the divine perfection in everything," the experience of "finding God in all things." One is to do so even in conflicts, failures, and tragedies by viewing each as that through which the Spirit persuades to the better.[53] For in such conflictive situations duty becomes a requirement to help reconcile the alienated, even becomes an exigence to atone and co-atone within a suffering servant community. Duty calls genuine loyalists to humble risk-taking and efforts at countering estrangements. Concretely, it calls for what Jesus meant by his example and command of feetwashing.

Goodness, Royce's final basic idea, took on the color of Christian blessedness in what he called "the Realm of Grace."[54] Thus the better was what promoted this teleological harmony more. In this realm, grace originates "as from above" in a way that philosophy cannot explain. Grace somehow comes from the Universal Community's Logos-Spirit who guides the universe and over all holds the initiative. The result is that the whole problem of evil is set within the Spirit's guidance. This supplies the ultimate ground for the bold hope that to all personal immorality and treason, to all impersonal accidents and chance events, there corresponds a counterbalancing healing and integration.[55] The life of grace within the Beloved Community is good through and beyond all evil.

Besides Christian ideas, there is the Christian way of life. A Christian does not turn his experiences into a system, but allows himself to be led through the variety and surprises of reality. But reality is sometimes dark and obscure, and surely not fully comprehensible to human selves. Meeting such reality, Royce created an ethics that paralleled the spirit of Newman's Christian ethics. Royce, too, prayed, "Lead, kindly Light" with just enough light for the next "step . . . amid the encircling gloom."[56] After doing all he could, he surrendered in openness to the fuller vision and caring healing of the Universal Spirit.[57] Such a response fitted that docility which Royce had situated between sensitiveness and initiative as the three pivotal dynamics of psychological life in human selves.[58]

When emphasizing the need to undergo lost causes, Royce struck another Christian note. Here Royce taught that Christian life is a passage through dyings into risings, that expectably life will be hard, dark, and full of deadly risks, but that only through actual death do we move into the life which dies no more.[59]

Finally, by realistically grasping people's actual moral situation—as caught in misunderstandings and alienation, in struggles and tragedies—Royce came to tailor his humanistic and philosophical approaches to fit this situation. He thus opened it to, and made it consonant with, a Christian approach to ethics. He showed this especially in the central role he gave to atonement in his ethics. He thus paralleled closely Christianity's identification of itself in the Paschal Mystery of Christ's dying and rising as this is carried out in the members of Christ's community throughout the ages.

In these ways, then, the mature Royce modeled a Christian ethicist who engages in his or her reasoning in openness to the Logos-Spirit who teaches, reconciles, and draws humankind towards further union. By inserting in his mature ethics an openness to grace, to forgiveness, to the reception of atoning energies, Royce created an "ethics on the boundary," a *grenz ethik*. He revealed the limits of philosophical ethics and showed the need of the latter for an explicit relation with religion. Thus he kept ethics from becoming itself an absolute. In brief, he effected a Kierkegaardian transcendence of the ethical.

Some Remaining Questions for Evaluation

John E. Smith believes that Royce's ethics is for the few, not at all for the many.[60] Perhaps some qualifications are needed which limits of time prevented Smith from adding. Royce certainly aimed for the multitudes in *The Philosophy of Loyalty*. As we saw, he did not accept Nietzsche's "morality of the lordly class." His hundreds of public lectures tried to reach any Americans interested in learning. In his 1915–16 Extension Course on Ethics, he reached beyond his usual Harvard audience to Bostonians—mostly women who sought to recognize better moral living. This late move suggests Royce's aim to teach more ordinary folk, even if his audience did not include the dock-hands and hired girls of Boston.

On the other hand, in favor of Smith's view, Royce's late doctrine of loyalty lacks an explicit preferential option for the poor. It needs a strong counterweight against the systemic favoring of the first beneficiaries of the free-enterprise regime dominant in Royce's environment. In an age prior to one that currently speaks of "unjust systemic structures," Royce floated along with his colleagues, largely out of touch with "the fetishism of the commodity" and the particular patterns of greed which then marked the suppositions of Harvard capitalism.[61]

Then too, Royce's mature ethics did not start from the lives of most Bostonians of his day—the immigrant Irish and Italians—but from the established power-holding white Anglo-Saxon Protestants. Boston's poor majority might have instanced for Royce his focus on suffering servanthood but it seems not to have led him to a greater emphasis on social justice for the laboring classes. A bias for the power of investors may have unduly exerted itself within his ethics.[62] In brief, Smith's view that Royce's ethic aimed at the few rather than the many needs further research and discussion.

There is another and final unsolved question: has the present work failed to point out certain significant constrictions in Royce's mature ethics? If Royce did not, as just seen, fully transcend the perspectives and biases of his culture, what effect marred his ethics? Admittedly, his mature ethics was marked by a fecund method and ideas, a religious catholicity, and an outreach to Eastern thought. Yet with the advantage of an eighty-year hindsight, we can notice certain constrictions. Royce's encounter with Eastern ethical thought was limited—as he would be the first to acknowledge. He knew that his doctrine of the invisible church called any genuine loyalist to seek its embodiment in some visible church. Yet as an adult, he never brought himself to make such a commitment.[63] Finally, Royce would readily admit that his mature ethics needs updating, particularly in its applications. His insights concerning racism, environment, peace, insurance, world community, and a wise provincialism remain illuminating. But if alive today, he would apply his ethical method, art, and content to current issues in business ethics—especially its international dilemmas—media manipulation, dysfunctional families, terrorism, and low-intensity conflict. In his own humble limits and service, however, Royce with twinkling eye would readily pass on the torch to the upcoming generation of American ethicists.

Appendix A:
A Letter On Loyalty

JOSIAH ROYCE TO HIS FUTURE
DAUGHTER-IN-LAW, ELIZABETH RANDOLPH:

November 16, 1910

Dear Elizabeth:—

...Perhaps what I now suggest may help to tell you, not so much what I chance to think, but what, as I believe, your own heart has been teaching you for a good while. I can only try to bring the truth as to such things to your notice, now that you already have that truth within you. Life teaches pretty much the same lesson to everybody. The chief question is whether or no you get your eyes open to what that lesson is.

You ask: "Why *must* we live?" You wonder whether there is some "definite purpose" in life. And you also wonder whether we have to "take all this for granted," without proof, and whether "faith or fear is the stronger" as a guide to life.

My answer to such questions you find at length in the book on Loyalty. But if you will accept a mere condensation of an answer into a few phrases, I may state the case thus:—"Why must I live?"—Well, first, take me just as I *happen* to be,—a mere creature who happens to have been born, and to want happiness, and who happens to breathe and to eat and to long vaguely for I know not what,—take me merely thus, as a creature of nature,—and the question has no particular answer. Any other creature might,—so far as the mere natural fact of existence goes,—any other creature might as well be living in my place. I shall die after a while,—and what will it all have meant? That, I say, is all that can be answered to your question, Why must we live?

See *Letters*, 547–551; quoted with permission; Royce's emphases. Elizabeth Randolph married Royce's second son, Edward [Ned] Royce, on December 29, 1911, in Germantown, Pennsylvania.

so long as you consider us merely as accidental creatures of nature. But let me look at my life otherwise. Suppose I come to see, or even just to imagine, that there is some good to be done in the world that nobody but myself can do. Suppose I learn that there is something or somebody who needs just me to give aid for worthy ends of some sort. Suppose that this world of people, all so needy, *needs my help.* Well then the question, Why must I live? begins to get its answer. *I must live because my help is needed.* There is something that I can do which nobody else can do. That is: I can be friend of my friends, faithful to my own cause, servant of my own chosen task, worker among my needy brethren. I can thus join with the world's work of trying to make the whole situation better and not worse. And because I can live thus, I am more than a chance creature of nature. My life has sense and meaning—That is the first and simplest answer to the question Why must I live?

But of course that *first* answer does not of itself tell you *what* it is which you are needed to do to help the other people. And a great many good people who want to be helpful do indeed pass much of their life in a more or less amiable ineffectiveness, because they have not yet quite defined the "purpose" which gives life its true sense. It is just that purpose which I have tried, in my book, to define by the word "Loyalty." *The* help which my friends really most want of me, is help in living "in the unity of the spirit," as lovers and faithful friends, as patriots and all those who together are devoted to art, to humanity, to their religion, or to whatever *binds the souls of men in the common ties of the spirit,*—as all such, I say, are, in their various ways, trying to live. Whenever and however I can steadily and faithfully live in this way, I am really helping,—helping not only my own nearer friends, but, by my example and my indirect influence, I am helping everybody who is even remotely related to me or influenced by me, to give sense to his life. Now thus to live,—to live for the sake of the "unity of the spirit," to live for some "cause that binds many lives in one,"—to live thus is to possess what I call Loyalty. Very various "causes," such as the service of a country or a church or a fraternity or a family, or a friendship or a love,—or a science or a profession or an art,—very various causes, I say, can for various people form part of their personal "cause," or be selected as the principal means of living in the loyal spirit. But the great principle of the art of giving sense to life, is the principle:—Have a cause, choose it, and having chosen it, be fearlessly and steadily faithful to it.

In my book I have stated this view of the business of life partly, also, in the following way:—

"By nature," that is, apart from some choice of a cause to which to be loyal, each one of us is a mass of capricious and conflicting longings, passions, impulses, motives. We want happiness, but do not naturally know how to get it. We want "independence," and yet are always dependent upon other people's company, good will, or admiration, or other help. We want "power," but grow weary with our struggles to get power. We are fond of our fellow mortals, yet constantly tend to one or another sort of conflict with them. And in countless other ways we find that the first thing to note about our merely natural desires is that they endlessly fight one another, and that every one of us is, "by nature," a mass of contradictions.

Now is there any one way of escaping from this sort of conflict of desires? There is. This way is suggested whenever we come to feel that there is in the world something that not only, as I just said, needs *our help*, but that is, in its own importance, so vast, so dignified, so worthy or so precious, that, no matter how we happen to feel at any one moment, and no matter what the present state of our natural desires is, that something is always *worth helping*.

Now that is exactly what we come to know whenever we fall in love with what, in my lectures on Loyalty, I have called a "Cause." What a "cause" is, my book has tried to tell and I have just suggested to you. There are countless special "causes." And you always have to find out what your own special cause is, and to find that out for yourself. Only with regard to choosing a "cause" there are two things to remember:—*First* that, however various the special "causes" are which people whom I call "the Loyal" serve, there is a sense in which all devoted people serve the same great "cause," the cause of helping mankind, by example and by service, to get out of the confusions and conflicts of our natural impulses, to stop fighting and rivalry, and hatred, and "selfishness," and to live in unity and the spirit of faithfulness. And *Second*, that *nothing* in life can be better than to find some cause to which, through your own resolute will, you *can* be devoted for life. For devotion, faith, giving ourselves to our chosen cause, isn't bondage. It is the only possible freedom. It is the only way, if not wholly to calm, then at least to control, to centralize, to unify, our naturally so varying and capricious selves. It is so, because, when I find what is *outside* of me, and *greater* than I am, and more precious than is my private happiness, that very finding of my cause begins at once to hold me together,—to give me sense and unity, to make me indifferent to my own moods and caprices. It is then no longer what I get, but what I give to my cause that I find valuable about my life. And so long as I have strength, I can give, whatever my luck. And so long as I can do something for my cause, life is worthwhile, and has sense, whatever my private fortunes. If I then ask: "Why must I live?" the answer is always ready: "Because my cause needs my help."—If I still ask: Why choose a cause?,—the answer is,—"Only thus can my life get sense, only thus can I help my fellows to give sense to their own lives."

As to "fear," there is nothing so much to be feared as aimlessness and chaos. As to "faith," there can be no faith more rational than the faith in the value of spiritual unity and faithfulness.

It is this sort of doctrine that I have long been preaching, and trying in my poor way to live out. . . .

Katharine sends love. We are glad to hear of Dec. 24 as the probable date [of the wedding]. . . . And whatever you tell us is most prized, and whatever we can do to help you our dearest desire.—

Yours Lovingly,
Josiah.

Appendix B:
Royce's Mid-Year Examination

UNIVERSITY EXTENSION COURSES
ETHICS

I
A Case Involving Problems of Loyalty

Years ago, the following "case of conscience" was stated to the lecturer by a young woman who wrote from a distance, who asked counsel about her duty, who explained her problem in a brief series of letters, and who then, although invited to ask further questions, and to furnish, if she chose, more facts, preferred not to continue the correspondence. The lecturer has never seen this woman, and has no knowledge of her later course of action, or of her fortunes since these few letters were written.

What can here be summarized on the basis of this brief correspondence, furnishes the topic for this examination. Read the case carefully; assume that the gist of this young woman's letters is here correctly reported; and then devote the rest of your three hours time to answering the questions stated below, in section II of this examination paper.

This young woman, the only daughter of a widow, was (to judge her solely from her few letters) a sensitive and somewhat brooding person, highly intelligent and thoughtful,—a sufferer from a great many "balked dispositions" (to borrow the phrase that Wallas has made familiar to the students of this course),—and a good deal troubled also with distrust of herself, and with some tendency to be too suspicious of other people's motives. But she was a very affectionate daughter, and had always tried to be a dutiful one. There seems to be no reason to think that her beliefs about her mother were founded upon any motives or feelings that one ought to call morbidly disordered. She may have been mistaken about the facts; she

---

may have exaggerated the importance of some of them; but she seemed to be writing not only with love for her mother, but with a not wholly ineffective effort to judge matters fairly.

The mother, represented as herself a loving, but also as a somewhat pedantic person, was proud, reserved, and fond of affectionately dominating this only daughter, who had therefore been accustomed, since childhood, to know very little about matters of the world's business, and to live too quiet and ineffective a life. Her companions (after early childhood was once passed), had been few. Her mother had been, for years, her only decidedly intimate associate; while this intimacy itself had been confined to the rather narrow range of their common interests,—in their household life and in their somewhat simple social doings.

The maxims upon which, as the daughter remembered, her own moral training had always been based, were simple but notable. Her father had been a man of mark, and of a somewhat prominent family. So she had been taught: "Never forget that you are a daughter of X," or "that you are an X." This maxim had controlled the young girl's manners, and to some extent her tastes and cultivation, which were good. As to her general social bearing, and her dealings with neighbors and friends, the maxim had been "Do not make trouble for people." An unaggressive aimiability had thus been early trained in her. That was why she had made no new intimates, and for years had seemed to need none. But at length this quiet life had wearied her. When she wrote these letters, she was restless, aspiring, and as rebellious as she also was, according to her lights, conscientious.

The mother and daughter had lived for years too much apart from other people, so far as general social relations were concerned. Meanwhile, the widowed mother,—an energetic woman, had come to be a trusted servant of some large corporation, had used her business opportunities with apparent success, and, at the same time when these letters were written, had some share in the conduct of important commercial enterprises.

But within a few years before the date when this story was written down by the daughter, the young woman had become, first suspicious, and then (as time went on) more and more certain, that the mother was, in various, and in rather complicated ways, secretly defrauding her own employers. The sums involved, as the daughter believed, were probably large, or would soon become large. Nor could the daughter venture to judge very confidently how great a risk of being detected in her frauds the mother was running. Furthermore, owing to her own very limited range of business knowledge, the daughter was also unable to tell how far she herself was personally dependent, for the means which she then enjoyed, upon the mother's supposed crookedness.

So far, the daughter had never ventured to mention to anyone her own surmises about these fraudulent doings, or even to allude to the topic in speaking with the mother. Had the daughter not learned in childhood that she must "make no trouble" for people? Still less had she as yet thought it possible to appeal to any of their family relatives. The family pride, the sensitiveness, and the long practiced aloofness of both women, stood in the way of frankness regarding so delicate a topic, unless some crisis should force a new policy.

Meanwhile, the whole situation, as between the two, constantly became more and more tense. The mother and daughter now lived on mutual concealments, evasions, and downright lies, whenever there was any question regarding the mother's business. Neither must suspect that the other suspected, etc., etc.

Yet the mother's business, whatever it was, must go on. The employers must be faced by both women, in frequent meetings. The daughter must bear the pangs of believing that she herself was dependent, for her daily bread, as well as for all her opportunities and for her luxuries, upon fraud. In addition, she must endure torturing fears lest her mother's frauds should any day be unmasked. Meanwhile the daughter could hope to get more certain evidences about the well hidden facts, and about the extent of the supposed frauds, only in case she undertook spying methods of her own, or else appealed to outsiders for help in the investigation.

At least three courses of action suggest themselves as, under these circumstances, possible for the daughter. Yet these three are not the only possible courses. Perhaps still other and better courses than any of these three could be devised. These three, however, may next be here set down in their order, so as to aid you in beginning your inquiry.

1. The daughter might break with her mother, once for all, by leaving home, and by undertaking some new calling of her own. If this calling succeeded, it would make the daughter pecuniarily independent, and would free her from any need of sharing the proceeds of the mother's frauds (if indeed there were any such frauds). But this course would, in unfilial fashion, abandon the mother to her fate. Her heart might be broken. This course then might lead the mother to a premature death, or drive her to worse frauds than ever, or bring the sensitively trained and naturally lonely and unworldly daughter herself into hopeless struggles with new destinies.

2. The daughter could drop all evasions, boldly call her mother's attention to the evidences of the frauds, and demand explanation, and a full knowledge of the facts. But this effort to fight the way to clearness of life for both these women would probably simply be another way of leading to a break of the daughter with the mother, and would thus probably involve evils at least as serious as those involved in course 1.

3. The daughter could say to herself: "Since I must not be enjoying the fruits of fraud without knowing what my position really is, and since, unless I am ready to break with my mother, I cannot hope to find out the truth by

open inquiry addressed to my mother, I will use whatever spying methods I need in order to unravel this whole mystery."

II
Questions Suggested by this Case

Suppose yourself asked to give counsel to this young woman, and invited to work out, upon a basis of further correspondence, or of conversation with her, a plan for aiding these two women to live a reasonably successful and loyal life.

1. What sort of further information would you try to get as a means of throwing light upon the problem whether the young woman was probably right in her judgment regarding the mother's supposed frauds?

2. What advice would you give to the young woman regarding the best and safest methods whereby she herself might, loyally and discretely, test whether her own suspicions of her mother's honesty were, or were not well founded?

3. If a closer knowledge of the case shows you that the daughter's suspicions were well founded, and that the mother was as deeply involved in the fraudulent transactions as the daughter had supposed, which one, if either, of the courses numbered 1 and 2, and stated above, would seem to you the loyal course for the young woman to follow?

4. Can you imagine or devise any other course, besides the courses of action named? Could you recommend this other course as the loyal one in case you had to advise the young woman?

5. These two women, the mother and the daughter, as these letters and as this sketch depict them, are obviously more or less completely "detached individuals," and are thus "estranged" both from one another and from the Great Community. How would you advise them to act so as best to "get together" and so as best to have these "estrangements" healed?

In answering these five questions, do your best to show how the various main doctrines of the course, so far as these doctrines are yet before you, would bear on this one problem of the young woman and her mother. That is, treat this one case as a sort of miniature illustration of Wallas's Great Community, of its estrangements, and of its problems of loyalty. In particular, show what bearing each of the three "leading ethical ideas" has on this case; that is, show how: (1) The idea of Independence; (2) The idea of the Good; and (3) The idea of Duty stand related to the ethical needs of these two women.

February, 1916

Appendix C

Milford, PA
1913 June 30.

My dear Royce:

I write to you for the definite purpose of asking whether you have any separate copy *to spare* of your review of Stout's *Analytic Psychology*[1] (which I possess) or of anything else you may have written (or which others have written, but I have James's "Experience of Activity") that will illuminate my mind about the consciousness of volition.

I have been ill since the middle of November 1911, and my powers are so much broken that I feel I ought to make such haste as I can to put my present opinions about Reasoning in a shape to do good. As for my *Pragmatism*, though it is all very well as far as it goes, it chiefly goes to improve the *security* of inference without touching, what is far more important, its *Uberty*.[2] It doesn't for instance seem to have any thing to say as to our exaltation of *beauty, duty,* or *truth*.

In regard to consciousness I think I see that it is of three kinds of elements. The first is pure *sensation* on which I have made an enormous amount of experiments. It involves no discrimination, not even that between the subject-mind & the object. It is the state of a new born infant or of a person half or quarter waked up in a strange place. The second element is Volition on which I made an elaborate series of observations about 1871 (I can't say certainly the exact year at this moment.) The most instructive were got in lifting a dead weight of just 1000 lb avoirdupois. I did not think anything would be gained by lifting more. Now sense of *desire* is quite a different thing, and so are various other things, such as *intention*. I came

---

Republished from *Transactions* 26 (Winter 1990): 141–143, courtesy of its editor, Peter H. Hare.

to the conclusion from these & a great variety of other observations that the only thing distinctive of volition is a peculiar consciousness of two-ness, *distension* [distension between a sharply-focussed object that volition "objects" to, though it can't *intend* to abolish since intention involves more than volition and a pushed-back back-ground that we call "Myself"] between the sharply focussed object and the pushed back-ground Self; and I believe there is no other consciousness of Self.[3] Of course, *attention* is the same thing & "unconscious attention" is a mere misnomer. Now I ask what I am asking of you in hopes of more light on this. The third kind of consciousness is *thought*, where there is always a *triad* (or a larger collection of relates.) I don't think this can take place without the help of a *sign* which stands for an *object* vaguely called up, and significant in a certain *respect*. So thought has those 3 parts at least that have to be held apart in consciousness of that third kind.

And I think I can show by logical analysis that the idea of *three* cannot result from any "2+1". For, in fact, 2, +, and 1 already introduces the idea of 3 as an essential part of it. 2 is already present in 1 and in the back-ground from which it is distinct. So I hold that 1, 2, 3 are three forms of thought, though I don't mean that they are *distinctly* present in their full qualities in the mere numerals. I find the whole doctrine of inference to be full of triads.

I am going to insist upon the superiority of Uberty over Security in the sense in which *gold* is more useful than *iron* though the latter is more useful in some respects. And also that the art of making explanatory hypotheses is the supreme branch of logic.

I began your book with great interest but was obliged to lay it aside until I can do more in a day than I can yet. You may be very sure that I shall study it unless my end overtakes me, on which missing that reading would be one of my principal regrets.

very faithfully
C S Peirce

NOTES

1. Royce's review of G. F. Stout's *Analytic Psychology* had appeared in *Mind*, n.s. 6 (1897), 379–99.

2. Uberty, from L. *ubertas*, means "fruitfulness, plenty," or literally "full-breasted abundance of goods." Royce's mature stress on the "fecundity of aggregation" (of minds, signs, interpretations, etc.) parallels Peirce's uberty.

3. In brackets: a note that Pierce added in the margin to the left of the third paragraph.

Notes

PREFACE

1. Royce to A. O. Lovejoy, December 30, 1912 (see *The Letters of Josiah Royce*. ed. John Clendenning [Chicago: University of Chicago Press, 1970], 586-587).

2. Royce's 1915-16 Extension Course on Ethics, Lecture III, "Wallas' Problem of the Great Society," p. 4. Five lectures from this course are extant in folios 94 and 95 of the Harvard Archives Royce Papers [HARP].

3. See Frank Oppenheim, "Josiah Royce's Intellectual Development: An Hypothesis," *Idealistic Studies* 6 (January 1976): 85–104.

4. For Royce's appraisal of his *Religious Aspect of Philosophy*, see Royce to George Holmes Howison, September 23, 1894 (*Letters*, 325–326). For his retrospect on *The Philosophy of Loyalty*, see the 1913 statement from his *The Problem of Christianity* (Chicago: University of Chicago Press, 1968), 38.

5. Royce to Katharine Royce, August 25, 1915 (HARP, 1989 Crystal Falls Collection, Box A: "Josiah Royce: Letters to Family"), quoted with permission.

6. See Extension Course in Ethics, Lecture II, "The Idea of Duty" (HARP 94, no. 1).

7. Ibid., p. 3.

8. Ibid., p. 5, emphasis added.

9. See Section III of Ralph Waldo Emerson's poem, "Voluntaries," in his *Poems*, ed. J. E. Cabot (Cambridge, Mass.: Riverside Press, 1893), 178–182.

10. Extension Course in Ethics, Lecture II (HARP 94, no. 1), p. 10, emphasis added.

11. From Berkeley on February 5, 1916, Jacob Loewenberg wrote Royce, "Do you intend to print these lectures soon [from your Extension Course in Ethics]? By the way, I still have the typewritten manuscripts of your first five lectures. I shall mail them tomorrow" (HARP-CFC, B, Box 2). Of these five, only the last four eventually found their way to the Harvard Archives (as HARP 94, 95).

NOTES TO CHAPTER 1

1. *Fugitive Essays by Josiah Royce*, ed. Jacob Loewenberg (Cambridge, Mass.: Harvard University Press, 1920), 7.

2. On this, see G. H. Palmer's report in *Contemporary Idealism in America*, ed. Clifford Barrett (New York: Russell & Russell, 1932), 6.

3. For a more detailed survey, see Gladys Bournique, *La Philosophie de Josiah Royce* (Paris: Vrin, 1988), chap. 8, "La Suite de l'Histoire." This work along with those of Smith, Clendenning, and Kuklick has strongly influenced the present chapter.

4. See *Philosophical Review* 25, no. 3 (May 1916); *Journal of Philosophy* 53, no. 3 (February 2, 1956); and *Revue Internationale de Philosophie* 21, nos. 1–2 (1967).

5. Bournique, *La Philosophie de Josiah Royce*, 324–326; she borrows "smear" from Bruce Kuklick.

6. See, for instance, I. Woodbridge Riley, *American Thought from Puritanism to Pragmatism and Beyond* (New York, 1923); Herbert W. Schneider, *A History of American Philosophy*, cf. 1st ed. (New York: Columbia University Press, 1946), 481–490 with 2nd ed. (1963), 415–424 and 566; John H. Randall, "Josiah Royce and American Idealism," *Journal of Philosophy* 63 (1966): 57–83; W. H. Werkmeister, *A History of Philosophical Ideas in America* (New York: Ronald Press, 1949), 133–168; and Joseph L. Blau, *Men and Movements in American Philosophy* (Englewood Cliffs: Prentice-Hall, 1952), 206–217.

7. *Contemporary Idealism*, 3–4.

8. Composed playfully for his friend William James; see R. B. Perry, *The Thought and Character of William James*, 2 vols. (Boston: Little, Brown, 1935), 1:819–820, which includes Dickinson Miller's remark, "Royce finds lecturing the easiest form of breathing."

9. John Clendenning, *The Life and Thought of Josiah Royce* (Madison, Wisc.: University of Wisconsin Press, 1985), 198 [hereafter *Life*].

10. See, for instance, Perry, *Thought and Character* 2:413.

11. *Life*, 164–170, 179–187.

12. 1916 Extension Course in Ethics, "Comments" (Harvard Archives Royce Papers [HARP] 95, no. 1, pp. 6, 8, and *passim).*

13. J. Royce, *The Hope of the Great Community* (New York: Macmillan, 1916), 130–131.

14. J. Royce, *The Problem of Christianity*, ed. John E. Smith (Chicago: University of Chicago Press, 1968), 38, 235; *Hope of the Great Community*, 131.

15. See lecture of May 20, 1916, in Royce's Last Lectures on Metaphysics 1915–16 (Ralph W. Brown's and B. E. Underwood's stenographic notes of this Philosophy 9 course, William Ernest Hocking Papers, Houghton Library, Harvard University).

16. The Rubens comparison is made in William James to Dickinson S. Miller, January 31, 1899; see *The Letters of William James*, 2 vols., ed. Henry James (Boston: Little, Brown, 1926), 2:86. For the quote, see Perry, *Thought and Character* 1:812, and for the other charges see William James, *The Varieties of Religious Experience* (New York: Collier, 1961), 354, and *The Writings of William James*, ed. John J. McDermott (New York: Modern Library, 1967), 519.

17. The popularization of James's kind of pragmatism emphasized practical results in present experience. By contrast, the kind of pragmatism advocated by Peirce and Royce clearly called a person to a more demanding process. One was to sum up all the conceivable consequences of one's plan of action and compare and contrast this sum with the sums of the conceivable consequences of one's other plans of action before choosing a way of acting.

18. See *American Philosophy in the Twentieth Century*, ed. Paul Kurtz (New York: Macmillan, 1966), 314–337.

19. See Perry, *Thought and Character* 1:824, and R. W. Perry, *Philosophy of the Recent Past* (New York: Charles Scribner's Sons, 1926), 222–223.

20. As usually told, New Realism began at the meeting of the American Philosophical Association at Yale in December 1909, with Ralph Barton Perry's delivery of his often touted address, "The Ego-Centric Predicament." (See Schneider, *History of American Philosophy*, 2nd ed., 510–512. See also *Life*, 338). For Royce's response, see Last Lectures in Metaphysics, 1915–1916, lecture of December 2, 1915, and *passim*. Far less trivial in Royce's eyes was the *logo*-centric predicament whose acknowledgment distinguished idealists from realists. Cf. also W. E. Hocking, "The Ontological Argument in Royce and Others," in *Contemporary Idealism*, 45.

21. See Arthur Lovejoy, "Present Philosophical/Tendencies," Parts I and II, and "Notes and Newsletters From Professor Lovejoy," *Journal of Philosophy* 9 (1912): 627–640 (esp. 634), 673–684, and 720–721.

22. *Life*, 380.

23. See Bruce Kuklick, *The Rise of American Philosophy* (New Haven: Yale University Press, 1977), 438–447, and esp. 495. Bournique moreover points out that this labeling of Royce as "foreigner" and even "enemy" continued into and beyond World War II because Royce was reputed to have imported dangerous German imperialistic thought (*La Philosophie de Josiah Royce*, 325–326 with nn. 52 and 53).

24. Santayana's "The Genteel Tradition" was first delivered in summer 1911, before Berkeley's Philosophical Union; for the text see *Documents in the History of American Philosophy*, ed. Morton White (New York: Oxford University Press, 1972), 404–428. See also *Winds of Doctrine: Studies in Contemporary Opinion* (New York: Charles Scribner's Sons, 1913), and *The Genteel Tradition at Bay* (New York: Charles Scribner's Sons, 1931). For the overall picture, see *The Genteel Tradition: Nine Essays by George Santayana*, ed. Douglas L. Wilson (Cambridge, Mass.: Harvard University Press, 1967). The quotation is from *Documents*, 407.

25. George Santayana, *Character and Opinion in the United States* (New York: Charles Scribner's Sons, 1920).

26. Perry, "The Ego-Centric Predicament," *Journal of Philosophy* 7 (1910): 5–14; see also Bournique, *La Philosophie de Josiah Royce*, 327–328.

27. See Perry's chapters, "The Battle of the Absolute" and "Friendly Opponents" in *Thought and Character* 1:797–824.

28. Mead's earlier essay appeared in *International Journal of Ethics* 27 (1927): 168–170; the later one was "The Philosophies of Royce, James, and Dewey in Their American Setting," *International Journal of Ethics* 40 (1929–30): 223.

29. For the text, see Kurtz, *American Philosophy in the Twentieth Century*, 368–371. The rest of the paragraph reflects Theses 1, 6, and 9 of the Manifesto. "[C]onvinced that existing acquisitive and profit-motivated society has shown itself to be inadequate," these religious humanists also "demand[ed] a shared life in a shared world" (Thesis 14).

30. John Dewey, *A Common Faith* (New Haven: Yale University Press, 1934), 87; emphasis added.

31. *Problem of Christianity*, 319.

32. *Collected Papers of Charles Sanders Peirce*, ed. Charles Hartshorne, Paul Weiss, and Arthur W. Burks, 8 vols. (Cambridge, Mass.: Harvard University Press, 1931–1958). Burks edited the final two volumes.

33. In 1940–41, E. F. Wells gathered these Royce papers into ninety-eight folio volumes and fourteen capacious boxes in the Harvard Archives. In 1956, Victoria Hernandez indexed the folios while Boyd Cruise listed the contents of the non-logicalia boxes. In 1958 Frank Oppenheim listed the contents of the log-icalia boxes, and having in 1967 discovered Royce's own catalogue for his non-logical papers, rearranged these papers according to their author's catalogue. In 1989, the Crystal Falls Collection added twenty more boxes to the Harvard Archives Royce Papers.

34. Bournique, *La Philosophie de Josiah Royce*, 2, 324, with notes. This and the next paragraph depend heavily upon Bournique.

35. From 1910–1950 other voices sounded generally positive appraisals of Royce—those of A. Aliotta, C. Bakewell, J. W. Buckham, R. C. Cabot, G. Dykhuizen, R. F. A. Hoernle, P. Johnson, W. W. Muelder, G. H. Palmer, and D. S. Robinson.

36. Of the 294 entries in Richard C. Gilman's "Bibliography of William Ernest Hocking from 1898 to 1964," however, only 9 (or less than 3 percent) deal with Royce. See *Philosophy, Religion and the Coming World Civilization*, ed. Leroy S. Rouner (The Hague: Nijhoff, 1966), 465–504.

37. See Hocking's "Preface" to Gabriel Marcel's *Royce's Metaphysics*, includ-ing a foreword by Marcel himself and translated by Virginia and Gordon Ringer (Chicago: Regnery, 1956), vii. In an interview with the author (August 17, 1958), Hocking pointed out that at work within the human self's grasp of the finite other there is also a grasp of the Infinite Other. This is a knowing that inseparably and inescapably includes a feeling and a willing. In such knowing Hocking saw that Royce was actually holding a Louvain-type knowledge of the Infinite Other which operates within the agent's union with the finite other as found in each distinctively human psychic act.

38. See Royce to W. E. Hocking, December 4, 1911, in the W. E. Hocking Papers, Houghton Library, Harvard University. For whatever reasons, Hocking did not publish this significant letter and Clendenning did not gather it into his *The Letters of Josiah Royce* (Chicago: University of Chicago Press, 1970).

39. W. E. Hocking, "The Holt-Freudian Ethics and the Ethics of Royce," *Philosophical Review* 25 (May 1916): 479–506, esp. 506.

40. W. E. Hocking, "Professor Josiah Royce," *Harvard Alumni Bulletin* 19 (1916): 4–6.

41. W. E. Hocking, "The Ontological Argument in Royce and Others," in *Contemporary Idealism*, 43–66.

42. In 1992, this text, with introductions by Richard Hocking and Frank Oppenheim, lies in the hands of a publisher.

43. Compare W. E. Hocking, *Types of Philosophy*, rev. ed. (New York: Charles Scribner's Sons, 1939), 377n., with Hocking, *The Coming World Civilization* (New York: Harper and Brothers, 1956), 93 no.18.

44. See W. E. Hocking, "On Royce's Empiricism," *Journal of Philosophy* 53

(February 2, 1956): 57–63. See also Hocking, *Types of Philosophy*, 358, and *Coming World Civilization*, 34 n. 3.

45. Hocking, "On Royce's Empiricism," 62–63. Thus Royce's passionate focus on life and what showed more life—his "interest in the *more* vital"—made his thought alternate from one level to another, from self to community, from ego to Alter, and from past to future. It also made his mind swing from symbolic logic to ethics or aesthetics, from pure mathematics to mysticism or religion.

46. W. E. Hocking, *The Meaning of God in Human Experience* (New Haven: Yale University Press, 1912), 351–352. Hocking pointed out that in his Last Lectures in Metaphysics Royce had chosen to lecture on mysticism from March 25 to May 9, 1916.

47. Hocking, "The Holt-Freudian Ethics and the Ethics of Royce," 506.

48. Previously Marcel had read Hocking's *The Meaning of God in Human Experience* and then F. E. Bradley's metaphysical works. In his late twenties, Marcel's health disqualified him from military service. Gathered into book form, these articles were published as *La Metaphysique de Royce* (Paris: Aubier, 1945). Eleven years later its English translation appeared as *Royce's Metaphysics*.

49. See the "Conclusion" of *Royce's Metaphysics*, 147–148, and Frank M. Oppenheim, "Josiah Royce's Intellectual Development: An Hypothesis," *Idealistic Studies* 6 (January 1976): 92.

50. When Marcel wrote in his 1918 introduction to his four articles that "although one cannot say that Royce's thought was actually transformed" (xviii), he seems to have stressed its perduring unity. This can be reconciled with Royce's own contrast, made two years earlier, between the "original form of my [Royce's] idealism" and its new form revealed in *Problem of Christianity* (see *Letters*, 645).

51. M. W. Calkins, "Royce's Philosophy and Christian Theism," *Philosophical Review* 25 (May 1916): 282–293, esp. 288 n. 1.

52. *Fugitive Essays* and *Lectures in Modern Idealism*, ed. with introduction by J. Loewenberg (New Haven: Yale University Press, 1919); "Interpretation as a Self-representative Process," *Philosophical Review* 25 (1916): 420–423; "Josiah Royce, Interpreter of American Problems," *University of California Chronicle* 19 (1918–19): 39–47; and "Royce's Synthetic Method," *Journal of Philosophy* 53 (1956): 63–72. For his memoirs of Royce, see his *Thrice-Born: Selected Memories of an Immigrant* (New York: Hobbs, Dorman, 1968).

53. M. R. Cohen, "Josiah Royce," and "On American Philosophy: The Idealistic Tradition and Josiah Royce," in *New Republic* 18 (Spring 1919): 264–266, and 20 (August-November 1919): 148–150; *American Thought: A Critical Sketch* (Glencoe, Ill.: Free Press, 1954), 201–203, 275–280.

54. Cohen, *American Thought*, 209.

55. Ibid., 277–279.

56. Ibid., 202.

57. C. I. Lewis, "Types of Order and the System Sigma," *Philosophical Review* 25 (1916): 407–419.

58. See E. Paul Colella, *C. I. Lewis and the Good Social Order: The Social Theory of Conceptualistic Pragmatism* (Lewiston, N.Y.: Edwin Mellen, 1992).

59. *Contemporary Idealism*, 3–9, 25–66.

60. Bournique, *La Philosophie de Josiah Royce*, 341–344.

61. John E. Smith, *Royce's Social Infinite: The Community of Interpretation* (New York: Liberal Arts, 1950).

62. John E. Smith, "The Eternal, the Practical and the Beloved Community," in his *The Spirit of American Philosophy* (New York: Oxford University Press, 1963), 80–114.

63. John E. Smith, "The Contemporary Significance of Royce's Theory of the Self," *Revue Internationale de Philosophie*, 21 (1967): 77–89.

64. Stuart Gerry Brown, *The Social Philosophy of Josiah Royce* (Syracuse, N.Y.: Syracuse University Press, 1950).

65. Max H. Fisch, *Classic American Philosophers* (New York: Appleton-Century-Crofts, 1951).

66. Daniel S. Robinson, *Royce's Logical Essays* (Dubuque, Iowa: Wm. C. Brown, 1951).

67. J. Harry Cotton, *Royce on the Human Self* (Cambridge, Mass.: Harvard University Press, 1954).

68. Bournique, *La Philosophie de Josiah Royce*, 339–340.

69. *Royce's Metaphysics*, x.

70. See *Royce's Metaphysics*, x, 129, and *Problem of Christianity*, chap. 14. This "Doctrine of Signs" does not seem to have alerted Marcel in 1918 to its radical existentialist presentation of three fundamental "attitudes of will."

71. *Royce's Metaphysics*, xii.

72. Jacques-Robert Duron pointed these out in *Revue Philosophique de France et Etranger* 138 (1948): 359–361, where he reviewed the 1945 French original of *Royce's Metaphysics*.

73. *Problem of Christianity*, 341–342.

74. See *Royce's Metaphysics*, x, and Bournique, *La Philosophie de Josiah Royce*, 338, with n. 89. By 1956, Marcel claimed that Hocking's work, *The Meaning of God in Human Experience* "was an advance on Royce's [earlier] thought." Nor did Marcel advert, in his 1956 preface, to Royce's transformation of thought revealed in the later *Problem of Christianity*.

75. Peter Fuss, *The Moral Philosophy of Josiah Royce* (Cambridge, Mass.: Harvard University Press, 1965).

76. Charles Hartshorne, "Royce and the Collapse of Idealism," *Revue International de Philosophie* 21 (1967): 46–59.

77. Kuklick, *Rise of American Philosophy*, 301–306. See also his *Josiah Royce: An Intellectual Biography* (Indianapolis: Bobbs-Merrill, 1972).

78. Kuklick, *Rise*, 401.

79. See *Life*, 395–396. Bournique (*La Philosophie de Josiah Royce*, 312 with n. 14) also criticizes Kuklick on this point.

80. For Royce's studies on Peirce and Nietzsche, see *The Basic Writings of Josiah Royce*, ed. John J. McDermott, 2 vols. (Chicago: University of Chicago Press, 1969) 2:1215–1220. For his seminar, see *Josiah Royce's Seminar, 1913–1914, as Recorded in the Notebooks of Harry T. Costello*, ed. Grover Smith (New Brunswick,

N.J.: Rutgers University Press, 1963). For his logic and theory of knowledge, see "An Extension of the Algebra of Logic," "Primitive Ways of Thinking, with Special Reference to Negation and Classification," and "The Mechanical, the Historical, and the Statistical," on scientific methods; see *Basic Writings* 2:1215–1217.

81. J. Royce, *The Religious Aspect of Philosophy* (Boston: Houghton, Mifflin, 1885; rpt. Harper Torchbook edition 1958), v (emphasis added).

82. See Reck's "Contemporary American Speculative Philosophy," *Revue Internationale de Philosophie* 26 (1972): 149–171 and Murphey's chapters on Royce in Elizabeth Flower and Murray G. Murphey, *A History of Philosophy in America*, 2 vols (New York: Putnam, 1977).

83. Murphey, *History of Philosophy*, 753.

84. *Problem of Christianity*, 73–74.

85. Ibid., 42.

86. See chap. 2, "Spires of Influence," of J. J. McDermott, *Streams of Experience: Reflections on the History and Philosophy of American Culture* (Amherst: University of Massachusetts Press, 1986). See also his "Josiah Royce's Philosophy of the Community: Danger of the Detached Individual," in *American Philosophy*, ed. Marcus G. Singer, Royal Institute of Philosophy Lecture Series 19 (London: Cambridge University Press, 1985), 153–176.

87. *Basic Writings* 1:12; for the quotation, see Royce's *California, from the Conquest in 1846 to the Second Vigilance Committee in San Francisco [1856]: A Study of American Character* (Boston: Houghton, Mifflin, 1886), 500.

88. I. K. Skrupskelis, "Royce and the Justification of Authority," *Southern Journal in Philosophy* 8 (Summer-Fall 1970): 165–170.

89. *Letters* offers Royce's major outgoing correspondence; his major incoming correspondence is now available in HARP-CFC.

90. Mary B. Mahowald, *An Idealistic Pragmatism* (The Hague: Nijhoff, 1972); Edward A. Jarvis, *The Conception of God in the Later Royce* (The Hague: Nijhoff, 1975); Oppenheim, "Hypothesis," and *Royce's Voyage Down Under: A Journey of the Mind* (Lexington, Ky.: University Press of Kentucky, 1980).

91. For a description of this discovery and some samples of its treasure, see John Clendenning and Frank Oppenhiem, "New Documents on Josiah Royce," *Transactions of the Charles Sanders Peirce Society* [hereafter *Transactions*] 26 (Spring 1990): 131–145. With the addition of the Crystal Falls Collection to the Royce Papers previously gathered in the Harvard University Archives, there arises the urgent call that all of Royce's manuscripts there be carefully appraised and reordered so that a critical edition of Royce's complete works can be begun.

CHAPTER 2

1. Extension Course on Ethics, 1915–16, Lecture II, "The Idea of Duty" (HARP 94, no. 1) 1.

2. Royce's Second Plan for this 1915–16 Extension Course on Ethics (HARP Box H).

3. On her '49er journey across the plains she refused to move on the Sabbath, although this "resting" isolated them from the common caravan, exposed herself, her child, and husband to Indian raids as well as to later entrapment in the early snows of the high Sierras. According to a family tradition, she also refused to marry any man who did not believe that baptism by total immersion was necessary for salvation.

4. Ruth Royce to R. B. Perry, February 28, 1928 (Harvard University Archives, R. B. Perry Papers).

5. This is a major theme in Clendenning's *Life*. On Royce's father, see also Robert V. Hine, *Josiah Royce: From Grass Valley to Harvard* (Norman, Okla.: University of Oklahoma Press, 1992), 4–16, 33–35, 48–49, 51–52, 100–101.

6. *Hope of the Great Community*, 122–127, the basis for this and the next two paragraphs.

7. J. Royce, unpublished "Andover Address on the Relation of Philosophy to the Clergyman's Profession," delivered June 7, 1904 (HARP 75, no. 1), 25–26.

8. Royce offered some recollections of his boyhood during his 1893 Lectures to Teachers (see HARP 64, Lecture VI), 76–81.

9. *Grass Valley Union*, May 11, 1865.

10. *Hope of the Great Community*, 125–126.

11. *Life*, 34–35.

12. *Hope of the Great Community*, 126–127, the basis for this paragraph.

13. For his later identification of this as an expression of the dynamic of original sin, see *Problem of Christianity*, 106–111.

14. *Hope of the Great Community*, 123.

15. Excerpt from Sarah Eleanor Royce's poem to her son Josiah, inscribed on inside front cover and first sheet of this Bible (see HARP-CFC Box G, no.1: "Notebooks, Diaries, etc."), original emphasis. To reenforce her witness to the vital importance of hearing the Word of God, Josiah's mother tucked notes into the corners of this Bible, containing best wishes for the holiday season and references to seven Scripture passages she judged pertinent for her high schooler: Mt 5:16; Phil 2:14; 1 Pt 2:12; Is 55:3; Jn 4:12, 7:37; and Rv 22:1.

16. See *Problem of Christianity*, 213. Royce drew the phrase from Ephesians 6:17.

17. Here Royce practiced what he later taught explicitly: "adventurousness—its role in ethics." He listed this as an ethical ingredient in his Plan for Extension Course on Ethics (see HARP, Box H, no. 1, "Outlines for the University Extension Course," Third Plan, Part V).

18. *Religious Aspect*, 425. By transmuting his religious insight of January 1883 into an expository form of argumentation, Royce created *Religious Aspect*. He fashioned the philosophical quilt of this book into one continuous piece by sewing freshly drafted accounts onto large patches from many of his previously published essays (see *Basic Writings* 2:1177–1189).

19. J. Royce, *The World and the Individual*, 2 vols. (New York: Macmillan, 1899–1901), 2:vii; or, as he described it in his Last Lectures on Metaphysics on January 11, 1916, "This [discovery] led me to the decided reversal of point of view

that followed"—from being previously an empirical, skeptical agnostic into becoming a critical religious philosopher.

20. Royce to B. Moses, September 7, 1883 (*Letters*, 128).

21. Royce wrote to H. L. Oak, September 17, 1885, "Again and again I write what I think I have just learned from a document or book, and, looking again at my source, have to tear up my MS in disgust. If California history were only philosophy!" (*Letters*, 178).

22. Royce to H. L. Oak, November 12, 1885 (*Letters*, 181).

23. HARP 89, no. 4, "Christian Ethics," 162–165. HARP 89 contains Royce's 216 pages of notes toward 20 lectures on the History of Ethics. In the "Radcliffe division," he continued teaching an ethics course regularly up until 1887.

24. Royce to D. C. Gilman, February 9, 1888 (*Letters*, 211).

25. For an examination of Royce's intellectual development during this trip, see Oppenheim, *Royce's Voyage Down Under*.

26. *Life*, 245.

27. *Problem of Christianity*, 91; see also *Life*, 364.

28. This love is shown in the correspondence contained in the Crystal Falls Collection; see Clendenning and Oppenheim, "New Documents on Josiah Royce," 143–145.

29. Royce to H. L. Oak [May 31, 1886?] (*Letters*, 189).

30. See HARP 69–70; *Basic Writings* 2:1200, no. 7; and the *Harvard Crimson*, February 11, 1898.

31. Royce to Mary Gray Ward Dorr, August 7, 1898 (*Letters*, 378).

32. For Abbott, see *Life*, 179–187; for Howison, see *George Holmes Howison, Philosopher and Teacher*, ed. J. W. Buckham and G. M. Stratton (Berkeley: University of California Press, 1934), 81.

33. *Letters*, 289–290.

34. For instance, Skrupskelis lists thirty-seven studies in ethics that Royce reviewed or wrote from 1891 to 1894 (*Basic Writings* 2:1187–1194).

35. G. H. Palmer describes Royce's reaction to this double blow of his mother's illness and death occurring as the Abbott affair peaked (*Contemporary Idealism*, 9).

36. The colleagues were Dean V. S. Shaler and Professor J. R. Paine. Concerning Royce's growing and personal "cult of the dead," see *Fugitive Essays*, 276–279; HARP 82, no. 3, p. 60; Royce's *The Philosophy of Loyalty* (New York: Macmillan, 1908), 235–236, 246, 239; *Hope of the Great Community*, 94–95; Last Lectures on Metaphysics, lecture of April 1, 1916, and Cotton, *Royce on the Human Self*, 7 (which might be Royce's last writing).

37. He revealed his alert appreciation of the changing seas in his final letters to Katharine (HARP-CFC Box A, "Royce MSS: Letters") and esp. in Last Lectures on Metaphysics, lecture of March 18, 1916.

38. *Letters*, 287, 610–611.

39. For the identification of "absolute truths," see J. Royce, *William James and Other Essays in the Philosophy of Life* (New York: Macmillan, 1911), 239–244. For his logical work, see *Logical Essays*, 379–441, 310–378, and 293–309, respectively.

40. This and the following quotation are taken from *James and Other Essays*,

172–173, excerpts from Royce's "What is Vital in Christianity?" first published in the *Harvard Theological Review* 2 (1909): 408–445.

41. J. Royce, *The Sources of Religious Insight* (New York: Charles Scribner's Sons, 1912), 215–254.

42. *Problem of Christianity*, 42.

43. Royce to the Macmillan Company, June 7, 1906 (*Letters*, 502).

44. Royce to William James, January 9, 1908 (Houghton Library, William James Papers)—the basis also of the next paragraph.

45. *Harvard University Gazette* II (1906), pp. 2–3, 27, and III (1907), p. 158.

46. Royce to William James, January 12, 1908 (*Letters*, 518).

47. Royce to William James, January 9, 1908 (Houghton Library, William James Papers; quoted with permission). This rendered the name "Christopher" so poignant that thereafter it became an unmentionable in the Royce home.

48. Royce to F. J. E. Woodbridge, March 15, 1912 (*Letters*, 563).

49. For Royce's letter to Elizabeth Randolph, November 16, 1910, see Appendix A, reprinted from *Letters* 547–551, by permission of both James Royce from whose private collection it derives and of the University of Chicago Press. In this letter Royce penned perhaps his most concise description of what it means to live loyally.

50. *Letters*, 576.

51. Some of this pain and concern seeps through Royce's letters to Stephen; see HARP-CFC Box A: "Josiah Royce MSS, Letters."

52. *Philosophy of Loyalty*, 221.

53. Ibid., 324–340; see also James's diary record of this (Houghton Library, William James Papers).

54. Royce's marginalia on James's circular are found in Perry, *Thought and Character* 2:735–736. Unfortunately, when publishing this text, Perry omitted Royce's underlinings, missed his linear arrow, and thus so displaced this general objection that he sandwiched it inside the second of Royce's nine specific comments.

55. *Philosophy of Loyalty*, x–xi, written March 1, 1908.

56. William James to Royce, April 11, 1908; published in *Thought and Character* 1: 822.

57. J. Royce, "The Problem of Truth in the Light of Recent Discussion," delivered to the International Congress of Philosophy at Heidelberg on September 1, 1908 and published in its *Proceedings*; republished by Royce in *James and Other Essays*, 187–254, and by others in *Logical Essays*, 63–97 and *Basic Writings* 2:681–709. Unlike James, John Dewey detected how important Royce's essay was but judged its presentation of instrumentalism extrinsic and slanted. See John Dewey, "A Reply to Professor Royce's Critique of Instrumentalism," *Philosophical Review* 21 (1912): 69–81 (republished in *John Dewey: The Middle Works 1899–1924*, vol. 7, *1912–1914* (Carbondale, Ill.: Southern Illinois University Press, 1979), 64–78.

58. In Last Lectures on Metaphysics, lecture of December 4, 1915, Royce again called attention to his Heidelberg Address, to the part that pragmatist F. C. S. Schiller had played in the subsequent discussion and to the heated debate that ensued. Then, referring to James's familiarity with this essay, Royce added: "All

James said by way of criticism of this essay was that he thought it more connected and effectively put together than most of my things, but could not accept it in the least as a correction."

59. According to the *Smith College Monthly* 17 (1909–10): 488, Royce's Lecture series there on "Modern Philosophy of Life" included two lectures (March 8 and 11) entitled "Sources of Religious Insight." The same title marked one lecture he offered to the Yale Theological Club on May 14, 1910. During the ensuing academic year, when lecturing at Yale, he had regular "casual talks on religion" with some New Haven ladies, to whom he later sent a copy of *Sources of Religious Insight* for advanced reading and suggestions—a service he also requested of Professors Hocking, Bakewell, and Bennett. In this way Royce gradually refined his text for delivery at Lake Forest College, November 13–19, 1911.

60. *Logical Essays*, 122.

61. Ibid., 123–124, emphasis added.

62. *Life*, 359.

63. See *Letters*, 583–587; *Life*, 365, and *Journal of Philosophy* 9 (1912): 627–640, 673–684, and esp. 720–721 for Lovejoy's assertive withdrawal.

64. *Sources of Religious Insight*, 10.

65. Royce to G. P. Brett, March 29, 1912 (*Letters*, 566–568).

66. Royce, "What is Vital in Christianity?" in *James and Other Essays*, esp. 180–182.

67. *Life*, 334f. One can grasp something of the depth which Royce's religious insight had reached at this time by musing over his letter to Mrs. W. E. Hocking of December 2, 1909 on the "work of God" in the world (see *Letters*, 536–537).

68. See *Life*, 361–362, based on Royce's First Berkeley Conference of 1914 (HARP 84, no. 3), 8–14.

69. *Life*, 362.

70. *Letters*, 587–592.

71. For a summary of these reviews, see Bournique, *La Philosophie de Josiah Royce*, 293, and *Life*, 380.

72. *Life*, 371. Notice esp. *Problem of Christianity*, 41:

If indeed I myself must cry "out of the depths" before the light can come to me, it must be my Community that, in the end, saves me. To assert this *and to live this doctrine* constitute the very core of Christian experience, and of the "Religion of Loyalty". . . . I have everywhere kept this thesis in mind. (emphasis added)

73. In the Middlebury College Archives, there are more than a dozen letters exchanged between Royce and John M. Thomas, the president of Middlebury, from June 2, 1913 to January 11, 1915.

74. J. Royce, "The Carnegie Foundation for the Advancement of Teaching and the Case of Middlebury College," *School and Society* 1 (1915): 145–150, and the *Bulletin of the American Association of University Professors* 2 (April 1916) on the formation of its Committee D on the "Limits of Standardization of Institutions, etc."

75. For this significant text, see *Logical Essays*, 254–259; see also *Letters*, 610–611.

76. B. Russell, "The Essence of Religion," *Hibbert Journal* 11 (October 1912): 46–62; "A Free Man's Worship" appeared in his *Philosophical Essays* (1910) and in a revised edition (London: Allen & Unwin, 1966). See also *Last Lectures on Metaphysics*, lecture of April 25, 1916, and Royce to R. B. Perry on Russell, in *Letters*, 590–592.

77. After getting medical advice, Royce declined this invitation which came so soon after his illness; see *Letters*, 568–569.

78. See Victor Lenzen, "Reminiscences of a Mission to Milford, Pennsylvania," *Transactions* 1 (1965): 4, and Bournique, *La Philosophie de Josiah Royce*, 322–323. See also C. I. Lewis's contrast of the two logics undergirding these two theories of knowledge in his "Types of Order and System Sigma," *Philosophical Review* 25 (May 1916): 418–419.

79. Letter of W. F. Kernan to the author, September 26, 1967.

80. *Life*, 368.

81. *Life*, 380, and HARP 84, no. 3, pp. 10–14; Peirce's letter to Royce of June 30, 1913, was published in *Transactions* 26 (1990): 141–143, and is included here in Appendix C.

82. *Life*, 301. See also HARP 84, no. 3, p. 17.

83. J. Royce and W. F. Kernan, "Charles Sanders Peirce," *Journal of Philosophy* 13 (1916): 701–709. For the story of the retrieval and first sorting of the Peirce Papers, see W. F. Kernan, "The Peirce Manuscripts and Josiah Royce—A Memoir, Harvard 1915–1916," *Transactions* 1 (1965): 90–95.

84. *Philosophy of Loyalty*, 16–17 (Royce's emphasis). For Royce's account of this effort, see his Preface to *War and Insurance* (New York: Macmillan, 1914), iv–v.

85. *Life*, 286f.; see also Royce to Kuno Francke, November 22, 1914 (Harvard University Archives, Francke Papers).

86. W. F. Kernan, Royce's companion during this "duckboard" incident, detailed it to the author in a letter of September 26, 1967. See also *Life*, 387–390. In this instance, Royce's risk-taking initiative embodied traditional moral teaching. Aristotle (*Nicomachean Ethics* VI, 1143a9–35) and Aquinas (*Summa Theologica* II–II, Q. 51, aa. 3–4) had recommended that on encountering exceptional situations, persons should shift from using ordinary moral understanding (*synesis*) and employ instead a perspicacious judgment (*gnome*).

87. Royce's Tremont Temple addresses, "The Duties of Americans in the Present War," and "The First Anniversary of the Sinking of the *Lusitania*," were delivered in 1916 on January 30 and May 7, respectively; see *Hope of the Great Community*, 1–13, 93–121.

88. HARP, Symbolic Logic Box 4, Autograph Notebook, "A. Triad Operation and Its Results," pp. 44–45.

89. Cotton, *Royce on Human Self*, 7.

90. *Life*, 397.

91. Royce, "The Spirit of the Community," HARP 91, no. 3, p. 20a.

CHAPTER 3

1. These include his *California* (1886), his novel *Feud of Oakfield Creek* (1887), *Studies of Good and Evil* (1898), *Race Questions, Provincialism, and Other American Problems* (1908), *William James and Other Essays on the Philosophy of Life* (1911), *War and Insurance* (1914), and *The Hope of the Great Community* (1916).

2. Paragraph based on HARP Box A and *Life*, 32–33; *Lincoln Observer* 2 (1869), no. 4; *Basic Writings* 2:1169–1170, esp. no. 34 and no. 2 under 1875.

3. *Fugitive Essays*, 34, extracted from Royce's diary for March 10, 1879. Both Goethe and Fichte laid stress on the principle, "In the beginning was the deed."

4. *Letters*, 108, emphasis added. This theme is maintained through *World and the Individual* (2:ix, xv, 289–294, 329–331) and through the key psychic stance of docility in *Outlines of Psychology: An Elementary Treatise with Some Practical Applications* (New York: Macmillan, 1903), on into the interpreter's sensitive submissiveness to the sign-sender in *The Problem of Christianity*, 2.

5. J. Royce, "A Monkish Chronicle", *Berkeleyan* 6 (December 1878), 279.

6. These three lectures, entitled "Certain Ideals of Right Conduct and Their Value for Society" (reserved in HARP Box E), were favorably reviewed in the *Harvard Advocate*. See *Life*, 137–138.

7. Royce judiciously abstained from placing these economically upsetting ideas in published form before the eyes of his largely Yankee audience. Almost the only statement Royce published on the ethics of a political economy came after his 1888 voyage to Australia. Even then he focused directly on Australia and New Zealand and only obliquely on systemic structures in the United States (see *Basic Writings* 2:1185–1188, nos. 10 and 11 under 1889 and no. 7 under 1891).

8. See *Letters*, 289–290. The two were entitled "The 'Law of Love' in Recent Ethics: Schopenhauer; the Utilitarians; the Philanthropic Spirit" and "The 'Law of the Healthy Social Order': Spencer, von Ihering, Wundt, Paulsen."

9. *Religious Aspect*, xii. Future references to this work in this section will be in the text.

10. *Problem of Christianity*, 39.

11. *Fugitive Essays*, 7.

12. Plato's Seventh Letter mentions the human need for a divine word (*theion logon*) as a second boat (*deuteron ploun*) to complement human reasoning.

13. Royce's "Autobiographical Sketch [1866–1886?]" HARP-CFC, Box A, "MSS of Josiah Royce," p. 5.

14. Royce's early emphasis on this Humean dichotomy between fact and value contrasts sharply with the clear claim of his final days, "The very recognition of Being is itself an estimate. The categories of metaphysics are from the first teleological." (See his final metaphysical lecture of May 27, 1916.)

15. In 1883 Royce required a person to escape from the illusion of a self-centered perspective in order to reach the moral insight. By so doing, he implied his later doctrine of the "transformation" of intellectual viewpoint and volitional attitude needed for genuine loyalty. (See *Problem of Christianity*, 291, 349.)

16. By the turn of the century Royce will describe this intimate purpose, inmost to one's Self and other Selves, as an "internal meaning." Later, in 1913, he will speak of "interpretation" as his way of grasping interiorly the minded being and its intent, which neither perception nor conception can grasp. His Peircean insight let him overcome his earlier groping for the right term.

17. For this illustration, see Bernard Lonergan, *Insight: A Study of Human Understanding* (New York: Harper & Row, 1958), 7–10.

18. See Kuklick, *An Intellectual Biography*, 50–52. Here, too, is foreshadowed Royce's distinction of two kinds of knowledge—concrete appreciation and abstract description—which he would render explicit in *Spirit of Modern Philosophy: An Essay in the Form of Lectures* (Boston: Houghton, Mifflin, 1892).

19. Thus Royce pointed out a higher-than-survival kind of ethics which presaged contemporary stress on an ethics of flourishing, taken in his sense. Out of this his atonement ethics of 1913 will arise—that is, his Christian ethics of the suffering servant who atones for the Great Community. Also see on this H. R. Niebuhr, *The Responsible Self* (New York: Harper & Row, 1963), 99–100, 106–107.

20. See *Letters*, 324–326, from which the subsequent quotations in the present paragraph derive.

21. How Royce clung to this central insight, even while modifying and supplementing it, can be traced in his revisions of it in *Spirit of Modern Philosophy*, 368–380, in *Studies of Good and Evil: A Series of Essays upon the Problems of Philosophy and Life* (New York: D. Appleton, 1898), 163–168, in later works, and even in his metaphysical lecture of January 11, 1916.

22. In this section, subsequent references in parentheses also refer to *Spirit of Modern Philosophy*.

23. *Outlines of Psychology*, vi–vii.

24. See *World and the Individual* 1:553 no. 1. Here Royce estimated that this insight was "of the greatest weight for any metaphysical enterprise."

25. See *Letters*, 185–186 and Bournique, *La Philosophie de Josiah Royce*, 122 n. 85.

26. In the same year, 1892, Royce stressed this theme of a "union of opposing elements" in "The Knowledge of Good and Evil"; see *Studies of Good and Evil*, 112.

27. See *Problem of Christianity*, 349–350. In 1898 he had already identified the "general [materialistic] presuppositions of modern naturalism" as an especially serious hindrance to an ethical interpretation of the universe; see *Studies of Good and Evil*, ix.

28. In *Spirit of Modern Philosophy*, Royce continued to revise that dialectic of choosing between optimism and pessimism which had marked some of his writing and lectures as a Berkeley instructor (e.g., *Basic Writings* 2:1176, no.7) and which he further purified in his essay of 1887, "Tennyson and Pessimism" (*Harvard Monthly* 3 [1886–1887]: 127–137). On this see Bournique, *La Philosophie de Josiah Royce*, 98.

29. Published in the *First Book of the Author's Club, Liber Scriptorum* (New York: Author's Club [of New York], 1893), 491. Other quotes in this discussion are from pages 495–497.

30. *Studies of Good and Evil*, "Introduction," viii. This essay was originally

printed in the *International Journal of Ethics* 4 (1893–1894): 48–80. It was reprinted in *Studies of Good and Evil*, 89–124, from which the following quoted material is taken.

31. *Studies of Good and Evil*, 98.

32. Ibid., 112.

33. See Royce's "Tennyson and Pessimism."

34. Ibid., 137, excerpted from a passage that Royce twice republished, in *Spirit of Modern Philosophy*, 231, and *Studies of Good and Evil*, 87.

35. Published later in *Studies of Good and Evil*, 261–297. The subsequent influence of this article can be traced in *World and the Individual* 1:42, 72, 78, 82, 176–177, 547; *James and Other Essays*, 162–166; and on into his Last Lectures on Metaphysics, lectures of April 6, 8, and 11, 1916.

36. In 1892, Royce had distinguished between the order of logic and that of spiritual worth. In logic the priority belongs to the "World-Self as a Thinker"; but "in the order of spiritual worth and dignity" the completed Self with its moral categories is "supreme"; see *Studies of Good and Evil*, 167.

37. Through Kuno Franke, Harvard expert in German Literature, Royce traced the source of Eckhart's idea of *Fünkelin* to Hugo of St. Victor (see HARP-CFC Box B, "Important Incoming Correspondence," Kuno Francke file).

38. Royce's endeavor to integrate consistently both *Fünkelin* and *Pünctelin* provides an interesting parallel to C. S. Peirce's efforts to use a Scotist *haeceitas* to account for unique individuals. For Royce's tussling with this problem, see his *Conception of God*, 230–247.

39. Eckhart's additional themes that genuine ethical life depends on grace, as exemplified in the life of Schwester Katrei (*Studies of Good and Evil*, 296) and that life's sorrows and griefs are calls from God to love God alone (286) reverberate in *Sources of Religious Insight* and *Problem of Christianity*. Subsequent in-text references are to the "Meister Eckhart" article in *Studies of Good and Evil*.

40. See *Philosophy of Loyalty*, 16–17.

41. Ibid., 357.

42. From Royce's article "Natural Law, Ethics, and Evolution" (July 1891); republished in *Studies of Good and Evil*, 137.

CHAPTER 4

1. *Letters*, 374.

2. See his Augustus Graham Lectures, 1896, Lect. 3, "The Moral World as the Revelation of God" (HARP 67, no. 3) 46–48. In-text references in this section refer to *The Conception of God: A Philosophical Discussion Concerning the Nature of the Divine Idea as a Demonstrable Reality*, 2nd ed. with Royce's Supplementary Essay, "The Absolute and the Individual" (New York: Macmillan, 1897).

3. *Letters*, 341, emphasis added.

4. Royce's 1898 Cambridge Conferences, Lect. VI (HARP 70, no. 6), 23. On this much neglected aspect in Royce's thought, see his *The Conception of Immortality* (Boston: Houghton, Mifflin, 1900), 37, and also HARP 76, no. 3, p.13.

5. *Letters*, 343.

6. Ibid. By assigning a dominant role to one's *instinctive feelings* (both for individualization and for each individual moral decision), Royce foreshadowed A. N. Whitehead's primacy of feelings in the self-constitution of each "actual entity."

7. Here I rely particularly on "The Problem of Job," the ethical chapters of *World and the Individual* and *Conception of Immortality*, and his 1903 presidential address to the American Philosophical Association, "The Eternal and the Practical," *Philosophical Review* 13 (1904): 113–142.

8. *Collected Papers of Peirce* 8:117; and C. S. Peirce to Royce, May 27, 1902 (first draft reserved in Houghton Library).

9. See *Collected Papers of Peirce* 8:117, n. 10.

10. *Outlines of Psychology*, xv–xxiv.

11. See his "Royce and the Justification of Authority."

12. Royce's 1907 Urbana Lecture, "Four Types of Personality" (HARP 76, no. 2), 2–3, ed. Peter Fuss and published in *Journal of the History of Philosophy* 5 (1967): 270.

13. *World and the Individual* 2:314.

14. An illustration of this can be found in a personal confession by the middle-period Royce, published in *Race Questions, Provincialism, and Other American Problems* (New York: Macmillan, 1908), 156–157.

15. Ibid., 157.

16. Mt 10:16.

17. First Cambridge Conference, 1898 (HARP 70, no. 1), 28–29.

18. "On Certain Limitations of the Thoughtful Public in America," Founder's Day Address at Vassar College, 1899 (HARP 71, no. 2), published in *Race Questions*, 143.

19. E.g., see *Philosophy of Loyalty*, 15–16, 117, 177–179.

20. Ibid., x–xi.

21. E.g., see ibid., 157, 178, 191, 294, and Royce to Frank Thilly, November 17, 1908 (*Letters*, 533).

22. See *World and the Individual* 2:359, and John McDermott on this in *Basic Writings* 2:831. The radical transformation will become clearer in *Philosophy of Loyalty* and most evident in *Problem of Christianity*, 351–357, in the choice between the three fundamental attitudes of will.

23. *Philosophy of Loyalty*, 78.

24. Because Roycean ethics most centrally requires one to achieve and maintain this conversion, I regard his ethics as primarily *transformational*, rather than, *pace* Fuss, as primarily self-realizational. See Chapter 13 of this present work.

25. *Studies of Good and Evil*, ix.

26. On Royce and "ecology," see the study by Robert V. Hine in *Californian History*, June 1987, p. 90, and Kevin Starr, *Americans and the California Dream* (New York: Oxford, 1973), 143–145.

27. Josiah Royce, "Impressions of Australia," *Scribner's Magazine* 9 (1891): 78. See also his "The Pacific Coast: A Psychological Study of the Relations of Climate and Civilization," in *Race Questions*, 169–225, to which subsequent citations

are made. In *Race Questions*, 192–199, Royce conveyed the emotional responses of sensitive minds to nature in central California by quoting poetic passages from Bret Harte, Millicent Shinn, and a Miss Coolbrith.

28. See *Race Questions*, 284–287.

29. Ibid., 22–26.

30. *World and the Individual* 2:283. Frederick Copleston, S.J., interprets the position which Royce called "realism" as "an extreme nominalistic empiricism, according to which the world consists of a plurality of entities that are mutually independent"; see his *History of Philosophy* (Garden City, N.Y.: Doubleday, 1967), vol. 8, Part 2, pp. 29–31.

31. *World and the Individual* 2:286. In the next two paragraphs, in-text references are also to *World and the Individual* 2.

32. On this, see Bournique, *La Philosophie de Josiah Royce*, 185.

33. *Conception of God*, 264.

34. Royce delivered an unpublished lecture, "John Fiske," to the Brooklyn Institute on December 11, 1901 (see HARP 72, no. 1, to which the in-text page numbers in this section refer). In this lecture Royce reflected even more fully on Fiske's contribution to American thought than he did in his two published articles on Fiske (see *Basic Writings* 2:1204, under 1901, no. 2).

35. As early as 1900 Royce stressed *atonement* as the positive creative complement to one's endurance of evils (see *World and the Individual* 2:370–373, 388–392). Among classic American philosophers, Royce distinctively highlighted, among other things, the need and role of atonement in ethical life.

36. "Introduction," HARP 52, no. 1, p. 10.

37. *Philosophy of Loyalty*, viii. In this section subsequent in-text references are to *Philosophy of Loyalty*.

38. Despite Royce's popular expository style in *Philosophy of Loyalty*, he evidenced how strongly he intended to make this work a critically sound and readily useful piece of moral philosophy. For its index he drafted a manuscript of eighty-seven pages (see HARP, Box G, no. 8). In *Basic Writings* 2:829–831, McDermott skillfully summarizes *Philosophy of Loyalty*.

39. Intermediate descriptive definitions of loyalty occur in *Philosophy of Loyalty* at 41–42, 46–47, 89–90, 97, 129–130, 137, 170–172, 185, 247, 260–261, 296–297, and 311. Besides his pair of "final" formulations of loyalty on page 357, he offers another on 377.

40. One is to remain faithful to one's cause "unless it becomes unquestionably evident" that continued fidelity to it means preying upon others or excluding others without good reason. (See *Philosophy of Loyalty*, 191.)

41. Royce's growing stress on human *fallibility* (*Philosophy of Loyalty*, 187–188, 196, 371) derived from his own starting point in philosophy, the possibility of error, and from his contact with Peirce's fallibilism.

42. See *Philosophy of Loyalty*, chapters V and VI.

43. See ibid., chapters VII and VIII.

44. See ibid., chapter VI.

45. Royce found James's theory valid as far as it went, but by omitting the whole universe of objective truth, it proved seriously inadequate.

46. Quotation based upon *Collected Papers of Peirce* 5:9.

47. See Royce's second Urbana Lecture. Of these five lectures, the first two were edited by Peter Fuss and published in *Journal of the History of Philosophy* 5 (1967): 60–78, 269–286. For the third lecture, see HARP 76, no. 3. The fourth and fifth lectures seem nonextant.

48. See, for instance, *Philosophy of Loyalty* 15, 123–124, 127, 132, 324, and *passim* on the "worthiness" of the cause.

49. Royce used the phrase "loyalty to loyalty" more sparingly in subsequent years. Apparently he found people resting on it as a double conceptual abstraction while missing the concrete and mature moral point of view he had first intended the phrase to indicate.

50. When addressing the "specially Christian terminology" of the "love of God and love of man," Royce commented, "My own common name for both these motives to which the higher life of man—whatever his religion or his nation—has been due is the term Loyalty." (Smith College Lectures of 1910, Second Series, HARP 78, no. 1, pp. 41–42).

51. In his third Urbana Lecture, "Loyalty as a Personal and as a Social Virtue," Royce offered a more detailed and expanded explanation of being loyal to universal loyalty (see HARP 76, no. 3, pp. 22–37).

52. Royce to Frank Thilly, November 17, 1908 (*Letters*, 532–533).

53. Ibid., 533.

54. First Pittsburgh Lecture (1910?), "The Conflict of Loyalties" (HARP 82, no. 1), 11–12.

55. Third Pittsburgh Lecture, "Loyalty and Individuality" (HARP 82, no. 3), 15–16.

56. Second Pittsburgh Lecture, "The Art of Loyalty" (HARP 82, no. 2), 3.

57. Ibid., 58.

58. See his *Summa Theologiae* IIa–IIae, qq. 47–52.

59. Second Pittsburgh Lecture, 57–58.

60. First Pittsburgh Lecture, 28.

61. Ibid., 35–36.

62 Smith College Lectures of 1910, Second Series (HARP 78, no. 1), 80.

63. *Sources of Religious Insight*, 181. In this section in-text references are to *Sources of Religious Insight*.

64. Royce had already insisted that the "work of God" in the world is "*identical with, [and] consists in*, the work of all rational beings" who have "the divine ideal genuinely, even if not abstractly, present to their minds" (original emphasis). See Royce to Agnes Boyle O'Reilly Hocking, December 2, 1909, in *Letters*, 536–537.

65. As examples of this heroic union of adversity and loyalty, Royce adduced Chaucer's Griselda (*Sources of Religious Insight*, 208–213) and the story of Peter Lannithorne (ibid., 241–250). If understood empathetically, these examples of loyal servants under oppression manifest the ongoing mystery of living redemptively for the ethico-religious conversion of the oppressors.

66. Among classical American philosophers, Josiah Royce seems to have entered most accurately into the problem of the oppression of the weak-but-loyal by the powerful and selfish. As the twentieth century comes to its close with an increasing oppression of the world's "little ones" by the powerful, Royce's concluding chapters of *Sources* become ever more relevant.

67. J. Royce, "Error and Truth," in James Hastings, ed. *Encyclopaedia of Religion and Ethics*, 13 vols. (New York: Charles Scribner's Sons, 1908–1927), 5:366–373; republished in *Logical Essays*, 98–124. A clue that Royce composed this article around fall 1911 may be found in *Sources of Religious Insight*, 109–110.

68. *Logical Essays*, 122.

69. See *Letters*, 645.

CHAPTER 5

1. E.g., *Problem of Christianity*, 38.

2. E.g., *Studies of Good and Evil*, vi; *Philosophy of Loyalty*, ix.

3. Royce hinted at this interconnection in *Philosophy of Loyalty*, vi–vii.

4. *Religious Aspect*, 461.

5. William James, *The Will to Believe and Other Essays in Popular Philosophy* (New York: Longmans, Green, 1899), 3.

6. In-text references are to the month and date of one of Royce's Last Lectures in Metaphysics (LLM); e.g., here 12/2 means his lecture of December 2, 1915.

7. C. S. Peirce to Royce, Appendix C, and *Collected Papers of Peirce* 5:121.

8. *Collected Papers of Peirce* 5:121.

9. See Robert Bellah et al., *Habits of the Heart* (San Francisco: Harper & Row, 1985), 334.

10. *Problem of Christianity*, 122, 138–139 with n. 3, 193–194, 218.

11. Ibid., 122; see also LLM 12/16.

12. John E. Smith, *America's Philosophical Vision* (Chicago: University of Chicago Press, 1992), 126.

13. *Fugitive Essays*, 349, 361.

14. Here Royce made prominent "this reflexive aspect of the world of Being."

15. *Problem of Christianity*, 349, 361.

16. Ibid., 200.

17. Letter of Peirce to Royce, see Appendix C, original emphasis.

18. *Problem of Christianity*, 298, 314.

19. Cf. this with his lapidary statement, "The very recognition of Being is itself an estimate" (LLM 5/27). This statement echoed his earlier emphasis on the moral element in the "interpretation of our knowledge of finite facts as largely due to an active 'acknowledgment,' whose significance is ethical, rather than to a mere passive acceptance of 'given' contents of present experience" (*World and the Individual* 2:vi–vii).

20. Royce's article "Negation" in Hasting's *Encyclopaedia*; see *Logical Essays*, 203. Including its "numerous not-relations," Royce's evaluative response here to Peirce's three ideals expresses that "principle of the nobler" which also animates

each of Aquinas's "Five Ways"; namely: *id propter quod unumquodque tale et illud magis* (whatever reality is the reason why some limited being has a certain quality possesses that quality in a yet more perfect way). See Aquinas's "fourth way" in *Summa Theologiae* I, q. 2, a. 3.

21. In his *Second Part* Aquinas does not seem to have remembered the kind of unchangeable God which he had described in the *First Part*.

22. *Religious Aspect*, 437.

23. Instances occur in *Religious Aspect*, 422–425, and 431–435, with a clear summation at 476. For some secondary expositions of this argument, see Smith, *America's Philosophical Vision*, 126–128 and Frank M. Oppenheim, *Royce's Mature Philosophy of Religion* (Notre Dame, Ind.: University of Notre Dame Press, 1987), 351 n. 21.

24. See, e.g., *Spirit of Modern Philosophy*, 469–471; *Conception of God*, 42–44, 203–216; *World and the Individual* 2:460–466; and *Philosophy of Loyalty*, 361–364.

25. First Berkeley Conference, 1914 (HARP 84, no.3), 31–32, emphasis added.

26. See Question 2 of the mid-year examination, February 7, 1916, in LLM, end of the first semester. For other adumbrations of his arguments in LLM, see 12/2, 12/11, and 12/18.

27. Royce's other 1915–16 *Encyclopaedia* articles, "Negation" and "Order" made some, though fewer, contributions to his last theory of knowledge than did "Mind." In LLM, he gave epistemology even greater prominence than metaphysics.

28. For Royce's late theory of *scientific* knowledge, see *Logical Essays*, 254–267, and especially his article of 1914, "The Mechanical, the Historical, and the Statistical" (35–61). The latter reflects the fruit of Royce's many seminars in scientific methodology at Harvard, his deepening grasp of Peirce, and especially his interpretation of Peirce's intent to insist on the fecundity of reasoning more than on its security (see Appendix C).

In this article, Royce also clearly adopted Peirce's idea of "thirdness" by frequently referring to nature's tendencies and habits—e.g., "some tendency to orderly cooperation" (*Logical Essays*, 60–61)—and by highlighting

> the statistical fecundity of nature's principal tendency . . . to that mutual assimilation which both defines . . . real classes of natural objects, and tends to keep these classes or aggregates permanent in the world and to increase both their wealth of constitution and their extent. (59)

Here Royce also pointed out that nature's seeming tendency to an unconscious sort of teleology—such as the Greeks and especially Aristotle held—is expressive of "the fecundity of aggregation" principle, which can be formulated in statistical terms. By the use of chance and "the habits which nature gathers as she matures" (61), Royce suggested a teleology in nature *without* having a provident god design a blueprint for its development.

29. To undergird his late theory of knowledge, Royce continued in 1916 to use his 1910 "Principles of Logic" with its System Sigma (*Royce's Mature Philosophy*, 43–87), even while he transformed it with Peirce's triadic theory of interpretation and doctrine of Signs. The presence of his *Principles of Logic* becomes clear in his 1916

Encyclopaedia article "Order" (*Logical Essays*, 204–231). For Royce, no theoretical or practical knowledge can exist without a grasp of order, which has a grasp of inference as a prerequisite, which in turn relies on negation as its basis (230).

30. In this section, in-text references are to "Mind" as published in *Logical Essays*.

31. See LLM 11/18 to 12/7.

32. See Peirce's detailed investigation of this in *Collected Papers of Peirce* 1:545–559.

33. For Royce's article, see *James and Other Essays*, 187–254 or *Logical Essays*, 63–97; for Dewey's "Reply to Professor Royce's Critique of Instrumentalism," see *John Dewey: The Middle Works 1899–1922*, vol. 7, 1912–1914, 64–78. My estimate is that here Dewey misunderstood Royce.

34. *Life*, 362.

35. See Royce's third principle of his philosophy of loyalty in his First Berkeley Conference, 1914 (HARP 84, no. 3), 31–32 and also *Sources of Religious Insight*, 197–213.

36. For Royce's refutation of other related charges, equally inaccurate, see *Problem of Christianity*, 339–340.

CHAPTER 6

1. Georg Habermas portrays a three-staged history of metaphysics: first, the study of beings (*onta*); secondly, the subject-centered kind of philosophizing that Descartes started; and finally, such metaphysics as starts from a community of sign-sending members and emphasized language, semiotic, and hermeneutics.

With Peirce, the mature Royce saw that the only gatewey to this third stage of metaphysics lay in a community of interpretation. E.g., "On the whole, the schools of metaphysical discussion have made quite an inadequate use of our social experiences and problems" (LLM 10/5). Subsequent in-text references are to LLM.

2. *Collected Papers of Peirce* 1:545–567, 5:213–357. Peirce's minute investigations into the usually unrecognized reasonings at work beneath ordinary human perceptual judgments unearth three types of inference (abduction, deduction, and induction), which expressed his three ultimate categories (Firstness, Secondness, and Thirdness) for both his logic and metaphysics.

3. LLM thus constitutes Royce's most mature and insightful commentary upon *World and the Individual*.

4. This is the mature and transformed version of his earlier purposeful "internal meaning"; see *World and the Individual* 1:22–23, 32–33.

5. Royce dedicated a total of twenty lectures to the First Conception of Being (fourteen at first, and then six more during his reconsideration of it in late April and early May). But to the Second, Third, and Fourth Conceptions of Being he invested only ten, five, and four lectures, respectively.

6. In 1881, Royce had already claimed that he was "no nominalist." Beside perhaps echoing his early reading of Peirce, Royce described classical nominalism

as holding "terms as mere names" without reference to connective realities. See his *Primer of Logical Analysis* (San Francisco: A. L. Bancroft, 1881), 4.

Pierce himself spoke of two kinds of nominalism: (a) the classical nominalists who, by regarding terms as merely the sound of words (*flatus vocis*), held that the only two realities were things and terms; and (b) the conceptual nominalists who, although acknowledging the existence of universal concepts, nevertheless held that these concepts were linked only to terms. Thus they did not acknowledge any "real connections between individual things regardless of mere formulae." In addition, Peirce noted: "to be a nominalist consists in the undeveloped state in one's mind of the apprehension of Thirdness as Thirdness"—that is, of "real generals" such as real laws, habits, and tendencies. See *Collected Papers of Peirce* 1:16; 5:48, 122, and also Paul D. Foster, "Peirce and the Threat of Nominalism," *Transactions* 28 (Fall 1992): 691–724.

A paradoxical cross-usage of terminology resulted. Whereas Peirce opposed his "scholastic realism" and nominalism, Royce brought his "realism" and nominalism to converge upon his First Conception of Being.

7. See W. E. Hocking, "The Ontological Argument in Royce and Others," *Contemporary Idealism*, 45–66.

8. Here Royce approached the role of *narrative* in identifying an individual, since the coherence of one's story expresses one's plan of life or overall purpose, which is the basis for self-identification.

9. Here Royce clearly followed Peirce's attack on claims of self-evident and immediate knowledges.

10. Here Royce's use of "realistic" approaches Peirce's meaning in his "common-sense realism"—hardly Royce's special sense of "realism" as found in the First Conception of Being.

11. Our source for this section is Royce's "Mind," to which in-text references refer.

12. See his Peirce-inspired article of 1914, "The Mechanical, the Historical, and the Statistical," in *Logical Essays*, 35–62, and *Seminar*. See also *World and the Individual* 2:1–242.

13. In 1901, Royce had already adopted the core of pragmatism: "my whole philosophy [lies in the position]. . . that all theories have a practical meaning" (*World and the Individual* 2:xv).

14. In 1902, Royce's view of mind in *World and the Individual* as a *dynamo of ideas* had already seemed "most suggestive" to Peirce; see *Collected Papers of Peirce* 8. 122, n. 19.

15. *Problem of Christianity*, 248, 256–260.

16. Ibid., 345. In this section in-text references are to LLM.

17. Extension Course in Ethics, Lect. II, 4.

18. *Problem of Christianity*, 401.

19. Ibid., 350.

20. R. B. Perry held that Royce's idealism was caught in an *ego*centric predicament; mainly, "that the being of things is a being in the mind of some thinker" (LLM 2/29). Insisting even more on objectivity than did Perry, Royce viewed

Perry's objection that knowing is centered in minds (Egos) as an obvious and trivial truism, basically irrelevant to Royce's attack on extreme realism and metaphysical nominalism. See also 5/20.

21. *World and the Individual* 1:22–23.

22. The teleology of certain basic ideas—such as those of being, truth, and genuine loyalty—seek their goals with such undeniable constancy that they ground Royce's use of performatory contradictions to validate and articulate several absolute truths.

23. *Problem of Christianity*, 337–339.

24. By "teleological," Royce means not merely cognitively, but also voluntaristically intentional.

25. In this course Royce had stated, "I cannot myself maintain that there is any such thing as an analytical method which can be carried on in distinction from a synthetic method in metaphysics" (LLM 2/15).

26. This reveals how Royce's 1883 insight into the reality of the All-Knower perdured to the end as both seminal and central.

27. *Problem of Christianity*, 351–357.

28. Royce called these elements "disteleological" or "anti-teleological" (LLM 5/27).

29. *Problem of Christianity*, 403–405.

30. Earlier in *Problem of Christianity* he had used this strategy of alternation by requiring the use first of the idea of Individual and then of the idea of Community to reach a richer interpretation. A similar strategy marked his Extension Course in Ethics of 1915–16.

31. In general, I here concur with Max Fisch's original evaluation of Royce's stature in his *Classic American Philosophers*, 1–7.

CHAPTER 7

1. See W. E. Hocking, "On Royce's Empiricism," *Journal of Philosophy* 53 (1956: 57–63. From Royce's 1915–16 Extension Course in Ethics, the first lecture on autonomy and the good is missing. Of the five extant lectures, four were delivered near the start of the course: Lecture II "The Idea of Duty," Lecture III "Wallas' Problem of the Great Society," Lecture IV "Pleasure and Pain; Happiness and Unhappiness," and Lecture V "The Self." The final extant lecture, "Comments upon the Problem of the Mid-Year Examination Paper"was delivered in the second semester on February 16, 1916. The typescripts of the four early lectures are preserved in HARP 94, nos. 1–4, and "Comments" in HARP 95, no.1.

Royce's three manuscript outlines for the course are preserved in a six-page appendix to a second typescript of Lecture II, in HARP Box H. His Programme for the course is published in the *Extension School Catalogue, 1915–1916*, pp. 18–19 (HUE 25.510 in Harvard Archives).

2. See *Extension School Catalogue, 1915–1916*, pp. 18–19.

3. Extension Course in Ethics, Lect. IV, pp. 5–7.

4. See Lect. II, pp. 17–20 and "Comments," 8–10, 34–36, 44–63.

5. Lecture II, pp. 7–24. Royce returned to this story in his final metaphysical lecture (LLM 5/27).

6. See Appendix B below for Royce's four-page mid-year examination, dated February 1916, which presents the mother-daughter dilemma under "A Case Involving Problems of Loyalty." Royce's subsequent observations on this case occur in "Comments," 5–10, 40–63. (An original printed form of this examination is reserved in the Josiah Royce Memorial Collection, UCLA.)

7. "A Case Involving Problems of Loyalty," p. 4.

8. For a detailed description of this method, see Oppenheim, *Royce's Mature Philosophy*, chaps. 12–14.

9. Extension Course in Ethics, Lect. III, p.4.

10. LLM 5/27, emphasis added.

11. See *Problem of Christianity*, 351–355. In the three years following the publication of *Problem* in 1913, Royce grew from simply a largely static presentation of these three "attitudes to will" into a far more dynamic way of portraying the self's progressive purification. In his metaphysical lecture of March 16, 1916, Royce suggested that the human self needs to pass through the first two attitudes of will successively, and by discovering their large areas of unwisdom, be disposed to adopt the third attitude of will which serves as the psychic precondition for genuine Loyalty (*Problem of Christianity*, 270).

12. First Berkeley Conference, "Illustrations of the Philosophy of Loyalty" (HARP 84, no. 3), 31–32, emphasis added.

13. Extension Course in Ethics, Lect. III, p. 4.

14. In 1907 Royce had asserted both that "we possess an innate power to become reasonable," and that conscience, when regarded as "within you, . . . is the spirit of your own self, the very ideal that makes you any rational moral person whatever" (See *Philosophy of Loyalty*, 178).

15. See *Problem of Christianity*, 122, 193–194, 218–219; *Letters*, 645; and Extension Course in Ethics, Lect. V, p. 12.

16. In its positive form, this willingness (genuine loyalty) constitutes the bond with community required for ethical life. Its logical root lies in Royce's basic *epsilon* relation, see *Philosophy of Loyalty*, 17.

17. Royce's first outline states, "all ethical ideas should be both socially and individually applied" (HARP Box H, no. 1), 1.

18. *Extension School Catalogue, 1915–1916*, p. 19, original emphasis.

19. By 1915–16 Royce generally avoided the phrase "Be loyal to loyalty!" Distinctive of his 1907 ethics, this slogan had become applied stereotypically to his ethics by others who viewed it as an abstract monolith. The fact that Royce usually avoided this phrase in 1915–16 suggests that by then he had found many people taking it so abstractly that they missed the concretized catholic ideal which he found functioning in moral life as lived.

20. LLM 12/4.

21. *Hope of Great Community*, 131.

22. LLM 12/4.

23. LLM 5/27.

24. Extension Course in Ethics, Lect. III, p. 17.

25. See *Philosophy of Loyalty*, 60–70, where before portraying and defending his own form of *rational* ethical individualism, Royce described its four *ir*rational forms, each involving a misinterpretation of genuine loyalty. The first deviant ethical individualism lies in a more enthusiastic than reasonable revolt against some oppressor. The second so emphasizes moral independence of judgment that it deafens itself against hearing traditional wisdom and long-range common hopes. The third type of individualistic self-assertion places an unbalanced emphasis upon one's own rights rather than giving an equal stress to one's duties. The fourth feels that an individual's mere possession of oneself in inner light and peace relieves such a "spiritual" soul of the need for any loyalty to externally visible causes. (See *Philosophy of Loyalty*, 68.)

26. Extension Course in Ethics, Lect. II, p.5.

27. "Outlines for the University Extension Course," p.1.

28. For Peirce's letter, see Appendix C. For Royce's acknowledgment that he "deeply prized" this letter, see p. 17 of his first Berkeley Conference of 1914 in HARP 84, no. 3.

29. For these deviant forms, see *Philosophy of Loyalty*, 60–70.

30. See chapter 16 of *Royce's Mature Philosophy*, 264–279.

31. Extension Course in Ethics, Lect. II; in-text references in the following paragraphs are to this lecture.

32. See HARP Box H. no.1.

33. Extension Course in Ethics, Lect. V, pp. 2, 12.

34. In his final year Royce referred his metaphysical students to *War and Insurance*, 44–46, rather than to chapters 11–13 of *Problem of Christianity* as his preferred source for clarifying the dynamics of a Community of Interpretation (See LLM 10/19–10/23).

35. See *Royce's Mature Philosophy*, 277.

36. On this, see W. E. Hocking, "Josiah Royce," *Encyclopaedia of the Social Sciences* 13: 451–452.

37. LLM 4/15, original emphasis.

CHAPTER 8

1. *James and Other Essays*, 190.

2. Compare *Problem of Christianity*, 351–357, with "The Idea of Loyalty," Extension Course in Ethics, Lect. II, pp. 22–24.

3. "Comments," 4–5, emphasis added.

4. LLM 4/11.

5. See *Sources of Religious Insight*, 239–240; also *Philosophy of Loyalty*, chap. 6, "Training for Loyalty," esp., 277, 283, 288.

6. On pseudo-individualisms, see *Philosophy of Loyalty*, 68–69. Among the types of disordered loyalties Royce included those that are blind or fanatical, fickle or indecisive, primarily militant or competitive, and especially those focused exclusively on some group—family, corporation, nation—without reference and openness to the Universal Community.

Royce also analyzed different basic attitudes behind our linguistic use of "I," "you," and "we" (see First Berkeley Conference of 1914, p. 44 [HARP 84, no. 3]). If members of a community of interpretation are animated by a genuine will to interpret *each other*, a genuine "we-consciousness" will arise from the unity-promotive "third attitude of will" then operating in the members.

7. E.g., in *Philosophy of Loyalty*, compare chapters I–IV with V–VI.

8. E.g., in *Philosophy of Loyalty*, 258–263, 263–268, and 268–295, respectively. In-text references in this section are to *Philosophy of Loyalty*.

9. Second Pittsburgh Lecture, "The Art of Loyalty" (HARP 82, no. 2), 12.

10. Ibid., 50–51, punctuation adjusted.

11. See, for instance, Extension Course in Ethics, Lect. III, p. 4, where Royce stated, "Nowhere is pedantry or a love of mere uniformity more out of place than in ethics."

12. Second Pittsburgh Lecture, p. 51.

13. First Berkeley Conference of 1914 (HARP 84, no. 3), 51.

14. On the demand for seriousness in ethics, see *James and Other Essays*, 289, 298; on the sense of childlike humility, humor, and play, see "Comments," 6–8; *Letters*, 638, 641; and *Royce's Mature Philosophy*, 26, 120, 141.

15. See *Philosophy of Loyalty*, 283–295, and *Sources of Religious Insight*, 215–256, "The Religious Mission of Sorrow."

16. See *James and Other Essays*, 295.

17. Royce had already said it was "this synthesis of individualism and loyalty which constitutes our whole ethical doctrine" (*Philosophy of Loyalty*, 200; see also 59, 98, 199). For the next eight years, the same integrating intent energized his interpretation of conflicts of loyalty. Notice how he handled, for example, the cases of Antigone and the mother-daughter in "Comments," 33–36, 44–67.

18. This insistence on the balancing of individualism and loyalty needs highlighting in our day. Moreover, if erroneous understandings of Royce are set aside, three imbalances mark most current, fairly accurate expositions of Royce. His theoretical philosophy has suffered from a one-sided emphasis upon the idea of Community to the soft-pedaling of his idea of Spirit. Similarly, his practical philosophy has suffered from a one-sided emphasis upon loyalty to the omission of his equal stress upon authentic individualism. His overall philosophy has suffered from a one-sided emphasis either upon the careful logic undergirding his philosophy or upon the practical embodiments of this logic in ethico-religious living, instead of insisting upon the difficult balancing of both. As noted, *Philosophy of Loyalty* and the Extension Course in Ethics often stress the need to balance all these pairs.

19. LLM 11/2.

20. LLM 11/16.

21. LLM 4/8.

22. Extension Course, Lect. III, pp. 1–5.

23. This followed as a corollary from his pathfinder's passional logic; see Royce's *Principles of Logic*, and *Royce's Mature Philosophy*, 48–53.

24. In *Problem of Christianity*, 387, Royce described this step-by-step procedure, using as a text the poem of John Henry Newman, "Lead, Kindly Light."

For Royce's 1916 practice, see "Comments," 61–63, where the tone of tentativeness emerges in his frequent use of "perhaps" which keeps hope-filled possibilities open without yet permitting them the status of fixed certainties.

25. "Comments," 63.

26. See *Philosophy of Loyalty*, 357.

27. "Comments," 5.

28. Royce surfaced this theme even in his final metaphysics course: "At present I act because my past demands of me this act with reference to my future. I must get on with this enterprise one step more." (See LLM 10/16.)

29. Admittedly, my study and use of Niebuhr's *The Responsible Self* has sensitized me to the role played in Roycean texts by the "detection of the fitting." Niebuhr acknowledged his own intellectual inheritance from Royce and called his responsibility ethics an ethics of the fitting or a cathecontic ethics to distinguish it from, and go beyond, goal-centered and duty-centered kinds of ethics. For his part, Royce rarely used the term "responsibility" as a contemporary substitute for "duty" (yet see LLM 3/16) and he never called his own a cathecontic ethics. I believe, however, that the late Royce's personal and philosophical practice shows him "discerning the fitting." He also supplied the vital seedlings for a cathecontic ethics which later thinkers, influenced by Royce, like Niebuhr, James Gustafson, William Spohn, and others, have developed into a mature ethics of responsibility.

30. See *Life*, 361–362.

31. *Nicomachean Ethics* VI, 11; 1143a20–21. The Greek term *epieikes* means what is fitting, meet, suitable and derives from *to eikos*, meaning what is reasonable, fair, or equitable. The latter term forms the compounds *to kathekon* and *ta kathekonta*, which mean "in accord with what is fitting, meet, or proper." These compounds are the roots for Niebuhr's term "cathecontic," used to distinguish his kind of ethics (see his *Responsible Self*, 87).

32. Accordingly, on grounds of its distinct object, this moral kind of discernment needs to be distinguished from discernment of "spirits," of "God's will," of "one's deepest desire"—however closely interconnected these modes of discernment are.

33. This teaching would become even more evident were a word-count undertaken of Royce's post-*Problem* writings to discover how frequently such words occur as "fit," "fitting," "adapted," "worthy," "suitable," "appropriate," "proper," "in accordance with," and so forth.

34. See, e.g., *Philosophy of Loyalty*, 179–196.

35. See, e.g., ibid., xi.

36. Royce stated, "One of the main purposes of these lectures is to simplify our conceptions of duty and of the good" (*Philosophy of Loyalty*, 149). His "and" suggests his effort to integrate both these chief ethical ideas.

37. See *Philosophy of Loyalty*, 15, 123–124, 127, 132, 324.

38. In-text references for the rest of the chapter are to Royce's "Comments." Besides the clues dropped in *Philosophy of Loyalty*, Royce indicated the need to find the fitting or the proper mean or the "between" ideas in six other late major sources:

(1) Smith College Lectures of Spring 1910, First Series, "Introductory Remarks," (HARP 77, no. 3), 2, 4, and in Second Series, "Recent Problems in Philosophy," (HARP 78, no. 1), 2.

(2) *Problem of Christianity*, 79, 376 (See also *Royce's Mature Philosophy*, 271).

(3) First Berkeley Lecture of 1914, "Some Illustrations of the Philosophy of Loyalty," (HARP 84, no. 3), 31, and Royce's prepared but undelivered lecture, "The Spirit of the Community" (HARP 91, no. 3), 5–6, 8, 10.

(4) Royce's article of October 1914, "A Plea . . ." (*Basic Writings* 2:1217 under 1914, no. 3), 12–14, esp. 13.

(5) LLM 10/15.

(6) In Extension Course in Ethics, Royce aimed to synthesize fittingly the three leading ethical ideas. He searched for the fitting adaptation of each of these ideas to its proper familial relationship. Overall, he was concerned for "the healing of estrangement" as the need to be met most fittingly—not only in the mother-daughter case, but in the ordinary situation of every isolated individual who needs salvation or deliverance (see *Sources of Religious Insight*, 8–17, and *Problem of Christianity*, 42, 75, 119, 128, 130, 194, 202).

39. Niebuhr's expression in *Responsible Self*, 127–145.

CHAPTER 9

1. *Problem of Christianity*, 38 and 41–42. In this section in-text references are to *Problem of Christianity*.

2. See also *Problem of Christianity*, 128, 130, 190, 194, 207, 224, and cf. *Philosophy of Loyalty*, 294, 388.

3. See "Essence of the previous [fifth] plan," HARP Symbolic Logic Box 4, no. 4, p.1 (according to the 1967 listing of box contents).

4. Royce's late interest in mysticism found expression in his "George Fox as a Mystic," *Harvard Theological Review* 6 (January 1913): 35–59, even before his two months of lecturing on mysticism during his Last Lectures on Metaphysics, in spring 1916 (see LLM 3/25–4/25).

5. First Berkeley Lecture, 1914, "Illustrations of the Philosophy of Loyalty" (HARP 84, no. 3), 31–33.

6. Ibid.

7. Contrast *Letters*, 587, with Royce to his wife Katharine, August 25, 1915. In the latter he wrote, "I have now written out the two opening lectures in full—*the hardest for me*—of my University Extension Course." The arduous labor here acknowledged contrasts with his other reports to Katharine, written on August 9th and 30th, that he was "pleasantly busy on my MS" and "making, for the moment, good progress." (See HARP-CFC Box A: Royce MSS, fol. "Correspondence," emphasis added.)

8. See LLM 5/27.

9. Here Royce paralleled William James's starting ethical question, "Is Life Worth Living?" See James's *Will to Believe and Other Essays in Popular Psychology*, 32–62.

10. See Royce's carefully balanced critique of the relation between mysticism and idealism in *Studies of Good and Evil*, xiii–xiv, and LLM 3/25–4/25.

11. *Problem of Christianity*, 269–270.

12. Ibid. See also 349–351, 401.

13. Ibid., 49.

14. See ibid., 125, 132, 197.

15. Stress on one particular leading ethical idea, in accord with a different relationship within the family structure, became distinctive of ethical maturation in Royce's late ethics (See "Comments," 20–37).

16. See, for instance, his 1879 "The Practical Significance of Pessimism," in *Fugitive Essays*, 133–154, or his 1885 "Ethical Skepticism and Ethical Pessimism" in *Religious Aspect*, 107–130.

17. Royce acknowledged, "For my own part the study of character saved me from pessimism" (HARP-CFC, Box A: "MSS of Josiah Royce," "Autobiographical Sketch, 1866–1886[?]," p. 19).

18. See *Philosophy of Loyalty*, 49–98, where Royce identifies four deviant forms of individualism (59–70), to which he adds that of the "moral hobo," the individualist who is loyal to nothing (202). For a more recent analysis, see Bellah et al., *Habits of the Heart* and Frank Oppenheim, "A Roycean Response to the Challenge of Individualism," in *Beyond Individualism*, ed. Donald Gelpi (Notre Dame, Ind.: University of Notre Dame Press, 1989), 87–119.

19. See his third outline for the Extension Course in Ethics where "intentions" replaced the "expectations" of his first outline (HARP, Box H, no.1).

20. *Problem of Christianity*, 248–256.

21. See LLM, 10/23; *Sources of Religious Insight*, 46; *Philosophy of Loyalty*, 14; *James and Other Essays*, 157; and *Letters*, 587.

22. Extension Course in Ethics, Lect. V, 2–3, emphasis added.

23. Ibid., Lect. III, 4.

24. See John E. Smith's Introduction to *Problem of Christianity*, p. 14, n. 12.

25. Extension Course in Ethics, Lect. III, 17.

26. LLM 2/15.

27. Even in 1916 Royce judged Eckhart's mystical doctrine of the "little divine spark" worth protracted exposition (see LLM 4/6–4/15, esp. 4/8–4/11).

28. See Royce's 1916 article "Monotheism," Hasting's *Encyclopaedia* 8:817–821.

29. LLM 4/25. See also *Studies of Good and Evil*, xiii–xiv.

30. First Berkeley Conference of 1914 (HARP 84, no. 3), 6–7.

31. LLM 4/11.

32. Although complete, this trust does not become Ekhart's "detachment of soul" (*Abgescheidenheit*) (See *Studies of Good and Evil*, xiv). Royce derived the view of God as "leader of the world" from Aristotle. In the outline for his proposed (but never delivered) 1916–17 Extension Course in Ethics, Royce listed "My Search for the Captain" as the seventh and final example of his ethical idea of "Attachment, Reconciliation, etc." (See HARP Symbolic Logic Box 4, Autograph Notebook: "A

272 Notes

Triad Operation and its Results," pp. 44–45. Professor Robert Burch called my attention to this outline).

33. Extension Course in Ethics, Lect. II, 10, emphasis added.

34. Before 1900 Royce acknowledged that for his work in the "psychology of character," he "had ransacked most of the popular literature on the subject; had read phrenology, physiognomy, chirosophy, and graphology, and even astrology. . . . In recent years I have been concerned mostly with comparative psychology, especially morbid psychology. From this I have obtained more than from any other subject" (HARP-CFC, Box A: "MSS of Josiah Royce," Sketch of his intellectual course of studies from 1866 to 1886 (?), pp. 3 and 7). Royce worked in Harvard's psychological laboratory, contributed to the American Society for Psychical Research, and published the articles on psychology catalogued in Skrupskelis's Annotated Bibliography (*Basic Writings* 2) under 1887 nos. 5–8; 1888 no. 1; 1889 nos. 1–2, 4, 7, 11; 1891, no. 11; 1892 no. 1; 1893 nos. 2–3; 1894, nos. 1–4; 1895, nos. 13–14, and so forth, up to 1909, no. 4, "The Recent Psychotherapeutic Movement in America," and beyond.

35. For deviant forms of individualism, see *Philosophy of Loyalty*, 59–70, 202. In his third Pittsburgh Lecture (1911) Royce scored as incomplete and inaccurate the five following *misinterpretations of loyalty*, namely, that loyalty is "just the same" as: (a) "unselfishness, as self-sacrifice, as concern for others," (b) "pure benevolence, as devotion to the general happiness," (c) "subservience—some sort of blind obedience to authority," (d) "conservatism [which] implies a disposition to resist reform and progress" and (e) "an absorption in mere tasks, opposed to inner personal and spiritual cultivation" (HARP 82, no. 3, pp. 15–16).

36. LLM 5/27. In-text references are to LLM.

37. See, for example, how unflinchingly Royce faced the evils of life in the special eleven-page introduction which he wrote in 1896 for Harvard's philosophy department as a prolegomenon, fit for their ears, to a reading to them of his "Problem of Job" lecture. This manuscript in HARP 52, no. 1, is still unpublished.

38. See *International Journal of Ethics* 1 (1890–1891): 503.

39. *Problem of Christianity*, 146–152.

40. Ibid., 269.

41. In his *Outlines of Psychology* of 1903, Royce already suggested this order of Sign-sending. Finding the self's psychological sheaths as ordered according to the degree of their psychic warmth, he arranged them accordingly: "sensitivity" as the outermost and least warm sheath, "docility" as mediating and warmer, and "initiative" as inmost and warmest. The self is called to receive Signs from human and non-human natural "others" through its sensitivity sheath and then through its more interpretive docility sheath before it uses the unique autonomy of its own initiative. Thus the self maintains proper relation to the world around it. On this, see *Outlines of Psychology*, vi–vii, and Frank Oppenheim, "Royce's Community: A Dimension Missing in Freud and James?" *Journal of the History of the Behavioral Sciences* 13 (1977): 173–190, esp., 183–187.

42. In *Problem of Christianity*, the Logos-Spirit communicates its doctrine of life to all selves through the Signs of Time, Interpretation, and the Community, integrated by the Sign of the World as a Universal Community (401). With its

"Christian" doctrine of life, the Logos-Spirit further communicates with finite minded beings through the Signs of Genuine Community. Lost State of Natural Man, and Atonement, all integrated by the Sign of genuine Loyalty (or Grace) (*Problem of Christianity*, 42, 193–194).

43. *Letters*, 645.

44. *Problem of Christianity*, 189.

45. Ibid., 318.

CHAPTER 10

1. *Philosophy of Loyalty*, 77–79.

2. Royce's original "moral insight" (that ultimately the human self could not escape willing to live in harmony with all conflictive wills) perdured to the end (see *Religious Aspect*, 168–170).

3. Extension Course on Ethics, Lect. V, 2, emphasis added.

4. In 1916 Royce dedicated most of his logical approach in metaphysics to investigate diverse judgments of identity and identification (see LLM 2/24 to 5/4).

5. In the lectures he wrote for his 1915–16 Extension Course on Ethics he employed the terms "motives," "interests" and "concerns" nearly synonymously. See Extension Course on Ethics, Lect. II, 5–8.

6. Extension Course on Ethics, Lect. II, 3–4.

7. Ibid., 4.

8. Ibid., 1.

9. For the full text of William Ernest Henley's poem, see *The Family Book of Best Loved Poems*, ed. David L. George (New York: Hanover House, 1952), 57.

10. In 1915 Royce dedicated his entire fourth lecture to clarify the psychological differences between two kinds of good and evil (see Extension Course on Ethics, Lect. IV, "Pleasure and Pain, Happiness and Unhappiness").

11. Extension Course on Ethics, Lect. II, 3.

12. This description occurs in Emerson's poem "Voluntaries," Section 3, found in vol. 9, *Poems*, of *Emerson's Complete Works*, 12. vols., ed. J. E. Cabot (Cambridge, Mass.: Riverside Press, 1893), 178–182.

13. In 1912 Royce had chosen to present his "three most fundamental Christian ideas" according to his audience's ease of receiving them: namely, first Community, then Lost State, and only thereafter, the puzzling and less palatable idea of Atonement—all three being integrated by the idea of genuine Loyalty (or Grace) (see *Problem of Christianity*, 72–73).

In 1915, Royce again measured the degree of his audience's readiness to receive his "three leading ethical ideas." He reminded them that for over fifty years, "the idea of duty has been . . . the most unpopular of the great and fundamental ethical ideas" (Extension Course on Ethics, Lect. II, 4). So he chose to present the idea of Freedom first, then of Goodness, and only finally, the idea of Duty. All three ideas needed to be integrated within the central idea of the genuinely loyal self.

14. Extension Course on Ethics, Lect. II, 4. In 1907 Royce aimed to balance true individualism and loyalty and to simplify the conceptions of good and duty

(*Philosophy of Loyalty*, 79–80, 149). By 1915, however, he had clearly identified the "three leading ethical ideas" and harmonized them within the idea of the loyal Self. This new development suggests one dimension of Royce's growth in ethical philosophy during his final year.

15. Extension Course on Ethics, Lect. III, 21.

16. Ibid.

17. Royce, "John Fiske" (HARP 72, no.1), 38.

18. *Problem of Christianity*, 202–206.

19. See *War and Insurance*, 36–37, 42–43, 49, 56, 71; LLM 10/25; and Extension Course on Ethics, "Comments."

20. "Comments," 34.

21. Ibid., 35.

22. See, for example, *War and Insurance*, 7, 9, 39, 92. Although Royce had used the term "responsibility" (or derivatives) with significant frequency in 1901 (*World and the Individual* 2:389, 393–394, 402–405), he used it rarely thereafter until his final years.

23. See *Race Questions*, 55–108; *Hope of the Great Community*, 51–52.

24. See, for example, *Problem of Christianity*, 247–248; *Hope of the Great Community*, 94–95, and Cotton, *Royce and the Human Self*, 7.

25. See *War and Insurance*, 79–81; *Hope of the Great Community*, 79–92, esp. 85–91.

26. *Hope of the Great Community*, 51; see also 53.

27. Ibid., 49, 55.

28. See his "Spirit of the Community" (HARP 92, no. 3) and "Comments."

29. "Spirit of the Community," 6. In-text references are to this work.

30. See 1 Tm 2:5, and also Heb 8:6, 9:15, and 12:24.

31. This tradition stemmed from the *Cur Deus Homo* of Anselm of Canterbury (1033–1109).

32. HARP 91, no. 3, pp. 3, 7.

33. Niebuhr, a close reader of Royce, skillfully elaborated this theme in *The Responsible Self*, 117, 134–143.

34. Extension Course on Ethics, Lect. II, 10.

35. See also *Hope of the Great Community*, 76. Royce called each wise mediator of commercial and economic transactions—bankers, insurance agents, brokers, etc.— a "spirit of the community" in the secular sense of "spirit" (e.g., *War and Insurance*, 54; "Spirit of the Community," 23; *Problem of Christianity*, 317). But he also used "spirit" in a superhuman religious sense referring to the Holy Spirit of the Beloved Community (e.g., *Problem of Christianity*, 198, 234–235). See also Frank Oppenheim, "The Idea of Spirit in the Mature Royce," *Transactions* 19 (Fall 1983): 381–395, esp. 385–386, 390.

36. *War and Insurance*, 84.

37. *Hope of the Great Community*, 52–53. In this Royce anticipated John Rawls's requirement in his *A Theory of Justice* that the least advantaged derive some benefit from each investment.

38. In *The Responsible Self*, Niebuhr developed this symbol through viewing

the human self in its manifold relationships—as social, timeful, absolutely dependent on the author of being and life, and called to respond as one situated in the tides of sin and salvation.

39. *Hope of the Great Community*, 25–27, 30.

40. "Comments," 20; see also Extension Course on Ethics, Lect. II, 4.

41. Extension Course on Ethics, Lect. II, 1–4.

42. "Comments," 19.

43. See *War and Insurance*, 26, 39–41; *Hope of the Great Community*, 63.

44. "Comments," 11–32; the three following paragraphs are also based on these pages.

45. A *cathecontic* ethics is sometimes called a "responsibility ethic." In 1882 Royce used the term "responsibility" (*Fugitive Essays*, 347, 362–363) and 1901 he employed this term several times. As yet, however, he had not raised it to central prominence in his ethics; see *World War and the Individual*, 2:391, 393, 400, 403.

46. Fourth Berkeley Conference of 1914 (HARP 84, no.1), 30–31.

47. *War and Insurance*, 26. In this passage Royce's use of "reasonable," "right," "worthy," and "saving" brought his norm of the fitting to an almost explicit formulation.

48. "Spirit of the Great Community" (HARP 91, no. 3), 12–35. Whether this agent be banker, insurer, counsellor, judge, salesman, or some other intermediary, her central role is to discover the fitting (*ta hekonta*). This includes listening discerningly enough to her principal to concur with the intent of the principal. It includes listening discerningly enough to the needy client to adapt to that person's mentality. It expecially includes her discoveries both of that suitable "third idea" which first bonds those two selves by means of some common interest of theirs, and then of those subsequent "fitting thirds" which will keep creating and inspiring the life and unity of this agent-community for as long a time as is mutually "profitable" for all its members. (See also *War and Insurance*, 55–64, 86–93.)

49. Royce speaks of "a faint and uncertain hope" (*Sources of Religious Insight*, 222) *solely* on the hypothesis that all sources of religious insight have been blocked and that no cause offers divine grace any longer to one's life. John Clendenning's statement that Royce in 1915–16 "was still unconvinced that the universal community was more than a faint hope" (*Life*, 392) is unfortunately ambiguous. If his "faint" points to "dim" or "barely perceptible," he signals accurately; but if he means "faint" in its prior senses of "feeble" or "lacking conviction or courage," then he seems to be sending a misleading signal. Hence, I here place a greater counterbalancing emphasis on the vigor in the hope of the mature Royce than does Clendenning.

In 1901 Royce intended to consider how the problem of evil related to "courage, endurance, resignation and hope" (*World and the Individual* 2:380). He carried out this intent, however, only as regards the first three virtues, while outrunning his limits of space when it came to the fourth. Thus in 1901 he left hope for later treatment—something he provided explicitly in 1915–16.

50. *Problem of Christianity*, 248.

51. *Hope of the Great Community*, 37.

52. Extension Course on Ethics, Lect. II, 10.

53. For Royce, radical pessimism showed itself clearly in Schopenhauer and the Southern Buddhists (*Problem of Christianity*, 354–355). Since they taught that any desire entraps a person in illusion, they urged all humans to eradicate from their hearts any desire for bilss, and in this way to "succeed" in reaching "Nothing."

54. Cf. Robert Bellah in *Habits of the Heart* and *Beyond Individualism: Towards a Retrieval of Moral Discourse*, ed. Donald Gelpi, S.J., with an Afterword by Robert Bellah (Notre Dame, Ind.: University of Notre Dame Press, 1989).

55. *Hope of the Great Community*, 48–49. In this section in-text citations are to *Hope of the Great Community*.

56. *War and Insurance*, 27. Here Royce reminded his audience, "We often do our best when we fix our mind on the thought which Kant expressed in the words: 'If justice meets utter wreck, then there is no worth whatever in the continued existence of human life in this world.'"

57. The Royce of 1912 experienced a hope that led him to direct the practical portions of the *Problem* "for the strengthening of heart" (*Problem of Christianity*, 40). It led him to close that work with the statement, ". . . we can look forward to a time when the work and the insight of religion can become as progressive as is now the work of science" (*Problem of Christianity*, 405).

58. *Hope of the Great Community*, 71–92.

59. Ibid., 66. I am indebted to John E. Smith for the following observation. Although Royce saw the centrality of mediation, he largely omitted the ambiguities of mediation. He did not touch on dis-interpretation. In *War and Insurance*, he did not weight how smaller nations are wholly endangered by major powers. In general, his attention was so focused on genuinely loyal persons and communities that he scarcely mentioned, let alone considered carefully, the vast number of people and nations who are not genuinely loyal, but merely professional functionaries or, if personally committed to an ethical cause, still lack norms for distinguishing between genuine and merely natural loyalties.

60. *Hope of the Great Community*, 132–136.

CHAPTER 11

1. For the effects of his Peircean insight on Royce's mature ethics, see James Collins, "Josiah Royce: Analyst of Religion as Community," in *American Philosophy of the Future*, ed. Michael Novak (New York: Charles Scribner's Sons, 1968), 209, and especially, Max H. Fisch, "American Pragmatism Before and After 1898," in *American Philosophy from Edwards to Quine*, ed. Robert W. Shahan and Kenneth R. Merrill (Norman, Okla.: University of Oklahoma Press, 1977), 100–101.

2. See *Problem of Christianity*, 43, 46, and 233–235, esp. 235.

3. See his Prefaces to *Religious Aspect, Spirit of Modern Philosophy, Studies of Good and Evil, World and the Individual*, and *Problem of Christianity*; LLM 1/11; and his autograph "Note on the Influence of Men and Books" (HARP 96, Student Notes, University of California); along with *Letters*, 68, 346, 460; and the indices of *Life* and *Letters*.

4. If someone wished to create similar tables for the *early* or *middle* Royce, the following lists, based on nationality, might be consulted. In the text, however, these thinkers are not listed among those who influenced Royce's mature period. (An especially strong influence is indicated by an asterisk.)

American Thinkers: J. M. Baldwin; G. B. Coale; John Dewey; John Fiske; *D. C. Gilman; G. H. Howison; *Joseph LeConte; George H. Palmer; Katharine Royce (wife); Ruth Royce (sister); and *Sarah Eleanor Bayliss Royce (mother).

British Thinkers: A. J. Balfour; *Bishop Berkeley; Bernard Bosanquet; *F. H. Bradley; Charles Darwin; *Shadworth Hodgson; David Hume; Thomas Huxley; John Locke; James Martineau; J. E. McTaggart; *J. S. Mill; Herbert Spencer; G. F. Stout; and James Ward.

German Thinkers: Karl Duhring; *Rudolph H. Lotze; Hugo Münsterberg; Friedrich Schelling; F. Ueberweg; Hans Vaihinger; *Wilhelm Wundt; *W. Windelband.

5. At times between 1875 and 1916 Royce studied and profited from the following logicians and philosophers of science: Boole, Cantor, Dedekind, DeMorgan, Enriques, Frege, Hilbert, Kempe, Klein, Maxwell, Mill, Peano, Peirce, Poincaré, Russell, Schroeder, Venn, and Whitehead.

6. Deserving notice among religious sources, over and beyond the Apostle Paul, are Amos, Job, John the Baptist, and John the Evangelist, along with the authors of the *Imitation of Christ*, *Pilgrim's Progress*, and the Hindu scriptures.

Worthy of mention among literary influences (mainly poets and novelists) are Matthew Arnold, Robert Browning, Thomas Carlyle, Dante, Dostoyevsky, George Eliott, Emerson, Goethe, Heine, Holderlin, Novalis and the other German Romantics, Poe, Schiller, Shakespeare, Edward Rowland Sill, Tennyson, and Tolstoy.

The composers strongly influencing Royce were Bach, Beethoven and Wagner.

7. The ranking in this column represents a tested effort to indicate the order of effective major presence to Royce's mature mind. At best, however, the ranking reflects an educated guess.

8. See esp., *James and Other Essays*, 257–298, for Royce's last published treatment on "immortality" written in 1906. In it, Royce states, among other things, "I am essentially the wanderer, whose home is in eternity" (295). He identified the rational warrant for his doctrine of the human self's intrinsic immortality as lying in the fact that "No finite series of these deeds [by an individual] expresses the insatiable demand of the ethical individual for further expression" (296–297).

Interestingly, however, Royce limited the bearing of this evidence exclusively to the intrinsic tendency of the purposeful self (in parallel with what some scholastic thinkers call "natural—*not* factual—immortality"). For as regards the self's factual future after its biological death, Royce simply opened the door to hopeful trust alone, without any demonstrated knowledge, when he added, "I pretend to no knowledge about my future fortunes, and to no rights whatever to demand, as a finite personality, any particular sort of good fortune" (298).

9. See Appendix C below. Peirce died April 19th, 1914. For Royce's account that Peirce gave general approval to the way Royce in the *Problem* used and applied Peirce's "simple ideas," see *Life*, 361–362, and the first Berkeley Conference of 1914

(HARP 84. no.3), 16–17. The letter and pertinent extracts from this conference were published in *Transactions* 27 (Winter 1990): 140–143.

10. For example, "Mind" is based on Signs within a process of interpretation; and in LLM 2/15 Royce informed his students at some length of Peirce's various threefold divisions of Signs, of which "his favorite is that of *index, icon, symbol*."

11. Royce's Second Plan for Extension Course on Ethics, Sect. IV, p.2.

12. *Life*, 69.

13. Lee LLM 11/11.

14. See Skrupskelis's listings under 1910, nos. 4 and 6, and 1911, nos. 3 and 4, in *Basic Writings* 2:1211–1212.

15. See Royce's Examination Questions for this course in the W. E. Hocking Papers, "Royce iii 1950 f," Houghton Library.

16. See Skrupskelis's listing under 1912, nos. 1 and 4; 1913, no. 8; 1914, no. 1; 1916, no. 6; 1917, no. 3 in *Basic Writings* 2:1212–1220.

17. See *Letters*, 539.

18. *Problem of Christianity*, 240–242.

19. *Life*, 75.

20. Long before this sharing with Lovejoy on December 30, 1912 (see *Letters*, 586–587), Royce had surfaced his perduring view of philosophy's dependence on instinct and the popular mind. Signs of this occurring 1892 (*Spirit of Modern Philosophy*, 11) as well as in 1899 when he said, "We are primarily creatures of instinct; and instinct is not merely the part of us that allies us with the lower animals. The highest in us is also based upon instinct" (*Race Questions*, 153).

21. See Royce's *Philosophy of Loyalty*, 59–70, and Oppenheim, "A Roycean Response to the Challenge of Individualism," 87–119.

22. LLM 11/11.

23. See, for instance, Royce's "Some Psychological Problems Emphasized by Pragmatism," *Popular Science Monthly* 83 (October 1913): 394–411.

24. Ibid. In his last letter to Royce (Appendix C), Peirce pointed out about his pragmatism that its inferential liberty "is far more important" than its inferential security. Royce may well have written his article, "Some Psychological Problems," after receiving this much treasured letter and thus using its hint about the richness of inference to apply it here to deduction. Royce soon viewed the pragmatists as so emphasizing Peircean induction as to shortchange the roles Peirce assigned to abduction (retroduction) and deduction (see LLM 10/26).

25. "Some Psychological Problems," 408, original emphasis.

26. See *Logical Essays*, 347, for Royce's 1910 treatment of this axiom and his reference to James's *Psychology*.

27. See *James and Other Essays*, 237.

28. See *Problem of Christianity*, 353, 359–361.

29. Ibid., 40–41.

30. Ibid., 240–242.

31. Ibid., 234–235; *Letters*, 647; and LLM 5/25.

32. See *Fugitive Essays*, 103.

33. "Tolstoi and the Unseen Moral Order," in *First Book of the Author's Club*, 488–497, esp. 491–492.

34. Royce to G. H. Palmer, October 28, 1910 (*Letters*, 547). See also 1 Cor 12.

35. *Sources of Religious Insight*, 293–297.

36. *Problem of Christianity*, 135; *Life*, 161.

37. *Sources of Religious Insight*, 293.

38. *Problem of Christianity*, 46.

39. Ibid., 46, 377.

40. Ibid., 46.

41. Cf. 1 Cor 12:12–31 with *Problem of Christianity*, 233–235 and 251–271.

42. Cf. *Problem of Christianity*, 344 with 268, and *Letters*, 645.

43. As found in Rom 1–2 and 7.

44. *Sources of Religious Insight*, 16; *Problem of Christianity*, 102–103, 154–156; *War and Insurance*, 30–41.

45. Cf. Rom 8 and 1 Cor 15:45 with *Problem of Christianity*, 139 and 218–219.

46. *Problem of Christianity*, 119.

47. Cf. ibid., 256–258 with 1 Cor 15. Cf. also *Letters*, 649, with 2 Tm 4:8, for further light on the Pauline roots of Royce's "community of hope" through the latter's Good Friday centering on "the memory of our Lord, and the hope of those 'who love his appearing'."

48. Josiah Royce, "Order" in Hasting's *Encyclopaedia* 9:535–536, or in *Logical Essays*, 212–213.

49. *Sources of Religious Insight*, 294–297, 202–205.

50. "Mind," Hasting's *Encyclopaedia*, 656–657, or *Logical Essays*, 177. Cf. this text with Paul's 1 Cor 13 and Gal 3, 5. Royce derived his conviction that loyalty has a trans-individual object—the community as a real person on a higher level—from Paul's discovery (Eph 5:25) of Christ's love for the Church as a higher level person more important than the human individual members comprising this mysterious grace-initiated unity in the Spirit; see *Problem of Christianity*, 95.

51. For Royce's community-based interpretation of the biblical story of reconciliation between Joseph and his brother, see *Problem of Christianity*, 202–204.

52. See Royce's 1899 address, "On Certain Limitations of the Thoughtful Public in America," *Race Questions*, 120, as well as its Pauline source in 1 Thes 5:21; see also 2 Cor 13:5.

53. See *Sources of Religious Insight*, 286, and Problem of Christianity, 376, along with 58, 84, 199, 234.

54. *Problem of Christianity*, 319. The Pauline quotation is from 1 Cor 14:13.

55. 1 Cor 10:31.

56. *Problem of Christianity*, 404–405.

57. For instance, Royce's final definition of loyalty is "*the will to manifest, so far as possible, the Eternal . . . in the form of the acts of an individual Self*"; see *Philosophy of Loyalty*, 357, original emphasis.

58. *James and Other Essays*, vi–vii.

59. 2 Tm 4:6–8.

60. See *Sources of Religious Insight*, 177–178, 181–183, and 198–199. Notice how even Royce's starting definition of loyalty (*Philosophy of Loyalty*, 16–17) combines human effort (the "willing and practical and thoroughgoing devotion") with two things that are at least partly "from above"; namely, the transformed "willingness of the loyal man to do his service" ("devotion") and the graced superhuman object (or "cause") to which he is devoted.

61. See Rom 15, and *Sources of Religious Insight*, chap. 7.

62. See Rom 14:19 and *War and Insurance*.

63. See Skrupskelis, "Royce and the Justification of Authority," 165–170.

64. In stark contrast to Paul, Royce made practically no applications, if any, to sexual and marital ethics. This corrects any suspicion of an unbroken parallel between the ethics of Paul and the mature Royce. Since Royce applied his ethics to so many other practical areas—such as racism, provincialism, sports, and the environment—this omission (or discreet silence?) seems significant.

65. *Basic Writings* 2:652 n. 4.

66. *Letters*, 49; *Fugitive Essays*, 290–299 with the *Johns Hopkins Annual Report* II, p. 56; HARP 58, "Lectures Introductory to Philosophy," Lect. 7, pp. 37–38, to which Royce added, "The best work of philosophical thought since his [Spinoza's] time might be looked upon as but a sort of rewriting of Spinoza."

The two addresses were entitled "The *Tractatus Theologico-Politicus* of Spinoza" and "Natural Rights and Spinoza's Essay on Liberty." The "Natural Rights" essay received Royce's special care, with footnotes inscribed in red ink, as if for an editor's eye. Its *full* form was eventually published in *Fugitive Essays*, 290–299, on the basis of the MS in HARP 40, no. 4. This amends *Basic Writings* 2:1174–1175, under the date of 1880, no. 1.

67. *Spirit of Modern Philosophy*, 41; see also 27, 75, and 41–67 *passim*.

68. *Philosophy of Loyalty*, 88–89.

69. *Basic Writings* 2:1198, and *Letters*, 485.

70. *World and the Individual* 1:579; see also 71, 544 n. 1, and *Logical Essays*, 105.

71. *Problem of Christianity*, 341.

72. *Logical Essays*, 198–203, esp. 203; see also *World and the Individual* 1:278.

73. *Basic Writings* 1:410 and 2:739.

74. See LLM 3/14, 3/16, and Spinoza's *Ethics*, Bk. V, Prop. 42.

75. LLM 3/16.

76. *Spirit of Modern Philosophy*, 56.

77. See *World and the Individual*, 1:283 n. 1. In the late 1880s Royce's reading of German philosophical journals kept him in touch with the "Nietzsche movement" then current in Germany (see *Letters*, 65, 109, and Royce's reference to this in his 1910 Smith College Lecture, Second Series, HARP 78, no. 1, pp. 8–10).

78. See *James and Other Essays*, 230–237, and Royce's "Nietzsche," *Atlantic Monthly* 119 (1917): 321–331, esp. 328.

79. Royce's 1910 Smith College Lecture, Second Series, 9–10.

80. See Royce's "Nietzsche." In this section in-text references are to this article.

81. See the draft of his preparatory MS, "The Teachings of Friedrich Nietzsche," in HARP 97, no. 1.

82. In 1915 Royce proposed Nietzsche's idea of eternal recurrence to his Philosophy 9 class by suggesting, "[W]e have been here in this classroom an infinite number of times before, exactly as today." Using his insight into individuality, Royce then rebutted Nietzsche's notion according to a Scotist idea to which Peirce had called Royce's attention: "The *haeceity* of the particular lecture is distinct and would remain so even in Nietzsche's fancied world of recurrence" (LLM 10/21).

83. Extension Course on Ethics, Lect. II, 3.

84. *James and Other Essays*, 213.

85. In his "Problem of Truth" address, which he personally esteemed, Royce called himself an absolute voluntarist and referred to Nietzsche more than ever before. For his references to absolute voluntarism, see *James and Other Essays*, 198, 208, 212–213, 235–236, and 254; for those to Nietzsche, see 190, 196, 202, 230.

86. See F. Nietzsche, *Genealogy of Morals*, First Essay, start of Section 10, in the Walter Kaufmann edition (New York: Random House, 1967), 36–37. In *Problem of Christianity*, 351–355, Royce explicitly associated these two attitudes of will with Schopenhauer. In the second attitude a Nietzschean presence would be verified if its root were shown to include "*ressentiment*" as well as a Schopenhauerian "resignation."

87. Royce referred explicitly to Nietzsche's "*Umwertung aller Werte*" in *James and Other Essays*, 190, and implicitly required this "transvaluation of all values" in his exposition of the *Uebermensch* doctrine throughout his "Nietzsche" article. (See also *Problem of Christianity*, 117.)

88. As early as 1898 Royce had signaled his new emphasis on "the philosophy of life," see his introduction to *Studies of Good and Evil*. The full title of his 1911 *William James and Other Essays on the Philosophy of Life* rendered explicit Royce's identification with the movement.

89. As he matured Royce increasingly expressed this theme of philosophers' dependence on the life-wisdom of ordinary folk; see, for instance, *Philosophy of Loyalty*, viii, 14; *James and Other Essays*, 157–158; *Sources of Religious Insight*, 46; and especially, *Letters*, 586–587.

90. See *Philosophy of Loyalty*, vii, where Royce spoke of loyalty as "the central spirit of the moral and reasonable life of man." He also regarded *Race Questions* as an effort to apply his "general doctrine about life" to "some problems of American life" (*Race Questions*, v, ix). See also *Letters*, 586–587.

91. If some philosophers currently insist on tightening their nets of refined conceptions and of intersecting relationships, they also need to confess how limited are their draughts from the ocean of life.

92. LLM 9/30.

93. LLM 11/11.

94. See William E. Hocking, "Josiah Royce," *Encyclopaedia of Social Sciences* (New York: Macmillan, 1935) 13:451.

95. See *Letters*, 644–648, from which the quotations in the rest of this paragraph are taken.

96. The ontological sense of "person" derives from Boethius's definition of person as an "individual supposit of a rational nature." Royce's non-ontological but ethical sense of "person" views the self as a temporal agent unified by a chosen life-plan and dedicated to a community. Detached from a community, one is an incomplete human self, no longer a "person" in the ethical sense.

97. *Letters*, 646.

98. *California*, 500.

99. *Problem of Christianity*, 38.

100. See "IV. The Ethical Ideas in their Relation to Communities," in Plan No. 1 of Royce's "Outlines for University Extension Course," HARP Box H, no. 1, Appendix, p. 2.

101. *Problem of Christianity*, 40, emphasis added. For Royce, the "religious" opened up a transcendent as well as an immanent sacred dimension.

102. *Life*, 362.

103. Alasdair MacIntyre, *Three Rival Versions of Moral Enquiry: Encyclopaedia, Genealogy, and Tradition* (Notre Dame, Ind.: University of Notre Dame Press, 1990).

104. *Logical Essays*, 61.

CHAPTER 12

1. See *Philosophy of Loyalty*, 238–241, *Problem of Christianity*, 39, along with Morris R. Cohen, "Neo-Realism and the Philosophy of Royce," *Philosophical Review* 25 (1916): 361, and James Collins, "Royce: Analyst of Religion as Community," in *American Philosophy and the Future*, ed. Michael Novak (New York: Scribner's, 1968), 217–218 n. 9.

2. Royce's critique of Hegel on mediation occurs in his MS, "The Spirit of the Community," his undelivered Berkeley lecture of 1914 (HARP 91, no. 3), 11–12. One stimulus for this lecture seems to have been Peirce's letter (see Appendix C), which highlighted, among other things, the liberty of reasoning.

3. Royce, "Order," Hasting's *Encyclopaedia* 9:540. The quotation is taken from the "literature" section of this article, a section omitted when this article was republished in *Logical Essays*.

4. See Vincent C. Punzo, "Royce and the Problem of Individuality," doctoral dissertation, St. Louis University, 1963.

5. Ibid., 372–373 n. 149.

6. LLM 5/20, 2/25, original emphasis. W. E. Hocking, E. G. Spaulding, and Peter Fuss have pointed to this realistic aspect of Royce's late thought. With this I concur.

7. This primacy becomes evident in Royce's treatment of the "three attitudes of the will," *Problem of Christianity*, 351–357.

8. See ibid., 285–286, 335, 346.

9. See *Hope of the Great Community*, 128 (or *Basic Writings*, 34), LLM 1/11, and Royce's "Autobiographical Note on the Influence of Men and Books," an undated MS of *ca.* 1877–1882 preserved in HARP 96. In addition to J. S. Mill, as an

undergraduate Royce read other British writers, particularly Spencer, and to a lesser extent, Hamilton and Mansel.

10. LLM 1/11.

11. See *Spirit of Modern Philosophy*; *Basic Writings* 1:444; and LLM 1/11.

12. See *Life*, 62, and LLM 1/11.

13. See *Life*, 61–62.

14. LLM 1/11.

15. See *Letters*, 460.

16. See Flower and Murphey, *A History of Philosophy in America* 2:863. See also James Gouinlock, *The Moral Writings of John Dewey: A Selection* (New York: Hafner, 1976), 18.

17. See John J. McDermott, *The Philosophy of John Dewey*, 2 vols (New York: G. P. Putnam's Sons, 1973) 1:60. The quotation derives from Dewey's *Creative Intelligence* (1917).

18. See Flower and Murphey, *History of Philosophy in America* 2:860.

19. Extension Course on Ethics, Lect. II, 10.

20. See John Dewey, *Human Nature and Conduct* (New York: Random House, 1957), 302, and his *A Common Faith*, 87.

21. *Human Nature and Conduct*, 302.

22. See *Sources of Religious Insight*, 29.

23. Ibid., 24–25.

24. Ibid., 19.

25. Niebuhr, *The Responsible Self*, 84.

26. Extension Course on Ethics, Lect. V, 17.

27. See Niebuhr, *The Responsible Self*, 101–107.

28. Ibid., 105–106.

29. Extension Course on Ethics, Lect. V, 2.

30. By selecting his three ideas and synthesizing them concretely in the "loyal servant of community," Royce reaffirmed, on the level of interpretive meaning, the serial development of the four moral ideals, which he had taught at Urbana in 1907. One may recall this series of symbolic self-images as those of the hero, saint, titan, and servant. Each of the first three of these moral ideals seem slight imbalances of one of the three leading ethical ideas. The final self-ideal thus seems to embody a harmonious emphasis upon all three ideas.

31. *Logical Essays*, 228.

32. Compare Royce's "Comments," 58–63 with Niebuhr, *The Responsible Self*, 61–63.

33. Evidence of the gratitude students felt for Royce's Extension Course on Ethics is available in the Harvard Archives.

CHAPTER 13

1. Royce's explicit strategy, announced at Smith College in 1910 (see HARP 78, no.1, pp. 41–44), preferred the term "loyalty" rather than "the love of God and man." For he found that the ambiguous yet traditional Christian term "love" primarily

emphasized feeling and sentiment. On the other hand, the term "loyalty," even while carrying secondary affective tones of devotion and attachment, went further than "love." Paralleling Aristotle's ethics, Roycean loyalty stressed the centrality of "right desire" in moral life. It did so without downplaying affection, even as it emphasized the needs for commitment to the whole universe and for innovative constancy (or "creative fidelity," as Marcel called it). For Royce, then, genuine loyalty had to include a twofold thrust toward communities and individuals, shown in a wholehearted practical service to both. In his words of 1910, it also had to integrate two motives: both a "loyalty to the unseen world" *and* a "loyalty to the visible world of mankind, loyalty to the higher human life, viewed just *as* human life, as the better life that we seek or find in the social world around us" (43–44, original emphasis).

2. See *Letters*, 586–587, 636–637, 642, 646.

3. See Guy W. Stroh, *American Ethical Thought* (Chicago: Nelson-Hall, 1979), 140.

4. See Peter Fuss, *The Moral Philosophy of Josiah Royce* (Cambridge, Mass.: Harvard University Press, 1965), 160–198, 228–242, 247–253, esp. 161.

5. *Philosophy of Loyalty*, 143.

6. See Duron's review of Marcel's *La Metaphysique de Royce*, 357–359, and McDermott's Introductions to *Basic Writings* 1:6, 319; 2:829–831.

7. "The Genteel Tradition," *Documents*, 407. For an illuminating study of Santayana's meaning of "genteel tradition" and the claim that "he was more affected by the genteel culture he slyly spoofed than he ever let on," see Daniel Aaron, "George Santayana and the Genteel Tradition," *Bulletin of the Santayana Society* 7 (Fall 1989): 1–7.

8. "The Genteel Tradition," 407.

9. In Royce's published works, I find only two references to Jonathan Edwards: *James and Other Essays*, 3–5, 121.

10. See Jacques Duron's review of the French version of *Philosophy of Loyalty, Philosophie de loyalisme* (Paris: Aubier, 1946), in *Revue Philosophie de France et Etranger* 138 (1948): 359–361.

11. *Philosophy of Loyalty*, vii–viii, 15, original emphasis.

12. LLM 1/13, original emphasis.

13. *Philosophy of Loyalty*, 16–17.

14. Ibid., 357, 377, original emphasis.

15. *Problem of Christianity*, 41.

16. For an illuminating critique of Richard Rorty's metacritique, see Richard J. Bernstein, *Beyond Objectivism and Relativism: Science, Hermeneutics, and Praxis* (Philadelphia: University of Pennsylvania Press, 1985), 197–207.

17. Royce thought it better to avoid the common expression "God exists" and say instead "God is real."

18. LLM 1/8. But Royce's ontological vocabulary in *World and the Individual* 1:47–54 differs since there he tried to make no systematic distinction in usage between Reality and Existence (*World and the Individual* 1:52 n). Unfortunately, both in *World and the Individual* and in LLM, Royce's usage patterns of this vocabulary lacked perfect consistency.

19. To discern the meaning of "is," Santayana had counseled that we have only to ask whether "is" is used:

essentially, meaning *is identical with this*, or
attributively, meaning *has this property among others*, or
existentially, meaning *has a place in the flux*, or
naturalistically, meaning *has this substance or origin*.

(Excerpted from the concluding paragraph of Santayana's "Some Meanings of the Word 'Is'," *Journal of Philosophy* 12 (February 4, 1915): 66–68, the text upon which Royce lectured in LLM 2/26.)

20. For Royce's last utterances on creationism, see LLM 2/17.

21. Yet in "Mind" he said a mind is interpretable both "as a substance" and as a sign. In LLM 2/17 he spoke of a person's "inalienable being."

22. See *World and the Individual* 1:50–51 n. 1, and LLM 2/29.

23. To know oneself as the knower who knows the difference between truth and error is to be able to grasp one's actuality of being (*esse*) as not wholly embodied in matter, space, or time. Some Thomists refer to this experience as the making of a metaphysical "judgment of separation." In it one recognizes that "to be" can be actual without necessarily being embodied in matter or space or time—however frequently this actuality is so embodied.

24. Here, according to Gilson, God supposedly told Moses to inform the Israelites that the one named "I am who am" sent him to lead the Israelites out of Egypt. But the text more likely indicates God's reluctance to let Moses have a name for God. Rather than being a revelation of *esse*, as Gilson took it, the passage more likely conveys the mysteriousness of God and calls for trust based on the "great events" soon to enter the Israelites' experience.

25. *Philosophy of Loyalty*, 185–196.

26. *Hope of the Great Community*, 131.

27. *Letters*, 616.

28. *Hope of the Great Community*, 10, 130–132; *Letters*, 628–629.

29. *Hope of the Great Community*, 130.

30. Neither "sex" nor "sexuality" appear in the index of James's *Briefer Course*.

31. Social pressures and sanctions kept Harvard academicians of the early twentieth century from speaking freely on sexual questions. In like manner, but long before Royce, Harvard Divinity School professors who favored the abolition of slavery in the 1820s and 1830s, before it became popular to do so, suffered heavy social disapproval.

32. See LLM 2/26 to 3/7, and Hocking, "The Ontological Argument in Royce and Others," *Contemporary Idealism in America*, 45–66.

33. Compare, for instance, Royce's mature ethics with Bernard Lonergan's chapter 28, "The Possibility of Ethics," in his *Insight: A Study of Human Understanding* (New York: Harper and Row, 1978), 595–633.

34. See W. E. Hocking, "Royce's Empiricism," *Journal of Philosophy*, 53 (1956): 57–63.

35. *Hope of the Great Community*, 4.

36. *Philosophy of Loyalty*, 251.

37. Ibid., 252.

38. See Duron's review of *Philosophie de loyalisme*, 361.

39. Bruce Kuklick confirms this in his *Intellectual Biography*, 50, 65.

40. On this see Smith, *Spirit of American Philosophy*, 106.

41. See LLM 5/27.

42. G. E. Moore carefully identified this fallacy in conceptualistic thinking, to which David Hume had first drawn attention.

43. *Philosophy of Loyalty*, 326; *James and Other Essays*, 254.

44. On this see Morris R. Cohen, *American Thought: A Critical Sketch* (Glencoe, Ill.: Free Press, 1954), 278.

45. William James, *Pragmatism* (Cambridge, Mass.: Harvard University Press, 1975), 19.

46. Almost spontaneously a mother usually prepares another meal for her family. Or habitually a good teacher usually lets his or her pupils know from the start the aim of the present class and a clear summary of it at its close.

47. First Berkeley Lecture of 1914 (HARP 84, no. 1), 40, 50–51.

48. See *Problem of Christianity*, 341–342.

49. For a detailed study of this sense, see Oppenheim, "Royce's Appreciative Sense of the More Vital," *Modern Schoolman* 44 (March 1967): 233–239.

50. See his 1916 article, "Monotheism," in Hasting's *Encyclopaedia* 8:818–819 or *Basic Writings* 1:408.

51. LLM 3/16.

52. *Problem of Christianity*, 234; *Letters*, 646.

53. LLM 3/16.

54. *Problem of Christianity*, 121–142, esp. 141–142. Writing conceptualistically in 1903, G. E. Moore said that the good could not be defined. Relying on a process of communal interpretation in 1916, Royce taught that one could "define" the good "simply in terms of the loyal identification of the true self with the aim and purpose of the community" (LLM 3/16).

55. *Problem of Christianity*, 342, 382; Extension Course on Ethics, Lect. II, 10.

56. *Problem of Christianity*, 387.

57. See Extension Course on Ethics, Lect. II, 10.

58. *Outlines of Psychology*, vii, 197–298.

59. This strikingly presaged the position of Karl Rahner in his *Foundations of Christian Faith* (New York: Crossroad, 1982), 404.

60. Smith proposed this view on June 4, 1988, at the "Frontiers in American Philosophy" Symposium held at Texas A. & M. University.

61. I have not discovered signs of Royce's familiarity with the writings of Karl Marx.

62. If so, the non-publication of his 1884 statements on social ethics and socialism becomes more significant.

63. Royce smarted from the wounds he had received in his youth from the controversy between religion and evolution and from the wounds inflicted later by the petty in-fighting between certain sectarian Christian groups and their ministers.

Select Bibliography

WRITINGS BY ROYCE

The Basic Writing of Josiah Royce. Ed. John J. McDermott. 2 vols. Chicago: University of Chicago Press, 1969. With an excellent bibliography of Royce's published writings by Ignas Skrupskelis, 2:1167–1226.

California, from the Conquest in 1846 to the Second Vigilance Committee in San Francisco [1856]: A Study of American Character. Boston: Houghton, Mifflin, 1886.

The Conception of God: A Philosophical Discussion Concerning the Nature of the Divine Idea as a Demonstrable Reality. 2nd ed. With Royce's Supplementary Essay, "The Absolute and the Individual." New York: Macmillan, 1897.

Extension Course on Ethics, 1915–1916. Harvard University Archives, Royce Papers, fol. 94, nos. 1–4, and fol. 95, no. 1.

Fugitive Essays. Ed. Jacob Loewenberg. Cambridge, Mass.: Harvard University Press, 1920.

Harvard University Archives, Royce Papers: 98 vols., 14 boxes, plus 20 additional boxes of the Crystal Falls Collection, acquired in 1989.

The Hope of the Great Community. New York: Macmillan, 1916.

The Letters of Josiah Royce. Ed. John Clendenning. Chicago: University of Chicago Press, 1970.

Last Lectures on Metaphysics, 1915–1916. Ralph W. Brown's and B. E. Underwood's stenographic notes of the Philosophy 9 course. William Ernest Hocking Papers, Houghton Library, Harvard University.

"Mind." In *Encyclopaedia of Religion and Ethics.* Ed. James Hastings. New York: Charles Scribner's Sons, 1916. 8:649–657. Reprinted in *Royce's Logical Essays*, 146–178.

Outlines of Psychology: An Elementary Treatise with Some Practical Applications. New York: Macmillan, 1903.

The Philosophy of Loyalty. New York: Macmillan, 1908.

"The Principles of Logic." In *Logic*, vol. 1 of the *Encyclopaedia of the Philosophical Sciences*, 67–135. Ed. Arnold Ruge. London: Macmillan, 1913. Reprinted in *Royce's Logical Essays*, 310–378, and by Philosophical Library, 1961.

The Problem of Christianity. 2 vols. New York: Macmillan. Reprinted, ed. John E. Smith. Chicago: University of Chicago Press, 1968.

The Religious Aspect of Philosophy. Boston: Houghton, Mifflin, 1885. Reprinted Harper Torchbook, 1958.

Royce's Logical Essays. Ed. Daniel S. Robinson. Dubuque, Iowa: William C. Brown, 1951.

Race Questions, Provincialism, and Other American Problems. New York: Macmillan, 1908.

Studies of Good and Evil: A Series of Essays upon the Problems of Philosophy and of Life. New York: D. Appleton, 1898.

The Spirit of Modern Philosophy: An Essay in the Form of Lectures. Boston: Houghton, Mifflin, 1892.

The Sources of Religious Insight. New York: Charles Scribner's Sons, 1912.

War and Insurance. New York: Macmillan, 1914.

The World and the Individual. 2 vols. New York: Macmillan, 1899–1901.

William James and Other Essays on the Philosophy of Life. New York: Macmillan, 1911.

WRITINGS BY OTHERS

Barrett, Clifford, ed. *Contemporary Idealism in America.* New York: Russell & Russell, 1964.

Bournique, Gladys. *La Philosophie de Josiah Royce.* Paris: Vrin, 1988.

Clendenning, John. *The Life and Thought of Josiah Royce.* Madison, Wisc.: University of Wisconsin Press, 1985.

Fuss, Peter. *The Moral Philosophy of Josiah Royce.* Cambridge, Mass.: Harvard University Press, 1965.

Hartshorne, Charles, Paul Weiss, and Arthur W. Burks, eds. *Collected Papers of Charles Sanders Peirce.* 8 vols. Cambridge, Mass.: Harvard University Press, 1931–1958.

Hastings, James, ed. *Encyclopaedia of Religion and Ethics.* 13 vols. New York: Charles Scribner's Sons, 1908–1927.

Hine, Robert V. *Josiah Royce: From Grass Valley to Harvard.* Norman, Okla.: University of Oklahoma Press, 1992.

Hocking, William E. "The Ontological Argument in Royce and Others." In *Contemporary Idealism*, ed. Clifford Barrett. New York: Russell & Russell, 1964.

Kuklick, Bruce. *Josiah Royce: An Intellectual Biography.* Indianapolis: Bobbs-Merrill, 1972.

———. *The Rise of American Philosophy.* New Haven: Yale University Press, 1977.

Marcel, Gabriel. *Royce's Metaphysics.* Trans. Virginia and Gordon Ringer. Chicago: Regnery, 1956.

Niebuhr, H. Richard. *The Responsible Self.* New York: Harper and Row, 1963.

Oppenheim, Frank M. "Josiah Royce's Intellectual Development: An Hypothesis." *Idealistic Studies* 6 (January 1976): 85–104.

———. "A Roycean Response to the Challenge of Individualism." In *Beyond Individualism*, ed. Donald Gelpi. Notre Dame, Ind.: University of Notre Dame Press, 1989.

———. *Royce's Mature Philosophy of Religion.* Notre Dame, Ind.: University of Notre Dame Press, 1987.

Perry, Ralph Barton. *The Thought and Character of William James*. 2 vols. Boston: Little, Brown, 1935.

Smith, Grover, ed. *Josiah Royce's Seminar, 1913–1914, as Recorded in the Notebooks of Harry T. Costello*. New Brunswick, N. J.: Rutgers University Press, 1963.

Smith, John E. *Royce's Social Infinite: The Community of Interpretation*. New York: Liberal Arts, 1950.

———. *The Spirit of American Philosophy*. New York: Oxford University Press, 1963.

White, Morton, ed. *Documents in the History of American Philosophy*. New York: Oxford University Press, 1972.

Index of Names

Index of Topics